Essential Horse Speak

Continuing the Conversation

Also by Sharon Wilsie

Horse Speak: The Equine-Human Translation Guide

Horses in Translation

Horse Speak: First Conversations (Video)

Essential Horse Speak

Continuing the Conversation

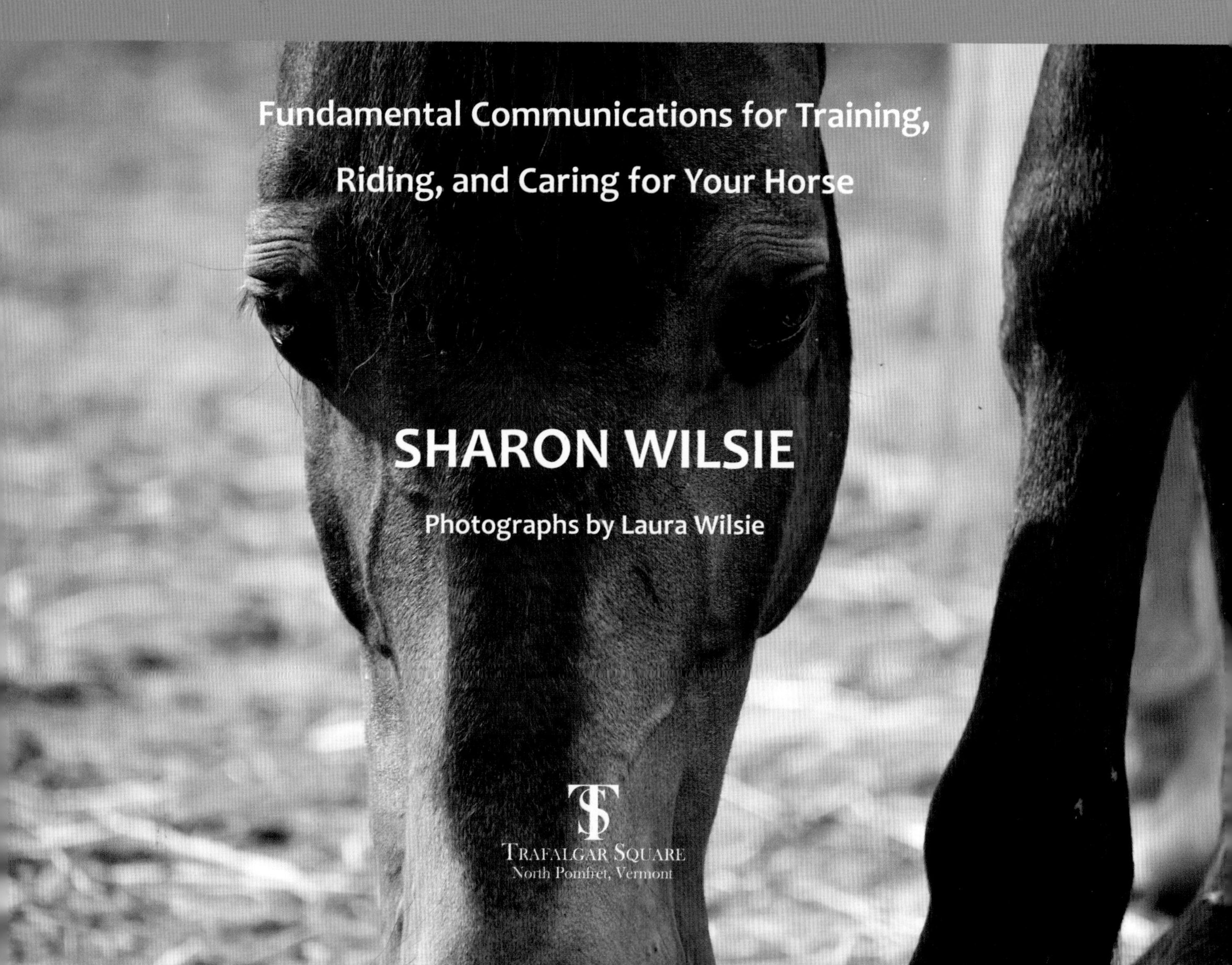

Fundamental Communications for Training, Riding, and Caring for Your Horse

SHARON WILSIE

Photographs by Laura Wilsie

TS
Trafalgar Square
North Pomfret, Vermont

First published in 2022 by
Trafalgar Square Books
North Pomfret, Vermont 05053

Disclaimer of Liability
The author and publisher shall have neither liability nor responsibility to any person or entity with respect to any loss or damage caused or alleged to be caused directly or indirectly by the information contained in this book. While the book is as accurate as the author can make it, there may be errors, omissions, and inaccuracies.

Trafalgar Square Books encourages the use of approved safety helmets in all equestrian sports and activities.

Library of Congress Cataloging-in-Publication Data
Names: Wilsie, Sharon, author.
Title: Essential horse speak: continuing the conversation : fundamental communications for training, riding, and caring for your horse / Sharon Wilsie with photographs by Laura Wilsie.
Description: North Pomfret, Vermont : Trafalgar Square Books, 2020. |
Includes index. | Summary: "Internationally renowned horse trainer and behaviorist Sharon Wilsie takes her ground-breaking Horse Speak techniques of communicating with the horse using body language similar to what he uses with other horses to the next level. She introduces new concepts on the ground and in the saddle that help people and horses better understand each other"-- Provided by publisher.
Identifiers: LCCN 2020030511 (print) | LCCN 2020030512 (ebook) | ISBN 9781646011476 (paperback) | ISBN 9781646010783 (epub)
Subjects: LCSH: Horses--Training. | Human-animal communication. | Body language.
Classification: LCC SF287 .W518 2020 (print) | LCC SF287 (ebook) | DDC 636.1/0835--dc23
LC record available at https://lccn.loc.gov/2020030511
LC ebook record available at https://lccn.loc.gov/2020030512

Photographs by Laura Wilsie
Illustrations by Sharon Wilsie
Book design by Lauryl Eddlemon
Cover design by RM Didier
Index by Andrea Jones (JonesLiteraryServices.com)
Typefaces: Candara, Myriad Pro

Printed in China

10 9 8 7 6 5 4 3 2 1

In Loving Memory of Zeke

Contents

Acknowledgments

I would like to thank my herd, the original horses of Horse Speak. Without Rocky's tireless teachings, Dakota's zeal, Jagger's selfless attitude, or Mommy and Luna's seamless contributions, I wouldn't have been able to finesse the nuances of this language. I love you guys!

Thank you to all the people and horses I have had the honor of meeting and working with since my first book *Horse Speak* came out. Each one of you have brought a piece of this puzzle together!

A special thank you to my partner Laura, who has dedicated countless hours to this mission of "Giving Horses a Voice." Without her efforts this book would not have been possible.

Thank you to the Horse Speak Team for your ongoing and amazing support.

Thank you, Trafalgar Square Books, for believing in Horse Speak.

Most of all, thank you to my family for your love and devotion.

Prelude

For those who have read *Horse Speak: The Equine-Human Translation Guide* and *Horses in Translation*, and who have seen my video *Horse Speak: First Conversations*, I want to say that it's a pleasure to have you join me again for another epic adventure.

To those who have picked up this book with no idea what Horse Speak® is all about, I am excited to introduce you to the notion that horses have a language system, and you can learn it! The goal of this book is for you to become fluent, or more fluent, in this language, and to learn how it may apply to any training practice.

Horse Speak is a result of many years of independent study and research. I share this story in detail in my book *Horses in Translation*. Here, I will tell you just a little bit about the events and discoveries that led to where we are with this work today.

Horse Speak's Inception

Early on I had some particular life experiences that opened doors of perception and awareness. I was a sickly child, spending most of my early years bedridden or hospitalized, which enabled me to spend hours reading books. My mother was a veterinary technician, and I spent a good deal of time with her in the veterinary hospital due to my condition. The veterinarian was a kind, warm human being who allowed me to play in his office and even sit fully gowned on a high stool in the surgery and watch operations. Everyone thought I would grow up to be a veterinarian. But animal behavior was more interesting to me. I was often allowed to offer the clinic's patients comfort and kindness, and in this way, I learned how to handle animals in distress.

We lived close to an urban zoo, and my family would go there for strolls on the

As a toddler, my meeting with a wild horse at the Capron Park Zoo in Attleboro, Massachusetts, set the stage for my later relationship with Rocky, my Mentor.

weekend, which I cherished. There is a photograph of me as a child, crouched under the guardrail of one of the exhibits—"Wild European Horses"—trying to extend my hand to the small equine on the other side. This encounter must have sparked something in me because I suddenly became smitten with horses.

As I turned 10 years old, new breakthroughs in medicine allowed me to begin to lead a more normal life. I was given a dog of my own, and even got to go away to summer camp—a *horseback riding* summer camp! Two passions now emerged: It was not enough for me to ride a horse or have a dog—I needed to know how to train both.

In my teens I was an apprentice to my riding instructor as well as a local dog breeder, where I learned to train for obedience trials and for agility. (Later, I branched out and worked with sled dogs, hunting dogs, and dogs who learned to carry packs on the trail.) I showed horses hunt seat, and then studied dressage on a schoolmaster. (Riding him was like tasting chocolate for the first time; I was hooked!) I took longe lessons to improve my balance and seat.

Years later, I found enjoyment riding reining horses and spent time as a trail guide. I learned to long-line and drive a pair.

My equestrian experience landed me eventually as a teacher at a local college for students with learning disabilities. There, I was asked to help design an equine-assisted learning (EAL) program for the school after the supervisor of the experiential learning department came to a clinic I was teaching at a local horse rescue. I had learned Reiki (a form of energy healing) over the course of my varied career, and offered classes in simple techniques to rescue volunteers, realizing that they needed more help coming up with solid rehabilitation plans for the horses in their care.

Training Meets Scrutiny

Over time, I had become an avid researcher of ideas about horses and training methods from all around the world. What I was so often up against at rescues was the fact that the horses there were frequently traumatized or angry or injured, and most trainers wanted to start working with them at a "place" that was miles away from where the horses were mentally and emotionally.

Meanwhile, I had begun to accumulate horses with their own complex stories in my backyard. Working with and studying them (which I talk about in detail in *Horses in Translation*), plus my work with the students at the college and the equine rescues, all came together, eventually leading me to asking more questions but having fewer real answers. *No one* I had studied with or learned from had any insights on how to help me *talk to* my horses. And my time at the rescues was pointing me in an ever-clearer path toward a *different* way to work with horses—one derived from studying how the elder, wiser animals were helping other "troubled" ones become calm. I began to sense how even when it looked like they did almost nothing, things happened. In addition, my autistic and nonverbal learning disorder (NVLD) students at the college were asking superbly pointed questions about equine body language, and I did not always have good enough answers for them. My students' desire to feel connected to horses was stunning; if I used typical equine training methods around them, they saw no reason to hold back if they found it counter to the ideals of bonding with a horse.

So, I postulated the dilemma all horse people face to them: "How can we improve the risks we take while moving around horses, without demanding obedience from them? Is it ever possible to build a healthy bond with horses when we use punishment and force?" This was a class that I taught early on, and it is where I began experimenting with training with levels of kindness and achieving standards of mannerly behavior *without* punishment.

A few years later, I took a year off to do nothing but sit in my field and study my own herd of horses. I recorded their postures, gestures, and signals, as well as *Breath*

BUZZWORDS

Breath Messages

Horses use breath as a communication tool. I teach a number of specific messages in my first book *Horse Speak.* The most important thing to know is that your breath is a foundational tool and deep breathing always communicates awareness of this to your horse.

Messages, eye-blinking signals, and single-foot-placement "intentions." I observed their angles of approach, movement in circles and arcs, and even ways they appeared to "apologize" or "re-harmonize" when things became grumpy. Letting go of my "Trainer Brain" was the hardest part of my studies, but it was necessary to figuring out how horses "begin" the "content" of their communication as well as how to they "end" it. I also wanted to figure out how I could approximate their gestures, postures, and signals back to them. Essentially, I wanted to discover if I could have a "Conversation" with a horse in his language. And if so, what would it be about?

When I went back to work, I brought my newfound information with me. I developed more programs with different schools, reached more rescues, and worked with private clients of different riding disciplines. Little by little, the way to teach the form of communication I believed to be "horse" and its practical application was polished.

Welcome to the Language of the Natural World

I have always said that Horse Speak is both a science and an art, and it is. All the equine movement patterns I now reference have been through scrupulous analysis, and organized and re-organized, until I could arrive at a universal platform of core meanings. I learned to witness the delivery of these messages under several variables: different settings, time of day, group dynamics, and interaction with the outer world. This is one side of Horse Speak: the science and mechanics of how it works.

The real usefulness lies in the art of Horse Speak, however. I call this "other" side the "world view" of Horse Speak. It incorporates a systematic approach to understanding what seems to actually motivate, drive and inspire horses—in other words, their wants, needs, and preferences... what they talk *about*. It is this aspect of learning Horse Speak that often caught me. Sometimes, the horse's world view—when you actually took the time to study it in and of itself for the purposes of seeing something from the horse's perspective only—went *completely against* conventional beliefs. In fact, I realized that, in some cases, the stuff I had done throughout my life as a rider and trainer went almost completely *against* how horses actually communicated, as well as being disconnected from their real motivations. With more and more certainty, I came to realize that a good deal of what had come to be conventional belief about working with and training horses was truly only "the rule" due to thousands of years of using horses as vehicles. I had always thought that I was a kinder, gentler trainer. However, a willing servant is still a servant.

I started to realize that in fact many of the techniques I had learned to use on horses had, inherent within them, qualities of traumatic layers of conditioning, ending with the effect in some cases of "learned helplessness." The more I worked with troubled horses and troubled youth, the more I came to understand the very nature of trauma-informed reactivity or stunted development. But in the end, I still was faced with very real, here-and-now problems: How do I get a halter on a horse who wants to bite me? How do I ride a horse who wants to buck me off? How can I have a horse learn to trust people again when an abusive owner put a pitchfork into his neck?

Horse Speak Can Make a Road Where There Was None

Learning Horse Speak is not just an entertaining idea or a new trend. In many cases, it can provide an avenue for progress where there has been none. When combined with solid, kind- hearted training systems that have the horse's health and well-being in mind, Horse Speak can be the "missing link."

However, Horse Speak is *not* a training system on its own. It literally is the language of the horse. Horses are not talking in a rigid protocol system like robots. You cannot just implement some aspects of Horse Speak and expect the machine of operations to spit out a predetermined result on the other side. Many systems of training teach us to expect the horse to comprehend and comply with a cue we have given. Having Conversations via Horse Speak means you *enter into an encounter with the horse as his own free agent.* Therefore, you must learn to watch the horse's response to a gesture, posture, or signal and then figure out: Is he asking a question? Is he thinking it over? Is he trying to come up with a good answer? Is he lost and confused?

Two Sides of Horse Speak

So, there are these two sides of Horse Speak: The direct mechanics of how horses combine their postures, gestures, and signals to form thoughts, share feelings, create boundaries, and bond and work together to keep the herd alive, and their "world

BUZZWORDS

Safety Objects

A Safety Object is the side of a wall, a cone, a barrel, a post, a rock, a tree, and interestingly, quite often a fresh pile of dung left in a strategic spot. The Safety Object represents a place to rest, reset, do nothing at all and just breathe, blink, and lick and chew. A horse is also more likely to take a nap in a designated Safety Object area (see more on Safety Objects on p. 72).

view." It is this second side that takes into account the horse's way of interacting with the area or spaces he lives and works in, as well as the other horses who are with him. There are some stark differences between a human's world view and a horse's—primarily, that he was born knowing he could be eaten by many things on this planet, while we were born knowing we could eat many things on this planet.

Horses see the world around them as a sort of "Chessboard of Life" (see more about this in chapter 2, beginning on p. 89). For them, the goal is to locate resources, *Safety Objects*, and areas of concern. How they move around the Chessboard is based on strategies they have learned from elders and betters; their brains do not have the design for imagination or projection, so they really must learn all the rules of the game from somewhere. Dogs and humans and other predatory creatures have brains that can strategize—you need this to hunt something. Prey animals need to know the ground they are covering to use it to their advantage, and they need to have practiced reflexes of escape. Their proprioception is designed to watch the micromovements of a predator. Adding to this form of awareness is the need for the herd to hold formation. Horses require other horses to be able to mirror each other's movements at lightning speed in order to move as one in a sharp change of direction, like birds or fish. This is one of the reasons leadership among horses not a militant, superiority complex; it is a shared algorithm of group harmony.

Horse Speak Lessons

This book covers the nitty-gritty "actions" of Horse Speak: how to convey or understand direct messages. It will also examine the world view of horses, as I have come to understand it, and help you begin to comprehend the way horses interpret what is happening around them. What most people who begin the practice of seeing the world from the horse's point of view tell me is that *it makes sense*. One of my favorite sayings from a clinic participant is, "Once you see it, you can't *not* see it." It is like one of those drawings with the squiggly lines and a hidden picture in the middle—you stare and stare, and finally, the hidden picture "pops out at you." Then, when you look at the drawing, you don't see the squiggly lines, but only the hidden picture. Horse Speak can be a little like this.

Training and Communication

Real communication with a horse can be hard for some people at first simply because most of us are into the idea of "push a button, get a response." However, the benefit of learning to actually talk to horses in their language instead of expecting them to understand ours is that it is a way to forge deep and lasting bonds of rapport. With troubled horses, a little Horse Speak can shave off an incredible amount of time and effort during retraining because the right message delivered at the right time can literally tell a horse, "I mean you no harm," and "I want to help."

In almost any training system, Horse Speak can find a comfortable place. It does not matter whether you are training driving horses or ranch horses or show horses or pleasure horses, or whether you are in Europe or North America or Australia—they are all horses, and they all share a common language. I now know trainers who recommend Horse Speak to their clients so they have the help they need in forging the day-to-day boundaries, "bubbles" (see p. 69), and bonding that is necessary to create safe, healthy, and happy relationships with their horses. I also now know trainers from all over the world who have found answers to certain questions or got a beneficial "nugget" of insight from Horse Speak, which took their own work to the next level.

Good, Better, Fantastic

What I like to say about Horse Speak is this: If you have a troubled horse, it can help you arrive at a better place. If you already have a good relationship with a horse, then Horse Speak can help make it *great*. And if you have an amazing relationship with a horse, then Horse Speak can help put some decorations on that cake. If you love horses, why not learn their language, instead of expecting them to know yours? I want to give you the gift that horses gave me, and that is the exact and specific nuances of how our body language can communicate clearly with them, if we just take the time to learn how.

How to Use This Book

If you have read my first book, *Horse Speak: The Equine-Human Translation Guide,* you have already learned a lot about what horses are saying. In this book, I am going to provide all the advancements that horses have shared with me since 2015, when *Horse Speak* was published. I am going to give you a path to take your work with Horse Speak to the next level.

If you are new to Horse Speak, you will find enough foundational information in the Introduction (p. 15) and pages that follow to get you started, but if you like what you are reading, then I suggest you pick up a copy of *Horse Speak* to receive the in-depth introduction to having Conversations with horses in their language.

Here, we will be building toward a more complete understanding of how to incorporate Horse Speak into our everyday interactions and training through the following steps:

1 Solidifying Basic Language Skills (p. 40): We all need to start with a general understanding of Horse Speak fundamentals. All of these were introduced in my first book, but I have learned more over the last five years that I am excited to share with you.

2 Observing the Horse's Environment and Movement Signals (p. 84): Most people are familiar with the game of chess. Don't worry, you don't need to know the specific rules, just that there is a board of equal-sized squares and that game pieces are placed on the board in a particular fashion. Each piece has a role and rules it must follow. I have determined that this theme can be applied to every group of horses and the environment they live in, yielding valuable information about how horses navigate around each other and around us. I call this *The Chessboard*, and we'll explore it, along with horse movement and expression, giving you important tools for taking your horsemanship to a new level.

3 Knowing the Buttons and What They Do (p. 116): Horses have many communication centers on their body—or *Buttons*, as I call them—and in *Horse Speak* I taught you 13 of them. Now I have added two more: the *Sit Button* and *Bridge of the Nose*. I have also shared all the new connections and Conversations I've discovered since my first book.

4 Understanding Herd Dynamics and Your Horse's Type (p. 156): Over the years I have put a lot of thought into how to present "personality types" in horses. While others have relied on such methods of categorization, I have been hesitant to do so because I do not like to "label" horses—or people, for that matter. I like to give all beings I meet the opportunity to learn, grow, and potentially sustain a transformation, from wherever they start to a "better" end result. The reason I have now decided to include personality types in Horse Speak is to better assist you in understanding the role your horse is playing in his daily interactions. When you understand who your horse thinks he is on The Chessboard, it can go a long way in helping you deepen your empathy and achieve greater success. I have, therefore, come up with three basic energy types and designated roles in the herd from what I have observed over time and experience.

5 Exploring the Circular Nature of Horse Conversations (p. 196): In my first book I discuss this idea and provide the stages of that Conversation as *The Four Gs: Greeting, Going Somewhere, Grooming,* and *Gone*. Now I will take this a step further with a related "container" of understanding to help you remember where you are in a Conversation with your horse. I call it *IINN: Initiation, Introduction, Negotiation,* and *Navigation*. How do you *initiate* a Conversation with your horse? How do you *introduce* yourself or an object? How do you *negotiate* getting out of a stall (for example), and how do you *navigate* together in movement?

6 Starting the Conversation Outside the Box (p. 222): In this chapter, we explore one of the marvels of Horse Speak—namely that we don't have to touch the horse to talk to him. With new tools that allow us to communicate from a distance, we discover safe and effective ways to initiate connection and source breakthroughs with tricky cases. In addition, we further the skills we've learned by using them to navigate around the Chessboard, giving us a means to communicate and work together in spaces beyond arenas.

7 Inviting the Horse to Come with You (p. 250): Here we apply Horse Speak protocols to the familiar realm of leading a horse. Haltering, leading, and backing up in hand can be less challenging and a more rewarding experience for both you and your horse when elements of Horse Speak are applied. I explain best practices for handling on the lead rope and illustrate the all-important Advanced Therapy Back-Up, which has lasting effects in many scenarios. I have come to understand it can be a door that opens the horse to better and better associations within himself, as well as in his connection to you. This chapter is full of strategies that improve communication between you and *all* the horse's Buttons.

8 Advancing Your Body Language at Liberty and on the Longe Line (p. 288): This chapter shares Horse Speak concepts for working with the horse on the ground at liberty and on the longe line, two keys to developing that rapport we desire with a horse. I find that time spent understanding the horse, and his balances and imbalances, on the ground translates to more success in the saddle. A key component of this is Dancer's Arms, which I introduced readers to in my first book *Horse Speak.* Now I expand upon its uses and the ways it can help us communicate with horses "more horizontally," as they might communicate with each other.

9 Riding with a New Perspective (p. 308): Finally, we take all that we have learned about communicating with the horse on the ground and bring it to our shared experience in the saddle. I explain that rather than having two worlds in our minds—one of groundwork and the other of riding— that we need to consider it all one, because the horse is talking to you, wherever you are. With new focus on a gentle Yoga Rein warm-up that can be incorporated into any riding session, and deep exploration of the kinds of things horses don't like about being ridden—and more importantly, what they *do* like—this section opens doors to a new awareness on horseback. Whether you do reining, ranch work, jumping, or dressage, the Conversations we can have for a happier, willing, more athletic horse are the same.

Throughout I provide *Skill-Builders, Myth-Busters,* and *Buzzwords* so you can have a profound learning experience and be able to cognitively understand the language of horse and explore the empathic link that you could share with them. Then, in Part Two, you will find "The Dictionary of Conversations"— some basic horse message "interpretations" that will be most useful as you begin or further your implementation of Horse Speak concepts. The Dictionary is broken into three sections: How to Say… (p. 340); How to Fix… (p. 348); and Messages from the Horse (p. 362). Please remember: These are generic and "middle-of-the-road" concepts that will have to be adapted to fit you, your horse, and your specific situation.

This book is like providing some spices, such as vanilla, cinnamon, and nutmeg, but also garlic, onion, salt, and pepper, in order to help you prepare a tasty meal. Some recipes will need more of one or the other, but a good cook knows how to combine the flavors to create a delicious dish. Too much of one or not enough of the other can only sometimes be determined by tasting along the way. You will find your particular combinations, but first you may need to try everything to get an idea and a feel for what the flavors even are.

Horse Speak in Training

Training is the act of educating horses about the jobs we are asking them to do for us. For too many people, taking a horse along the path of education gets confusing and difficult when the horse has difficult behaviors… or dangerous ones.

There is no "magic wand" that makes everything better in a day; if you have a horse, you need to think of your relationship as a "daily practice." But on the "bad days," if you know the basic protocols of Horse Speak taught in this book, you will at least have an improved understanding of your horse and be able to help him get to a "better place." What I personally love about this work is that not only can you have more effectiveness with less dust flying, but it can bring more qualities of bonding, affection, and connection to your relationship with your horse.

I think the reason most people are interested in applying Horse Speak to their training goals comes down to one thing: They want to know, *Is my horse happy with what is happening?* Or in other words, *Is my horse happy with me?*

Many people have confessed to me that they, at some point in their lives with horses, hit a crossroads in their desire to ride. The fact is, in varying degrees, some ethically minded folks often now question if riding and training a horse is actually okay.

I, too, had these questions. I can say it took years of solid investigation and all sorts of agreements and adjustments to my training goals for me to find a place that felt right. I even stopped riding for a year while initially researching Horse Speak. I had horses who were trained to bring themselves to the mounting block and come to me and slip under the saddle as I held it, waiting to place it on their backs. I thought that this must surely be a sign that they *wanted* to be ridden.

However, I still had a nagging feeling of discomfort… I thought again how a willing servant was still a servant. This is why I have continued my own journey with Horse Speak. Whatever reason you are drawn to it, and however much of this language you choose to learn or use, keep this simple reminder in mind: It is never a bad idea to try to both be understood and become more understanding. You and your horse will have all manner of topics and tasks you need to discuss and practice together, and while I cannot possibly know what all of these are or will be, I want to give you enough tools to be able to: try different "words" at various times, set up preventive maintenance tactics so you can problem-solve, and have fun exploring the new avenues that are sure to open up.

As you read and practice Horse Speak, the most important thing to remember is this: Horses want, deep down, to live in peace. Their inner craving is to have a calm nervous system and a feeling of safety and inclusion. If you approach everything you do knowing this, you will have greater success than if you think it is up to you to curtail your horse's outbursts or poor behavior. The goal in your human body language should be to remove tension, act welcoming, and offer your horse a "safe place to land."

PART ONE

Horse Speak Essentials

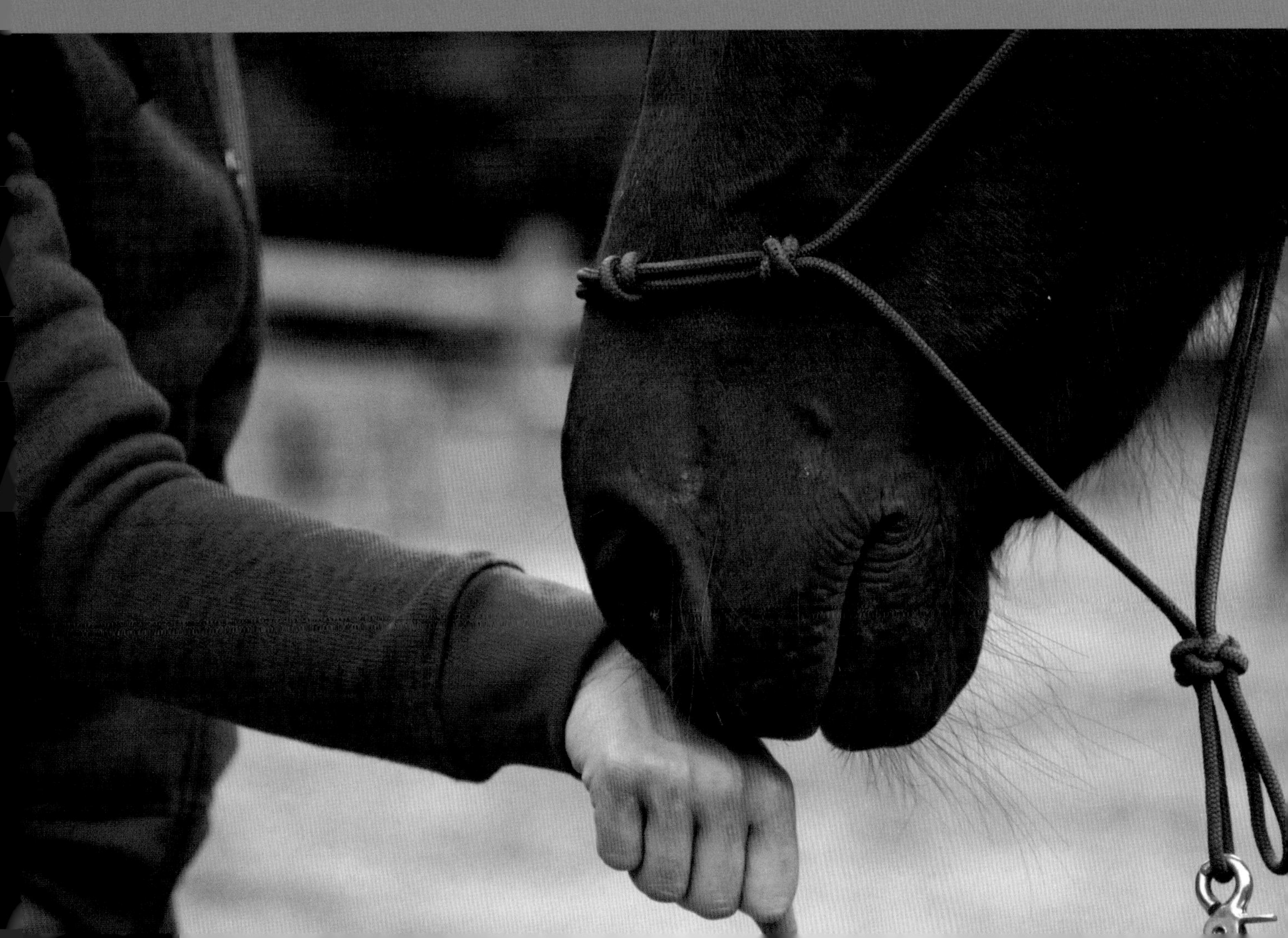

Introduction: Transitioning from an Old Model to a New Vision

What humans now seek more than ever from horses are relationships. In the past we used horses as vehicles, and our model of horse training reflected that: It was geared toward making a horse a useful tool. Any relationship that was gleaned was a benefit but not required. The more successful trainers could often get *both* done—relationship and working machine—but the relationship was a by-product of training, not its foundation.

In our modern world, the new paradigm is a desire to have horses engage in emotionally fulfilling relationships with us. The "horse as a vehicle" is a different mindset completely from "horse as my friend." There is a vacuum of knowledge between attaining what we used to want and what we now desire, and when we don't know an answer, we tend to fill in that space with projections, fears, frustrations, or misinterpretations. These may point us in a direction *away* from what we intrinsically value in our relationship with the horse. The benefit of understanding horse body language is that it can point us back *toward* our values (fig. I.1).

Being able to read and interpret the horse's postures, gestures, and signals, as well as understand equine expressions, means that you no longer have to ask *other people* about your horse… *you can just ask your horse*. Imagine what it would be like to

I.1 Training and communication have to go together, whatever exercise you are trying or discipline you are pursuing.

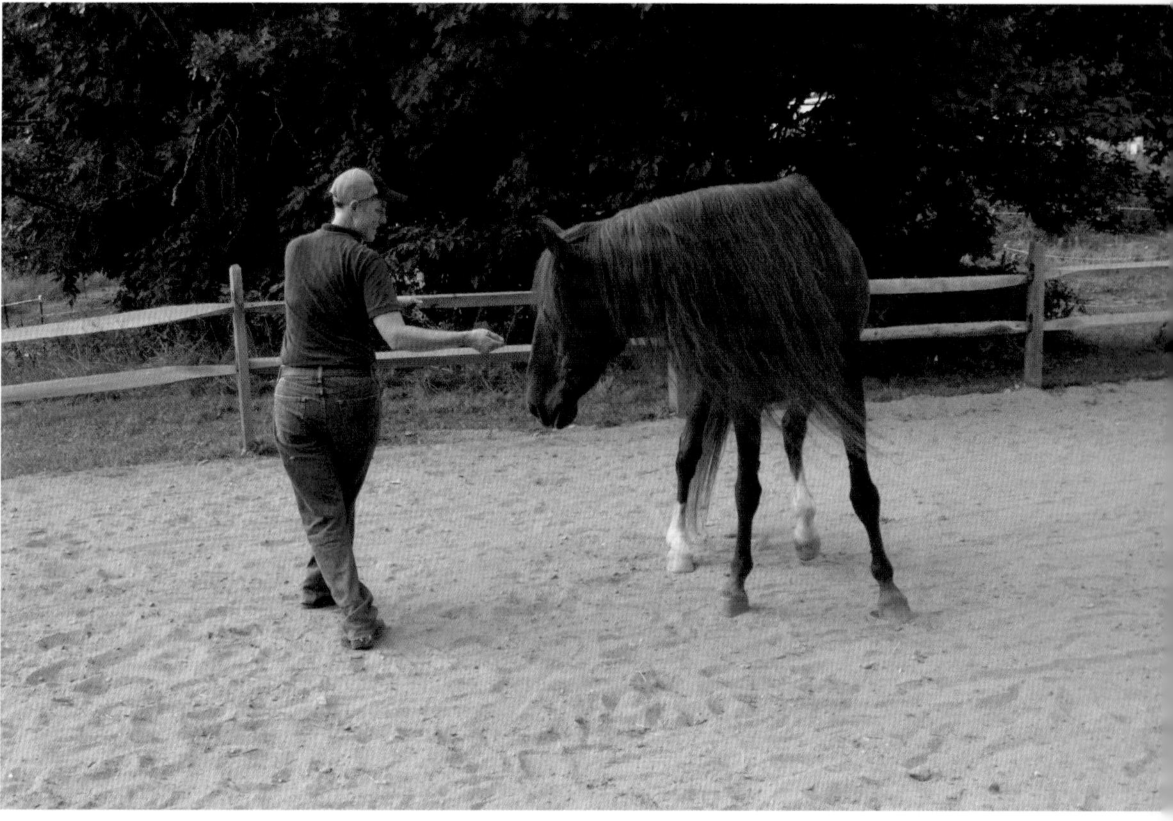

I.2 Being with your horse changes in compelling ways when there are no whips, no treats—just you!

work with a horse using nothing but your body language (fig. I.2). No whip, no special halter, no treats. *Just you.*

Imagine what it would be like if, at the moment you arrive at your horse's paddock, or drive up the driveway to the barn, or stick your head outside the back door of your house, you know, beyond a shadow of doubt, that the Conversation with your horse has *begun*.

I am not saying there is not a place and time for training tools. When fairly and safely used, whips, special halters, and treats can all be part of a good training repertoire. What shifts here is the idea of requiring these items to *begin* a Conversation with your horse. Body language only requires you to have a body. *You are enough.*

The Wisdom of the Ages

The famous horse trainer and Greek general Xenophon recommended that all green horses be quietly walked in hand by their grooms for up to two years. In this way, he believed horses would develop a wish to be with their handlers more than even other horses. Xenophon found that when the horse not only relied on a person for food and grooming, but also spent all day in the person's company, learning about the world, this fostered the sort of trust and respect the general cherished in a good cavalry horse.

I.3 The language of Horse Speak is so complex, and the nuances of the mechanics of the body movements so precise, that over time the potential door-opening experiences could be quite profound.

Here we have an interesting juxtaposition: We have a famous cavalry commander setting up the conditions through which a riding horse could not only learn to trust and respect a person, but also would become trustworthy and have the necessary loyalty to a human being to be counted on in the heat of battle. This same sentiment is often echoed in ranchers' tales of relying upon good cow horses: When you really have a partner in dangerous or perilous work, the burdens are shared and needs on both sides can be met. Humans instinctively understand that a tremendous bond can be forged between horse and human (fig. I.3). English novelist R.S. Surtees famously wrote: "There is no secret so close as that between a rider and his horse."

With all that being said, riding was still, of course, something that was done for a purpose: to fight or flee the enemy, to get from here to there safely, to fulfill whatever task the rider needed. Bond or not, there was still a component of teaching a horse to be compliant and obedient to human desires, cues, and "mastery" (fig. I.4). In today's world, we tend to still have this desire, especially in the arena of sports and showmanship. We want an obedient horse to run faster, jump higher, perform more beautifully—or simply, carry us safely along the trails.

I.4 There is a place and time for training tools.

We can acknowledge, however, in most situations we find ourselves in, what we do with our horses tends to fall under the banner of "things I love to do with a horse," not "if my horse doesn't get me there, the medicine won't get delivered." This changes the nature of our desire for obedience in the horse. Obedience was once paramount in any training protocol. To be fair, this made sense. But I have found a way to incorporate a healthy

I.5 Horses have their own sense of orderliness.

set of mannerly standards in the horse by learning how, why, and when horses create them *within their own herd dynamics*. We can have healthy, well-balanced, and mannerly relationships with horses, whatever it is we enjoy doing with them, by learning to understand and utilize their own protocols for creating the very same thing (fig. I.5)!

The Process of Horse Speak

When I was discovering the protocols of Horse Speak, I organized the material in a very specific manner. The information was overwhelming, and the "translation" required long hours of trial and error. Understanding this process will be helpful to you as you learn and apply Horse Speak with your own horse.

Basically, I began by studying a precise gesture between two horses. Let's use the muzzle-to-muzzle touch as an example. (I'll call it "M to M" in the paragraphs that follow to simplify.)

I might see M to M in the morning, when a pair of horses was first turned out together. However, I might also see it later, when horses were coming together to share a pile of hay. Then, I might notice it occurring after the two horses had separated for a while and then come back together, or after an altercation, when it seemed like they were "making up."

After a while, I began to notice that M to M happened much more regularly than I previously recognized—because the variables of this contact also included "distance contact," when the horses aimed M to M from far away. From this, I realized that it was not only the M to M that was significant, but also the flaring of nostrils that occurred during the interaction. Now, not only was I watching for M to M, but also for nostril flaring.

As I tuned into this added element, I noticed there were distinct nostril flares, and while some were related to M to M, some were not. In addition, some included an audible breathy sound.

For the purposes of my research, I tracked the baseline of M to M, both close up and far away. I noted the frequency, timing, and delivery, whether it included nostril flare, and if it did, then the frequency of nostril flare.

Now, another component began to be apparent: raising and lowering of the head while engaged in M to M. The nostril flare seemed to change with the raising and lowering of the head.

By now, I would have a range of context: high or low head, loud or soft breaths from nostrils, M to M that includes direct contact or indirect (distance) contact, both of which could occur when the horses were directly in front of each other, or when they were side by side (often at a 45-degree angle). Sometimes there was the addition of hoof strikes, stomps, or displays.

Finding Context

In order to fully understand the content of these messages, I had to ask a new series of questions:

- What led up to such displays (why did they happen)?
- What happened during the interaction?
- What happened after (what was the end result)?
- When two horses engaged in such a way, how did the engagement affect the social order, if it did?

- Did the behavior offer benefits to the herd and its overall well-being? Did it seem to serve to create bonding, settle a dispute, engage in play, or promote problem-solving activity?
- Did the behavior occur only at specific moments or did it happen frequently throughout the day?
- Can I witness this behavior in 10 horses I have never met before?

The Bell Curve

With the answers to these questions, I had a range of data about M to M engagement between horses. If organized and plotted out on a graph, from most to least intense, the resulting image was what I call the *Bell Curve* (fig. I.5).

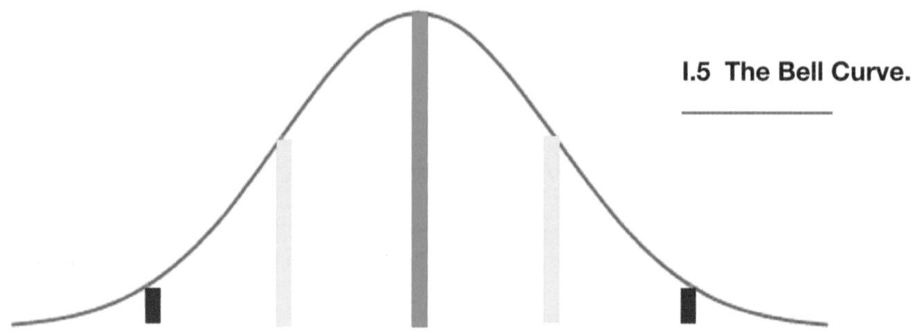

I.5 The Bell Curve.

At either end of the Bell Curve is an equine *Red Zone*: extreme withdrawal on one end and extreme engagement on the other. Both of these are reactive zones, when a horse's behavior can be unstable, and he isn't primed to learn or communicate. In the middle of the Bell Curve are the *Yellow* and *Green Zones*—think of a traffic light and when you should stop, when you can proceed with caution, and when you can go with confidence. When looking to engage with a horse, it is difficult if he is in one Red Zone (fearful and hesitant) or the other (in your face), but in Yellow or Green, the middle of the curve, you would find a reasonable middle range of predictable patterns in interactions related to M to M (as well as others). It is here, in the middle of the Bell Curve, where it is easiest to teach humans how to enter into a Conversation with a horse. It is extremely difficult to teach the extremes (the Red Zones) when first learning Horse Speak because of the range of variables and the sheer number of potential responses and outcomes that exist. The middle range is just plain easier to comprehend, imitate, and teach. This is why most of the target information I share in the pages ahead is set to this middle range. (Note that I will dip a little into the extremes—both Red Zones—when discussing certain topics.)

From Human to Horse

The next step was determining precise body language that accurately mimicked what the horses did. I practiced long hours of *Mirroring*, moving my own body in close harmony with a particular horse during a particular activity—grazing or social grooming, for example. I memorized how each horse used his body relative to the specific message: How did Horse A do the M-to-M touch? How did Horse B do it? I tested the Bell Curve with at least 10 other unfamiliar horses to find what might be considered "middle of the road" generalized activity versus Red Zone activity.

Over time, it became clear that horses preferred life in the Yellow or Green Zone—that Bell in the middle was where the inner *Zero* (a state of inner calm) I'd identified as terribly important to them was located (see p. 41 for more about Zero). The real breakthrough for me came when I could begin to see how a horse who was clearly in the Green Zone could effect a change in a horse who was in the Red Zone (calm a fearful horse, for example). Sometimes the messages a Green Zone horse shared were "slow and steady," which I translated to be messages of comfort, such as, "Let's have a 'Low-Calorie' Conversation" (fig. I.6). Other times, there were messages of

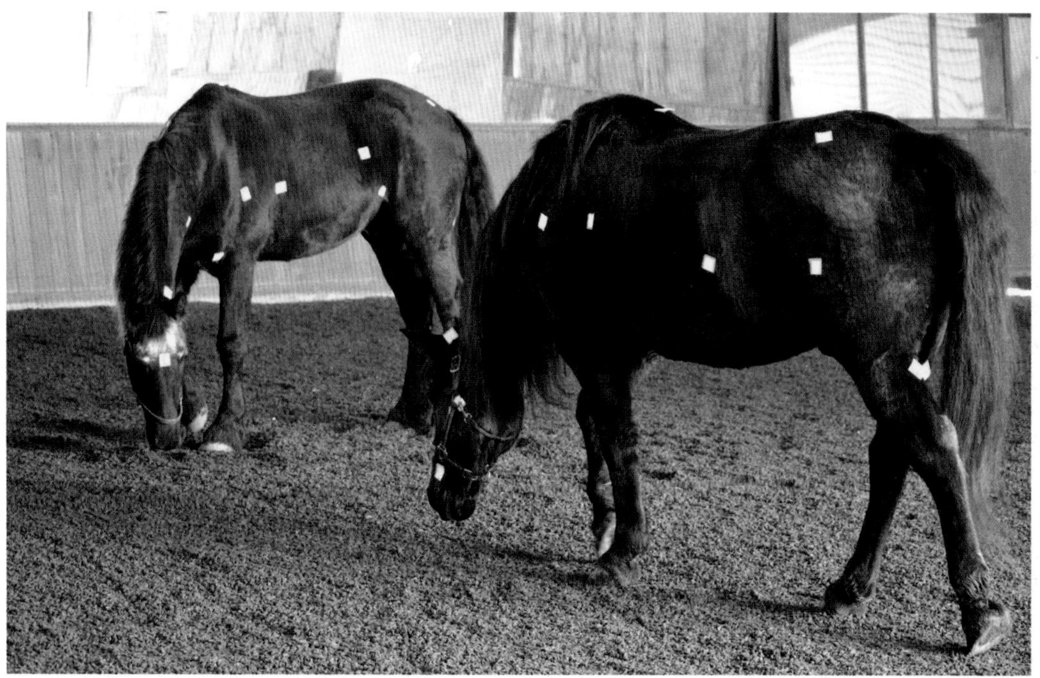

I.6 Horses use a low posture to initiate quiet communication. I call this a "Low-Calorie Conversation." (Note: The white squares mark the 15 Horse Speak Buttons, which I explain beginning on p. 117.)

protection: "Before I say 'Hi' to you, let me make sure there are no coyotes." And still other times, there were messages about resources: "Let's share a meal together." *Mirroring* these *Initiation Rituals* (p. 75) allowed me to get closer, sooner to many Red Zone horses. It helped me set the stage for working with difficult horses without ever needing to touch them. By copying these methods, I could introduce myself to horses in a totally different way than ever before, with profound results.

BUZZWORDS

Mirroring

We can match our horses' breath, footfalls, eye blinks, and position of other body parts to gain a deeper understanding of how they go through their day. When we let go of our human agenda and tap into the horses' agenda, we begin to see and feel the world from their perspective.

It Isn't About Behavior

While developing Horse Speak, I stopped thinking exclusively of the word "behavior." Although the word "behavior" has long been used as a common standard of describing what animals do, what I was not only witnessing but also beginning to take part in felt more like *language*. Certainly, behaviors were shown, but I was watching how one horse could visibly change the mental or physical state of another horse, or was seemingly able to influence another horse's decisions by asking things like, "May I share this hay with you?" or "I desire to go to the water tank, can I entice you to join me?" I was experiencing the primary state and group mind shifts that we normally associate with language, which is the ability of one being to communicate clearly to another the wants, needs, fears, and affections of the moment.

If I could recognize a horse's actions when he was "asking questions," and I was able to not only answer his questions, but "ask questions" of my own, then I believe the threshold between "behaviorism" and "language" was crossed.

Takeaways

The development of an awareness of the language of Horse Speak also awakened in me an understanding of other factors integral to being with horses and working with them in a positive and fulfilling manner.

Find the Right Role

Horses are not always in a happy state, and some horses appear grumpy and pushy much of the time. There are plenty of videos of horse bullies; I've viewed one of a wild stallion killing a lame foal in order to get his mares moving away from perceived danger. There is always a range of action and reaction in any group of living creatures. Despite this, there is a certain overall effect one can find in horse herds, and it is one of peaceful relationship. The horses within the herd have roles (which I discuss further later in the book—see p. 164), and we can model our own behavior in ways that reflect those roles. Do we want to be like a bully horse? Or do we want to be more of what I call a Mentor who creates a blanket of security and confidence in those following us. When you bully something, most living creatures either fight back or just give in. When you model healthy behavior, most living creatures match and mirror it, creating harmony.

Horses Have Emotions

As I learned the horse's language, I witnessed a wide variety of emotional signaling, as well. This had nothing to do with anthropomorphism (assigning horses human feelings and intentions). Mammals use emotions to form bonds, to manage crisis, to nurture their core group, and to resolve conflicts. Today, this is a considerably basic premise. What I was interested in was nailing down a solid baseline of equine emotional signals so that I would have a better range of understanding of the facial expressions and messages that were delivered to me. Ultimately, this would impact what I could offer in response.

MYTH-BUSTER

Do Horses Plan?

Because of the written and spoken word, humans can reflect on things from years ago and dream about tomorrow. Our language allows us to create complex strategies and build structures and containers (both literally and figuratively) to manage resources, emotions, and pace toward desired outcomes.

Horses do not build anything, nor do they bury hay in preparation for winter. They are more prone to "problem solving" what is in front of them in the moment rather than "strategizing" outcomes. But just because their language is based on solid, here-and-now needs, wants, and values does not mean that it is any less valuable than a language based upon time and imagination.

The Role of Expression

When I really began to fully comprehend the enormous impact facial expressions had between horses, it dawned on me that *this was a missing link*. Consider how, when first drawing a face, little children often sketch a big round circle, then two eyes and a long mouth, turned up or turned down… maybe some fuzzy hair (fig. I.7). One of our brains' first identifiable insights is that round faces have expressions, and we need to discern what they are.

What all this boils down to is this: Horses have faces, not just "heads." Human beings are more comfortable forming relationships with cats and dogs because they, like us, have eyes on the front of the head with a clearly defined nose and lips. When a cat or dog looks at you, you see a "face." In contrast, a horse's skull structure is exceptionally long, with a "muzzle" at the bottom, a long jaw and nasal structure, and a wide-set pair of eyes positioned on either side of the head—not in front like a predator. Also, animal size and head position impact our reactions: When a dog or cat looks up at you, they are broadening their focus to include you in their awareness. But when a horse raises his head up, he is moving into a state of hyper-focus. The only way the horse can strategically focus on the horizon or a specific object is to use the position of his head to adjust his vision. In contrast to dogs and cats, he *lowers* his head for connection and inclusion.

I.7 Early childhood drawings often feature eyes and smiles from a frontal perspective.

The Art of Communication

The art of Horse Speak becomes evident when the memorization of body language signals, postures, and gestures is ingrained, and the Conversation can begin to flow in both directions. You can interpret the horse ("decoding") and send messages back to him ("encoding"). At first the process is slow and a bit mechanical, but the good news is that horses tend to absolutely love it when you start to "speak" with them. They often assist, mature, blossom, and even begin teaching you new things.

Many of the body language messages you learn are truly the language of nature. Since committing myself to Horse Speak, I have had interactions with zoo animals, wild deer, fox, raccoons, and even seals. I have also adapted many of the basics to communicate with domestic animals: cows, sheep, goats, pigs—and, of course, dogs and cats. There are differences, as you might expect, but what is fascinating is that

SKILL-BUILDER

Developing a Relationship

Imagine you have to go to "marriage camp" before you get married. There, the head counselor ties both you and your partner to a dinner table and forbids you to get up until you have mastered the art of eating dinner in a polite manner. Then, the counselor presents you both with several tasks and hits you if you fail to work together to complete them. However, if you *do* complete the tasks, you get apple pie. Next, you have to solve puzzles with your partner, and if either one of you gets frustrated, you are tied up in a corner, and possibly made to repeat the puzzle 100 times. Only smiles are allowed, no frowns, and you cannot ask for help or clarity, or confront the actions taken against you, or you will be punished. You have to say, "Good morning, Teacher," every time you see the head counselor, regardless of how you feel. There are bars on the windows of your room, and you are locked in there whenever you aren't practicing the tasks required by the counselor.

When you complete the month of camp, you can get married.

How would your relationship turn out? How would your feelings about your partner turn out? What personal gains and losses can you imagine experiencing? How much would you project the experience onto your partner? Would every time you see your spouse, some element of "marriage camp" flash through your mind? Would you decide you do not want to be married anymore? And if so, would the counselor be called in to "refresh" the earlier conditioning?

On the other hand, what if you are sent to a different camp, where you have the completely opposite experience? You start your day by having coffee with your partner in a lovely garden, where you are given the ingredients to prepare a nice breakfast together. As you eat, you are allowed to negotiate what your plans are for the day and are encouraged to navigate the tasks and to-dos in ways that ensure that your needs and those of your partner are met. The counselor at this camp sets up skill-building exercises that demonstrate how you can navigate through a Conversation and gives you tools to help troubleshoot breakdowns in communication. You are provided a path to understanding what your partner might be feeling at any given moment during the Conversation.

A month after this camp you can get married. What do you imagine the results would be? Any different than if you attended the first camp?

This illustrates the cognitive dissonance that is often at the root of misunderstanding the role of training in the *art* of a relationship with a horse.

there are more similarities. How is it that farm animals can all get along? Why is it that animals so often connect better with children than adults? I now understand that, as children, we learned about and relied on body language to entrain our nervous system to know who and what provided safety, nurturing, and security, and who and what did not. We existed in a world of experience, not a world of ideas, and animals exist there, still.

I.8 The truly balanced horse exhibits what can be called a sense of pride in his body, mind, and heart, and he is open to communicating with us.

The Role of Balance in Communication

In Horse Speak, you will learn to pay strict attention to the way horses use their feet: how they walk, how they halt, and what foot is doing what. Horses talk with their feet—that is where imbalances of every sort show up.

Some training traditions have sought to create "four-square" foot placements out of the understanding that a well-balanced horse seems to also behave better. This is because all three balances—*mental, emotional,* and *physical*—go together for

horses. In-hand techniques and lateral movements often try to teach horses how to balance their bodies in particular ways that allow us to ride them in certain advanced maneuvers. There is an old saying, "Shoulder-in fixes everything." It can be effective for improving physical balance; however, we need to remember that forcing a horse into a frame or teaching a horse who is unfit for a particular exercise to do it anyway, does not improve his sense of well-being (his mental or emotional balance). A horse can learn to hold a frame through rote learning, but there is an evident sense of *pride* that comes with a truly well-balanced horse. When the old masters referred to "self-carriage" as a goal of training, they were referring not only to the look of a horse in balance, but also to the horse's sense of inner mastery and pride as he executed the skill. The truly balanced horse exhibits this characteristic in his body, mind, and heart, and in addition, he is open to communicating with others—including us (fig. I.8).

What Builds Rapport?

Rapport is a "soft skill," meaning it is a result of mutual understanding, tolerance, kindness, and a willingness to work together. Rapport has to be cultivated, and the conditions of it require trust, honesty, and open-heartedness.

You cannot force rapport. You *can* force compliance. The two are not the same (fig. I.9). We have two main settings: "friend" or "foe."

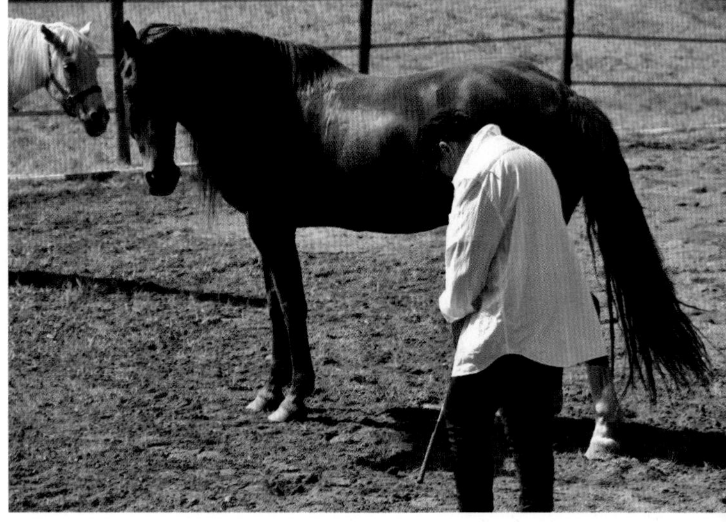

I.9 I use my posture to create a low-energy (what I call 'Low-Calorie'—see p. 41) Conversation, even with a whip in hand.

- If "friend," then what kind of friend? Are you a parent, child, lover, partner, follower, leader, student, teacher?
- If "foe," then what kind of foe? Are you an annoying irritant to mostly ignore? Someone to dislike and possibly rebel against? Someone dangerous to avoid? Or someone with lethal intent to do battle with or escape from?

A friend seeks rapport, a foe forces compliance.

When two beings understand each other, their nervous systems can switch off hypervigilance (worry about foes) and switch on agreements about connection (assurance of friendship). If you would like to have an epic relationship and build rapport with your horse, then Horse Speak is the place to start.

What *You* Need on this Journey

No One Has to Be Perfect

I encourage people to take some time off from their usual activities when learning Horse Speak. It is important to relearn some things about yourself, including your own three balances (physical, mental, and emotional). If you swing way out of balance with one, it will be reflected in your horse. He "reads" your body language like CliffsNotes®—if you cannot adapt and enhance your own body language to communicate more clearly, then he can only respond to the unconscious cues you and your three balances (mental, emotional, and physical) are delivering.

You do not have to be mentally, emotionally, or physically perfect to be with horses. It is more important to be *congruent*, meaning what is going on "inside" matches what is going on "outside." When you are congruent the horse can overlook your limitations and listen to what you really intend to say to him. Beginning this exchange can be as simple as talking out loud to your horse, from a healthy distance, all about whatever is really going on in your life. Note that this is different from the "chatterbox" tendency some people have or using "baby talk." I mean really *let it go* in front of your horse, preferably without touching him so as not to discharge all that intensity into his body. When you say what you mean, and really allow yourself to be vulnerable, horses can see an integrated version of you. When you try to hold stress inside in the back of your mind, your unconscious body language will act out, although you will be unaware of it (*incongruency*). The horse *is* aware, however. It then becomes muddy as to what he is supposed to pay attention to—the "inside" stuff, bubbling over in the background, or the actions you are taking and cues you are giving him on the outside?

SKILL-BUILDER

Ask a Better Question

Instead of, "What do I do to make my horse stop pawing on the cross-ties?" you have to learn to ask a better question, such as, "How do I help my horse feel more secure on the cross-ties? How do I express to him that I am here to protect him, and nothing will harm him as long as I am around?"

The Gap

All too often, this juncture is where what I call *The Gap* shows up. When we are out of touch with our own basic emotional state—out of habit, fear, anxiety, or even past traumatic events— then how are we going to be able to accurately assess the horse's, especially when a hallmark of a prey animal is to conceal much of its frailty? In nature,

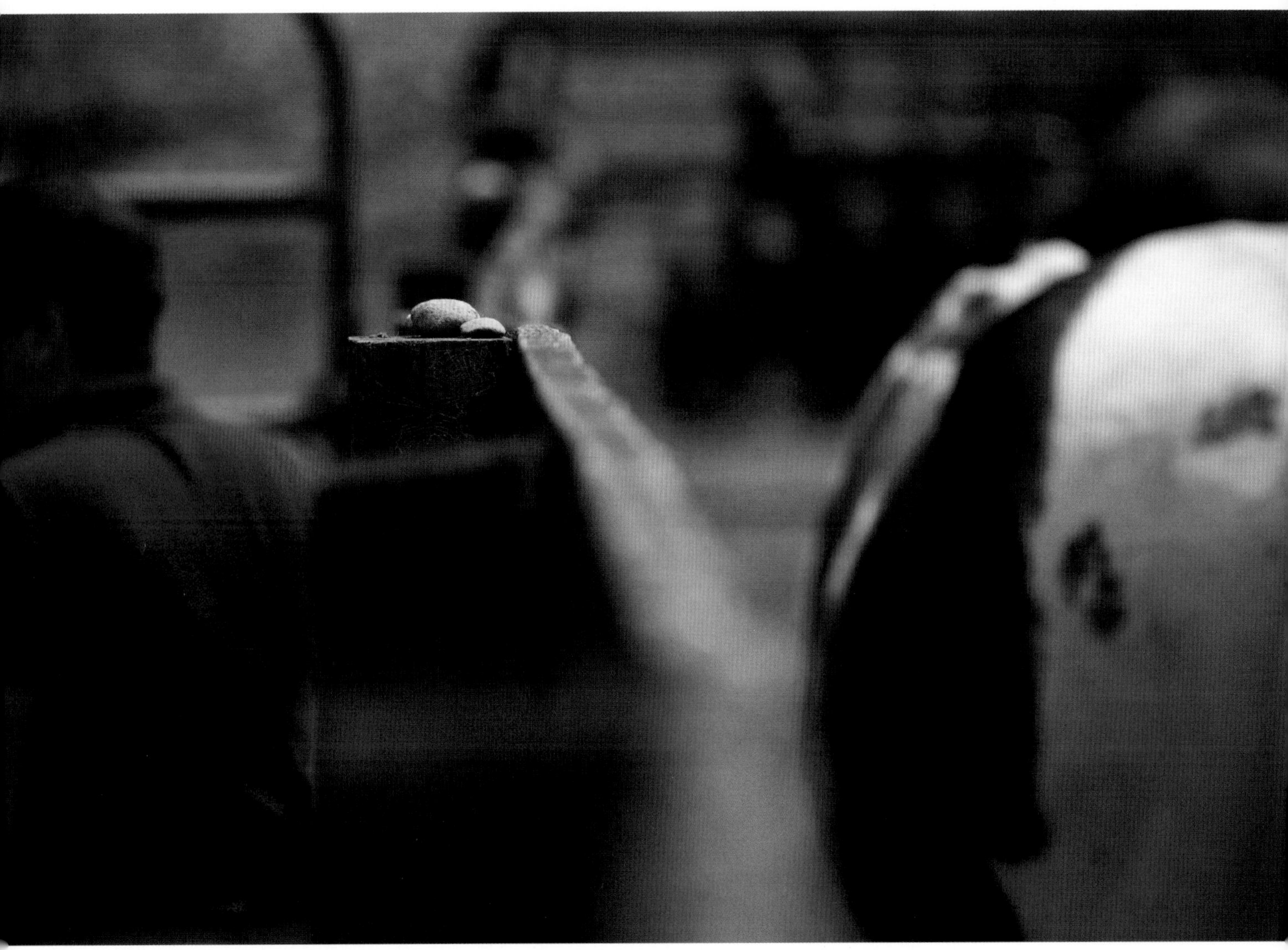

the horse that is obviously weak or wounded is the easiest target for a predator. Horses are not incongruent in the way we are, but one of their survival tactics is to hide injury or stress (fig. I.10). When they are hiding fear, stress, illness, or injury out of instinct, and we are taught to hide what we are really feeling, then who gets to "get real" first?

I.10 Mind *The Gap*—the space between what we know and what we don't know about horses.

This "Gap" is why I so often hear the words, "All of a sudden, the horse just blew up." When neither the horse nor the human is able to be present enough to de-escalate rising tension, something has to give.

Arriving at Balance: Finding Inner Zero

Humans have such developed imaginations that our minds can literally be in very different places from wherever our bodies are. We can be sitting on a city commuter train and lost in a story about wide open spaces and faraway places. Luckily, the basic functions of our brains usually work well enough "in the background" to prevent us from walking onto the train tracks or missing our stop. We are usually still aware on some level of the people around us (friend or foe?) and maintain the ability to sit upright and carry our belongings, despite being distracted by a fictional adventure.

This ability to be in two places at once is pretty unique to our species and part of what makes our world so interesting. However, if we are "lost in thought" while around horses, we can get into all sorts of trouble.

Horses are vulnerable creatures. It is a fact of prey-animal life. This means that, not only do they not mind if you are vulnerable in front of them, but they also often soften and relate more fully. (It is important to know that, of course, not all equine personality types will react the same way. Some horses really need us to be a competent leader.) Allowing yourself to "let go" with your horse helps ensure your resources are not split between being present and being distracted. All horses need us to be in a state of readiness and congruency when we are with them.

I have found I am most successful in spending time with my own horses or the

SKILL-BUILDER

How Do You Learn?

As you embark on learning the language of the horse, know that it is not like learning to speak Italian (for example) to another human. You are learning to use your body to speak to another species. It is important to your journey to know how you will be able to learn Horse Speak best. Career and management learning-solution provider MindTools.com indicates there are three models of learning style: *audio, visual,* and *kinesthetic. Visual* learners need to be taught with visual aids (tools that can be seen); audio learners love to listen to lectures (and typically like to talk!); kinesthetic learners need to have the physical experience to "get it." Everyone uses all three learning styles to some degree, but you have one that is the "strongest" (the easiest way for you to learn), one that is your comfort zone or "grounded place," and lastly, one that is the "deepest place" (it helps what you learn resonate and become part of you).

I want you to have success as you explore Horse Speak. My students have found determining how they best learn useful to their journeys, especially those who are, in turn, professional instructors or trainers, because it helps them understand their own clients much better.

horses I meet at clinics and expos when I "get present." I must allow the happenings of my day and the thoughts that are running through my mind to go to rest as I prepare to head into the world of the horse. Your horse will thank you if you can find an activity or exercise—meditation, yoga, breath work—to do before you interact with him that helps you "be here now."

I.11 Horses who endlessly chew on objects may be showing signs of displacement—a strategy of addiction and distraction.

One thing that is different between our species is that horses, by nature, seem to crave a state of inner and outer balance. This is in the energy of Zero (a state of inner calm) that I mentioned in the section about the Bell Curve (see p. 20). Zero also allows you to feel *physical* well-being. As we have already discussed, the horse's physical, mental, and emotional balance are deeply connected. In truth, ours are, as well, but we human beings tend to become very detached from our bodies and distracted by what is going on "inside." Perhaps this is one reason why we want to be with horses—to "get back into" our bodies in a direct and meaningful way. I have long wondered if humans have developed strategies of addiction and distraction (*displacement activities*) to deal with this basic disconnect. Horses may show levels of displacement activity as well, such as weaving, pacing, and cribbing. There are no real vices in human or horse; it is all displacement (fig. I.11).

When we show up to the barn dissociated and "out of our bodies," then that is the model of behavior we demonstrate to our horses. This is also the model of communication we offer—distracted, internally focused on our own thoughts, and generally anxious, guilty, or discouraged about the many things we are having internal dialogue about. A horse cannot know what our internal dialogue is, but the horse will react when we are saying with our unconscious body language, "Something is wrong," or "I am not happy."

The fact is, *Zero makes your strong, stronger*. If you have a good Zero—a good state of inner calm—then you have the baseline from which all other things spring. Zero is not *empty quiet*; it is actively choosing to remain centered. This is an act of power and determination. The horse with the best Zero is the most reliable (Green Zone) horse. And horses recognize a good Zero in humans, too. I teach you how to practice your Inner Zero in chapter 2 (p. 41).

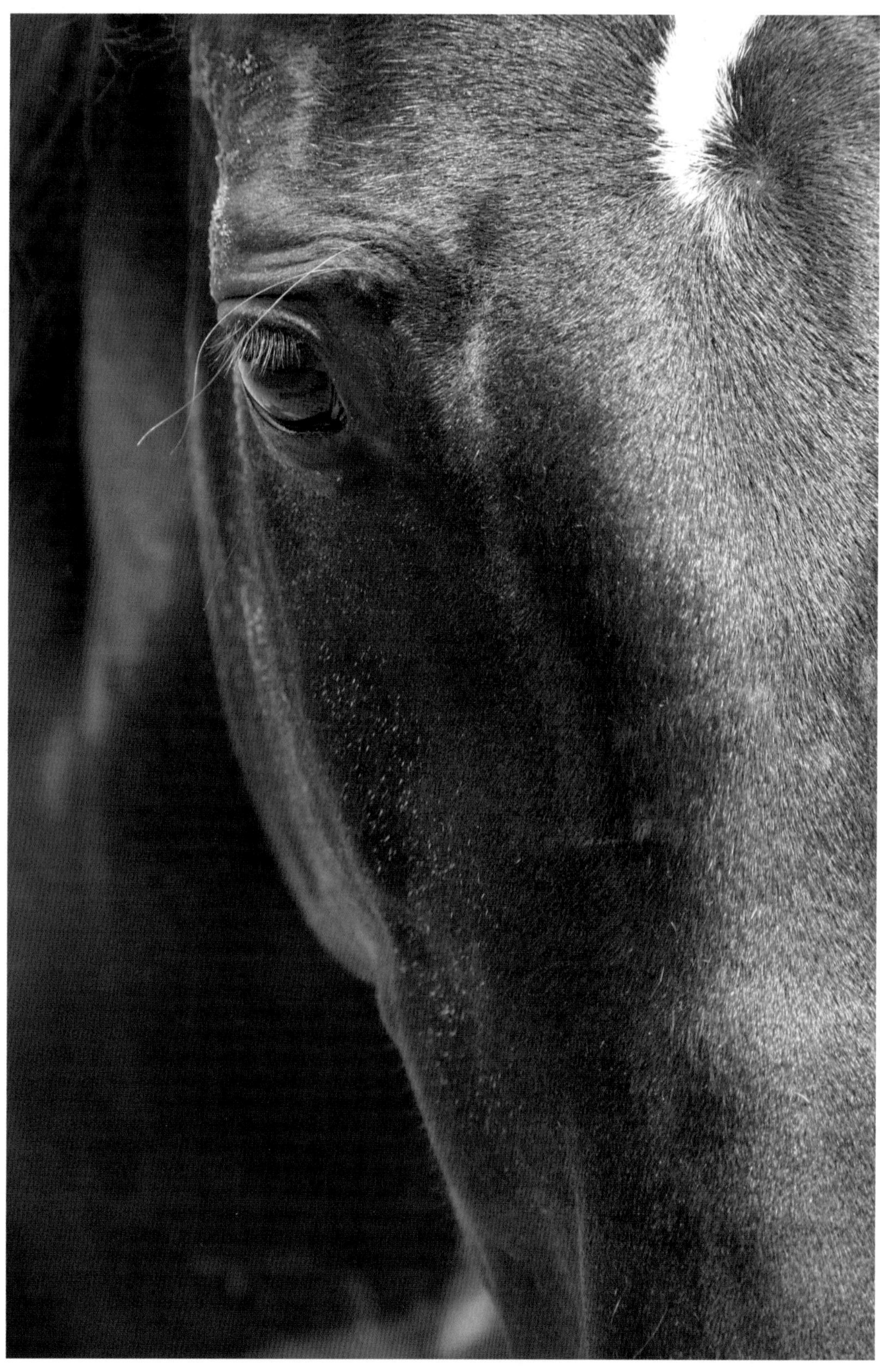

I.12 What is the *Feeling State* of the human versus the horse? Reading facial expressions—especially the eyes—can help determine what the horse may be feeling or experiencing.

The Three Pillars of Horse Speak

Developing the First Pillar: Cognitive Understanding

You must train your eye to observe *what is really there*, not what your thoughts tell you is there. In addition, cognitive understanding of Horse Speak also means memorizing a certain number of data points.

You will probably come up against previously held beliefs about what horses are doing and what they mean by certain actions. "Seeing is believing," as they say, and as you learn to really see horses communicating, your eyes will witness the reality of Horse Speak—your understanding will not be based upon my words teaching about it.

This stage of learning requires your eyes to work a little differently: You need to use your peripheral vision to see both ends of the horse at once. You will learn to focus on one body part doing one thing, yet still be able to shift your gaze as needed to other body parts. Taken as a whole, the entire horse is used in communication: postures, gestures, and signals like eye contact, Breath Messages, single footsteps and raising and lowering of the head all mean something. There can be a wiggling muzzle, with an eye blink, a single step, a lean into a direction, and a tail swish. Each has individual meaning, and together they have collective meaning.

BUZZWORDS

Feeling State

We tend to substitute the word "feeling" when we mean belief, preference, or like or dislike. I using the word "feeling" to describe awareness of both physical sensations and emotional responses.

For instance, using the word in a casual manner, I may say something like, "I feel that my life has meaning. I feel like eating a hamburger today. I feel like I liked your hair when it was pink, but the new color purple makes me feel uneasy."

Becoming aware of the *Feeling State* is checking for congruency and sensation in your body verses perceived sensations from the horse's body. For example, let's say I step into a horse's *Bubble of Personal Space* and my heart begins to race, and I become tense. When I step out of the Bubble, I am restored to neutral. I ask myself the question: "Is it me, or is it coming from the horse?" This is checking for the Feeling State.

Developing the Second Pillar: Empathy

To begin trusting your ability to empathize with your horse, which gives you the ability to accurately read his *Feeling State*, you have to be able to read and work with your own authentic Feeling State. You (and the horse) have both a physical Feeling State (what you notice about your body at any given point in time) and an emotional Feeling State (the emotion you sense at any given point in time). The primary reason the Pillar of Empathy is so important is that you want to tune in to these aspects of your horse in order to both perform better risk assessment *and* have a better chance for bonding (fig. I.12). If you are completely unaware of the emotional elements at play behind a horse's messages, then you may miss an entire side of a Conversation between you.

When we talk to other humans, we use our tone of voice, word choice, and body language to communicate the feelings behind the Conversation. Our most impactful communications are the emotional ones. In fact, when you learn the skills needed for a job in, say, sales, mediation, or psychotherapy, you are taught to pay attention to emotional language and subtle gestures—what are called "tells." In contrast, we have long been taught to ignore what horses might be feeling and the signals they might share to communicate those feelings. This makes sense when a horse is a vehicle or a war machine; however, in modern society, we want to know that our horses are happy and comfortable, or even if (dare I say it?) they *love us*.

Not only have *we* been taught to ignore their feelings, but *they have also* been taught to ignore their feelings. Standard training looks at what the body of the horse is doing: Is it performing in the frame we want? Is it going the speed we want? Is it clearing the jumps or working the cow or spinning the way we want? If not, how do we make this happen? What do we do to the horse's body with our riding, or with training techniques, to make the body of the horse work and look the way we want it to?

None of this has anything to do with the horse's feelings. We may notice that a horse has a "good work ethic" or is "relaxed and forward" or is "calm and quiet," but none of these statements says much about what the horse is *emotionally feeling*.

Of course, many people still get the heebie-jeebies when it comes to using words like "emotion" when talking about horses, because we have an outdated scientific model that is completely spooked by anything to do with feelings. When I was hospitalized in the sixties, the term "patient care" didn't exist. Believe me, I had my fair share of "Nurse Ratcheds." The very idea that a nurse should show empathy to a patient as part of the healing process was not only discounted, it was also frowned upon. This same attitude informed early scientific norms where animals were used in vivisection and behavioral experiments that many of us would now acknowledge as akin to torture. With the development of a field called *ethology*—the scientific and objective study of animal behavior under natural conditions—we have a movement toward understanding animals in their own world and studying them in far more conscientious ways.

The important thing about developing empathy in your life with your horse is

BUZZWORDS

Bubble of Personal Space

This is the circular realm of personal space around a horse, and around us. If you watch horses move in a group with each other, you will see them walk around each other in arcs, tracing the borders of their Bubbles.

that, while your nervous system will not lie, it *can* be swayed by your projections and beliefs. If there is trauma in the horse or the human, the nervous system can *also* overreact. I have worked with many traumatized horses, and being able to know my own emotional Feeling State and trust my own nerves while tuning into theirs has kept me from getting killed more than once. Learning to read their body language gave me a way to realize when a horse was getting triggered (in the Red Zone), and it is *this* that I want you to learn. I have had many reports from people who were able to avert catastrophe because they could read the signs in their horses and were able to trust what their own bodies, inside and out, were telling them about those signals.

Feel

The Pillar of Empathy is about "feel," but more than just the sensory "feel" of limited, body-centered awareness, like you have when balancing a bicycle, walking on a balance beam, or even playing sports. You do not really need empathy to have a better shot in basketball or to ride a bike. Horsemanship, on the other hand, requires more than tactile skills.

Some trainers or instructors may have said to you, "You just need to get the feel." You may have seen amazing equestrian performances, of either the athletic or entertainment kind, where it certainly looks like the humans involved have some kind of feel. "Finding a feel" has been long associated with the mysteries of attaining "oneness" with a horse. Many books and clinicians, over many years, have tried to illustrate this elusive sensation. The conundrum here is that old saying, which we often hear in relation to feel: "You either have it or you don't." Well, I am not satisfied with that answer. I want all my students to embody that mysterious word, *feel*, and one of my goals of this book is to teach it to you! And, if you already have good feel, I want to help you to have *great* feel (fig. I.13).

Treating horseback riding like a mostly tactile skill leaves out the other side of the coin: the fact that both humans and horses are highly emotional creatures. When asked what initially drew them to horses, one of the top reasons people cite is generally something like, "I like how they make me feel," not, "I like the sensation of using my calf muscles on a horse's flanks." What so often happens when learning to ride, however, is the student is told to "make" the horse do whatever it is she wants (trot, for example) and to ignore emotional feelings related to getting a horse to do it (such as kicking). We go to a lesson to feel, and we are often systematically taught *not to* feel.

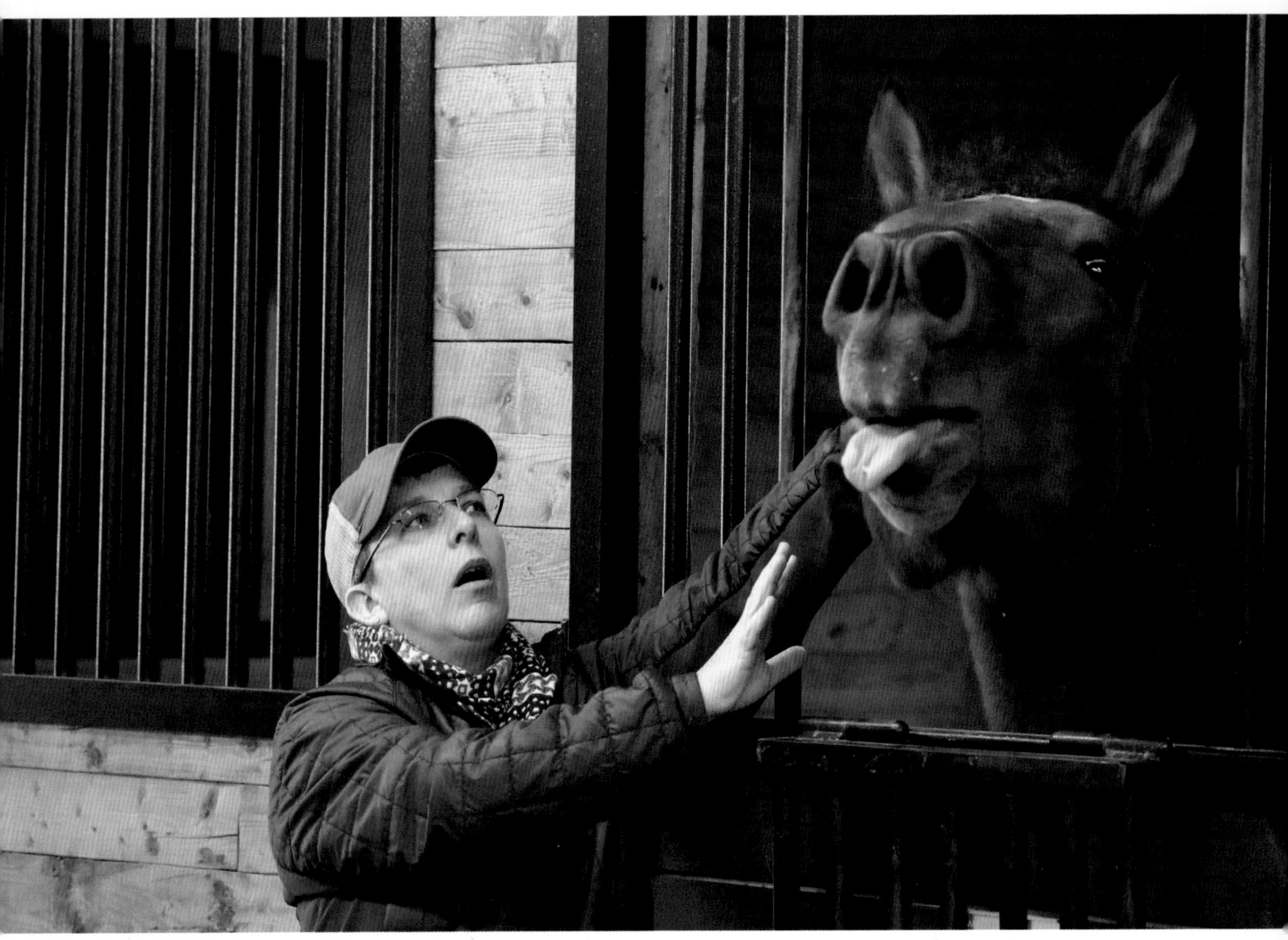

I.13 Trying to make the same facial expression that a horse is making can help you get the "feel" of a horse.

What Is "Feel," Anyway?

When horsemen talk about the word "feel," they are generally referring to awareness achieved through both *proprioception* (perception of the body's balance, locomotion, and physical expression) and *sensory perception* (processing of input related to the experience the body is having via sight, sound, smell, taste, or touch). Let's imagine a yard stick. On one end are people who have a difficult time decoding body language, and on the other end are people who are masters of body language. The increments between them indicate the varying degrees of ability to decode and encode body language. In many ways, "feel" is simply the ability of the brain to decode and encode correctly and quickly, along with the understanding of what to do with the coding to further your goals.

For example, if your brain sees an angry human face and responds correctly to that face by staying out of trouble or even preventing trouble from happening, then the next time you see that angry face "brimming" (meaning a second before it even happens), your brain will start initiating the coding process to keep you out of trouble. The physical sensation might be that intuitive "hit" you feel in the pit of your stomach, which seems to help tell you what to do in the situation. Some researchers who study neuroscience and Polyvagal Theory teach that the nerves of the brain are connected to the gut, heart, and lungs via the vagus nerve, and that the vagus nerve plays a role in emotion regulation, social connection, and fear response. This is oversimplifying it,

SKILL-BUILDER

Developing Your Feel

When with your horse, ask yourself good questions like:

- How do I feel inside my belly?
- How do I feel inside my heart?
- Do I feel dizzy in the company of this horse, or do I feel centered and calm?
- Am I scooting off into internal dialogue in six seconds, or can I linger longer with these feelings? (We sometime feel uncomfortable trying something new, so we need to be patient with the process and stick with it.)

Assign non-escalating language to what you believe to be your horse's "moods." For example, instead of, "He's angry!" try "He appears to be feeling a *level of stress*, which I can see due to his facial expressions, the fact that he is holding his breath, and his tense posture." Or, rather than, "She's happy!" try, "She appears to be feeling *comfortable and relaxed* because of her deep breathing, her cocked hind leg, and her droopy ears."

This language can help you "feel" what your horse really needs and begin to understand how best to react to his state or actions in a moment in time. If you say to yourself, "He appears to be feeling stressed," you can then consider whether, in response to his mood, you are shutting down, feeling tense, or beginning to feel negative, as well. Likewise, you could sense your body feeling warm and comfortable as you watch your mare in her relaxed state.

Cultivating an ability to identify with the horse's state of being, and then learning to pay attention to the back-and-forth empathetic share, is vital to coming to a more accurate conclusion about what is real for your horse and what is a projection of your own mental or emotional state on him. With practice, this exercise can help you be more "in the ballpark" with regard to what your horse is telling you.

SKILL-BUILDER

Inspired Coaching—Getting into the Mindset

Did you grow up participating in your school band, play sports, or perform with the drama club? Typically, these types of activities involve a leader or coach. Do you remember a leader who inspired you but made you work hard and held you to a standard, which created a path to be the best you could be, both individually and as a team? Or was there a coach you liked just fine, but you only stayed with the program because you liked the activity, not because of what the leadership offered?

My partner Laura grew up playing sports—mainly basketball, but she loves to play anything where you can throw, hit, or muscle your body around. She says her high school basketball coach had a passion for leading. He got his players physically fit, worked on their foundational footwork and other practical skills, prepared them mentally, and emotionally inspired them to put their hearts into the game. He also let them know that he had their backs. His team trusted that, no matter what, he would give them the direction they needed to succeed, which they did by winning a state championship.

On the other hand, Laura tells me about other coaches who were mediocre at their jobs. They set a timer, went over a list of drills every day, and shouted plays during practice. The experience was empty—there was nothing enriching about going to practice.

What Horse Speak represents is a playbook. It is a strategy that can be adapted to anything you are doing with your horse, and it enables you to do more than provide drills and shout plays. Instead, you can be the inspirational coach and mentor for your horse. I want you to be like Laura's high school coach. I want you to understand the world from the horse's perspective, be able to speak his language, and inspire him to feel encouraged, confident, and full of pride with every step.

Like a good coach, we do need to work with horses in a way that keeps both us and them safe. They are big creatures on the outside, but so many of them are like tiny little hamsters on the inside. We do need to have a sense of control, and we do need to act like healthy, sane leaders. Sometimes we need to draw a line or give a reprimand. That is just life. However, I do not think we really want to live every day like it is a battlefield. Since developing Horse Speak, all I need to do is snap my fingers, and my horses know, "Mom means business!" This is like the kindergarten teacher who gets her rowdy class to focus by whispering, until all the kids are saying, "SHHH!" to each other... because they want to hear *everything* she has to say.

but basically the brain and nervous system do things we do not always know about to ensure our survival. One of those things is to accurately predict outcomes based on subtle signs and cues that our system is "reading" from the world around us. If your eyes perceive movement on the ground that wiggles like a snake, your body is inclined to jump up and away without it being a conscious choice. This is an intuitive reaction to stimulus; however, on more subtle levels, you are also reacting to the messages you have come to believe or been conditioned to respond to from all your sense perceptions all the time (remember the angry face example from earlier—see p. 24).

Developing the Third Pillar: Mechanics

The Mechanics of Horse Speak are the nuanced gestures, postures, and signals that we use in Conversations with horses. This book gives you the opportunity to learn them and put them into practice in your day-to-day interactions with your horse.

Three Pillars, One Goal

The Pillars of Cognition, Empathy, and Mechanics are needed to create balance in the interpretations of equine body language. You need to be able to read signs and also interpret the feel of the messages in order to reply. Most people are stronger at one Pillar or another, but all are needed for a well-rounded communication to take place. I go into more details of how to develop your empathy, your sense perceptions, and your mechanics later in this book, but know that the outcome I want for you is to take whatever discipline you are already pursuing with whatever style of horsemanship you already practice, *and make it better*. The number-one reason I focus primarily on getting readers to Zero and to be able to use the Three Pillars is to train them to become more present and have their insides match their outsides. The reason I want you to learn all the steps of "speaking horse" is to gain access to rhythm, timing, and harmony. Taken all together, these are the components that help create the horsemanship term of "feel." These are the pieces that will move you from one end of that yardstick to the other.

1 Solidifying Basic Language Skills

What Is Zero and Why Do You Need It?

1.1. A & B Horses at play may show X posture (see p. 47)—the posture of intensity (A). When intensity is over, they use a "Low-O" posture (showing a state of relaxation—see p. 47) to show it (B).

In *Horse Speak: The Equine-Human Translation Guide* I teach the concept of *Inner Zero* first, and because it is the most important tool you will have (and one that you should always return to), I will do the same here. Since horses are always watching your body for clues, you need to be aware of your basic posture.

Zero is the term I use to represent an inner state of calm. I use the word Zero because in Horse Speak there are levels of intensity that range from Level One to Level Four. Zero is what comes *before* any intensity, and it is where we need to return *after* intensity. When one horse moves another one, the mover uses the appropriate level of intensity for the situation (the lowest level necessary) and goes back to Inner Zero when it's over (figs. 1.1 A & B).

We have to cultivate our Inner Zero. Most of us lead hectic lives, and as I've already mentioned, this inner stress is read by horses and can make us incongruent to them. More problematic is that when you are stressed on the inside and trying to be a horse's leader, then in effect you may be telling him, "Follow my lead and get stressed out."

I have found a commitment to Inner Zero and the Low-Calorie Conversation to be the absolute best way to establish new "ground rules" for improved manners. *Things are going to take time no matter what you do.* Modeling the calm, centered, and focused behavior you expect from your horse from the get-go can have surprising and long-lasting effects.

How to Get to Zero

Getting to Zero can be a very personal activity. You may have a specific practice in your life that brings you to Zero, and if so, it is beneficial to engage in it when preparing to spend time with your horse. For instance, if you like yoga, then do some in the paddock. If you like artwork, then draw your horses. To further cultivate your Zero while with your horse, try this:

1 *Focus on your senses,* especially your senses of hearing and smell. Listen to the sounds of nature; inhale the natural smell of your horse or the barn. Play the same song before you go out to see your horse to get yourself in the right mindset.

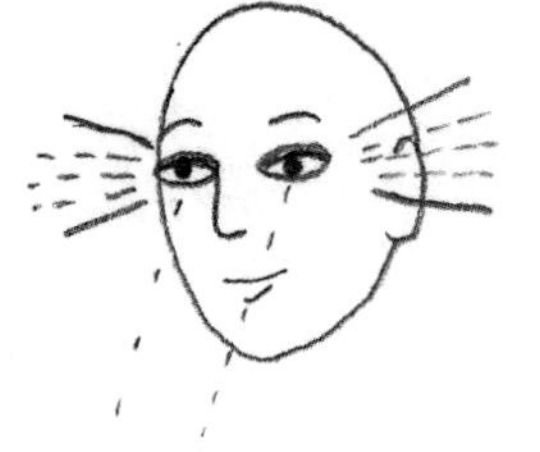

1.2 Peripheral vision is important to develop. Horses can see around themselves, so we need to pay closer attention to what is around us.

2 *Focus on your eyes,* specifically your peripheral vision. Raise your palms so they hover on either side of the corners of your eyes. Expand and contract your hands until your peripheral vision becomes engaged (fig. 1.2). This does two things: First, it may relax you. How we use our eyes affects the chemistry of our brain and the levels of stress or relaxation we feel. Second, it prepares you to be able to take in the image of your whole horse, from nose to tail, instead of hyper-focusing on one area of his body at a time.

3 *Focus on your breathing,* and make sure that you take full breaths. Holding your breath is a symptom of latent stress. It does not matter what sort of breathwork you do, just pay attention to the fact that when you inhale it represents what you "take in," and what you exhale represents what you "let out."

4 *Place your hands in your lap* with your middle and ring fingers touching. Relax your hands, elbows, and shoulders. Just doing this signals your nervous system to switch from *sympathetic* (the involuntary response to dangerous or stressful situations) to *parasympathetic* (the "rest and digest" system).

5 Do all these things at the same time.

Notice that in the steps just illustrated I did not mention anything about *what to think*. There is a reason for that. The state that your body is in—meaning the posture you are using—affects your mental and emotional function. What this means is that you do not have to try to grapple with the "monkey in your mind" when you have made a habit of changing your physical, mental, and emotional state using body-centered awareness. This is a form of practical mindfulness and learning to "be present."

SKILL-BUILDER

Building Awareness of Your Senses

Getting familiar with which sense is your strongest and which is your weakest is part of gaining the "feel" that I talked about in the Introduction (p. 35). When you are able to perceive the sense that is strongest or most dominant, take a stroll and practice focusing on that sense for five minutes. So, if you are very sensitive to smell, allow yourself to really engage in all the scents of your environment. Then, take a break for five minutes. When you are ready, take the same walk while focusing on the sense that seems to be your weakest. The goal is just to explore without judgment and build an awareness of how you take in the world around you.

Continue to practice shifting your state to Zero on a regular basis. Our bodies like homeostasis; when you point the body in the direction of a better state of well-being, it tends to want to go there all by itself.

Take Zero to Your Horse

Your next step is to practice Zero in the presence of your horse. For the best results, start on the other side of a physical barrier from your horse but close enough that he is paying attention to you. A small paddock or stall is great; a larger arena or round pen is acceptable. The key is to notice if your change of state (condition you are in at a specific time) to Zero has an effect on your horse. If so, what did you notice?

When a horse gains a better Zero (moves from Red Zone to Yellow or Green—see p. 20), it means he comes to understand that you not only want his body to perform tasks for you, but you also want him to have a better sense of overall well-being. This often results in the horse investing more in building a relationship with you. And, more than anything else, it allows a horse to mature and blossom into his potential. A horse who has matured is better able to express agency over his life and therefore can begin to "self-regulate" (or do a better job of it). A horse who is able to self-regulate is better able to monitor his level of arousal and find ways to ease his reactions to stress through an internal ability to do so—not from you correcting or regulating him through techniques. (I will give you some skill-building practices that help your horse embody Zero, beginning on p. 45.)

What a Horse Looks Like When He Is Going to Zero

- Eye blinking: Staring is fear, worry, or concern; blinking is thinking.
- Soft, relaxed ears or "perky," engaged ears.
- Licking and chewing, temporomandibular joint (TMJ) release.
- Lip wiggling: Wiggling the upper lip, or flapping the lips together is a signal of resetting emotionally and also a signal to others of having pleasant feelings. (In *Horse Speak* I call this "Having a Nice Day.")
- Drooping lips: Often a sign of really relaxed facial tone. Occasionally *extremely* droopy lips on a listless horse is a sign that the horse is not feeling well.
- Head nodding: As the horse's nervous system shifts down into "rest, digest, and repair," it is common to see him make little nodding motions. (I tell people to make gentle "Yes" and "No" head-nodding gestures to encourage horses to do the same.)
- Scratching the front leg with the side of the face: I call this "Learning Something." You will see horses do this when they seem to be understanding current events. Humans touch their own faces during similar "Aha!" moments when something is either understood or integrated.
- Relaxed shoulders: When a horse is in an intense or "high" posture, his whole skeleton shifts into "run position" with a rotation of the shoulder blade. This makes horses look inverted (like a banana) and as if they are on their tippy toes. When they shift into a truly relaxed state, the shoulder blades have a more rounded and "comfortable" look. The horse's whole skeleton then resumes "rest, digest, and repair," often making him look shorter and fatter as the adrenaline leaves his body.
- Tail release: In Zero, the horse lifts the tail into a comfortable position, as opposed to clamping it down or flagging it high. Sometimes this is combined with a little wagging motion indicating a release or the passing of gas or manure.
- Re-adjusting feet: As they shift into Zero, most horses will rebalance their feet. Becoming mentally and emotionally balanced is reflected in adopting better

physical balance. (It is interesting to note here that the better a horse's three balances, the higher in herd hierarchy he will usually be because a balanced posture states competence to others.)

Pay strict attention to all these signs. Seek to find them when doing your Mirroring practice (see p. 102). The better you are at seeing the signs of Zero, the better you will be at sending these messages yourself, and the better you'll be at helping your horse to either find Zero or stay Zero.

SKILL-BUILDER

Use an Artificial Barrier to Help You and Your Horse Find Zero

It can be a good idea to practice finding Zero with your horse on the opposite of a barrier. The reason is simple: The physical barrier ensures a Bubble of Personal Space for both you and your horse. For this phase of learning, your only concern is to be able to safely practice your Zero and notice whether it has any effect on your horse without raising any personal space issues. This is beneficial for all horse types, no matter where they are on the Bell Curve, and is especially useful for an extremely sensitive (Red Zone) horse or a too friendly or too high strung (also Red Zone) horse. Having a barrier means both you and the horse do not have to adjust to accommodate each other's Bubbles yet. In my experience, this is an important step that should not be skipped (fig. 1.3).

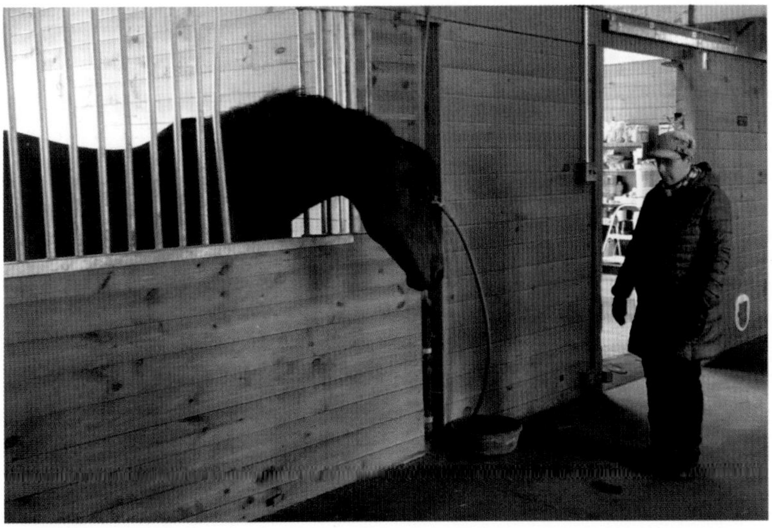

1.3 This stallion was defensive of his space. Working across the barrier of his stall allowed me to gain his trust by approaching and retreating while staying safe.

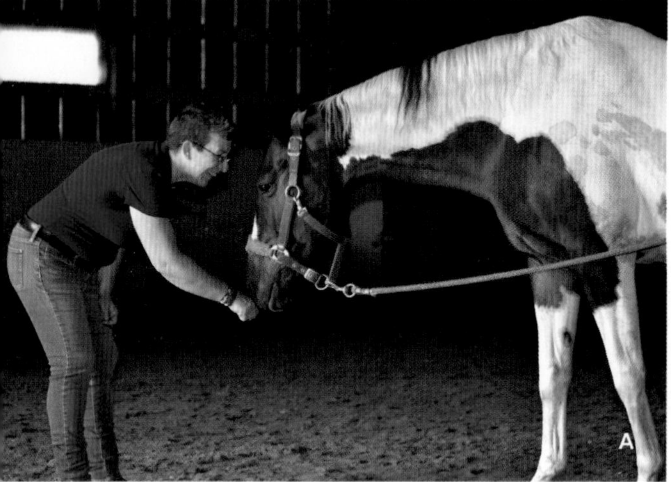

1.4 A & B A welcoming posture is similar in both humans and horses (A). A beckoning expression—relaxed ears, a steady soft gaze, a lowering of the head or head nods, and soft breaths—is shown by both the horses in Photo B. It is easy to see once you know what you are looking for.

Drawing, Driving, and Halting Forces—Getting to Know X and O

We are tall, thin creatures, so by offering hand gestures, we can better describe the space around us and what we want to do with it. A *welcoming posture* may involve opening your hands wide, softening your chest, and smiling at another. A *defensive posture* may involve hugging yourself tightly, looking downward, or making other "unwelcoming" gestures.

The horse cannot make gestures with hands, but he does have a long head and neck, and he does use their length and height changes, along with changes in the angle of his body, to express his own feelings of being welcoming or defensive (figs. 1.4 A & B).

Here we must address the two main postures of body language: *X* and *O* (figs. 1.5 A–D). The *X posture*—when you face the horse directly with your eyes, shoulders, hands, belly button, and feet, shoulders back, feet spread, hands raised—represents intensity; the subject in X is awake, aware, and alert. The *O posture*, on the other hand—rounded shoulders, hands together in front of your belly—represents relaxation and reprieve. The subject in an O could be neutral, or possibly even welcoming or beckoning.

Our beliefs or habits related to correct posture or stance can be inherently at odds with the creating of rapport around horses. Many of us were taught that a tense, upright posture is a sign of confidence, and we must walk around with this X,

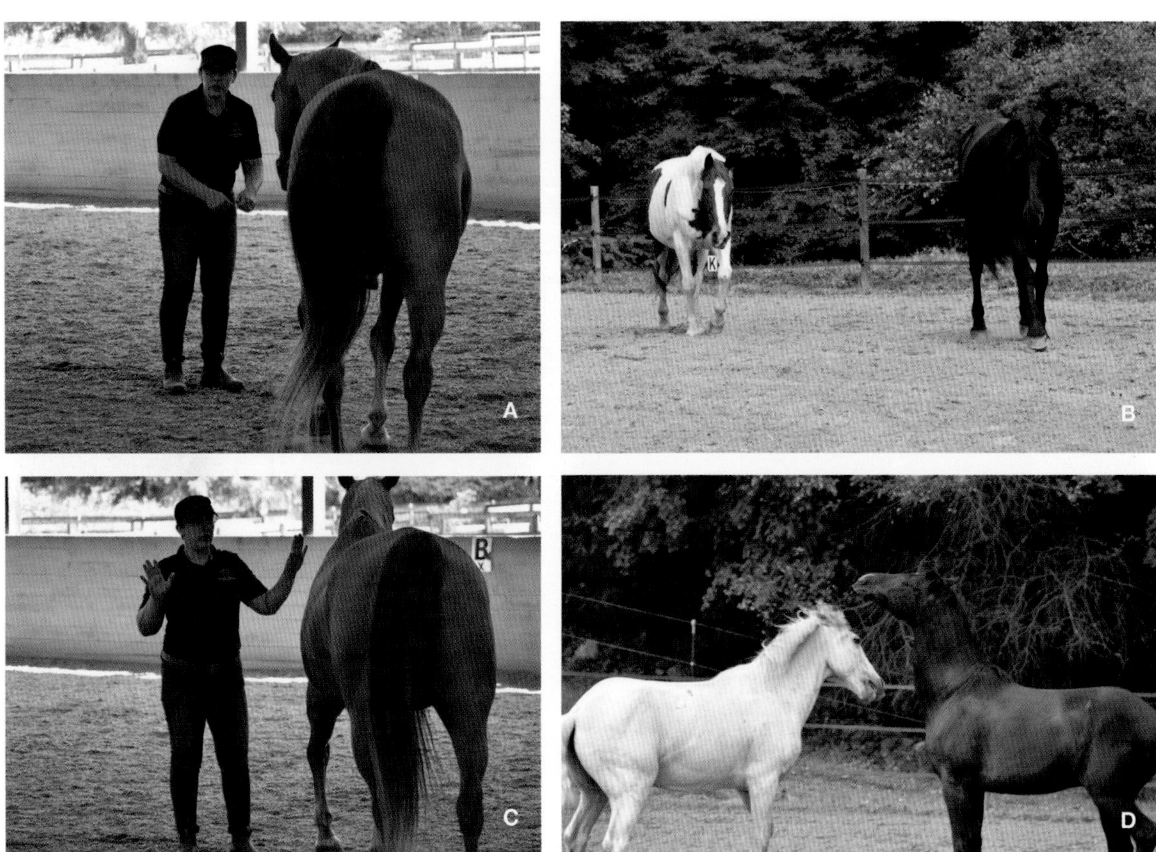

1.5 A–D In Photo A, I am in O posture, drawing the horse to me and connecting with him. In B, you see horses in O posture, either coming together or moving in connection. Photos C and D show me and a pair of horses in X, which is used for driving a horse forward and asking him to halt.

especially with horses. Too much X, however, has a driving effect; it is not beckoning or welcoming as there is no softness in it. It can also indicate hypervigilance, chronic anxiety, or hostility. The O can also be taken to an extreme and become a sort of "apologetic posture." Too much O can make it difficult to set appropriate boundaries. It doesn't provide a partner a solid "place to land" nor does it volunteer a strong membership in a team, group, or couple.

The right amount of X and O can make all the difference in your ability to communicate with your horse. A *balanced* X in a person represents someone who is awake and aware, not overly tense but fully present, and in a level state of both self-awareness and self-control (fig. 1.6). The *right* amount of O represents someone who is open-hearted, welcoming, and nurturing.

1.6 A balanced X, as shown by Laura in this photo, is awake and aware. Laura and Zeke are in *Matching Steps,* moving in harmony together.

1.7 Laura's O posture can be athletic, too.

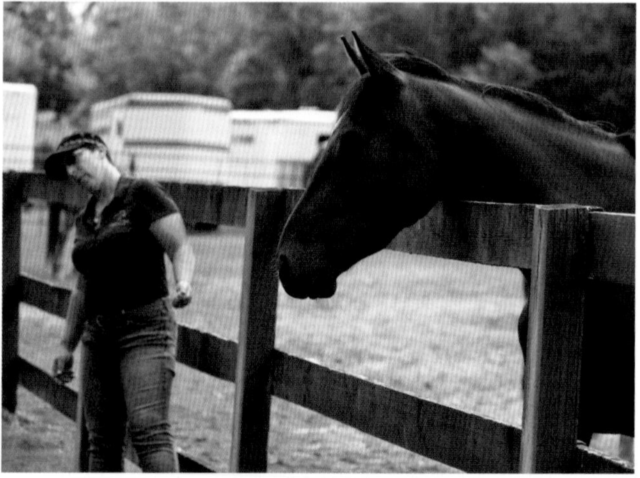

1.8 Scooping with my head, neck, and shoulder, with a beckoning gesture from my hand, invites this young gelding into my space.

The amazing thing about these two postures is that in communication, they can denote levels of action, levels of intensity in those actions, and even levels of adjustment, such as a change in direction (fig. 1.7). You have to make some X postures if you are going to kick the ball in a soccer game, and you have to make some O postures to change direction at speed and alert your team that you are going to a new position where you will be ready to receive the ball. These postures happen so fast as we play and are so practiced because of the many hours team members spend with each other, that even a subtle hand gesture or slight turn of the torso can be read in a second. This is how it can be with your horse, too (fig. 1.8).

BUZZWORDS

Matching Steps

A Conversation with your horse where you tap into his sensitivity regarding hoof placement and rhythm by mirroring his stride and then asking him to change his stride with you (see p. 273).

X and O in Your Horse—and How It Relates to Inner Zero

Identifying the X or O posture in the horse enables you to determine an overview of the horse's physical, mental, and emotional state. If the horse moves into an X posture (high-headed and stiff-necked), is he becoming alert? Is he becoming alarmed? If he moves into an O posture (low-headed, lower-set neck), is he also inwardly calm, or do you feel a mysterious tension around him? (Some horses use a Low-O posture when they have "surrendered," which means they could still be anxious internally.)

The goal for me when I am having a Conversation with a horse is to *always be Zero*. Even if I ask his energy to go up (by using X, like the soccer player kicking a ball), he should stay Inner Zero (internally calm and focused). I want his X to be athletic, not stressed out or defensive. I also want to be able to ask his energy to go back down, and Inner Zero makes that possible.

Too often, horses are made to move faster and perform more intensely when mentally and emotionally they are not calm and focused, which can either create poor ability or lead to resistance—and even breakdown. If I want a horse to perform in a proud and balanced manner, then focusing on his X and O posture in *all* the activities we do together is a good place to start. To help him become Zero on the inside, I can begin with X and O on the outside. As you learn more Horse Speak, you will be able to give your horse the gestures, postures, and signals that encourage good self-regulation (Zero) on the inside.

SKILL-BUILDER

Are You X or O?

Try this exercise without judging that a posture is right or wrong. You are simply gathering information about yourself.

1. Look at yourself in the mirror. Observe the set of your shoulders. Are they more upright or rounded?

2. When you sit in a chair, do you tend to sit up straight or slouch?

3. Do your peers or family members view you as a take-charge type or more of a pushover?

If you observe that your shoulder position tends to be more upright, that you sit up straight in a chair, and you have a take-charge kind of personality, you can assume you are more of an X-posture type. If you answer the opposite, you are more an O-posture type.

Why is this important? If you have a tendency to be more X, you could be accidently driving your horse away. If you are more O, you may not be able to ask your horse for space when you need to. The goal is to have balance between the two postures and to know how to modulate them, depending on the activities you practice with your horse.

X, O, and Breath

Breathing is also X and O. A sharp outward breath is a strong X message to encourage movement or halting. A soft, huffing, or gentle blowing breath is an O message of welcoming.

Imagine shouting at a person who is about to step into oncoming traffic—your hands will probably make a big X toward the person, while the breath you intake or release will be loud, sharp, and make them pay attention to you, even if they do not hear the words that follow. In fact, in such cases, we usually just shout sharp-breathed sounds like "HEY!"

Now think of leaning in to coo to a little baby, maybe making soft "shushushu" sounds. Your body will be rounded, a gentle and soft O posture, and your breath will be audible in whispers.

We can add these X and O breaths to every single element of the Horse Speak gestures, postures, and signals to take it to the next level.

X, O, and Hands

There are three primary hand gestures: *Hold, Activate,* and *Draw.* Making X with your hands is Activate, making O with your hands is Draw, and Hold is right between X and O—enough O in your posture to signal, "Relax," but enough X in your hands to signal, "Stay there," or "I've got this." Let's talk about Hold Hand first.

Hold Hand

In a horse, the Hold position is often a *neutral* posture, in which the head and neck are held up, not aimed down (as they might be when grazing), and looks similar to when a horse is napping. However, the horse is not napping; he is holding still. This Hold position is an important message to the others in a herd. It combines enough O to say, "There is no problem," and enough X to say, "But, I am on guard, watching out." It says, in general, "*You* can go about your business—eat, nap, move around." If a leader horse does the Hold position in front of a troubled, young, or restless horse, then the message is more pointed: "I will hold still and be here for you. I will watch out... you are safe."

We can adapt this position to work with our bodies by holding a palm or both palms upright toward the horse. Your shoulders should be relaxed and your elbows bent (figs. 1.9 A & B). This is enough O to say, "No worries," but your palm in the air also says, "I am actively considering things." Hold Hand can be used as a signal of protection (aimed toward a loud sound or stray dog) or can be used directly on the horse (aimed toward him to say, "I've got your back," "I just want to share space with you," "I am open to listening to you," or "I see you.") You can offer Hold Hand to an

1.9 A & B Hold Hand, with your palm upright toward the horse, creates a boundary and a connection at the same time (A). Make sure you have a relaxed shoulder and bent elbow (B).

individual Horse Speak Button for site-specific meaning, or to all the Buttons in a slow, fluid motion (see p. 117 for a discussion of the Buttons).

Hold Hand is less about tension and more about awareness—a firm self-awareness, as well as a clear awareness of the other being near you. Your palm can be higher or lower, depending on the need of the moment. Imagine you have an eyeball in the palm of your hand: What is the eyeball seeing? What is it looking at or what is it seeking? Do you want the horse to feel protected by the eyeball or witnessed by it?

Hold Hand is a precursor to touch and friendly contact (from a distance or up

SKILL-BUILDER

Become the Gatekeeper

Think of your Hold Hand position as being the "Gatekeeper" or "Guardian." A friend of mine who is a professional equine body worker was working at a new barn. She wanted the barn staff to benefit from the Hold Hand but she was short on time to explain all the details, so she simply told those who were bringing her horses to work on, "Pretend you are the Gatekeeper." She gave very basic instructions: "If you see the horse's head going up, lift your hands into the Gatekeeper position, and spread your legs. This lets him know nothing is going to 'get' him as long as you are around. Once his head starts to drop, lower your hands, too. When the horse is calm, you are on 'standby'" (fig. 1.10).

1.10 Picture yourself as a Gatekeeper or guardian when you are doing the Hold Hand.

In every single case, the horses settled and received the bodywork session she was offering with double the efficiency, and before long, the word spread through the barn about being the Gatekeeper. No one could believe how immediately effective this one simple message was. By the end of the day, the barn workers were calling to each other things like, "Can you come be my Gatekeeper at this door?" or "Can you be the Gatekeeper while I walk Big Al to the paddock, so he doesn't flip out like he usually does?"

Try it at your barn!

close). It also signals the edge of the Bubble of Personal Space (see p. 69 for more on this). Think of Hold Hand and the Bubble like the fence between your lawn and your neighbor's. The fence is the boundary, but it is also where both yards meet.

When horses use Hold position for each other, it is about normal horse-related activities. When a human does it, the horse is now relating to the human world, and what *can* happen is that any trauma, confusion, or bad feelings that the horse has had *while with humans* may be reviewed somehow and released. I and many others have witnessed this direct effect. Whatever the reason, horses receiving the Hold Hand often slip into a state of *processing*, which means they are reviewing their internal map of reality. In my head, I "hear" it like this: "Hmm… no person ever gave me the Hold signal before. How do I feel about this now? Do I trust this human and this message enough to release old baggage? Let me consider…"

> **BUZZWORDS**
>
> **Processing**
>
> Horses need to pass all information through their entire body when they are problem-solving or assessing new information. I call this "processing," and I discuss it in more detail on p. 69.

Activate

Activate is an X message. I use the term *Activate* to mean you want a horse to move. I stay away from the word "pressure" as much as possible. Even though the phrase "pressure and release" represents the simple act of applying pressure or removing it to motivate movement, humans tend to confuse this idea. Simply put, when it comes to people, the word "pressure" can also refer to internal feelings or sensations of stress, as in: "The boss put a lot of pressure on me to get this assignment done for Friday's meeting," or "I am feeling a lot of pressure to get this essay finished for school," or "As a single mom, I am under a lot of pressure." Pressure is often paired with feelings of being trapped or getting into trouble or being forced into a sort of behavior (think "peer pressure").

Activation in this context refers to the use of *applied or implied physical contact coming from your fingertips* (fig. 1.11). Whether in the air or via touch, the desired outcome is that the horse

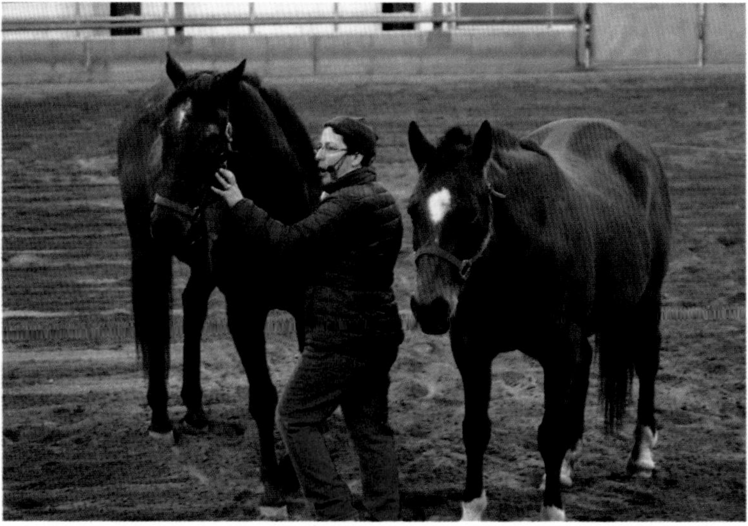

1.11 I am using what I call "Prong Fingers" (see p. 54) at the location of Buttons on the horse's cheek and shoulder to ask for space.

understands your request, rather than being cajoled into action. The better you get at this, the lighter and brighter your horse will tend to become.

You only need to Activate contact to the degree that the horse responds, and then immediately *quit Activating.* Think of it like turning a key in your car ignition: If you keep turning after it starts, the engine makes an awful noise, and you damage the starter.

I always wanted to be a Paint!

1.12 We all know how to make Laser Beam Eyes when something doesn't go our way. The trick is learning to do this on purpose.

Now, activation can be delivered in two ways: *in the air* in the form of a pointed finger or even a finger snap, or *in full contact*, with your fingertips touching the horse. In my first book *Horse Speak,* I explained the *Five Levels of Intensity:* Zero (which we've already discussed in this book) through Four. As the intensity numbers increase, so does the size or emphasis of your movement. In the case of Activation, Level One intensity is in-air contact. Think of the principal at school or your stern grandmother pointing the "Finger of Doom" at you! They would not need to touch you for you to get the message. This is masterful Level One intensity, and the equivalent in horses is often dealt with their eyes (the "Stare of Doom"). You can also learn to use your own *Laser Beam Eye*, which delivers the same no-nonsense meaning (fig. 1.12). Either way, this is in-air Activation, and with sensitive horses, this may be all you need.

Levels Two through Four intensity involve full-contact or touch Activation, starting with barely touching the coat, then getting close to the skin, then contacting the muscle, until finally your fingers may make a visible dimple. I call this "Prong Fingers." I try to use simple Prong Fingers for 90 percent of whatever Activate message I am giving horses—either in the air or on their bodies. Adding intensity to an air message can include using Laser Beam Eyes along with them, or it can mean using both hands to send a stronger message that you want *action now*; you want the horse's feet to move (fig. 1.13). It can mean using a stick to swish *upward* toward the horse. (Note that an overhand, downward motion is a punishing or "attack" gesture. Upward gestures "get the energy going." You can see horses do both upward and downward gestures

BUZZWORDS

Laser Beam Eye

I have seen many horses redirect the eye path of another horse, which then redirects where that horse's body goes. We can Mirror this Conversation: Look a horse right in the eyes and imagine a beam of light shooting out and blocking or redirecting his forward momentum.

SKILL-BUILDER

Practice Intensity for the Horse

In my book *Horse Speak*, I detail how to learn to move through the Levels of Intensity. It is true that some horses need a good Level Four intensity—but what is important here is that it is *for* them, not *against* them. This means that many horses like to see their leader as strong enough to drive away a boogeyman with a breath and to step up to a spooky object and kick it. This is *X for the horse*. To my surprise and delight, many times making a big Level Four "show"—for example, yelling at a scary wheelbarrow left in the wrong place—has encouraged a horse to fall in line with me immediately afterward.

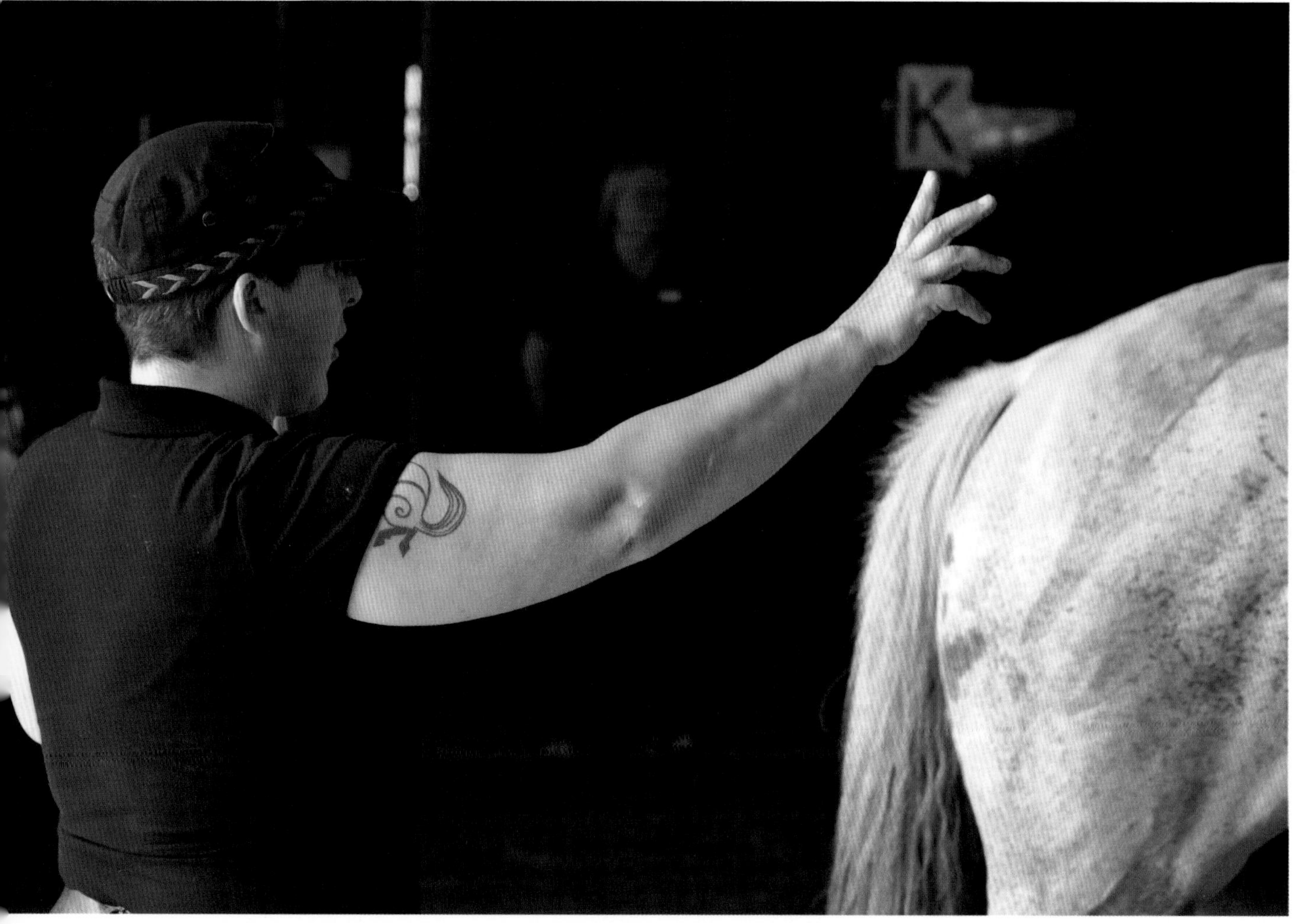

1.13 I add intensity to air Activation, aiming my Prong Fingers and Laser Beam Eyes at the horse.

PSST-
I missed this in class-
what does it mean?

1.14 Waving your hands or making flapping gestures is startling to horses. They often freeze, not knowing what to do. If they do move away from flapping, it is a reflex rather than a reaction due to understanding. In Horse Speak we learn to make single, pointed Activations, and then add intensity with your feet, breath, voice, energy, and maybe the movement of a stick.

toward each other with a swish of the head and neck, and even the tail.)

You can use Activate from a distance; I have even done so from clear across an open paddock or field. To do this well, use your whole X message—your whole body. Stand with your feet solid and grounded, and perhaps add a stomp and Laser Beam Eye. Aim at a Button or the whole horse you intend to move. (This distinction may seem odd at first, but as you get to know the Buttons, you will become familiar with which Buttons move the horse in certain ways. But when first learning this, you may just show X to a horse in general—see p. 117 for more about the Buttons.) Add a straight arm with a pointed finger, or even a snap of the fingers, and perhaps make a loud noise like, "Shwaa!" or "Cheeee!" Collectively, all this adds up to a very strong X message. If you are already an X person (see p. 50), you may need only the noise, or only the stomp, or only your eyes.

Activate should be one solid message, *not* a bunch of "flapping" motions, which can and do startle horses

MYTH-BUSTER

Is It Okay to Slap a Horse?

The palm of your hand should never be used to slap a horse as a correction or to shove him aside as this dirties the purity of the palm's message in Hold Hand. In addition, enthusiastically slapping a horse on the neck to tell him he did well does *not* actually feel like praise to him. The palm is a gesture of connection, either implied as when held in the air, or direct as when placed on the horse's body.

When you need to move a horse over, use Prong Fingers, and add a snap for more energy. If you need to scold a horse, make a loud noise or stomp your foot, but try not to strike the horse if you can help it. You will still get the point across, but you won't risk the horse having a startle reflex the next time you lift your hand for different reason.

and have been used by trainers for that reason—to cause a startle and use that startle to move the horse away (fig. 1.14). However, if what you are trying to create is a thoughtful, quiet, attentive horse, startling him with flapping, slapping, or waving does not achieve the result you want. It makes the horse feel like he never knows when you are suddenly going to "bite." It makes you appear insolent and irritable.

Draw

Draw is a hand gesture connected to the O posture and can be done in a number of ways. First, you can put the fingertips of your hands together while in your Low-O posture, and this by itself can act like a draw. You can sit on a low surface, like a mounting block, or stoop over, bending your knees as though calling a puppy to your lap—a good posture to offer a really hesitant horse (figs. 1.15 A & B). The next level of Draw can be a little tugging motion in the air, as though you are pulling a string or indicating the "Come here" signal from your curled finger.

When a horse comes to you in response to your Draw message, he is looking for "a place to land." When he approaches, you need to provide your knuckles for his muzzle to touch (the "place to land" is your knuckles, not some other part of your body), or put your Hold Hand up so he knows where to halt on the edge of your Bubble (see p. 119 for more about Greeting with your knuckles).

Turn the Key, Come to Me

One Draw Conversation horses seem to like the best, and that I have had the most success with, is called "Turn the Key, Come to Me." This is not a command, like

1.15 A & B Sitting on a mounting block encourages a relaxed O posture, which helps this unsure horse feel beckoned (A). Adding a gesture of greeting to Draw her in was the next step (B).

training a dog to "Come." Rather, it is a direct invitation for the horse to approach you. Most horses at least take a step or lean in toward you. (Outgoing horses will often walk right over. Hesitant horses may look like they want to come but remain shy. Stoic horses may take one step and call it a day. I talk more about all three of these personality types in chapter 4, p. 164.)

Here's how you do it: Let's say you are "talking to" the Mid-Neck Button (see page for more about the Buttons):

1.16 "Turn the Key, Come to Me" uses a rotation of your hand like you are turning an actual key. Horses find this motion very inviting.

1 Put the fingertips of one hand "on" the middle of the horse's neck—this can be a direct contact "touch message" or an "air message" from some distance away.

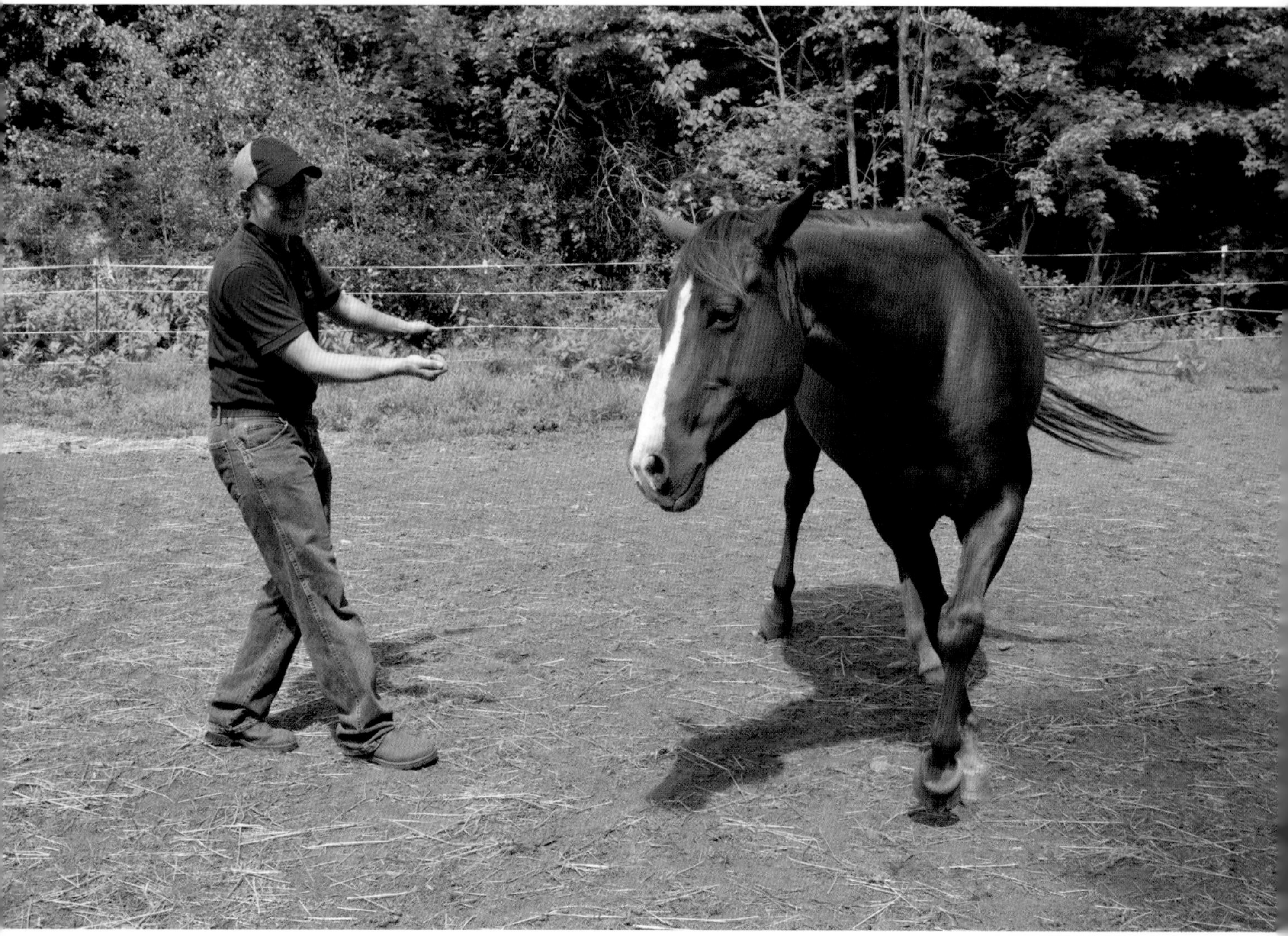

2 Turn them like you are turning a key in a keyhole.

3 Pull your hand back toward your belly button while stepping backward three steps. You must step backward to make space in front of you for the horse to move into. Some horses need more space, so if nothing happens, take three more steps backward. (Note: If your angle backward is too sharp, they may wait until you ask again from a better position.)

4 Often, the horse will seek to put the Button you are "talking to" in the palm of your hand, so offer a Hold Hand as a "place to land" (fig. 1.16).

Targeting

Horses use what I call "Targeting" to show intention. Picture a horse looking at where he wants to go—let's say the water tank—then back at his pasture buddy, and then once again at the tank. Perhaps he drops his nose to the ground in *Aw-Shucks*, removing the pressure, and then takes a step while his head is low, saying, "I want to keep it cool, but I am ready to start going there." Horses first look at or "target" an area where they would like to move to. Then they signal to others with appropriate gestures. Combined, this is how they show the overall intention—what they pay *attention* to helps to display their *intention.*

You can model this Targeting by inviting the horse to follow you with your O posture and the pointing of a finger toward where you want to go. Combined this shows where *your* attention is focused and sends a clearer picture to him about *your* intention.

In Horse Speak, a closed fist with knuckles up simulates a horse's muzzle. I use it whenever I am connecting with a horse or upon entering his personal space. (Like a human handshake or giving someone a high-five, it is also what is used for Greeting, which I discuss in more detail on p. 119.) You can also use your knuckles as a "target" for the horse to follow in a Draw Conversation (figs. 1.17 A & B). You can progress to asking a horse to follow this *Target Hand* at liberty or when longeing. Some horses will happily follow your Target Hand when you offer it, and some may need encouragement, such as incorporating clicker or treat training.

Part of an invitation to come or follow is the indication of when to stop. When you

BUZZWORDS

Aw-Shucks

The expression is seen in the horses when he puts his nose to the ground as you approach, not to eat, but to ask you to take the pressure off. We can share this message with the horse with a human version: pausing, scuffing the ground with one foot, and looking down.

1.17 A & B Target Hand uses your knuckles as an extension of Turn the Key, Come to Me (A). It's important to keep your *Soft Eye* on the horse's eyes to stay engaged (B).

ask your horse to halt, he needs to know what part of your body he should line up with, stop at, and check in with. The easiest way to do this is to keep your knuckles as active as possible for all these communications. He can follow them with his eyes, place his nose on them when he stops, and then line his feet up with your feet to rebalance at the halt.

Your Hold Hand can be used for Targeting, too, by moving with it aligned with a particular Button. To stop the horse with Hold Hand, use *Drop It to Stop It* to signal a halting motion with your body.

You can also advance your Target Hand, turning it into *Invitation Hand*: Open your palm upward, indicating the direction you would like to go (similar to a host or waiter indicating, "Right this way, please") as you aim your intention in the direction of the hand gesture. Invitation Hand can be used to request any level of movement, including beginning to longe at liberty or change directions. This is a nice progression in both liberty and lead- or longe-line communication.

BUZZWORDS

Drop It to Stop It

This basic movement looks like you are going to sit down suddenly. Drop your weight and attention into a sitting motion with your pelvis. Horses often use a similar movement in their hind end to ask others in the herd to halt with them.

SKILL-BUILDER

Combining Hold, Activate, and Draw

With Hold, Activate, and Draw you can really begin to have what I call "Fun with Feet." Horses adjust their space with each other by positioning and repositioning their hooves. So, when we use our feet to claim and yield space, they understand our language. This is a Conversation you can have, trying some deliberate steps and seeing if your horse Mirrors you.

To create some interesting movement together with your horse—whether on a lead or longe line, or at liberty—set up an obstacle course to have reasons to use Hold, Activate, and Draw. Practice problem-solving with objects or in corners and see how many messages you can use as you ask for movement forward, backward, left, and right, as well as halting, "Come to me," and "Move away from me."

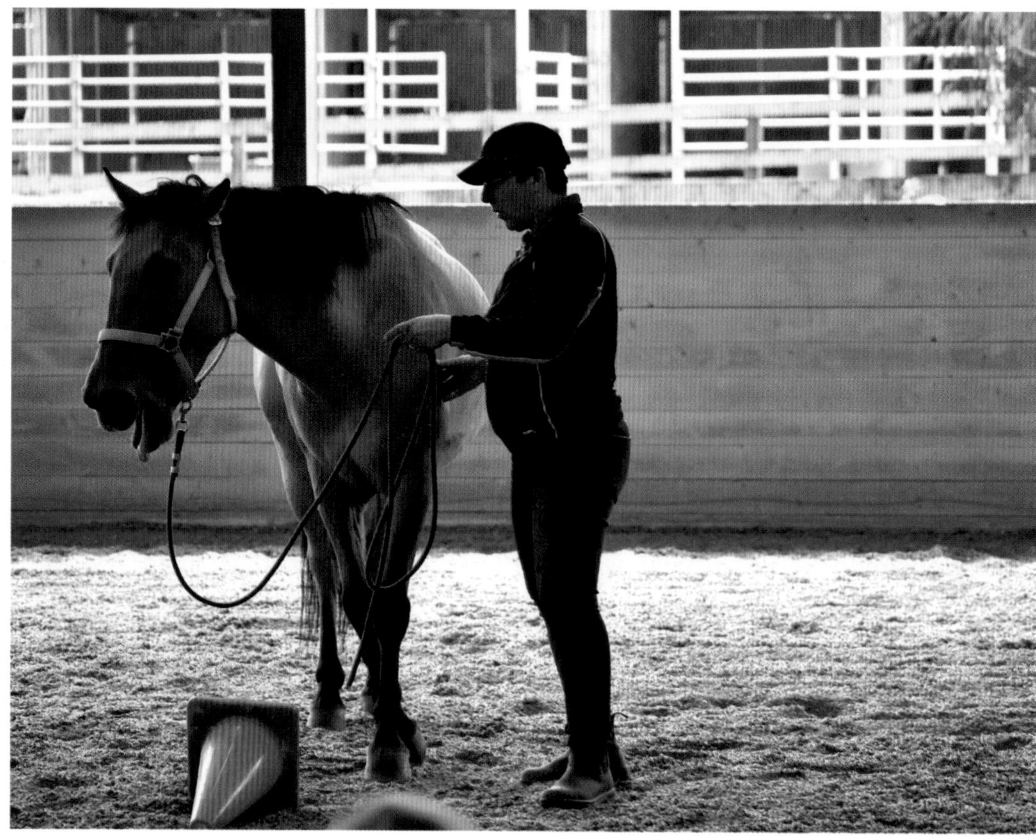

1.18 The Core Energy that is directed from your belly button area is where you show intention to move, change direction, engage, or disengage.

Understanding Core Energy

As I explained in *Horse Speak*, your true "center" or "balance point" is located behind and a little below your belly button. In other words, from your pelvic floor to your belly button area is where the brunt of your core strength comes from. *Core Energy* is emitted from your belly button area (fig. 1.18). This is the outward manifestation of attention, intention, and direction, and a projection of power or powerlessness, and animals look to your belly button to determine your level of intensity. A person can puff out her chest, but the true show of strength comes from her gut.

Similarly, the horse's core strength comes from the pelvic floor to where the umbilical cord was severed. The difference between horses and humans is that a horse's Core Energy is expressed through his *chest*. This body part is visible to another horse (the horse's navel faces the ground). Think of a stallion with a proud chest, showing off.

BUZZWORDS

Soft Eye

You can see a calm horse has a Soft Eye when the muscles around his eyes are relaxed. We can mirror this with our own expression.

What Does Core Energy Do?

The Core Energy that is directed from your belly button area is where you show intention to move, change direction, engage, disengage, or increase or decrease intensity. Imagine walking down the street, looking into storefront windows as you go. When your Core Energy is pointed forward, you can still walk straight ahead even though your head is turned. If you stop to really look at something you see in a window, you will probably also turn your belly button toward the window—and now all of your attention and intention is on that window. Similarly, horses can move with their heads and necks bent to look in a certain direction, but as long as their Core Energy (chest) is aiming forward, they remain on that trajectory.

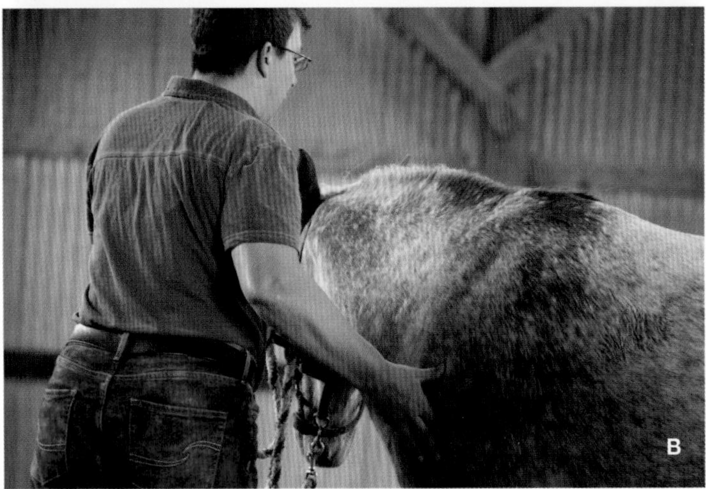

1.19 A & B In both human and horse, there is an expression of Core Energy in every X and O posture, which denotes not only the intention of movement, but also the level of intensity put into that movement. The rearing horse's X (A) has different intention and intensity from my X quietly asking a horse for space (B).

In both human and horse, there is an expression of Core Energy in every X and O posture, which denotes not only the intention of movement, but also the level of intensity put into that movement (figs. 1.19 A & B). For example, a proud horse's chest lifting upward as he strikes out toward an opponent or engages a friend in rough play (X) is quite different from a panicked horse's sunken-in chest (fearful X) as he scurries to get away. A martial artist may crouch in a Low-O to get ready to spring. His Core Energy is coiled and ready to go even though he is in an O. In contrast, the nervous grade school kid may try standing up to a bully by adopting an X posture, but a lack of Core Energy may still be apparent.

Learning to pay attention to the Core Energy of the horse is one more way to gather information and add to your growing list of how to discern a horse's Feeling States by interpreting their postures.

1.20 A horse may be showing off, like the horses in my herd do with arched necks and expressive tails when they are feeling good or playing.

Translating the Body Language in Collected Movement

In collected movement, whether at liberty or under saddle, horses are more in an X posture with higher intensity and a higher level of being alert. Their *core strength* may be engaged like that of a bodybuilder; however, this does not automatically mean that their *Core Energy* is in a state of pride.

There are three main emotional states a horse may be demonstrating while in this high-intensity posture:

- First, a horse may be excited… and unsure. This form of collection is a display that says, "Who goes there? Are you friend or foe?"
- Second, a horse may be alarmed—more of a, "Yikes! We better run for the hills!"
- Third, a horse may be showing off, such as when a stallion prances before the object of his affection, or two stallions prepare to do battle, or two horse friends in play (fig. 1.20).

For our purposes, we really only want a horse in the third category, whether at liberty or under saddle. We do not want an over-aroused, nervous horse, nor do we want a hypervigilant, frightened horse. We want a horse that is invested in his play drive or his sense of showing off—we want a horse that is proud (fig. 1.21).

Understanding X, O, and the role Core Energy plays is an essential ingredient in determining if your horse is in a state of well-being, happiness, and therefore Inner Zero (which we are always aiming for!), or if he is in a state of submission or even triggered into one of *The Four Fs.*

1.21 You can see my horse Rocky's sense of pride as he carries his body with power over the snowy pasture.

The Four Fs

I have several dear friends who are psychotherapists, and we have had many fascinating conversations about therapeutic models and the human brain. One day, after one of my friends returned from a conference about Polyvagal Theory (see p. 37), she enlightened me about something. We were talking about her horse, and I mentioned that he tended to get "stuck" in a state of *fight* or *flight*. She lit up with enthusiasm and told me that she'd learned that there were two more survival states into which nervous systems could be triggered—there were actually *four* "Fs"—and that there was a good deal of current research regarding the effects of stress on animals.

This is an oversimplification of what she explained, as I am not a neuroscientist; however, what I now know as *The Four Fs* is an important backdrop for understanding how Core Energy, body language, and emotional states are linked. The Four Fs are:

- *Flight*: the instinct to run away from danger.
- *Fight*: the instinct to duel it out with danger if running is not an option.
- *Flock*: the instinct to group with others to find "safety in numbers" or to get to a place of safety. (With horses, we see this when they are "buddy-bound," "herd-bound," or "barn-bound.")

- *Freeze*: the instinct to not move at all (perhaps the predator won't see you). We often call this the "deer in the headlights" syndrome; however, it can also happen when an animal senses it is doomed. In this case, the freeze mode creates a disassociation, which nature seems to have provided to spare the pain of death to some degree.

For the purposes of educating a horse, we need him to be able to self-regulate. This means he needs to develop a tolerance for stimulation and gain the ability to not be triggered into one of The Four Fs when we are working with him. Unfortunately, there are many training methods that do the opposite: They flood the horse, hoping to trigger him into a *freeze* state because people misunderstand what that really means. A "frozen" horse can melt a little, learning to live in a sort of "slushy" state in which he goes about his day, not complaining and doing his job, but he is not fully awake, nor is he capable of building a rapport with us.

In the book *Waking the Tiger* by Peter Levine, the author, who holds doctorates in biophysics and psychology, describes the *freeze* state as one of the fundamental issues underlying the condition we call PTSD (post-traumatic stress disorder). His book details many animal cases, including a section on horses who had been "sacked out" and slipped into a "death state"—stuck in *freeze*. Levine mentions the connection between "dead-broke" horses who are actually living out life in the *freeze* state, and why they may react to "normal" conditions in a violent manner—triggered into *fight* or *flight*—when and if they do "wake up."

This is why my commitment to Zero, to proper use of X and O and Core Energy, is so important. Many horses can be skating on the edge of that "slushy" place. Some have not settled into *freeze* and instead are triggered into one of the other Fs, perhaps being hostile, panicked, or unable to go without a buddy or to travel any distance from the barn. When I meet this type of triggered horse, I put a lot of effort into offering messages of safety, protection, and nurturing. I slowly demonstrate my X and my O. I thoughtfully turn my Core Energy on the horse and then away from him. Everything is done in slow motion and with extreme diligence. This is to try to shift the horse out of the point of the trigger and into the moment with me. I have to look like someone the horse can safely begin communicating with before I ever try to catch him, touch him, or lead him. Zero is the state of well-being that is the opposite of being triggered. Both horses and humans need to find Inner Zero to lead full, rich and healthy lives.

All About You

As much as we want to decode the language of horses, we also must know what our everyday body language is projecting. The steps to success for beginning the journey of discerning body language are as follows:

1 To be able to be calm and objective enough to let go of old habits of thinking and feeling, you must find your Inner Zero (see p. 41).

2 To be able to develop the powers of your "feel," you need to be able to keep your Zero while practicing X and O and directing with your Core Energy.

3 Quiet your mind: If you notice inner dialogue creeping in, quiet it down.

4 You need to feel comfortable with self-assessment: If nothing else, can you pay attention to your own habits? Do you tend to be more X or more O? Do you have

SKILL-BUILDER

What's Yours and What's Mine

We have feelings and postures, and so do horses. It is necessary to be able to tell if we are projecting something or if the horse is projecting something—or both. This exercise is designed to help you develop discernment in this area.

1. Approach your horse slowly.
2. Notice any change in your thoughts, feelings, or physical sensations.
3. Notice any change in your horse's X, O, or breathing.
4. Notice any judgments, criticisms, or negative thinking you have about either yourself or your horse.
5. Now, observe how close you are to your horse. Exactly where were you in relation to him when you started thinking or feeling something?
6. Back away.
7. What do you think or feel when you are back to where you started the exercise?
8. What does your horse do?
9. Repeat this at least three times.

Most people discover that by the third time, there are definite changes in their awareness. Many find this exercise enlightening because you can begin to identify faulty projections and discern what energy or emotions are yours and what is coming from the horse.

too much Core Energy around your horse? Or do you find yourself collapsing around him?

5 Remember to practice getting in touch with *all* your senses (see p. 43). Also, notice what sensations you get in your body in different scenarios: "warm and comfortable," "sharp and hard," "cold and withdrawn," "cool and relaxed." Note the sensations *without* judging them. Try to assess whether the sensations you are experiencing are yours or your horse's, or whether they are shared.

1.22 A & B Horses move and think in terms of circular motion, which you can see in these two photographs showing horses moving in their space and around each other in arcs. (Note the curve of the horses' bodies seen from overhead in B.). These circular areas they define are what I call *Bubbles of Personal Space.*

Why is having awareness of your body important? We are about to talk about *Bubbles of Personal Space*—ours and our horses'. Our Bubble is created partly by our body posture, which often belies our personality. For instance, "huggers" may typically be more O posture (welcoming energy), while Type-A personalities may be more X posture (high intensity).

Bubbles of Personal Space

In my book *Horse Speak*, I describe how horses not only see in a circle almost all the way around themselves (because of the position of their eyes on their heads), they also move in circles and arcs, and think in terms of circular, repetitive patterns and cycles. In addition, they live inside their own special Bubbles of Personal Space (figs. 1.22 A & B). The horse's Bubble is the only thing he truly possesses. In general, horses need their space clearly defined and respected for them to have a sense of well-being.

SKILL-BUILDER

Move Like a Horse

1. Take a long pole—a broomstick will work—and hold it low on one side of your body, about in the middle of the stick (fig. 1.23).
2. Walk around your house and property with the stick extending both in front and behind you, making the space you take up longer like a horse.
3. What is it like to navigate with a long front end and a long hind end? Move near your horse like this and see if it changes your perception of him or his of you.

1.23 Consider the body shape of a horse. Walking around with a long stick, like a broom handle, can help your awareness "tune in" to what it might be like having a longer body like a horse.

Much of what horses do in moving around each other has to do with outlining their mutual Bubbles of Personal Space. Moments where one horse may "pop" another horse's Bubble (move into another's space without asking) have what I call "rituals" associated with them (see, for example, the Greeting Ritual—p. 119). For our purposes, we have to start by understanding Horse Speak from *outside* the horse's Bubble. This means learning to observe where the outside of a particular horse's Bubble may be. For instance, one horse may be very comfortable with people and therefore has a small Bubble when around them. Another horse may be very timid and will flinch when you are 20 feet away.

How to Find Edge of the Horse's Bubble

Place your horse in an enclosed area if possible, like a stall or a small paddock. Begin approaching from 20 feet away outside the barrier, and take notice when the horse indicates being aware of your presence. Typical responses are as follows:

- The horse looks at you.
- He looks away from you.
- He takes a step toward you.
- He takes a step away from you.
- He turns his haunches toward you.
- He swishes his tail at you.
- He reacts with a very refined signal, such as a flick of the ear or a twitch of the skin on the shoulder or flank, or he lets out a breath or starts holding his breath.

When you see any of these signs, stop and back up at least three steps. Turn so one shoulder is facing the horse, and sigh out loud to release any tension. Approach and retreat several times in a row and from different angles to test your awareness.

This is an exercise in finding the edge of the Bubble to see if you can sense where it is—that is all. Your goal is a heightened awareness of your horse's personal space. When you demonstrate this observation skill, many horses begin to feel more comfortable in your presence.

The Bubble and You

When working with horses, we have Bubbles, too. Our Bubbles are defined by human standards. When we went to school, we learned to walk in a line, single-file. We learned to sit at our own desks. In a crowded space, we may use the edge of a shoulder to define personal space, but we definitely keep our hands to ourselves in public. In other words, our Bubbles expand and contract, just like the horse's.

When we are with a horse, we have to change our awareness of what a Bubble is to accommodate that of the horse. As we explored in the Skill-Builder on p. 69, the horse's body is much larger and longer than ours, so his Bubble extends farther and requires greater physical distance to prevent "popping" it (entering the space before the horse has agreed to it). In fact, we tend to "pop" horses' Bubbles because we want to touch them, brush them, and ride them, and we usually do so without asking first. In response, it is actually pretty common for horses to "pop" our Bubbles. Why? Because:

- We humans usually aren't aware of horses' Bubbles and "pop" them all the time (that is, there is no mutual respect), so the horse "pops" ours, too.
- We have treats.
- We will scratch itchy spots.
- We tend to just do what we want to horses, so they may adopt this behavior back to us—for instance, turning us into a scratching post.

Just like when we were in school, we have to learn some of the social rules that horses require in order to get along better with them. They really are the same rules we learned related to our own Bubbles:

- Stay in your own space.
- Don't just reach out with your hands and touch another whenever you want to without asking.

MYTH-BUSTER

Are Horses "Disrespectful"?

I want to clarify the word "respect" and how I use it in this book. Human beings conceptualize, so we have an *idea* of "respect" that encompasses a psychological profile—for example, someone being "disrespectful" could just be talking to us in a certain way. However, in the horse's world-view, respect means simply that Bubbles of Personal Space are operating in harmony, while disrespect means they are colliding.

Harmonious movement means both parties respect each other's space and can work together. ONE single step toward a horse or ONE single step away carries significance. That one step takes space or gives it back. One step can connect or repel, and one step can mean, "Thank you," or "No, thanks," depending on whether and how you are giving or taking the space. Mutual respect is necessary for harmony.

Horses are not scheming about "disrespecting us" because of some sort of grudge or one-upmanship. They are responding to whether *we* are congruent or not (see p. 28).

- Be able to politely ask for healthy space when you've had enough, too.

Horse Speak ensures that we learn to respect equine personal space and how our body language impacts it. By respecting the horse's Bubble, we can open doors to communication that were previously locked.

Now that you have completed the first steps of developing an awareness of basic equine/human body language and the state of mind needed for ultimate success, I would like to enter the world of the horse, from the horse's perspective.

What Horses Value

Have you ever thought about what you personally value on a daily basis? Maybe you like to wake up every morning with a cup of coffee and then read the news, go for a walk with the dogs, and take a hot shower. Now consider what your horse may value on a daily basis. The list is going to look a bit different, but there could be some similarities. Does he like to hang out with his horse friends while having breakfast? Does he like you to put his halter on him a certain way? Does he enjoy a long, leisurely warm-up? Does he like a walk in the woods after a training session?

When asked this question, many people begrudgingly say things like, "Well, he cares about food more than me." This sentiment is so misguided. I care about food a heck of a lot, too. And if I came over to your house when you were sitting down to lunch and told you to spit your sandwich out and pay attention to me, you would probably show me the door.

Horses have a set of values and learning what they are sets us up to provide a compassionate training environment and better enrichment. Here are the six basic values I have identified as most important to most horses. When all six values are balanced, the horse can return to a state of Zero—or at least begin the journey.

The six basic values are:

1. Safety
2. Protection
3. Resources
4. Connection
5. Comfort
6. Clarity

SKILL-BUILDER

How to Make a Safety Object

As I've already mentioned in this book, a Safety Object can be any object that represents a safe place to rest and reset. Horses make their own safety objects by dropping manure piles in designated "safety zones." I have even witnessed them running back to the same place a manure pile was removed from and making a fresh pile, then standing by it, or sniffing it for a long time, as if saying, "Hey, that is my 'safety poo'—I need that there to make a scent mark about that spot."

In order to create a Safety Object for your horse, you must know ahead of time what and where it's going to be, point to the object upon approaching it, and when you arrive at the object with your horse, you must touch the object first and let out a big sigh, as if you are saying, "We made it, now it's time to relax." It's critical to not ask anything of the horse while at the Safety Object because it is meant to symbolize a time to pause, regroup, and "take a load off." The horse does not have to touch the object, but you should allow him to explore it with his muzzle if he wishes to. (You may find that your horse likes to rub his muzzle on the object as a way to "reset" because of the acupuncture point that is in this location.)

Do *not* directly treat at or clicker train a Safety Object. Horses naturally make these for themselves *away* from food. It is a specific spot to shift down into deep relaxation, not get stimulated. If you horse wants to nibble the object or some grass near it, that is *his* choice. Just do not use a hay net, feed dish, or direct treating.

Safety

Horses first and foremost want to know their environment is safe. This is more pressing than even food. In nature, the horse's food is on the ground; however, putting his head down means he is vulnerable to attack. Safety trumps food.

Horses can display issues related to feeling a lack of safety in many ways, and Horse Speak provides a number of messages and actions specific to helping a horse feel safe, including:

- Making *Safety Objects* (see Skill-Builder above).
- Offering predictable patterns, routines, and times.
- Repeating messages three times to ensure the horse understands your request.

- Pacing yourself and allowing space for the horse to process.
- Offering comfort messages (see below).

Protection

Safety and protection might sound the same, but they are not. Horses need you to provide protective messages to help them feel safe. But what we have to understand is they might ask if you will act like a protector even when they do not actually feel unsafe in the moment.

Some insecure, traumatized horses may not readily accept you in the role of protector, and some are very self-protective and won't "let you in" right away. Horse Speak has many messages you can share with a horse seeking protection, which you will learn later in this book. Here are a few of the ways to communicate your willingness in the role:

- Secure the Environment: Touch three items on the outside of his stall or enclosure.
- Scan the Horizon: Look into the distance for danger (see p. 98).
- Blow a Sentry Breath: A sharp, forceful, audible breath out, like a horse's warning snort (see p. 229).
- Touch items in the horse's environment before the horse does. (I call this "looking for bees, bears, and boogeymen.")
- Display a "Big X" for the horse: Throw a stone or a stick away from the horse, yell at a dog, tell someone to move. This is a display of leadership or power *for* the horse, not against him.
- Walk from Safety Object to Safety Object.
- Pay attention to what the horse pays attention to.
- Manage your breathing and Breath Messages (see p. 4).
- Take heavy, slow steps to show there's "nothing to get worked up about."
- Offer Hold Hand to the horse's hip to say, "I've got your back."
- Rock the Baby on the Bridge of the Nose and Follow Me Buttons or while pointing at the horse's feet (see pp. 124 and 129).

Resources

It goes without saying that horses love food. However, food is not always the resource they value most. Sometimes the resource is a companion (related to the values of connection and comfort, which we will discuss next). Sometimes it is shelter, water, or a good place to lie down.

Sometimes it is you.

In nature, equines have to constantly move around to be able to ensure they get enough to eat. Domesticated horses remain highly motivated to walk and chew and search for food. Leading a horse through a grassy pasture would be like you walking across a field of freshly baked bread with melted butter, and not being allowed to taste it.

So, how can we learn to value resources in a way that works with how the horse values them?

- Learn to be an effective hand-grazer or allow yourself to wander about with your horse while he grazes loose.
- Stand near and "share a hay pile." This is an important part of being "inside" his world—it is the equivalent to having lunch with a friend. (Have common sense—do this over a barrier if you are at all concerned about food aggression.)
- Establish rules about "no eating while working" *if that is important*.
- Establish rules about how many nibbles of grass are okay when walking your horse.
- I normally allow three places to have a nibble. After the third one, the horse knows to walk along.
- Horses lift their heads and journey for some distance in search of better fare all the time. Do note, however, that if a horse on a journey with his gang wants to grab a bite to eat, *no other horse stops or corrects him*. The consequence he faces for his snacking is that he gets left behind!

The promise or presence of treats should *not* cause or increase a horse's anxiety. Remember these important points:

- Only offer a horse treats if you fully understand the proper use of them, such as in incentive-based or positive-reinforcement training.
- Do not use them as a lure.

- My recommendation is to offer them in a bucket at the end of work, or occasionally as a special reward.
- Hand-feeding must involve good manners. Never allow "mugging." Mother horses don't allow their foals to mug the udder, and neither should you!
- When feeding, use your Hold Hand in more of an X to negotiate space when delivering hay.
- Do not try to fix grain anxiety at one time. Make a logical plan and use all the X and O postures needed to slowly work on better manners around feeding. Give yourself and the horse a *reasonable* amount of time to see improvement.

Pay attention to what your horse pays attention to when hand-grazing or sharing a grassy field with him. As we've already discussed, his *attention* will often help you understand his *intention*. Learn what your horse craves, what he seems to seek out, and how he acts in relation to it. Horses with resource fears may show signs of being food aggressive, buddy sour, barn sour, and demanding. They lack a certain level of trust that their resource will always be there. I have found that in some of the worst cases of food aggression, for example, simply offering Protection (see p. 74) around a horse's Bubble while he ate revealed how worried he was about *resource loss*. That protection resulted in a deep sigh of relief and behavior indicating the horse didn't want me to leave his side.

Connection

This value is about the need for others, which can mean other horses, dogs, cats, people, goats—the list of potential sources of companionship goes on. Horses are herd animals by nature and need to be social. Even when they have "learned" to live alone—stallions kept apart, or racehorses or show horses who are never turned out with others—they still have this latent need. A horse that displays a deficit of connection, breaks connections, is overeager to connect in a way that seems infantile, or has an indifferent attitude toward connection is demonstrating symptoms of an issue with this value. Once a horse has lost his essential ability to connect, it can be hard to help him get it back.

- If you have a kind, gentle soul of a horse who seeks you out and displays nice manners, this is a sign of a healthy connection, and nothing to worry about. You can still respect his Bubble and "walk in your own lane" because that will add to this horse's trust in you.

- In some cases, the horse's need for connection is projected on you. When this is the case, you may have an equine who "pops" your Bubble, looks for treats, and acts babyish and immature.
- Some "Bubble poppers," however, act out of deep-seated insecurities and underlying fears or worries about not having access to the connection with you whenever they need it.

We can learn to handle these connection value issues by watching horse herds interact. I will introduce ideas for negotiating Bubbles of Personal Space and connection in the pages ahead.

Comfort

Some horses seek connection without obvious physical affection, and others truly seek to nuzzle, scratch, play with, and lie down near each other. Just as with humans, every horse is an individual—and some are "huggers" while others are not.

When a horse has experienced a deficit of comfort—physical or emotional—then he may actually seek to stand alone and not enjoy any comfort offered from horses or humans. He may even drive away touch. Often something has gone awry with the horse's level of physical contact, evident when he seeks too much or tries to avoid it.

- Some horses receive the most comfort from Breath Messages or facial expressions around the mouth. Use of your breath can say, "All's clear," licking your lips (I call this "peanut butter mouth"), and an out breath can be strong comfort signals.
- O posture, nodding your head gently to release stored neck tension, and eye contact with blinking are all messages of comfort, too.
- Even just taking one step outside the horse's Bubble can make him feel more comfortable by "giving him his Bubble back."

Some horses like physical comfort that induces deep relaxation and has been linked to emotional or protective messages, such as stroking the area around the vagus nerve located near the jugular vein while linking it to a verbal cue or sound. This encourages the same neuropathway to activate when you say the word, even without the touch that brings a deep state of calm, which can be helpful when riding. I call this action "Linking and Layering"—linking a sound or word to physical relief, in this case a long, relaxed stroking down the neck, so that later the same sensation can be induced, even without the physical touch.

Other horses are more comforted by offering messages of protection and safety, two of the six basic values we have already discussed (see pp. 73 and 74).

Clarity

This value refers to the need equines have to simply understand what our signals mean. A lack of clarity can cause some horses to become so frustrated that they buck, bite, strike, paw, pin their ears, and any other number of expressive behaviors. Nine out of ten times, these basic "vices" (displacement activities—see p. 31) are cured when "muddy" communication between human and horse is cleared up.

This can mean:

- Clearly demonstrating your X and O.
- Keeping your Core Energy off the horse's body when you are not moving him.
- Using the correct level of intensity. (Horses are generally not that upset with the use of intensity, but rather with the incorrect level of it—that is, the intensity should fit the situation. I talk more about levels of intensity in chapter 6—p. 230.)
- Becoming more aware of the horse's Bubble of Personal Space. The horse prefers a very distinct "line" between your body and his, much in the same way a line runs between cars on the road. The motto is *Stay in Your Lane.* Although it can seem like the horse is the one changing lanes, I guarantee user error is most often the cause. Horses who cross the line usually do so because the human unconsciously told them to!

It is not uncommon to have a very intense horse *actually* be stuck in one of The Four Fs, as we discussed on p. 65. You may have inherited this "stuck" state from the horse's previous owners or trainers. In this case, clarity is the keynote to

BUZZWORDS

Stay in Your Lane

I use this phrase to indicate rules about personal space when working around horses. Imagine two lanes of automobile traffic and the rules of the road that keep everyone safe. The concept applies to handling a horse and moving together from one place to another.

helping the horse become "un-triggered" so his real personality can emerge and he can begin to get his Zero back. If a horse did not get good socialization, was trained too intensely at too young an age, has been roughly handled, or has been forced to perform in a rigid and mechanical form, then he may be expressing a sense of either "learned helplessness" or utter frustration with a lack of personal space.

Working Through the Value List

I have provided a basic summary of the six values that horses need to find their Zero. Depending on their roles in the herd or "type" (see p. 158), their experience, and their level of emotional maturity, every horse will have some values that they look for more obviously. Once you identify and help them address their top issues, don't be surprised if they switch and become concerned about a different value. Eventually, most horses go all the way through the value list. When all is well with one, they may suddenly become irritable as they bring up another issue that was more latent.

Make a habit of going through the value list in your head as you send and receive messages. The more you do, the more "up to date" your Conversation with your horse will become. The more you are able to fulfill this list for him, the easier it is for your horse to focus on the training you wish to do with him. It has been my experience that horses with a "satisfied" list of values are not only more interested in their education, but they often have valuable insight to offer to the training process. Many seem to be thinking about their last lesson and eagerly start right where they left off once they don't have to waste so much time trying to communicate their basic needs.

As mentioned earlier in this book, asking good questions is a part of practicing Horse Speak. Hopefully with this list of equine values, you will have a starting point from which to do just that!

SKILL-BUILDER

Customize Your Horse's Value List

From what I have observed from the many horses I have been around, the six basic values are a great start. But, of course, there could be more values on the list, depending on the horse. I invite you to make a list of what you can perceive your horse to value. Whether a favorite brush, a specific type of grass, or where he likes to stand to take a nap, these are all pieces to getting to know your horse on a deeper level.

What Balance Means to a Horse

We've already touched on the idea of balance—both outer and inner. Why is balance so important it bears repeating? From the moment of birth, a horse's physical balance is his greatest defense; newborns need to be on their feet and able to move with Mom within a few hours of birth. To horses, balance also represents personal power. When they play or problem-solve at speed, you will often see them rear, spin, buck, and bolt. Even older horses can still often be enticed to play like this. When a horse cannot balance well physically due to illness or injury, he is more likely to be easily triggered. The horse's primary need is good physical balance to maneuver, and when this is removed, he is going to instinctively be in a higher state of alert: An injured wild horse is an easier target for predators, so he will be more vigilant and nervous.

As we've discussed, for horses, all three balances—physical, mental, and emotional—go together. Being physically out of balance puts them mentally and emotionally out of balance, as well. When a horse is confused, his body will brace, and he will be physically off balance. When a horse is scared, his body will tense, and he will be physically out of balance. Likewise, if a horse is pulled or thrown physically out of balance, that can confuse or scare him.

All three go together.

Consider how you may lead your horse from the barn to the mounting block. Due to the physics of your body's movement, you can, and probably often *do,* literally pull your horse off balance on the way there.

When what you are doing as a matter of course accidentally makes the horse feel like his body is unbalanced, then you put his mind and feelings out of balance, too. Now, it is likely you get on and expect the horse to be balanced while you ride, *but* you are starting from a position where, as far *as the horse is concerned*, you have pulled him all out of balance before expecting him to perform.

One of the easiest ways for horses to deal with constantly feeling like they are knocked off balance is to tune us out. In some horses, tuning out the humans around them produces anxiety, in others aggressiveness,

SKILL-BUILDER

Walk in the Horse's Shoes

Just imagine if someone led you around every day and didn't care if you felt like you were constantly slipping, tipping, tripping, or feeling worried about it all. How would you bond with such a person? If your friend or teacher slapped you to move you over, tugged on you in an unbalancing way, or dragged you along behind with your hands tied, how would you feel?

while some horses just become dull. They learn to ignore our body language in an effort to preserve the balance they have. Some horses are very forgiving and figure that we are just silly and don't get it. They seem to love us anyway and enjoy our company as best they can. Others are not so forgiving and may even be freaked out by this, resulting in a range of issues, from panic to aggression.

Providing Enrichment

An important step in Horse Speak is changing your mindset: Instead of getting to the barn and thinking about what your horse can do for you today (clear that course, nail that flying change, beat that time), include what *you* are going to do to add value to *his* day. Consider the value list on p. 79; in addition, each horse has his own "sweet spot" or favorite things. Some "valuable" activities to try:

1 Share resources: Go "grass-hunting" for the best spots or offer bits of hay. Lower-value food items are less exciting than grain or carrots, for example, so offer a better opportunity for you both to find Inner Zero—and balance—together (fig. 1.24).

2 Set up an obstacle course made of your horse's favorite things. Play in it with him.

3 Allow your horse to roam free in the arena while walking along casually with him. Use this as a chance to observe his body language, Mirror it (see p. 102), and play Copycat (see p. 105).

4 Figure out which is your horse's favorite brush, and only use that one.

5 Learn some equine bodywork—there are a number of methods that are safe to apply yourself once you know basic techniques. Offer your horse bodywork on a regular basis.

6 Try some basic trick training.

7 Take a walk in the woods together with an eye for finding as many Safety Objects—trees, stumps, rocks—as you can, to exclaim, "Ooh... *another* place to feel wonderful about!"

8 Sit with your horse while he eats or naps; enjoy a glass of wine or cup of tea.

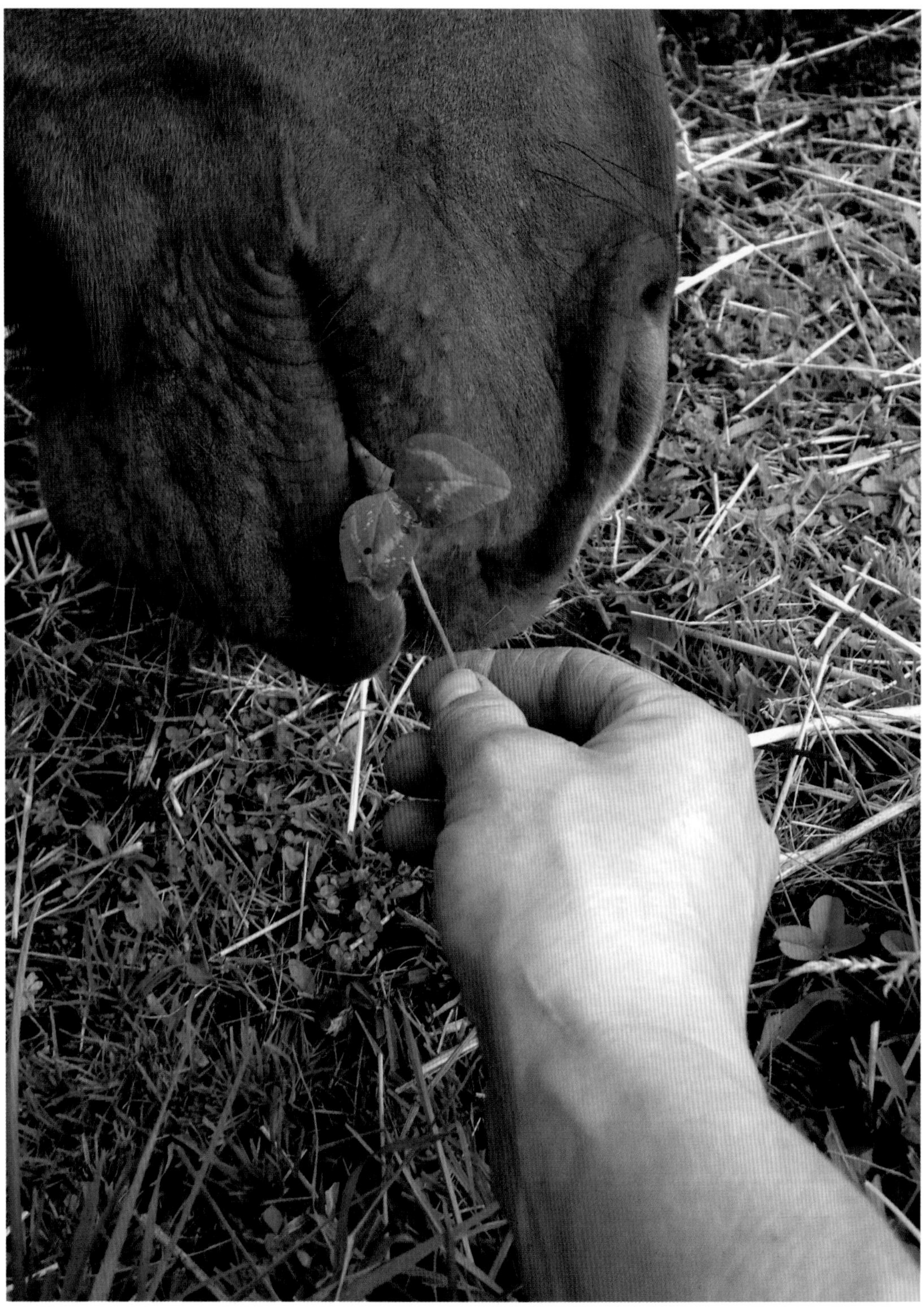

1.24 Laura goes grass-hunting with Jag. Perhaps your horse loves four-leaf clover?

SKILL-BUILDER

Enrichment Self-Assessment

Notice the sensations in your body when you incorporate enrichment activities in your time with your horse. We value sitting together with our friends and family eating a meal or watching a show. Horses have their version of this.

Many of us have tried to do enriching things with our horses out of a vague understanding that it's probably a good idea. So many times, however, the enriching activity becomes another "task," or is even a training method in and of itself. On the surface, a horse may seem to like what we are doing, so it is important to consider the following:

- When you try trick training, do you notice your energy going up or your horse's energy going up? (If so, he could be lightly triggered by the activity itself or possibly the use of treats to do the training.)

- Are you able to pick through a flake of hay and find what nibbles your horse might favor without thinking about what you are going to do next?

- Can you let go of "the agenda" of enrichment and settle into a still, quiet moment with your horse, just for the sake of it?

- Can you smile at him, just because?

- Can you think about the fun you will have today instead of the work?

Being aware of what you are thinking and feeling from moment to moment will assist you in becoming more present and congruent with your horse.

2 Observing the Horse's Environment and Movement Signals

The key to Horse Speak is pretty simple, really. You just need to *pay attention* whenever you are with your horse. Since horse language is predominately visual, horses watch each other closely, even when it doesn't seem like they are doing much of anything. Horses are always watching you closely, as well, when you are with them.

Seeing vs. Looking

"Looking" at a horse is what we usually do. Learning to "see" a horse means we move past a casual, noncommittal use of our eyes, to a heightened awareness in which our eyes read the messages from the horse much like they read the messages on a billboard. This skill allows you to move on to more direct and clear moment-to-moment messages, such as you would absorb when reading a book.

The Conversations horses have with each other are very fluid. So much can happen so fast that it gets away from you at first (fig. 2.1). Luckily, once you start to catch on, your brain will take over. Our brains actually use body language as a source for

2.1 These horses are observing everything about me. They are "seeing" me. The trick is to learn to "see" them, too.

2.2 Because of the location of the horse's eyes on his head, his peripheral vision typically far exceeds ours. We can practice becoming less "forward focused" and more "peripherally focused" to see the world more like the horse.

up to 80 percent of all information gathered—we just don't *know* we are doing it because it is largely unconscious.

Go slow at first. Learn to *see*. Learn to observe. Expand your peripheral vision (see p. 42) and begin to memorize what your horse offers (fig. 2.2).

Red Light, Green Light

When you were a kid, you may have played the game "Red Light, Green Light," where the player in the "command" position has her back to the other participants who race to try to be the first to reach her while following the commander's instructions of "Red Light" (stop) and "Green Light" (go).

You may be asking yourself, "What does this have to do with horses?"

Remember the Bell Curve (see p. 20)? The Bell Curve illustrates how we can think about the ranges of Conversations we may have with a particular horse. There are many variables that come into play during a Conversation, and depending on the subject, we may need to make adjustments in order to stay in the middle of the Bell Curve where communication is optimal (fig. 2.3). A Red Zone horse can be difficult to communicate with, while a Green Zone horse is ready and willing. Similarly, Red Light, Green Light is a way to think of the signals, postures, and gestures you observe when seeing a horse. A Red-Light signal could be ears that are pinned backward or a horse's head that is high in an X posture. On the other hand, a Green-Light signal could be the

SKILL-BUILDER

Noticing Small Changes

One of the goals of honing your observation skills is to begin to notice the physical, mental, and emotional changes that your horse goes through in the course of the day. I suggest that you take a series of photos during a one-minute period while your horse is grazing, moving alone or with others, or even just standing in one position. Study them. I think you will be amazed to see how many subtle changes the horse's body language makes in such a short period of time.

2.3 Getting horses to Zero as I am doing here at a clinic helps to communicate with them from the middle range of the Bell Curve in the Green Zone.

horse's drooping lower lip, sideways ears, or soft eyes.

Like the Yellow Zone from The Bell Curve, Yellow Light refers to the place between Green and Red. A horse is often okay to work in the Yellow Zone; many school horses, for example, can be found here. The key is to discern whether Yellow Light signals are heading toward Green or on their way to Red (figs. 2.4).

2.4 Yellow Zone means the horse is not totally engaged but not engulfed by the Red Zone. In most cases, you can still get things done in the Yellow Zone, if your goal is Zero. When a horse is totally engulfed by the Red Zone like the horse here, he can no longer relate to you. In this case, I am keeping my Zero to help this horse find his.

As you work with a horse, it is important that you learn to read his zones and signals. Many of us were taught to push past subtle signals and try to enforce the training we want through repetition and insistence alone.

Repetition is, in fact, especially important with horses, but this comes from the safety it creates in the horse's world by providing predictable patterns, rather than the idea that you have to just teach the horse's body to "do the thing." There are moments to hold steady and stay the course in a horse's education. The horse will predictably ask, "Why?" from time to time, often by resisting something he normally does. This resistance is out of the horse's need to find out what his options are. Horses do this with each other, as well. However, holding steady *for the horse* so that he arrives at a point where he realizes what you are asking for is not going to hurt him is part of helping him to the Green Zone where Green-Light signals abound. This is different from holding steady *against the horse's will* in order to force him to do the task even if he is in a Red Zone. Pushing a horse through his Red Zone usually goes one of two ways: The horse is triggered into Freeze (or at least becomes "slushy" and gives up or gives in—see p. 66), or he is triggered into the other Fs and takes off bucking, running for the hills.

MYTH-BUSTER

Should I Force My Horse to Do Things He Doesn't Like?

Manners are the bottom line. There are certainly moments when we have to have our children brush their teeth even though they don't want to. There are moments when a horse needs to be able to develop a solid Yellow Zone about a certain task. I am not asking the horse to love the task; I am only asking that he tolerate it reasonably well (like getting his hooves trimmed, for example).

It is better to Linger Longer (see p. 153) and aim for short, positive-attention sessions when dealing with something a horse doesn't like to do. Consider the things your horse values (see p. 79). If he is going to pull away in three seconds, let go in two. Praise him. Make the deal as good as you can. Then, after all that, if your horse still acts out, a correction or reprimand may be in order. It's not that we never, ever need to use a correction—just make sure you have done all the rapport-building activities first.

Learn to Look for Red

When any task repeatedly creates a clear Yellow-toward-Red Signal (a higher X posture, facial expressions of discontent, tail swishing, holding the breath, bracing), it is wise to stop and work on simply arriving at a Green Light for the task. Training is only as strong as its weakest link. Some horses may not like having their girths cinched up or may indicate displeasure when longeing (as examples), but they can learn to have a greater *tolerance*. To me, this is a decent, working Yellow Zone. A horse can only change his tolerance level by experiencing enough positive associations related to the task to allow new pathways of learning to sink into his brain. No one, horse or human, learns when under stress.

Green Light and Manners

When I worked with rescues, there was one trainer I spent time with who was incredibly good, and we sometimes compared notes. She once said to me,

"Sharon, you know that many of these horses are really limited due to injuries or age. But, if we can help them to be such good equine citizens that they are just lovely to have around, then they will get good forever homes, even as someone's backyard pet."

It was true—for all the horses we reconditioned and found homes for that were riding horses, we also found homes for those who couldn't be ridden. Some became "babysitters," and others went off to people who no longer wanted to be in the saddle but whose lives were empty without horses in them. We used a variety of approaches, depending on the horses and what worked best, but in the end, if they had good manners, we knew they were going to be treated well and stay in the homes they went to, rather than being sent back to the rescue. I felt it was my duty to ensure that the horses I was helping developed softness and gentleness with human beings, and this was sometimes a real undertaking if they had come to us with a history of abuse.

To me, it is worth it to devote an entire afternoon, or realistically, a whole month to helping a horse "Green Light" whatever is the task at hand. The horse will be more likely to have a good home, a good life, and be treated well no matter where he is if the attitude, he brings with him is mannerly and positive.

You can force obedience; you cannot force gentleness.

MYTH-BUSTER

Flooding—Does It Work?

The most typical approach for forcing horses into the Yellow Zone these days is to "flood" them—a form of desensitization where animals (or humans) change their behaviors to avoid negative stimuli. With horses, this often involves getting their adrenaline going with some sort of running. Think of flooding like this: You are afraid of spiders, so a therapist ties you to a chair and throws rubber spiders at you for a half hour. You may get over your fear...or you may get worse. Either way, you probably won't love that therapist.

I *do* want to "get through to a horse" in the Red Zone. I *do* want to get the bug spray on, or the fly mask on, or the girth on, without having him spook, bite, or kick. In the pages ahead, I will teach you alternative ways to work with horses with phobias or injuries or severe behaviors, using techniques that allow you to learn so much about that horse, you can work together to get to that Yellow Zone. Some tasks may *never get a Green Light,* but a solid Yellow means the horse can at least "self-regulate" his survival instincts and stay present enough to handle what may be triggers.

The Chessboard

Horses are totally aware of their environment in a way that is different than we are. They are on constant alert about possible danger in their world. For them, food is on the ground: "Put your head down, there is probably something to eat on the ground." On a simplistic level, humans are

2.5 The Chessboard is a metaphor for how horses see and experience the framework of their world, which includes everything around them.

in the predator category, so rather than looking at the world and thinking, "What can catch me?" we have the viewpoint "What can I catch?"

In addition, our brains have the ability to *label* all the things in the world, giving us two cognitive abilities: distancing from objects and establishing ownership over objects. Horses, on the other hand, *directly experience* the environment and cannot cognitively say, "Oh, there's a deer foraging in the underbrush! How lovely." When they see or hear something in the woods, they don't label it—they do have a reaction to it. And typically, the reaction is to be ready to get far away from whatever it is.

I like to think of how horses experience the environment as a river of flowing consciousness—but not in a sort of dreamy internal way. Their world is totally practical, and their language reflects that practicality. You may imagine a spooky thought and then remember it and decide to tell someone about it: translating this thought in all its detail into a book, a movie, or campfire story. A horse has a spooky thought when something is happening in the here-and-now that makes him feel uncomfortable. He may remember a scary moment, but he does not form a narrative around it.

He cannot distance himself from it like we can, nor does he "identify" with the event, the way we can. His brain makes something more like an "emotional map" of the moment, which is woven into the fabric of the actual map he makes of his physical world. This is why understanding *his* map of the world is so important.

Thinking of a horse's scope of awareness like a Chessboard—a game board with 64 squares of alternating colors—can help people gain a larger perspective about how horses move through their world (fig. 2.5). Everything surrounding them is part of the Chessboard: their stalls and all the objects outside of them; the other horses sharing the same pasture or in the surrounding pastures; the pasture fencing; the run-in shelter—basically everything they can see and interact with is part of the Chessboard. When one thing, object, or creature that is part of the Chessboard moves or changes, it affects the horse and his position on the board in some way.

The position of your horse in a certain environment is his position on the Chessboard, and everything else plays a role in the game. Let's say you are riding in an indoor arena and your horse does not like to go to the far corner. From the horse's perspective, his movement on the Chessboard places him far away from the exit—too far. His emotional map remembers that is a spooky corner where a bird once flew down from the rafters, or where there was a bad smell, and his emotional map remembers his last "safe place" to be was outside with his friend. The closer you get to the physical trigger (the corner), the more he gets triggered emotionally. One of the Four Fs starts to engage (see p. 65).

Horses work with these emotionally laden physical maps in their herd dynamics. When you remove a key player or object from the Chessboard, all the horses in that game have to reassign roles. They will move around on the Chessboard and start a fresh game without that player. Of course, it is not a "game" to them at all, but a profoundly serious, never-ending stream of communication related to safety and connection.

Fire Drills and Sports Maneuvers

At Horse Speak clinics I often have two or more horses brought into an indoor arena and turned loose while attendees watch. It is then very easy for me to explain to the audience what is happening as the horses explore their Chessboard, because the patterns of movements are so predictable that this sequencing becomes very easy to see over time (figs. 2.6 A–E).

There are two primary types of movements you see horses making when they explore their Chessboard, whether it be a new one, or a part of their daily routine.

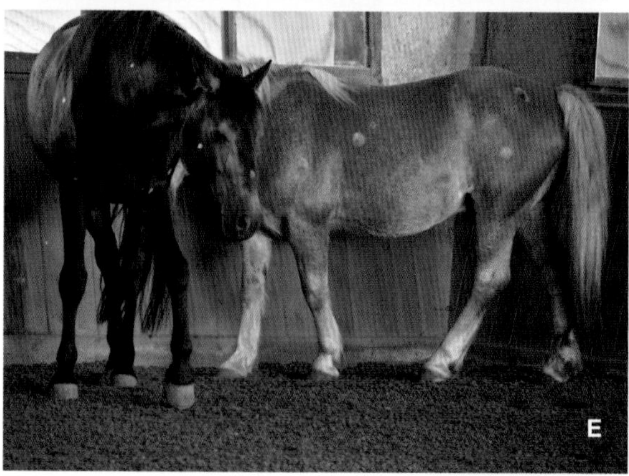

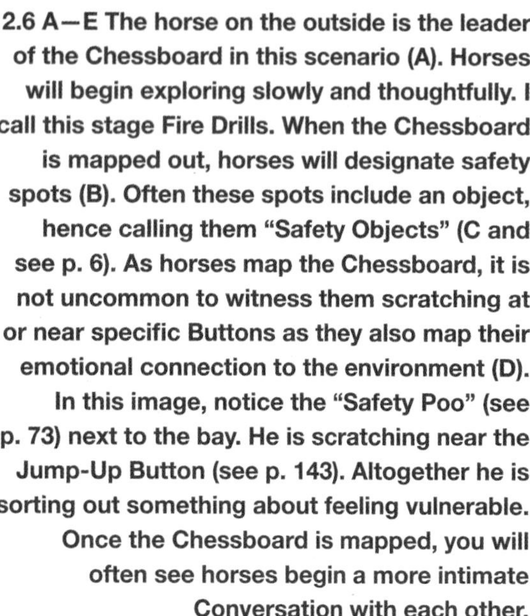

2.6 A—E The horse on the outside is the leader of the Chessboard in this scenario (A). Horses will begin exploring slowly and thoughtfully. I call this stage Fire Drills. When the Chessboard is mapped out, horses will designate safety spots (B). Often these spots include an object, hence calling them "Safety Objects" (C and see p. 6). As horses map the Chessboard, it is not uncommon to witness them scratching at or near specific Buttons as they also map their emotional connection to the environment (D). In this image, notice the "Safety Poo" (see p. 73) next to the bay. He is scratching near the Jump-Up Button (see p. 143). Altogether he is sorting out something about feeling vulnerable. Once the Chessboard is mapped, you will often see horses begin a more intimate Conversation with each other.

2.7 A & B It is totally naturally for horses to give it a "team effort" and navigate the Chessboard as a group (A). During Fire Drills, they are inclined to check out everything on the Chessboard (B). When we can imitate this process, we insert ourselves into a kind of primal communication. Working with this instinct can also help us understand better ways of introducing horses to new objects.

- When a horse uses a corner or feature of the environment to get "stuck in" or explore purposefully and move in and out of it on his own, or with a buddy, slowly, I call this a *Fire Drill* (figs. 2.7 A & B). This is the slow, predictable patterns of movement, usually regulated by the lead horse.

- When a horse moves around the environment and the features of it with speed, I call it a *Sports Maneuver* (fig. 2.8). This is the next level of movement. It often includes the main "topics" from the Fire Drill phase, but now one or two of the horses will want to move at speed, roll on the ground, and even buck and kick in mock defensive maneuvers. This is still typically overseen by the leaders who often do not move into Sports Maneuvers themselves, preferring to "hold their ground" as a governing body.

2.8 At a certain point, horses will usually test the Chessboard at speed. They practice forward, backward, left, and right evasive maneuvers. They also practice sticking together. This stage is what I call *Sports Maneuvers.*

Like an athlete preparing for any big game, horses practice both fast and slow maneuvers on the Chessboard so that in an emergency, they can "snap to it" without having to pause and think. Most horses will model both their levels of leadership and their evasive maneuvers in the form of play, which can include running, rearing, kicking, biting, and quick changes of direction (Sports Maneuvers) rather than slower exploration (Fire Drills). Humans can in no way match this degree of speed and intensity as a regular form of communication with horses, although things like longeing, round-penning, and liberty work do, in some ways, mirror these kinds of Chessboard negotiations.

What I have learned is that because horses actually prefer to have slow, self-regulated negotiations and navigations around their Chessboard with a calm, centered leader watching and governing their speed, I can use this to my advantage. In the past, I had been taught that I needed to get a horse moving around the Chessboard and focus on showing him I could control his actions while he galloped. I believed he needed to get tired and "get the bucks out" in order to focus on the day's lesson. I believed that the actions were strictly about the activity we were doing, be it longeing or round-penning or whatever.

I didn't know that this was inaccurate. I didn't know I needed to provide the Fire Drills *first* in order to have a thinking, low-intensity, Inner-Zero horse who would be able to pick up speed for practice, education, and even fun, but not out of fear or because of pressure.

Why does it help us to identify Fire Drills and Sports Maneuvers? When we realize that we can enter into direct communication with horses with the knowledge that they want to problem-solve the Chessboard, then we can begin to problem-solve *with* them, and they begin to see us as their leaders. Instead of exposing horses to artificial obstacle courses and trying to teach them not to fear certain things, we can use their own strategies to deal with *any* obstacle life throws at you both as you negotiate the Chessboard together (fig. 2.9).

MYTH-BUSTER

Can You Work with a Horse's Fear?

In my past as a young trainer, I was taught to push horses through fear, ignore their fear, and punish them for not paying attention to me. I learned how to sack out a horse, and I also learned how to use positive conditioning with treats, too—all with the aim of teaching horses not to be afraid.

The thing is, horses do not need to put on a show of fearlessness when you know how to tell them all is well, and they are safe with you. There are many ways to work with a horse's fear, and we will talk about a lot of them in the pages ahead.

2.9 Horses do not need to be "fearless" if you know how to tell them that all is well, and they are safe with you.

Entering Your Horse's Chessboard

Begin by familiarizing yourself with your horse's Chessboard:

1. Make a list of all the items and other players that you find within the space in which your horse lives. Everything you can see they can see plays a role in the game—not just the stall but all the things around the stall, the aisle that you walk down, the rack of pitch forks, the wash stall, the tree at the end of the pasture, and the goats next door. Take all of this into consideration.

2. While spending time with your horse, whether you have him on a lead line or you are visiting out in the field, begin to notice if there are certain places where your horse may be giving you a Red Light and going into X posture, or a Green Light and an O posture. Try to see what may have caused the change in the horse's state and how his body is positioned to the object—for example, whether the horse is facing it or has his hip to it.

SKILL-BUILDER

Chessboard Self-Assessment

As you walk around the environment, pay attention to any of the sensations that you feel in your body. For example, perhaps, you get "butterflies" in your stomach as you approach the wash stall—this is good information because maybe your horse feels uncertain about the wash stall, too.

Once you insert yourself in the Chessboard, remember that the horse knows you are there. You don't need to "get his attention" or tell him.

The Myth of "Getting Their Attention"

Have you ever noticed that when you are doing something in a paddock, like mending fences or picking out the run-in shelter, or some other time-consuming activity in which you don't really need or want to be helped by horses, it is not uncommon for your horse or horses to line up and watch you (fig. 2.10)? Have you ever turned around to grab a tool as you work and realized your horse is standing right there? Have you ever wondered why the maintenance guy who knows virtually nothing about horses can go out and catch the runaway horse in a matter of minutes?

I wondered. So, I watched. It turns out that the attitude we have when looking intent on getting a job done—such as mending a fence, cleaning a run-in, or catching a horse when you really don't care—and the attitude a true lead horse has who is "securing the environment" for all the other horses in a herd is expressed in a similar fashion: it appears as self-driven purpose when moving through Bubbles of Personals Space (see p. 69). In other words, when we look like we are desperate for attention from our horses, we send an intense message of "Gotcha," while the attitude of "I'm busy; stay out of my way," sends the message, "I don't need or want anything *from* you, but I am making sure your Chessboard is okay."

2.10 When we "look busy," horse find us interesting. Horses that are leaders look busy when they are exploring the Chessboard—"checking fences" while looking out for the herd.

I've mentioned before that most training systems insist that you have to get and keep a horse's attention. Perhaps this is simply because no one until now has been able to outline the precise micromovements horses are in fact using to demonstrate their focus of attention, as well as communicate their subtle Conversations to other players on the Chessboard. The Earth-shattering news is that you *do not*, in fact, *ever* need to force your horse's attention to be upon you. The very moment you show up, whether you are busy with chores or preparing for a lesson, the horse knows you are on the Chessboard and adjusts his own position to reflect that. The arrival of a human often changes the very mood of a horse. When you learn to see the changes in a horse's awareness, attention, and communication, you will also see him shift and adapt the moment some other human arrives. Many people are shocked to realize this.

Why do we think we have to "get" our horses' attention even after we enter the Chessboard? I think that because we are "eyes in front" hunter types, we recognize (and like) the greeting other "eyes-in-front" types give. For example, a dog will bark, wag his tail, and run up to you. A cat may meow, come near, rub against your leg, or even try to get onto your lap. There is no mistake that a cat knows you are there. Even if he chooses to ignore you, you still know about it.

But horses are "eyes-on-the-side" types. They are prey animals with careful approaches, often zigzagging, changing direction, and doing little more than showing you one or both shoulders to ensure approach is welcomed. When a prey animal walks right up to you, either the animal is very secure in himself or he's very secure with you.

In addition to orienting their Greeting according to the Chessboard and your Bubbles of Personal Space, horses need to continue to pay attention to the environment. If, for instance, a mountain lion crept to the edge of the pasture just as you were going to greet your horse, your horse will no longer be paying attention to you... he is going to deal with the lion. This is how the equine brain is designed—it is nothing personal. In fact, communications indicating, "I will *Scan the Horizon* to check for danger" are essential messages of protection between horses. The best "scanner" holds a higher rank. (See more about Scan the Horizon and how we can learn to use it to make the horse feel safe with us on p. 98.)

By adjusting our expectations about what horses should look like as they include us on their Chessboards (meaning they do not tend to look like dogs, running

MYTH-BUSTER

Can Horses "Tune You Out"?

Neuroscience News reported in 2018 that research done by Dr. Karen McComb demonstrated that horses not only recognize faces, but they also remember the *expressions* on people's faces. Dr. Janet Jones (author of the book *Horse Brain, Human Brain*) and Dr. Steve Peters are both neuroscientists who have worked to dispel various myths about horses' brains and how to train them according to their brain capability. In his workshops, Dr. Peters mentions the "Reticular Activating System," which is a part of the brain that is "scanning the environment" for possible threats. In the horse, it never really rests until deep, REM sleep.

All of this means that the horse's brain is literally *incapable* of tuning a human being out once that human is on the Chessboard.

BUZZWORDS

Scan the Horizon

This is a term I introduced in my first book, indicating the act of a horse lifting his head and looking to the distance—essentially scanning for danger.

up to us and wagging a tail), we can have more success noticing when they are, in fact, giving us Green Light signals to approach and be with them, or even requesting to connect with us. Remember, horses are never, ever *off* the Chessboard. This would be like taking a fish out of water or a bird out of the air. They are a part of the Earth and all that's around them, just as surely. If you want to keep your horse's attention squarely on you, then learn to see the Chessboard the way he does. "Playing Chess" means you can "paddle downstream": You do not need to force the horse's attention or punish him for getting distracted. You do not need to lure him with food or trap him into a corner to create conditions of surrender. Instead, your body language and how you use it in relation to the other players on the Chessboard is enough. *You are enough*. You never *need* a bag, flag, tag, or treat to trick, force, or cajole. You just need to learn to read the signs of attention that are already there.

You are enough.

Making the Chessboard Safe

At first glance, it may seem like "clearing" the Chessboard and setting up a safer game for your horse will take massive effort; some people even wonder if it can really be done.

MYTH-BUSTER

Does Looking Away Mean My Horse Is Bored with Me?

Don't think a horse that looks away from you isn't paying attention to you. Learn to see when a horse is looking away out of fear, out of concern for a real or imagined boogeyman, or even just as a sign of respect for your Bubble of Personal Space. Some may even be offering to Scan the Horizon (see Buzzwords above) as an offer of protection to *you.* Sometimes, horses look away just to clear their heads or to invite you in: Once you understand when a horse looks away as a request for "a minute to think," you will take it as a cue to give him the all-important "soaking moment." Also note: Sometimes a head turn away actually invites you in closer, like when a friend leans away to make space for you on a bench.

What I can say is this: I believe that most of the "corrective" horsemanship skills that flood the market were invented to deal with a horse's spooky maps of the Chessboard.

The standard approach in horse training today is to do things to the horse until he is inclined to stop panicking about the world around him and pay attention to you and only you. In my experience, even when these techniques are effective, they either simply distract the horse from his true inner fears (by replacing them with the fear of getting in trouble with *you*), or in the case of positive reinforcement training, the horse may learn to see many elements of the Chessboard as possible "paychecks" (that is, sources of treats, for example).

The bottom line? Instead of "making" a horse pay attention to us, we can pretty easily become the reason the horse *wants* to pay attention by becoming the key player on the Chessboard—the one who makes it *safe*. In the upcoming chapters, I will provide insights and concepts, and teach you skills, that will all lend themselves toward working with the horse's Chessboard. What I explain to you will allow you to insert yourself in the horse's game in a way that encourages him to choose to follow you... because when you show up, *all is well.*

MYTH-BUSTER

Are Treats Stress-Relievers?

While treat training for engaging on the Chessboard does work on some levels, it can also build a new stress into the horse's nervous system. Horses by nature are designed to seek to gobble up high-value food in times of plenty (midsummer) and to store fat for lean times like midwinter when food is scarce and temperatures plummet. Mother Nature tells horses to eat as much as they can of rich food while it is available. So, delivering high-value treats can trigger a latent "gobble syndrome" and accidently create a state of equine anxiety.

In addition, treat training can create a fixation, which can mean making a Safety Object or spot a place of deep rest and Zero that much more difficult. When over-treated, there are no Safety Objects; each object is a potential high-value food source due to "gobble syndrome." In certain horses, this can trigger other underlying anxiety that leaks into the horse's overall sense of well-being.

Learning to Play Chess

Appreciating all pieces of the game can help you gain a deeper understanding of how your horse is experiencing the Chessboard. It is also a way to notice if you are having certain reactions to elements of the environment that you were not aware of. Remember you are just information gathering *without judgment* toward yourself or your horse.

We will explore more explicit ways you can manage your movement on the Chessboard to optimize your connection with your horse in chapter 7 (p. 250), but now consider what the horse's movement is telling you.

2.11 A & B Since horses will naturally seek Safety Objects, we can work with this on purpose and turn a previous unpleasant object into a Safety Object, as this clinic participant is doing with the mounting block (A). Gates, in the meantime, are notorious for being spooky places on the Chessboard (B). I blow *Sentry Breath* and "claim" the gate by touching it. I allow the horse to stand quietly. Altogether I am telling her, "Nothing bad will happen here." (Only a moment before, she had spooked when asked to approach the gate.)

Movement Messages

There are two main types of equine *Movement Messages* that can be observed on the Chessboard.

- The first type deals with securing the environment and creating a safe space on the Chessboard directly. These messages can be for the individual horse or for the horse's group if the horse is a leader type (figs. 2.11 A & B). They are useful for us to observe and identify because then *we* can learn to give these all-important messages to horses.
- The second type of Movement Messages are those that deal with the inner workings of the *hierarchy* of the herd—whether that herd consists of two

horses in your back yard or multiple horses at a boarding barn. These messages are about relationships and have a direct impact on moment-to-moment levels of trust and respect, which can lead to better overall rapport. Learning to model them can therefore improve your own relationship with your horse.

BUZZWORDS

Sentry Breath

A short forceful snort out at something in the environment that is of concern. To Mirror this behavior, hold your head up, look in the direction of the area of concern, and blow out as if you are blowing out many birthday candles (see more about this on p. 229).

Human beings are designed to be attracted to movement, and our ability to hyper-focus reflects this. On the whole, though, we pay attention to big movements. Think of how we always notice when horses sprint and buck or run a race. Like it or not, we tend to only register this high-intensity movement (fig. 2.12).

This propensity, along with the desire to make horses our useful vehicles for thousands of years, has made us neglectful of the more subtle movements horses offer as signals. However, the subtle signals are what afford us a unique opportunity to craft highly effective and impactful encounters with horses in which our body language is enough—big, energetic driving forces, like whips or long ropes, are unnecessary. Horse Speak makes the most of the small, quiet signals.

2.12 Humans are good at noticing high intensity Sports Maneuvers, like when horses sprint or buck or play-fight, and we often miss more subtle movement.

2.13 If you and your horse are Zero on the inside, then you can have more fun on the outside because of the rapport you have built together.

It is my sincere opinion that most high-intensity training—such as dressage schooling, jumping, cross-country, reining—should only be done as an end result of a great deal of kind and open groundwork, which has instilled in both the human and the horse a deep level of trust (2.13). When you have laid a proper foundation, built on both of you being able to find and return to Zero, then, of course, the high-intensity work many of us enjoy pursuing can be interesting and fun for *both of you*. Your chosen activity or sport is then an advancement of a solid baseline of mutual trust and respect, rather than struggling to achieve the latter as a result of the first.

We tend to get this thing I like to call "Task Tunnel Vision." Remember, you have to stay in touch with your sense perceptions and with what you are feeling to better assess the messages you horse is trying to give you. Communication is a two-way street; *listening* is part of every Conversation.

Mirroring

I teach *Mirroring* as the first and foremost aspect of body language: looking where the horse looks, stopping when he stops, and so on. My students are always shocked to find that, when they focus on copying every movement that the horse is making, the horse is surprisingly doing a lot, all the time (fig. 2.14). I ask them to focus on a single body part of the horse for about five minutes; after the time is up, they often say they are exhausted by how much the horse is doing, even while simply grazing.

I consider Mirroring the most important stage of learning horse body language. This is because small children mirror everyone around them to learn human body language and social skills, so our brains actually learned this all-important lesson early. However, we then moved on to verbal speech, so we need to have a "homecoming" of sorts within ourselves as we return to nature's way of communicating with the other beings in this world. We normally overwhelm whatever a horse is doing and have him follow *our lead*. The best leaders know what it is like to follow. We need to step back and learn more practical and empathic relating.

SKILL-BUILDER

Practice Movements That Create a Safe Space

1 Pick three things that you will take your horse to investigate—for example, the wall of the indoor arena, a wheelbarrow, and a tree.

2 With your horse in hand, *point* to the first object you are planning to go to, and when you approach it, touch it first and act as if that object is the most interesting thing you have ever seen.

3 Repeat with the next two objects. The goal is to be the horse's mentor and inspire him to check out the object, too—after you do.

4 If you have an enclosed space where it is safe to allow two or three horses loose, just watch and observe how the horse's move and problem-solve in the new environment. Everything they do is saying something.

5 I would recommend either taking photos or video so you can revisit the experience and perhaps watch it in slow motion.

2.14 I invite you to practice Mirroring to learn about your horse's rhythm, feel, and timing.

Mirroring Practice

1 Find a comfortable spot outside of whatever enclosure your horse is in—his stall, paddock, pasture, or round pen, for example.

2 Go to Zero.

3 Do not try to influence the horse in any way.

4 Remember, the little signals and nuances actually carry *big meaning*. It is the little nuances that create maximum effect with minimal effort. Watch for them. Studying little nuances is a huge gain for human beings; you can then memorize and "keep up" with the horse's state changes (see p. 86).

5 Activate your peripheral vision and try to see the horse from nose to tail. (Please keep in mind that observation does take practice; allow yourself space to learn.)

6 Then, begin to focus in on one part—say, facial expressions, or the position of one front foot—but do not lose sight completely of the rest of the horse.

7 Mirror the signals externally by moving along with the horse, as well as internally, by doing it in your mind. Both have value.

8 Eventually, attempt to "take in" the Movement Messages of a few horses at a time, and see all of them nose to tail, Mirroring their signals.

Mirroring is an essential step to developing your natural inclination for your subconscious mind to memorize equine body language. I am teaching you the *cognitive* pieces of Horse Speak, but you have to teach your body to get to the point where the postures, signals, and gestures become second nature, and you will no longer have to *think*—you can just be with the horse and be fluid. Luckily, like when driving a car, the brain likes to memorize all the data, then switch off and run on automatic. There will come a time, where someone will come to visit your horse and comment that your

SKILL-BUILDER

Mirroring Self-Awareness

Notice any sensations in your body while you are Mirroring your horse. If you are focusing on his face, be aware of the feeling in your own face. If you are Mirroring your horse's breath, see if you have you started to breathe in the same cadence as the horse. It can be helpful to record your Horse Speak journey in a notebook to track your progress. As with other areas of observation, you may also want to take pictures, video, or sketch what you see.

2.15 In Copycat, I ask for *just one thing,* wait to get a response, and stay Zero.

relationship looks like "movie magic"— and you will have forgotten you were even doing anything at all.

Copycat

At first what I call *Copycat* should be done at a distance. Here you offer the horse a gesture and watch to see if the horse copies you on some level. This is based on a similar exchange horses use with each other to determine who will lead and who will follow. If, for example, you lift your right leg to see if the horse will copy you, you may be watching his right front leg, but the key is to notice *any* movement—an ear, eye, flinch of the skin, or swish of the tail (fig. 2.15). Any movement, however subtle, is a reply to your suggestion. Sometimes we think we are being totally clear, but our X is too weak, or our O is too strong, or our Core Energy is pointed in the wrong direction. The horse may be answering *the real question* your body is asking, not the question you *thought* you were. Have a sense of humor about it and have some fun. Horses have both a sense of curiosity and humor. Go ahead and laugh.

SKILL-BUILDER

Copycat Self-Assessment

Are you able to ask *just for one thing*, wait to get a response, and stay Zero? Remember, a reply to your suggestion *may not* be what you asked for specifically.

How did you feel while you were waiting? You are developing your feel, and it's important to notice the different sensations and thoughts that you may be having during the skill-building exercises. This stage is essential in moving forward into how Horse Speak is useful within any training modality.

One of the tougher things about being human is having patience.

Copycat Practice

1. Go to Zero.
2. Ask for a movement.
3. Watch the *whole horse* for *any response*.
4. Often the horse needs a full minute to "process" the information (see p. 113).
5. Try again if necessary. Perhaps change one thing about your movement: for example, give more space, change your angle, or use a different gesture.

Facial Expressions

In my first book, I cover a great deal about equine facial expressions (figs. 2.16). The human lips, chin, and nostrils can make surprisingly similar motions. Even

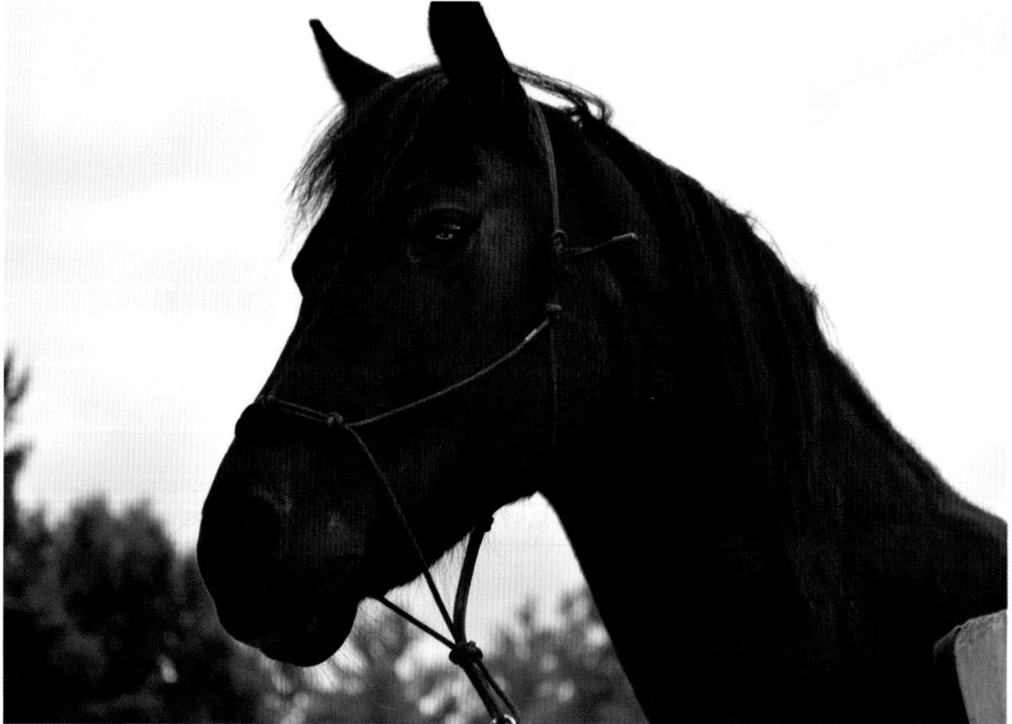

2.16 We were all taught to notice a horse's head and look for conformation. This may be a pretty head, but what does her facial expression say?

our eyes can make similar expressions, and raising, lowering, and tilting the head can have similar meanings.

Expressions Quick Reference

Using your observation skills, study your horse's face, one aspect at a time. Though expression can be specific to the horse, here are some common features and what they might be saying:

- In general, I use the terms "X messages" and "O messages" to describe what the facial expressions taken together might indicate (figs. 2.17 A & B).
- The *ears* tend to be an accent of feeling—for instance, there are a few stages of backward-facing ears before "flat-back" (pinned) ears (fig. 2.18 A & B). Most

2.17 A & B **The expression includes the ears, eyes, nostrils, lips, chin, and even the jaw or throat latch. X messages in the face represent higher intensity in the Conversation (A). As horses move toward Zero, their facial expressions become more rounded and softer—what I call O messages (B).**

2.18 A & B In photo A, the horse's ears are in concentration. But if you look carefully, you can see he is also holding his breath, which is visible in the tight or tucked look of his belly. In addition, his eye is worried, shown by the tented lines where his eyebrow would be. His muzzle and lips are pinched tightly. Collectively, this is a tense moment of concern for this horse. In photo B, two playmates are engaged in high-intensity Sports Maneuvers, which include play-fighting strategies. Notice that despite the drama there is an invisible line between them, and they are each in their own Bubble of Personal Space. Look at their ears (and other facial expressions), Core Energy, and expressive tails. This level of concentrated body awareness is hard for us to imitate at first.

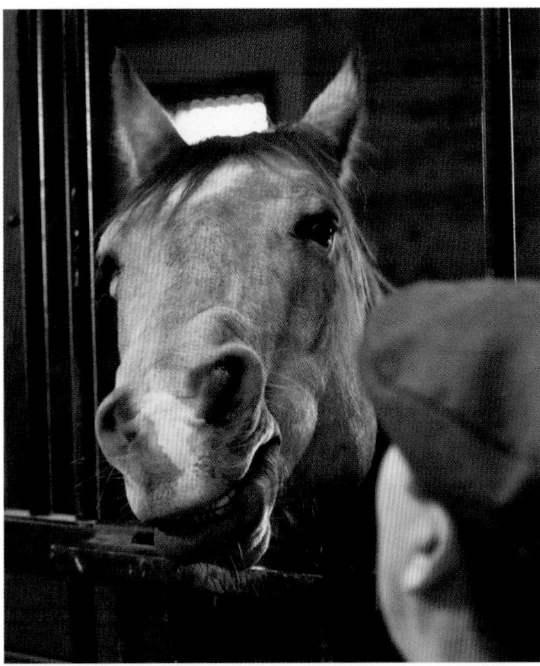

2.19 The nostrils will sometimes swivel so that one is more pronounced than the other. This often implies that the horse is sorting things out.

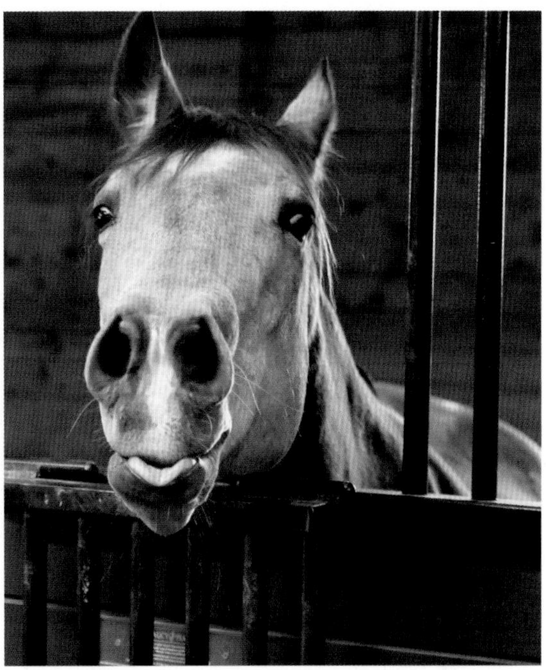

2.20 It seems horse lips can move in as many ways as our own lips can. Really watch your horse's lips for nuances of expression.

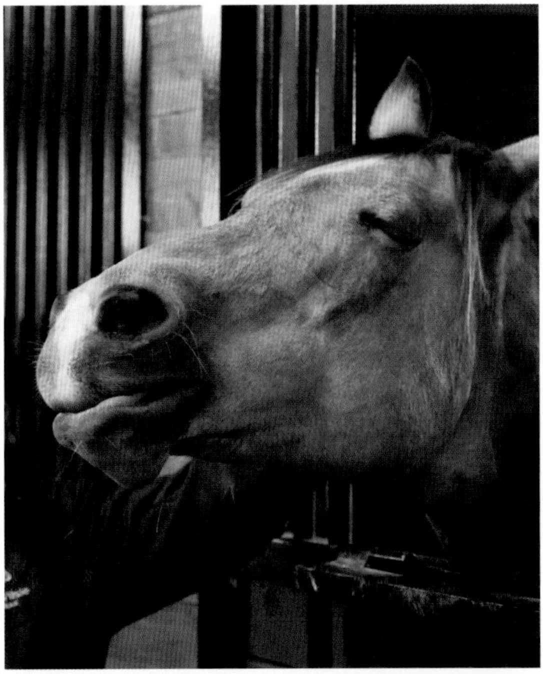

2.21 The horse's chin can tell tales of latent tension or represent that he is still chewing things over.

2.22 In this photo, you can clearly see the lines in this horse's cheek. Generally, lines like this represent "gritting the teeth," just like we might do. It can also be a sign of pain or anxiety.

2.23 The throatlatch can become tense when a horse feels uncomfortable or anxious. On the other hand, some horses like to have us stroke them there, presumably because it is relaxing.

2.24 A & B "The eyes are the window to the soul." This seems to be true for horses as well. Learn to notices the wide variety of eye messages that horses use, including "staring eyes" (A) and "blinking eyes" (B).

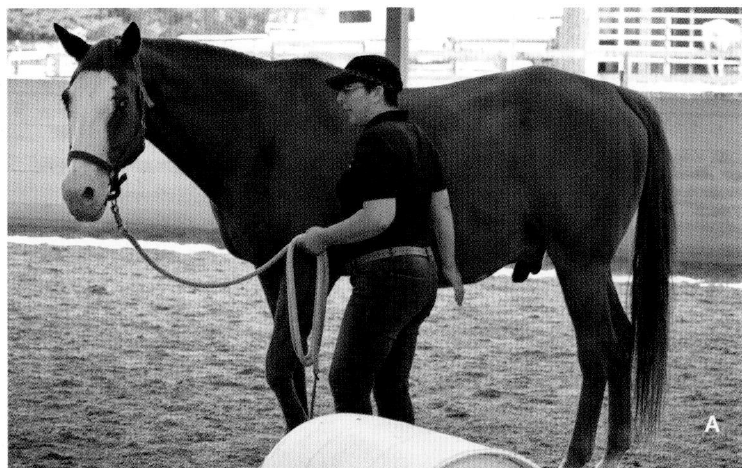

2.25 A & B X and O shown in the height of the head: X posture includes a high set to the head and neck (A), and O posture includes a low set to the head and neck (B).

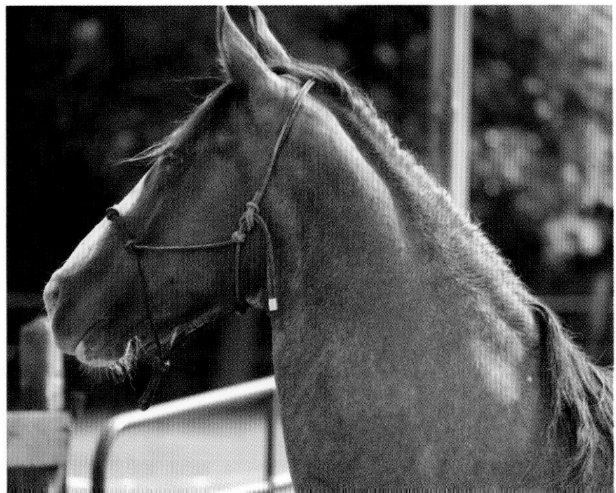

2.26 Pay attention to the level of rigidity in a horse's neck. A really stiff neck, as shown here, tends to indicate a horse feels overwhelmed and cannot process.

2.27 A yawn doesn't necessarily mean your horse is tired. It can be a sign of tension or release.

of the backward-facing stages represent seriousness and concentration, not *necessarily* anger or aggression (which flat-back ears mostly *do* signal).

- The *nostrils* have a wide variety of expressions, along with the Breath Messages they often share (fig. 2.19). You need to become aware of both.
- The *lips* make many defining expressions, most similar in nature to our own (fig. 2.20).
- The *chin* is a final "test" to determine if the horse is reserved and tense, or engaged or relaxed (fig. 2.21).
- The *jaw* shows lines if it is clamped or grinding teeth, while it is smooth when relaxed and open (figs. 2.22).
- The *throatlatch* shows us if the horse is tense and not breathing, or if he is relaxed and open to communicating (fig. 2.23).
- The *eyes* display a wide variety of expression, but "staring eyes" and "blinking eyes" are the most important to recognize (figs. 2.24 A & B).
- The *height of the head* denotes whether the horse is in or moving into X or O (figs. 2.25 A & B and see p. 49).
- The *neck muscles* signal the horse's Feeling State: rigid and inflexible denote tension, while relaxed and flexible signal acceptance and calm (fig. 2.26).
- *Yawning* can be a sign of tension if the horse has no way out of his situation, or it can indicate a deep release when he feels understood (fig. 2.27).

All these parts taken together as a whole tell the full story of the horse's "inner feelings" or thoughts in the moment. Many of the specific expressions that are typical of a horse also indicate his "type" and role in the herd (more about this in chapter 4—p. 158). In my experience, a horse "looks like" his personality.

Seeing a Horse "In Process"

We've talked about the Chessboard, movement, and expression, but you also need to observe when the horse is still—or when he needs to be. The best trainers all over the world know that horses need to "soak" on a lesson. How many maestros, old cowboys, and compassionate equestrians have said the words over and over again, "Give horses a minute to think about things"?

You can train your eye to watch the passage of this "internal processing." Horses need to pass all information through their entire body when they are problem-solving or assessing new information. You will memorize what processing looks like and feels like in a horse, and by degrees, you will come to see that allowing a horse a full minute to pause and think means he will be able to memorize the new information you have presented, compare notes with old information, and come to newer, more current conclusions about his relationship with you, as well as whatever it is you are asking him to consider.

When you know how to help a horse process, then you are setting yourself up as a benevolent leader. You are encouraging a horse to use his head, not just his instincts, while with you. Then, when you do up the intensity levels in your work, you are more assured that you are not throwing gasoline on a brewing ember.

Horses "in process"—whether on their own or with others—adopt what I call the *Hold Position*:

- Squared up.
- Head and neck in "neutral" (extended out naturally from the withers, neither high nor low).
- Eyes softly blinking.
- Lips relaxed or touching a Safety Object.

Once you see these signs of a horse processing information, you should go to inner and outer Zero for a minute (you will come to realize how much horses really do need a full minute—sometimes five whole minutes) to allow the information to

SKILL-BUILDER

Facial Expressions Self-Assessment

While practicing looking through the specific lenses of the horse's facial features, do you notice any sensations in your own face or perhaps other parts of your body?

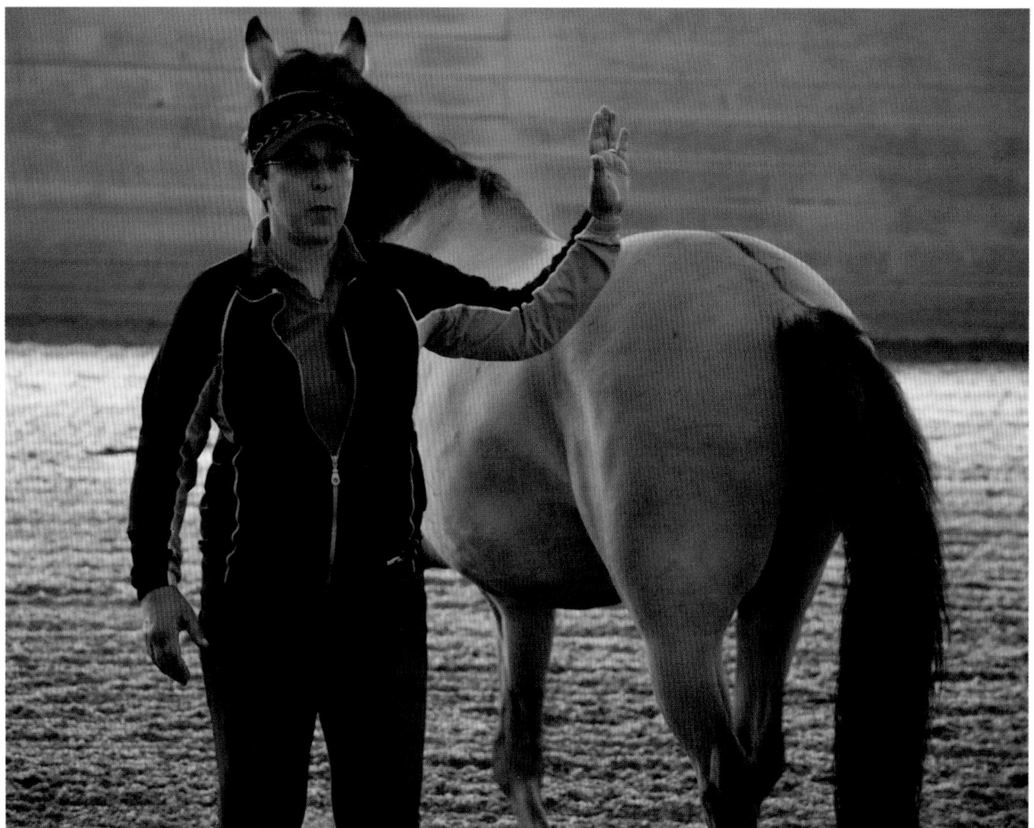

2.28 **When horses stand nose to tail, they are watching each other's backs so both can rest. Offering this message to a horse (facing his tail and raising your Hold Hand) can help him relax and process.**

travel internally from the tip of the horse's nose to his tail. Note also that some horses need to process on a regular basis and will tell you with their position. Once you learn to see a horse process information, it will begin to look like completely obvious body language. You will be amazed you never noticed it before.

The horse is done processing when there is stimulation in the hind end or tail; the final factor of a horse's Feeling State is the illustration of the tail. The tail acts a bit like punctuation at the end of a sentence—arched, flagged, swished all says something (fig. 2.28).

Observation Is Very Important

It may seem like this process is tedious or slow, but keep in mind there are a lot of levels of unpacking a typical human being needs to go through to get out of her own way! Horses are already *masters* of body language; we just began kindergarten level of something that they have a PhD in.

Give yourself and your horse a few weeks to practice all these steps. It will be more than worth it in the long run. It took me a solid month to begin to start to see something other than "horses just grazing," so be patient with yourself! With this chapter, I am trying to save you the hours of sheer struggle that I went through as I tried to get my "trainer's mind" to back off so I could learn something new. If you were to decide to learn a new sport or musical instrument, watching professionals in these activities would be an important piece of the learning process. The same is true for learning Horse Speak.

Whatever your agenda is with a horse—winning a blue ribbon or winning a horse's trust… or both—you need to be able to perform all these skills if you are going to be able to shape the horse's behavior in a way that both protects his dignity and promotes your ultimate goals. You are now showing up as an aware witness and demonstrating an interest in seeing the world from the horse's perspective. The horse will probably have some internal shifts just from you behaving in this way. Most horses love to be "joined" in their experience. We so often grab a horse, put a halter on him, and drag him into whatever we are doing. For the horse, just having the freedom to express himself, and be witnessed and even Mirrored, is normally a relief… and sometimes a breath of fresh air.

3 Knowing the Buttons and What They Do

The complexity of the *Horse Speak Buttons*—"zones" on the body that horses use when talking to each other—has taken me down a path of deeper understanding of the way horses are really and truly communicating with each other. The more I have observed horse-to-horse conversations between different breeds and all over the world, the more respect I have gained for their nuanced language.

I could probably write a whole book on the subject of the Buttons alone. In these pages I have done my best to deliver enough information about the Buttons to give those who are new to Horse Speak a solid working understanding and those who are returning to this work a deeper level of comprehension.

In my first book, I cover the basic premise of each of the 13 primary Buttons of Horse Speak. Here, I am pleased to be able to give you two more Buttons to work with (fig. 3.1).

What Are the Buttons?

A Button is an interactive area on the horse's body, which I've identified based upon watching horses talk to other horses (fig. 3.1). The Buttons indicate specific intention, wants, and needs, and also add to group dynamics. Each Button has its own range of meaning, and a collection of Buttons all used at once contain a more refined communication usually targeting a very specific agenda.

3.1 Horses "talk" to each other's Buttons by aiming their muzzles, eyes, or their own Buttons at them. Because we have hands and often have horses on lead ropes, we must learn how to communicate with the Buttons effectively, as I am here.

All you have to do is observe horses (as we covered in the last chapter) to see them using the Buttons to communicate with each other. Human beings have long co-opted many of these "hot spots" for our own uses, depending on the training system or systems you use. In Horse Speak, we use them to have Conversations.

The thing about the Buttons is that a horse can communicate with them in multiple ways: from one Button to another Button, or with attention aimed toward a Button (looking at one, or pointing the muzzle toward one, for example). The focus of attention between the Buttons depends upon the horses involved and the intention between them. For instance, let's say a horse wants to *Buddy Up* with his pal. He will aim the flat surface of his shoulder at his friend's Shoulder Button (p. 134), and perhaps yield his head away. This creates a beckoning gesture and also removes intensity. It

BUZZWORDS

Buddy-Up

This means to be friendly, standing quietly together, sharing space. When a horse shows you his Shoulder Button (see p. 134), he is asking you to come over and "Buddy-Up." Horses often Buddy-Up when they take a nap. They can Buddy-Up shoulder to shoulder or shoulder to hip, which is more of a message of, "You watch my back and I'll watch yours while we rest."

would be like patting the chair next to you and leaning away from your friend to "make room" and invite her to sit down.

In fact, although the Buttons are the seat of the intention of a gesture, posture, or signal, the horse moves his body in relation to the Button he is displaying and responds to the Buttons being displayed by other horses at the same time. Because we need to learn to both recognize these displays and also gesture toward Buttons in order to "talk" to our horses, let's review the location and use of all the Buttons (fig. 3.2). (Note that with regard to explaining the Buttons, I need to use human terms and definitions at some junctures, but keep in mind this is simply because I have to use human ideas to talk to other humans.)

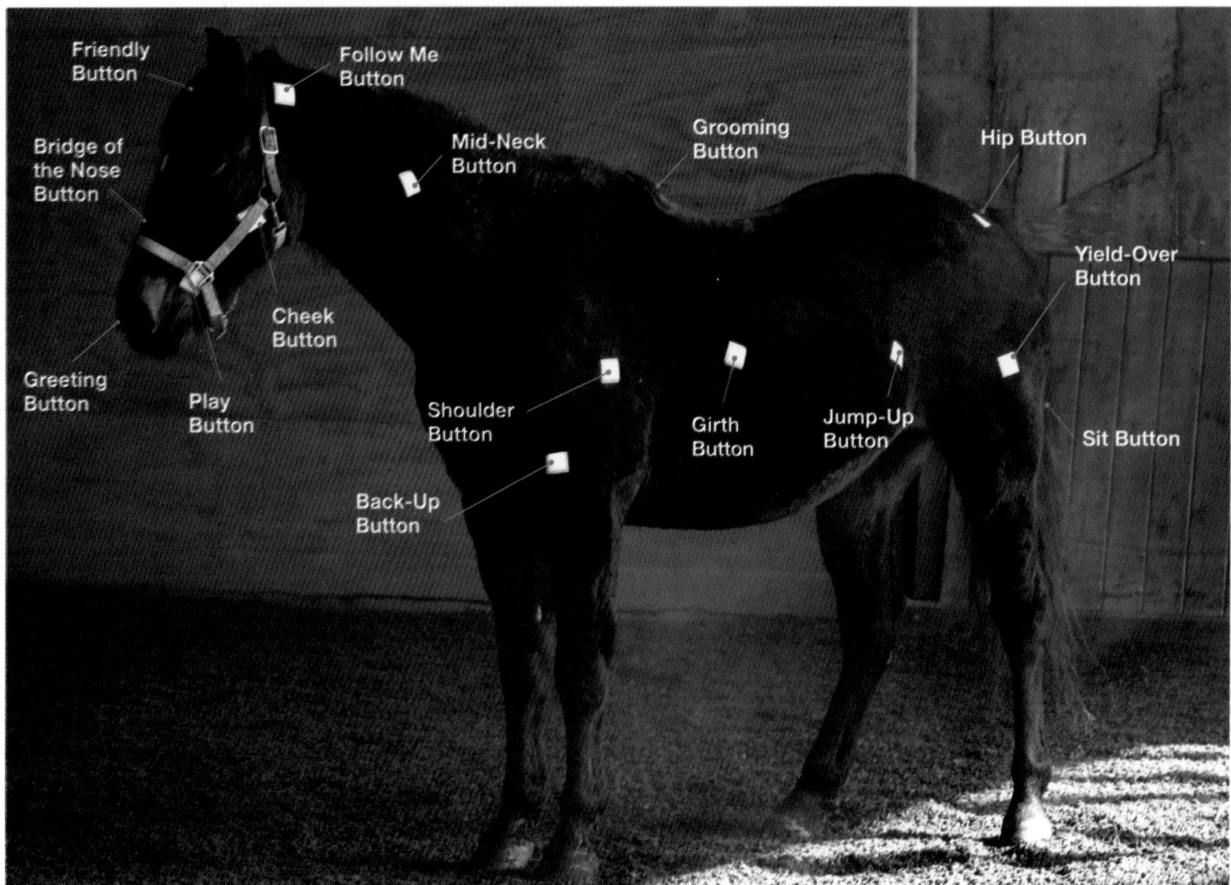

3.2 The 15 Horse Speak Buttons I am teaching you to use in this book.

Buttons of the Head and Neck

3.3 A & B Muzzle to Muzzle contact is how horses introduce themselves, using the Greeting Button. Horses use beckoning expressions to invite Greeting. When they first come together, it is usually at the front of the Bubble.

Greeting Button

This Button is at the tip of the horse's nose between the nostrils. Horses who are connecting with each other use this Button as the first point of contact on each other's bodies. Just as humans shake hands, horses greet each other with their muzzles. Aside from its role in the formal *Greeting* and informal *Check-In*, which I'll explain, this Button also shows curiosity, trust, interest, and is the "testing" Button that "checks things out." Greeting can happen both from a distance and up close (figs. 3.3 A & B). Sniffing and *Breath Messages* are part of this Button because of the nostrils' presence. I describe various breaths in *Horse Speak*, but if you practice a good Mirroring session in which you focus on the horse's nostrils, you should be able to pick up on the *soft breaths* that are welcoming, the *hard breaths* that are threatening, and the *blowing breaths* that indicate a warning or wariness.

The Nuances of Greeting and Check-In

Depending on whether you are new to Horse Speak or have already spent time exploring its possibilities, what follows will either serve as an introduction to the Greeting Ritual and Check-In, or a review.

In a *Formal Greeting*, horses display three primary touches of the Greeting Button. A Formal Greeting can occur between horses when the situation warrants a higher intensity of connection or more details need to be sorted out.

What can be tricky at first to witness is the speed at which the three touches occur. In some cases, horses may even linger near each other, only separating by a shadow of space between moments of contact. This shadow separation often includes more intense nostril-on-nostril breaths and higher, arched polls. The three touches can occur in the space between each out-breath. This high-intensity Greeting is often seen between horses meeting for the first time, or between rivals, mares in heat, or playmates inviting a romp around. I have also seen occasions in which horses perform type of Greeting several times in a row. Often this is a more serious debate about hierarchy, mating ritual, or some sort of dispute.

Luckily for us, there is also a *"Low-O" Formal Greeting*, such as one may see between friends or from one horse to his leader. The Low-O Greeting is the best one for us to try to emulate. We do not wish to display that we are a rival or in any sort of contest with a horse.

Approaching a horse in a lower O posture from the start signals that you are requesting the Low-O Greeting.

Your knuckles simulate a horse's muzzle and should be used whenever you are connecting with the point between the nostrils. Touching there signals you wish to have a solid, gentle connection. Only touching the Button for the space of one single breath says that you want a formal contact, which implies formal rules of "connect and respect." When your horse appears to linger and not retract his muzzle from your knuckles, he may be "skipping that part" (the formal contact) and in his mind may have performed the shadow Greeting I just described. Most of the time, however, horses will move their heads to the side slightly, and then come back for all three touches if you space them out with a breath between each one.

Usually, the third touch is the one where "lingering" is now acceptable. Many horses offer a gentle "kiss" on the back of your knuckles at this juncture, which means, "I am ready for more connection with you." Long, deep breaths from you at the third touch tells the horse you would like to have kinship and rapport with him. Be sensitive to not overstaying your welcome. Just like with a human handshake, lingering too long becomes uncomfortable.

Some horses may be very relaxed or feel very comfortable with you and will not feel the need to perform a three-touch Greeting. Other horses are mouth shy, head shy, or experiencing pain in their bodies and may not want to touch your knuckles with their muzzles. In such cases, they may offer the Greeting from a few inches (or even a foot) away and use it as a signal only. Accentuate the breath out with each knuckle offer, and this will suffice as a Greeting. Over time, most horses settle into a comfortable Greeting Ritual with their humans. Everyone is different, and where some may like a formal "How do you do?" others will prefer a "high five."

After an initial Formal (or what will pass for formal between you and your horse) Greeting, horses will seek to press their muzzle to your knuckles at every juncture in which there is a change. For instance, during leading, many insecure horses try to reach around to give what I call a *Check-In* to their human leader. They are seeking comfort and safety. When they don't get it, they may chew on the lead rope, nibble on the person's jacket, nuzzle into the person's belly, or become more and more restless. Simply offering a solid "place to land" on the back of your hand every time the horse draws his muzzle toward you will go a long way to improving the feelings between you. When we realize this muzzle Check-In is the equivalent of a friend or family member reaching for our hands when they need reassurance, the change of perspective helps us to see this as an important message to share with a horse.

Over time, offering healthy Check-Ins with horses can single-handedly improve your connection with them. However, unruly, immature, emotionally traumatized Red Zone horses can be nippy, jumpy, or demanding. There is a way to offer this important message of security and still maintain a "good manners" boundary between you. This involves knowing how to work with the Cheek Button, which I explain on p. 124.

Play Button

This Button is located on the side of the horse's lips. Too often, people push this area when they want the horse's head to move over, only to have the horse come right back and mouth them—because that is the spot horses target to invite play. You may see friendly horses nibble each other at this Button or share hay by sneaking bits out of the side of each other's mouths (fig. 3.4).

3.4 The Play Button invites *play*. It is best for us to leave this Button alone, unless we want the horse to open his mouth.

You will often observe two horses, typically geldings, licking or chewing on the side of each other's mouth. I once watched a mother lip the side of her newborn foal's mouth to encourage him to suckle.

We can use this Button when we want to offer a horse a mouth, gum, or tongue massage, or if we want to teach him to relax when getting his teeth floated. However, we must be sure to have a very clear Zero and use a lot of out-breaths or sighing to indicate relaxation, not over-stimulation. Because this area has such a direct message about high-intensity activity, it is best to avoid any correction or casual contact with it for the most part. Since riding with a bridle places the bit in this zone, ideally, we want to have a gentle, Low-Calorie connection with it to ensure the best contact when in the saddle.

It can be a tender, affectionate area—*but*, in general, it is best to leave it alone.

*** NEW BUTTON ***

Bridge of the Nose Button

This Button is located at the same main contact point as where the strap of the halter sits on the horse's nose. This sensitive, subtle, and nuanced Button has different meaning than the Friendly Button (under the horse's forelock, and which I discuss on p. 127) and is geared to invite deep trust and intimacy with the *entire body* of the horse. It's location on the skull sets up a powerful message that is felt through the entire skeleton of the horse. This zone is basically delicate bone and a thin layer of flesh, with some cartilage that expands toward the nostrils. Engaging with this Button induces deep flexion in all the joints and "scoops" the horse's energy into collection when you target it while moving either backward or forward. This Button can also be used when two horses are playing and one wants to lower the intensity. Think of it as two people wrestling for fun, and one puts up a hand and says, "Whoa—that's enough, let's quit this."

The Bridge of the Nose Button is primarily used to request calming down, getting centered, and "resetting." Note that this Button is extremely refined and powerfully emotional. We put halters right on top of it, so many horses have become cautious and even defensive about letting us touch it. Move slowly and carefully. Once a horse trusts you to use and hold the Bridge of the Nose, they begin to find a very deep Zero—I like to say they get "melty." It can also be used to redirect the intensity or energy of a horse, such as one horse pressing this Button with his lips or aiming his eyes at it to create a "yield" of the space in front the other horse (fig. 3.5). This is most often done when a youngster needs to back down and concede space to an elder. In humans it would be like a coach placing a firm palm on the shoulder of a player who needs to settle himself. Mostly, it is an unusual or "special situation" Button for horses to use with each other, but due to the position of the nosebands on halters and bridles, it is overly used by us. I have been able to translate our use of this Button into something that reinforces manners, adds emotional value, and enhances well-being and health in the horse (fig. 3.6).

3.5 Between horses, the Bridge of the Nose is an emotional and sensitive Conversation.

3.6 If we want the emotional sensitivity of the horse to emerge, then we must be very aware of our contact with this Button.

*** NEW NAME ***

Cheek Button (formerly the Go Away Face Button)

When I first wrote *Horse Speak*, I needed to come up with names for many of the aspects of this language. In my own mind, the phrase "Go Away Face" has a tint of humor in it. I first coined the phrase after watching a mother horse nibble her young colt on this Button (located on the large, round cheek of the horse) over and over again during one of his afternoons of rearing, fussing, and generally not allowing her

SKILL-BUILDER

Establishing Trust with the Bridge of the Nose

- Begin by making conscious and kind contact with this Button. This in itself can be a process of gaining the horse's trust. I will sometimes stabilize the halter in one hand with light but firm contact and reach repeatedly for the Bridge of the Nose Button with my other hand, removing it as soon as the horse stops flinching.
- Next, learn to use a feather-light touch on the Button, resting your cupped fingers across it. No pressure, no gripping, no grabbing.
- Now, do what I call *Rock the Baby* there. In my first book, I introduced the term Rock the Baby to describe a mild rocking sensation that creates deeper relaxation in the horse and is good for helping him stand still, prepare for mounting, and deal with stress (see p. 268). Do not use your arm exclusively or "shove" the horse back and forth. Instead, just rock your own body while your hand rests on the Bridge of the Nose. If it seems like the horse will pull away in three seconds, then stop in two seconds. Less is more.
- Step away (give the horse his Bubble space back), sigh out loud, and go to O posture, or hold a light X posture to say, "Stay in Your Lane, and I'll stay in mine."
- Repeat a few times. If the horse lowers his head, release the Button. If he yawns, go sit down somewhere and let him process. If he backs away, allow it. If he "declines" your touch by pulling his head away after your initial contact and movement, then he is "done."

Bridge of the Nose contact is incredibly useful for working with the horse's balance—all three of them (emotional, mental, and physical). Understanding how twisting the head slightly with Rock the Baby impacts the rocking of the entire skeleton will really help you see how the whole horse is affected by changes in balance. (Note that this is the prerequisite to obtaining a really good Therapy Back-Up, which I teach you later in this book—see p. 255.)

3.7 The Cheek Button is the first Button and the most Low-Calorie Button used between horses on an everyday level.

to rest. I imagined her saying, "Could you just *go away with that face*?" As I've taught Horse Speak over the past six years, however, I could see that this phrase was confusing to some and perhaps didn't accurately capture what this Button is about and the potential it has to create mannerly communication.

Let's define the Cheek Button now. Between horses, it is the first Button used in the stages of negotiating hierarchy and status (fig. 3.7). Therefore, it is also the first Button to be used to define the line between you and your horse, instruct a change of direction, and invite more personal connection (using Turn the Key, Come to Me—p. 57). You can also invite the Cheek Button toward you in a *Horse Hug,* which fosters trust and kindness, and can help with haltering and bridling, as well as preparing for ridden work (see more about the Horse Hug on p. 215).

The basic purpose of this Button is to provide a mannerly way to define the front part of the horse's Bubble. (I explain more about navigating *Bubble Quadrants* in chapter 5, p. 206.) The Cheek Button is the governing Button for messages to contract or expand the Bubble. When one horse wants another horse to join him, he will yield his Cheek Button far away to the side and hold it still. In my first book I called this *Deferring Space.*

When a horse wants to move through what would be the front of another horse's Bubble, either to pass by or to ask the other horse to move out of the way, he will make a "pointed expression" toward the other horse's Cheek Button. This can be a simple *look* at the Button, it can be *aiming the muzzle* at the Button, or it can have a higher level of intensity with pinned ears and a pushing motion forward with the whole head. The pushing motion resembles a person using her hands to push the air in the direction of loud children when telling them, "Go outside and play!"

When horses are eating hay together is the easiest time to witness the Cheek Button being used in a Low-Calorie manner. Horses eating together are often merely requesting "face space" at the dinner table, so this is also the best motion for us to memorize and copy.

In motion, the Cheek Button is the first to be engaged when either a leader is changing the direction of a group with a pushing or driving message to the Cheek of another, or a member of a group is indicating, "Follow me this way." When horses want to "steady the course," it is also this Button that adopts a "Hold" position and remains still to tell the other members, "Stay in Your Lane."

SKILL-BUILDER

Leading with the Cheek Button

Knowing how to use the Cheek Button can really help us when leading our horses. Holding one palm to the Cheek Button during the entire leading session not only defines to "Stay in Your Lane," it also helps you understand where the "line on the road" is between you. Like when driving a car, we need to know where the line in the road is in order to remain in our own lane. When we swerve from our lane to our horse's, due to lack of understanding of where it is and how to address it, we make the horse feel uncomfortable, frustrated, and often out of balance. We have "popped" his Bubble. This can result in a horse who lacks confidence, acts nippy or is outright difficult to lead. Imagine you are driving down the highway and someone begins swerving in the lane next to you, and then darts back and forth between lanes. How frustrated do you become? We do not mean to give our horses this feeling, but because our bodies are two-legged and their bodies are four, we lack the perception of what it is like to be in their Bubbles. I will talk more about how to practice Stay in Your Lane in Chapter 5 (see p. 216).

3.8 Horse friends may rub their Friendly Buttons on each other as a sign of comfort.

Friendly Button

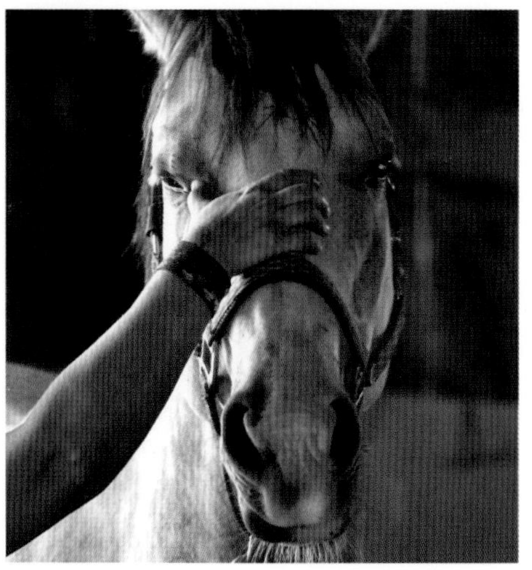

3.9 Some horses can be sensitive about us rubbing the Friendly Button at first. I am drawing my thumb along this mare's eye. She enjoyed that contact and gradually lowered her head.

This Button is located on the horse's forehead and is the area most often used for friendly contact (fig. 3.8). For a long time, people have walked up to horses and offered to rub their Friendly Button as a first sign of connection (fig. 3.9). I have witnessed professional horse trainers approach and rub on the Friendly Button to signal to the horse that "all is well now." This is offered with positive intentions, of course, but it isn't like rubbing a dog on his head. Horses do not rub heads as a form of Greeting. It is not a horrible misunderstanding, but it is not the Button horses use with each other for initiating contact (they use the Greeting Button—see p. 119). The Friendly Button is used later after the first stage of "Connect and Respect" has occurred (see p. 140).

Some horses rub their Friendly Button on people; I always ask for the *6-Inch Rule* of space first, then allow some rubbing. A horse who rubs his Friendly Button on you

BUZZWORDS

6-Inch Rule

Imagine there is a glass wall between you and the horse. The horse's head and neck should not break the glass. Think of "6 inches" not as an exact measurement, but as a metaphor to say, "Please do not cross this line, and keep your face out of my space."

when you are with him may be using you as a scratching post, although I have also noticed that a horse will do this to his person when he notices the person is tense or in a bad mood. This is like a friend patting you on the shoulder saying, "Hey, are you okay?" Some horses rub the Friendly Button on you because they have a literal headache. This form of rubbing is extreme, and I consider it displacement (see p. 31). Horses can get headaches from poor handling in a halter, a tight bridle, ulcers in the mouth due to sharp points on the teeth, tooth abscesses, poor bite alignment, or temporomandibular joint (TMJ) issues (meaning a tight jaw). There are 12 cranial nerves and two of them surf through the flesh of the horse's head: the *trigeminal nerve* and the *facial nerve*. Locating the pathway of these nerves can make you more sensitive to why some horses don't want to be bridled or haltered, or rub on you really hard when you take the bridle or halter off (fig. 3.10).

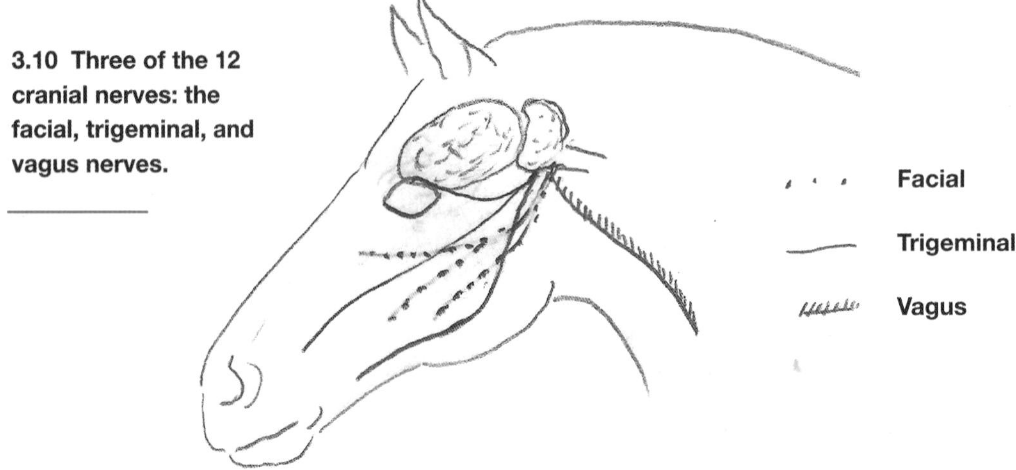

3.10 Three of the 12 cranial nerves: the facial, trigeminal, and vagus nerves.

Follow Me Button

This Button is located at the top of the poll, ironically where the strap of the halter or bridle sits behind the horse's ears (fig. 3.11). It is often used by mothers with tiny babies who are just learning to follow. Her lips will tug, turn, or lick this area to encourage her foal to step with her. Fighting horses may bite this Button because it is a sensitive location on the skeleton that could knock an opponent down.

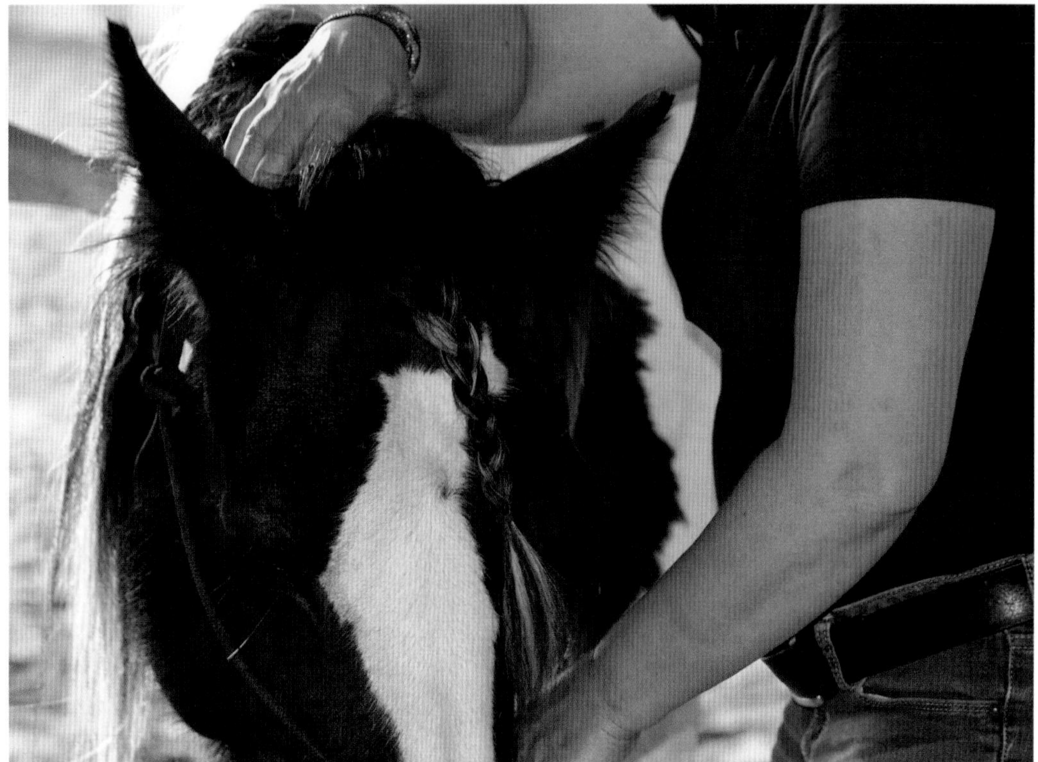

3.11 The Follow Me Button rests at the base of the horse's skull, right where the head strap of the halter sits.

The Follow Me Button often induces a deep state of relaxation when you Rock the Baby there (see p. 137). Many horses will naturally lower their heads into an Aw-Shucks position (the position of releasing tension and intensity—see p. 59) when you touch them there (fig. 3.12). The Follow Me Button can also request a horse literally follow you: if you tap it lightly and then slowly walk in front of the horse, he will often follow along. Forward or pushy horses on the lead line often relax and settle with this step. Under saddle, you can reach up and tap this Button while sighing out loud to ask your horse to settle down. In this case you are telling him, "Follow me into a relaxed state."

SKILL-BUILDER

Asking Yourself What Rubbing Signifies

When a horse wants to rub his head on me, I wonder:

- Does he have a headache?
- Is he stressed?
- Is he alerting me to a mouth condition?
- Does he think I am stressed?
- Is he a "space invader" and do I need to say, "Stay in Your Lane"?
- Does he just want to connect?

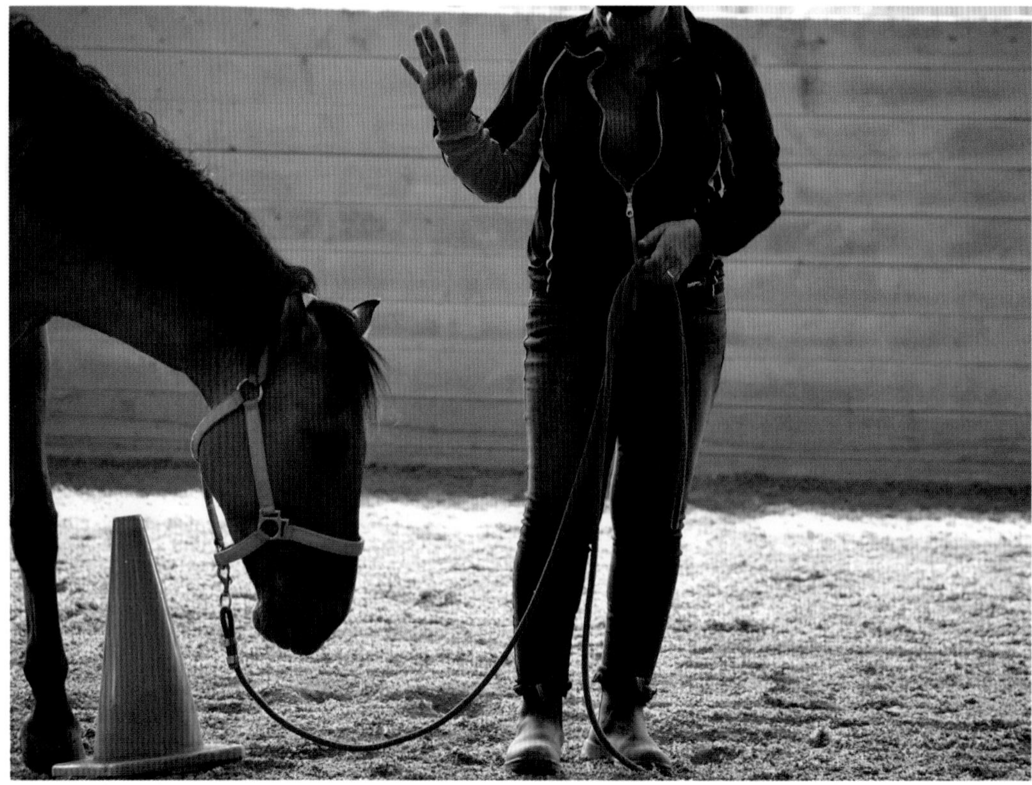

3.12 Hold Hand toward the Follow Me Button was enough of a signal for this horse to want to lower his head.

In one case, I worked with a very high-energy jumping horse who would get more and more worked up as he went over the jumps, becoming progressively difficult to ride. After a good jumping round, I told the rider to tap the Follow Me Button. At first, she was nervous because she was afraid he would plunge ahead when she reached up and forward from the saddle, but she prepared him from the ground, so when she did try it, he stopped in his tracks and lowered his head. She realized this was what she had been missing—a way to interrupt the high intensity and help him settle.

When so much of a horse's world can frighten and shock him, having a number of "Calm down" signals make sense. Many of their Buttons can have this effect; sometimes it is only a matter of finding a particular horse's "sweet spot."

Mid-Neck Button

This Button is located in the middle of the neck on each side. This is not a precise Button like some of the others, but rather a general location in the center of the meaty part of the neck. The horse's neck moves both side to side and up and down. When he flexes his poll, the neck becomes firm and tends to hold a more rigid position used

SKILL-BUILDER

How to Ask for Deep Trust

You can combine the Bridge of the Nose and the Follow Me Buttons to ask for a deeper, more trusting connection with your horse.

1 Obtain permission to lightly place your hand on the Bridge of the Nose and Follow Me Buttons. For best practices, I like to place my hands in these positions and three times in a row before I do anything more. These two Buttons are leverage points for a big predator to flip a horse, and I do not want to inspire any fear in the horse.

2 Gently begin to Rock the Baby while holding these two Buttons and sighing outwardly. Release after only a few breaths and step away from the horse's Bubble, noticing what he looks like as you do.

3 Repeat while facing the horse's tail so you can see his whole body. Watch what happens as you Rock the Baby on these Buttons.

- Does he sway?
- Does he relax his back?
- Does he lower his head?
- How do you feel in your body as this is happening?
- How would you describe the horse's state?
- How do you feel emotionally?

When you understand how this feels in your hands and body, you will be able to induce the same feeling while riding. I believe that when we spend quality time learning to feel our horses relax in specific ways while we touch them, our nervous system memorizes more and better information about what our connection to our horses *could* feel like. In turn, we are more likely to seek this connection in other situations with them—and they seek it with us as well.

The Bridge of the Nose and Follow Me Buttons together have a strange, almost trance-like effect on many horses.

for more intense athletic activities, like rearing, bucking, pivoting quickly, striking, and leaping. This posture is mainly used during play, displays of power, fighting, or defending the herd from predators. Stallions use this display to "show off" around their mares, while mares use it to settle hierarchy disputes, attack predators, or drive off unwanted visitors. However, a mare's primary choice of "weapon" in a fight is her powerful hindquarters, not rearing and striking as a male horse will do.

When relaxed, the Mid-Neck Button should be seen moving in a lovely swaying motion in a comfortable walk. Horses who have become rigid and tense can often develop a very tight Mid-Neck Button as a result of both poor conditioning during riding or work and a sense of chronic stress from which the horse cannot escape or change. I have met many horses with extremely rigid Mid-Neck Buttons, and more often it is a result of mental stress. However, when a trainer does not fully understand the needs of a particular horse in terms of the healthiest way for him to carry a rider, the horse can have overdeveloped muscles in the neck as he loads his forelegs with weight and basically drags the rider along with his shoulders. This shifts any tension from the horse's back to his shoulders, and you will see him using his neck like the stiff handle of a hammer as he plugs along. Sometimes it is hard to say what came first, poor balance and incorrect weight-bearing or mental tension and stiffening up the neck in response to chronic stress. "Bracing" is a term often applied to horses with very stiff necks and equally rigid attitudes.

Between horses, the Mid-Neck Button is the next in the line of hierarchy communication and change of direction signals, after the Cheek Button (fig. 3.13). The Cheek Button moving left is logically followed by the Mid-Neck Button moving left as well. This part of the neck can be seen "scooping up" another horse in an invitation to

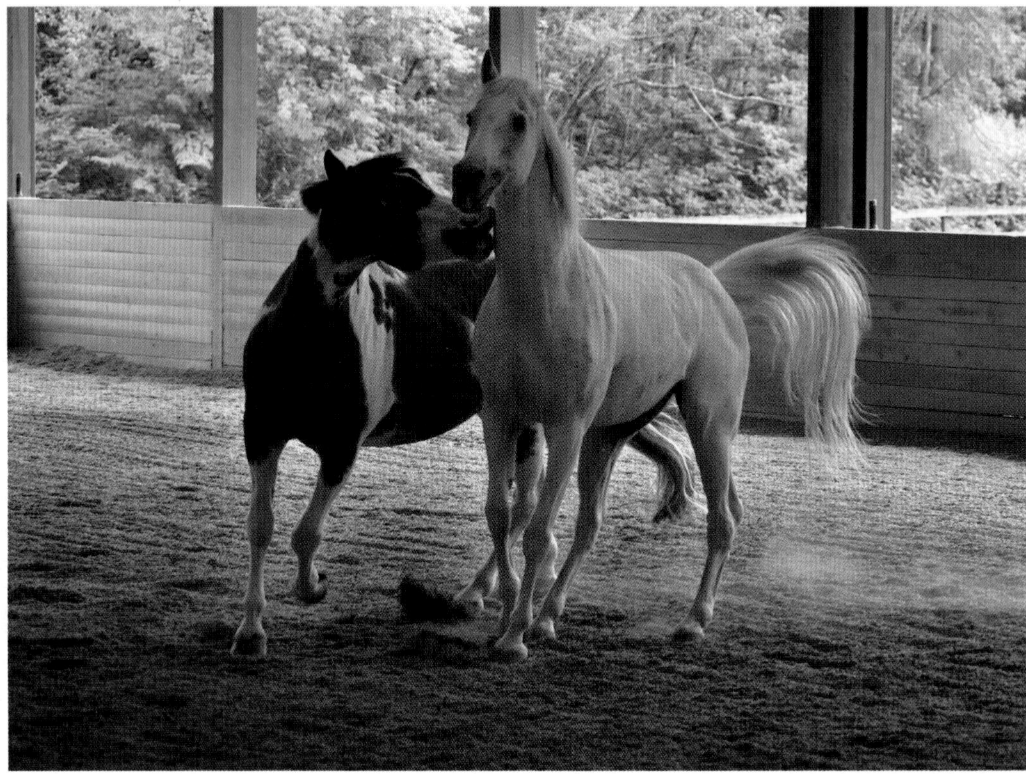

3.13 After the Cheek Button, the Mid-Neck Button is the next in line in determining direction and hierarchy, as the horses are in this game.

"come along" or "turn this way" and can be used as a strong show of friendship. Horses sniff each other on the Mid-Neck Button to show deep comradery ("I won't bite you here and drive you away"), and they also will "hug" each other by placing their necks over one another in a form of embrace (fig. 3.14). This part of the neck can also be attacked during more intense disputes.

3.14 Horses "hug" each other by connecting with each other's Mid-Neck Buttons. Here they are also sniffing necks, which is a message of friendship.

You learning to use the Mid-Neck Button to help navigate in hand is important to your horse because the point is so vital to his ability to balance while changing direction. A relaxed horse needs to swing his head and neck into a turn in a thoughtful way. A defensive horse counterbends his neck, driving his inside shoulder down as a pivot point and even using that shoulder as a "weapon" to smack into an oncoming attacker. Driving the inside shoulder down allows the horse to make his body into the U-shape needed to protect himself (fig. 3.15).

If we want the "pretty look" of a collected horse, but not the tension that goes with it, then relaxing the Mid-Neck Button is essential. In addition, the Mid-Neck Button is vitally important when a horse is trying to process information (see p. 113). Think of the energy of information as flowing water through a soft hose. When the neck is rigid or braces, this indicates the horse is having some sort of block in his ability to "think things through."

3.15 Horses use their inside shoulder to help counterbend into a U-shape when they feel defensive or threatened. This works well when a pack of wolves is coming from the side for attack: the horse's instinct is to keep the vital parts of his head high and away, and lift his belly and hind end in a ready-to-kick position.

3.16 The Shoulder Button, when Activated, is the next in the line of determining hierarchy and direction (after Cheek and Mid-Neck). As these horses play, there's a constant theme: "Who gets to drive?" and "Who gets to steer?"

Buttons of the Front Body

Shoulder Button

This Button is located at the point of the horse's shoulder, where the shoulder bone makes a bony projection. The trick with the Buttons of the front body, like the Shoulder Button, is that they tend to include the front legs (fig. 3.16). Let me explain: When a horse uses his front legs in some way, such as taking a single step toward another horse while sharing a hay pile, then the entire movement of the Shoulder Button through the front hoof is a total message. In the case of stepping toward a desired object, like hay, it is a claim to the space. In the case of a strike, it is a more dramatic claim to higher rank. In the case of rearing, it is now the highest intensity drama a horse can show.

Horses also *give* space with the front leg. Say a horse steps into another's spot on the hay pile, and the other horse backs away. The first horse will often then take his foot back and away—opening the door for the lower-ranking one to come eat comfortably again. In this case, the foot placement of the higher-ranked horse is "making sure" that the lower-ranked horse will not cause a fuss. When he concedes with ease, the "point is made." A return to harmonious eating is the follow through.

So the Shoulder Button has multiple meanings. When connected to front foot

3.17 A & B The Shoulder Button is not always as precise as other Buttons. Anywhere along the shoulder blade will do. In this picture, the chestnut Paint is sending a message of Buddy-Up to the black-and-white Paint (A). He then settles the black-and-white Paint by placing his Friendly Button on the Shoulder Button (B).

movement, it is about taking and giving space, or a display of wants, needs, or desires, and a broadcast about choices and directions. Horses who paw while tied or when food is coming are in a stressed or overexcited state. They want something *other* than what is happening: "I want to be off the cross-ties," "I want to go over there," "I want the food faster than it is coming," and so on. This Button is also used when lining up in tandem movement, when horses are going somewhere together (Buddy-Up—figs. 3.17 A & B and 3.18, and see p. 118).

3.18 When I make contact with the Shoulder Button, I prefer to have a Low-Calorie Conversation. In this picture, I am asking for Buddy-Up.

Grooming Button

This Button is located on the horse's withers. You can often observe horses using this Button in casual contact. It is the most common area of social grooming or offers of direct affection and intimate contact (fig. 3.19). I sometimes see my horses begin by sniffing the Mid-Neck Button, then they move to the Grooming Button and begin chewing on each other's withers in a clearly affectionate manner. I have watched them get an almost "dreamy" look on their faces when they begin to scratch this Button on each other, so it may have some very positive sensations.

For our purposes, contact with the Grooming Button is a great way to ask, "May I groom you now?" In sensitive horses or horses with troubles being touched or even a traumatic history, lightly tapping the Grooming Button three times then stepping outside the horse's Bubble to wait and see if proceeding is okay, is a fantastic way to work through layers of the horse's discomfort. I like to arrive at this Button after a reasonable Greeting and *Connect and Respect* phase (see p. 140). Horses follow this exact pattern, so to me it makes sense to move through their protocol to ensure greater acceptance and understanding between us.

Note this is also one of the Buttons where you can use Rock the Baby (see p. 137).

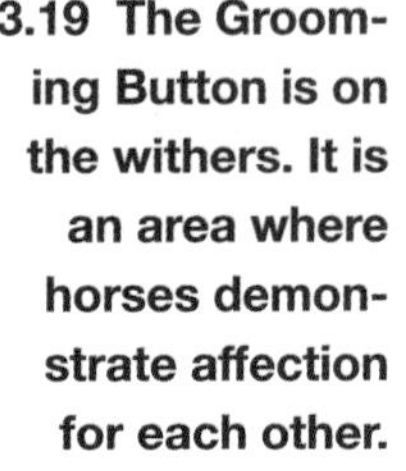

3.19 The Grooming Button is on the withers. It is an area where horses demonstrate affection for each other.

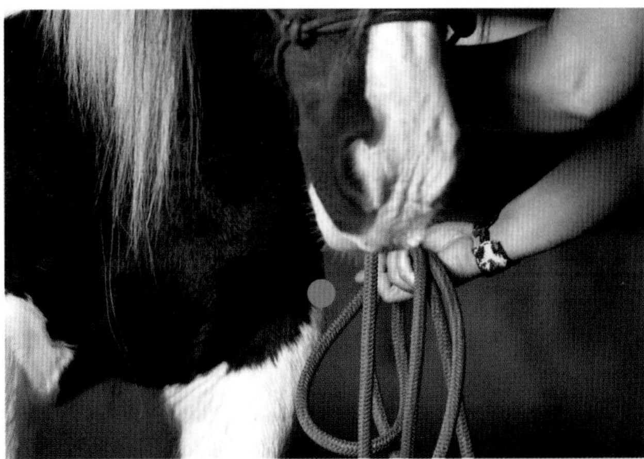

3.20 When we aim for the Back-Up Button, it is best to "scoop" your hand, palm facing up, with one pointer finger aimed at the Button. I find this gesture delivers the best "feel" to this Button and inspires the horse to willingly back up.

SKILL-BUILDER

Rock the Baby

Here's how to use this sweet Conversation with the Grooming Button to connect your horse's sense of balance to your own:

1 Stand with Inner Zero at the horse's Shoulder Button, facing the same direction the horse is.

2 Place your hand closest to the horse across his withers.

3 Slowly shift your weight from one foot to the other, connecting your shift to your breathing.

4 As you begin to feel your horse shift his weight from one front leg to the other, join him in the movement.

Note: Horses with laminitis or neurological conditions may find Rock the Baby difficult, so only ask for the tiniest little rocking motion that the horse is comfortable with.

(Note that this is the prerequisite to obtaining a really good Therapy Back-Up, which I teach you later in this book—see p. 255.)

Back-Up Button

This Button is located in the crook of the horse's elbow. Pointing or pressing here creates a pressure in the joint that makes it difficult for the horse to resist yielding that leg backward (fig. 3.20). Since this part of the horse's body is significant in relation to physical balance, the tendency will be for the horse's whole body to shift backward as well. As an added benefit, when this joint is "tickled" gently backward, the horse is inclined to relax all his other joints. This is an observable phenomenon that can add enormous potential to relaxing and conditioning the entire body of the horse in profound and surprising ways.

Horses use this Button on themselves to induce this same whole-body tension release. It seems to act like a "reset" Button for them after certain kinds of stress. I sometimes describe it as "getting back inside their bodies." I take this description from a human sense of becoming dissociated from certain kinds of stress and our own need to "get grounded." It can also be used in similar "self-talk" by the horse to help himself "get back" into better Zero or balance (fig. 3.21).

SKILL-BUILDER

How to Ask if a Horse Is Ready for Grooming

In *Horse Speak*, I introduced The Four Gs: *Greeting, Going Somewhere, Grooming, and Gone*. I take these a step further in chapter 5 (p. 208), but for now, here's what you need to know: *Greeting* is initiating contact (see the Greeting Button, p. 119). *Going Somewhere* doesn't necessarily mean taking steps—it can be as simple as the horse yielding his head away or even turning in toward you. It is simply the mutual respect dance at the front of the horse's Bubble. Some horses *do* need Going Somewhere to include walking with you and changing direction at least once. For them, this is to ensure that "we know how to move together if a tiger shows up." For this type of (Red Zone) high-strung, sensitive, nervous, or outgoing horse, a more dramatic Going Somewhere is important for their sense of security.

Once this phase is complete (which can literally be the span of a few breaths in a secure rapport with a comfortable horse or just a few minutes with an insecure one), then the Grooming Button can be asked, "Are we ready for a *Grooming Ritual*?" In Horse Speak, Grooming does not always include touching. *Social Grooming* simply means sharing affectionate energy on any level. So Grooming can be just sharing space, or it can be actually making contact. If a horse shivers, resists, steps away, or otherwise refuses contact on the Grooming Button, there may be a bigger issue at hand. For many horses, the environment around them can play a key role in their lack of trust in the Grooming Ritual. In nature, horses do not simply get "entangled" in each other's Bubbles until they are certain the Chessboard is cleared, all is well, everyone has been fed and watered.... "*Now* we can relax and enjoy Social Grooming."

Some horses are more "touchy-feely" than others. Some prefer a Grooming Ritual that is more about sharing space comfortably and resting or napping together. Others prefer to nibble bits of grass or hay in a relaxed manner close to another horse. Still others do like to rub their bodies on another horse (or an object) where they are itchy.

Asking the Grooming Button, "Are you ready?" means working with the answer that you receive. If it is a simple measure of not having completed the Horse Speak protocol (Greeting and Going Somewhere first), then knowing this can make a world of difference. If there is an underlying issue, going through the Horse Speak protocol allows the horse room to move into a position where he can display the Button that needs attention or the area of his body that is uncomfortable. By removing the emotional tension that can be the result of the horse feeling his space has been invaded, the horse is often in a better position to reveal what else may be happening.

3.21 Horses will scratch their own Back-Up Button. This can be a message to themselves about "getting grounded" after something that was unsettling. It can also be a message to others to literally back up.

Another use is to signal to other horses to literally back away from something or someone. I have a video of such a moment: a lead horse bites his own Back-Up Button to tell the two horses near him to back away from the person holding the camera, filming them. The other two horses turn their heads to look at the lead horse, then do just that. One backs away to the hind end of the leader, and the other, who is a little more fearless, needs to be cajoled into backing away by the leader who reaches to the Yield-Over and Jump-Up Buttons as well (see pp. 148 and 143). So, this Button can literally be used to ask other herdmates to back away.

Activating the Back-Up Button is used in what I call the *Therapy Back-Up,* which we will explore in detail on p. 255. This is because this Button is a powerful signal about yielding the space in front of the horse, meaning that only lead horses can pass in front of another horse. When we claim the space in front of a horse, we are suggesting we are that leader. Using the Back-Up Button not only makes this claim, it has the added advantage of relaxing the horse's entire body—so in effect we are saying, "I am the leader, and that should make you relaxed and comfortable."

Because of the location of the elbow joint in the movement plane of the horse's body, it is in direct connection to another significant joint: the stifle. When the stifle yields backward, it engages the Button located behind this joint under the rump of the horse, which I call the Sit Button (see p. 150). These two Buttons can move in

SKILL-BUILDER

Connect and Respect with the Head, Neck, and Front Body Buttons

The Buttons we have discussed so far are the first line of what I call "Connect and Respect." These Buttons deal with building rapport through both trust and mutual respect. If you do not have good connection and boundaries established with these Buttons, then the other Buttons are not going to work so well. Here are seven ways to establish Connect and Respect with these Buttons:

Knuckle Touch Greeting: As we've discussed, your knuckle simulates a horse's muzzle and should be used whenever you are connecting with your horse upon entering his personal space. The Knuckle Touch is similar to a human handshake or giving someone a high-five.

Hold Hand: Your Hold Hand (see p. 51) can be used to define your personal space and for scanning the horse's Buttons. Horses are aware of what our hands are doing at all times, and we can have an effect over their well-being when we have the right intention.

Stroking: Long slow strokes on the horse's neck send a soothing message to him. If your horse likes to be touched, it's best to practice long slow strokes rather than scratching because the latter is stimulating and can be irritating to some horses.

Asking for Space: The only thing a horse owns is his Bubble of Personal Space. When amongst other horses, a horse asks for his personal space to be respected, and when we show up, we ask the horse to please respect *our* personal space. Typically, we can use the Cheek or Cheek and Mid-Neck Buttons to discuss "My Space, Your Space," and to ask a horse to please "Stay in Your Lane." (We explore the how-to of My Space, Your Space in detail on p. 216.)

Inviting the Horse to Come Back into your Bubble: You can use Turn the Key, Come to Me on the Greeting, Cheek, Mid-Neck, and Shoulder Buttons in your O posture to invite the horse into your space.

Asking the Horse to Step to the Side: When you combine the Cheek, Mid-Neck, and Shoulder Buttons, you are able to ask your horse to step to the side.

Claiming the Space in Front: Using the Back-Up Button to claim the space in front of the horse relays to your horse that you would like to do so *respectfully*. You can also use the Bridge of the Nose and the Back-Up Button together as a stronger message.

unison, and when they do in both backward and forward movement, there is deeper, healthier flexion in the whole horse. Many forms of collected movement are more easily accessible and better understood by the horse when we wisely use these two Buttons in conjunction.

The Back-Up Button can also be used in conjunction with other Buttons to have more complex Conversations with a horse. When my horse Rocky was sick and in the hospital, he had to be tubed and have his stomach pumped several times. The first time, he lifted a front leg and struck out. This was not a hierarchy claim but a statement of pain and, "Leave me alone." I used the point of the Shoulder Button (p. 134) to calm the leg that struck out, then touched the Back-Up Button on the same side to ask him to leave that foot down. Despite his discomfort, he did.

Later on, one of the nurses was worried Rocky would strike out during another procedure, and she was twitching him. I showed her the two Buttons, and she used them instead. To her surprise, they worked amazingly well, and Rocky was not twitched again while at the hospital.

Buttons of the Barrel

Girth Button

This Button is located at the horse's girth area. Literally the whole line of the girth, all the way around the horse, can be indicated, but most commonly horses use a lower plane to signal this Button, near the lower part of the barrel. The first use of this Button comes when a foal is born. He learns to focus his eyes on his mother's Girth Button to follow her around. By keeping his eyes aimed here, he remains in the most protected area relative to her body. She can bite, strike, leap, and kick at a foe, and he remains on the inside of the sphere of her Bubble. In addition, by keeping his eyes on her Girth Button, he can follow her at the right speed, and turn or stop with her as well.

When horses grow up they still orient movement between each other's bodies with awareness on this Button. It can be helpful to think of the horse's body like a kayak. We sit in the center of the kayak, and from there we can shift the front or back of the boat. To remain balanced, we need to stay in the center of the vessel. Similar effects could be thought of on a bicycle, surfboard, skateboard, and skis. Basically, horses use the Girth Button centerpoint on their own and each other's bodies as a fulcrum to not only balance their own movement, but to move deftly around and with the other bodies in the herd.

3.22 The Girth Button allows horses to move at speed and remain aware of how they are lined up with other horses. By Navigating through awareness of this Button, they can change direction, speed up, and slow down, without losing track of each other.

The bottom line is that horses use a display of this Button for a more serious Conversation: basically, "Line up. We are Going Somewhere." This Button tends to be reserved for the times when horses intend to move in harmony at speed or over some distance (fig. 3.22). They may shift to a single-file position for a longer trek as a group, which makes the path that much easier to follow. However, when a large enough herd is on the move, you will often see a few horses side by side for the journey. These may be close friends, or relatives, or mother and child. Typically, this is when they practice Matching Steps and Mirroring each other.

For our purposes, knowing the Girth Button carries such intimate and protective meaning can be a real asset when working toward gaining a deeper rapport with a riding horse. If a horse saunters by you and stops so that you are lined up at his Girth Button, take this as a real compliment. The horse is saying, "You are part of my herd. We can move off together."

Troubled horses often regress with this Button and take it to be the "Mommy Button," which means they go all the way back to feeling like they can line up with a human "mother" to follow and be protected. Because of this, I like to use the Hold Hand gesture aimed at the Girth Button to ask, "Are you ready to line up and travel with me?"

Given that longeing and liberty in a round pen ask the horse to stay oriented to this Button while the horse travels around you in a circle, gaining permission, connection, and trust at this Button before doing either is essential in helping the hose understand that you are not chasing him away but rather inviting him to travel along with you. Because leader horses have the right to drive a lower horse away from them, it can sometimes follow that insecure or low-ranking horses can mistake a signal to "Go out on the circle" as being driven away. At best, they may feel scolded, and at worst some horses feel terrified or defiant at the prospect of being driven off for reasons unknown. In fact, occasionally a high-ranking horse can misinterpret this request as humans "picking a fight." I have witnessed a wide variety of longeing, liberty, and "free-schooling" or round-pen work that has stressed horses out and left the owners or trainers scratching their heads. Connecting with the Girth Button first could prevent that result (fig. 3.23).

3.23 I want to have a Low-Calorie Conversation with this Button before asking a horse to stay connected with me at speed.

Gaining access to the Girth Button as a gentle connection point and open communication center for movement that is in harmony and "with each other," not in competition or as a result of dominance, is important in having this Button also be accepting and relaxed when you are riding your horse. Since we mount at the girth area, and our heels touch this place as well, it really serves the riding relationship to pay special attention to how the horse feels about it.

Jump-Up Button

This Button is located at the lower part of the end of the horse's ribs, where the belly is round, just in front of the stifle. I used this name for this zone because it is easily triggered, and a defensive horse may jump forward, kick out, or leap sidewise.

Foals nurse under this Button, mating couples scent each other here, and friends show bonding and security by sniffing here (fig. 3.24). Some horses will show concern for another troubled horse by sniffing him here (fig. 3.25).

Issues such as illness, insecurity, injury, loss, grief, and suffering can be addressed between horses from concentrated attention on this Button. I have witnessed grieving horses sniffing each other here after a herdmate has died. Unwell horses may display this Button to a leader, or an elder horse may come and sniff an unwell horse here in a deep,

3.24 The Jump-Up Button is a naturally vulnerable area. In this picture, the chestnut is moving the black-and-white forward from this Button so his friend will feel more secure with his guidance.

3.25 The Jump-Up Button represents intimacy. The bay horse in the background was older and not feeling well. The Haflinger remained still and quietly breathing at this Button until the bay relaxed.

prolonged way. Insecure horses will sometimes try to sniff this Button on a leader horse—in this case, they seem to be admitting, "I am weak and vulnerable... can you help me?"

Unlike humans, horses are deeply aware of their vulnerability. If a predator grabs a horse at the Jump-Up Button, the horse can be easily gored. And yet humans often try to engage this Button when asking a horse for lateral work or to "lift up his belly" in attempts to get the horse's core muscles engaged. This is also where we often apply spurs or a whip. If you don't have permission from the horse to work with this Button, and if he doesn't trust you, he will hold his breath and get rigid, or collapse emotionally and feel bullied. This is a Button that you want to develop a *good* relationship with: Once you have permission from the horse, you can "tickle" it or "sparkle" it with a whip or the end of the lead rope, or by aiming your eyes or fingertips, which can tell a nervous horse, "I know you're scared, but I've got you... move ahead now." When done with care and understanding, asking the Jump-Up Button for forward movement can, in this case, sometimes "unstick" a horse who has planted his feet and won't go.

I find that this Button is amazing when dealing with any issue of tension, nervousness, or weakness in a horse. Offering the Hold Hand (see p. 51) to this Button with deep out-breaths, sends a message of "I am with you. Whatever you are experiencing or feeling is okay with me." I have seen troubled, worried, or traumatized horses lie down from this message. It seems it can deliver an amazing amount of compassionate witnessing of any difficulties a horse may have experienced.

Buttons of the Hind End

**** NEW NAME ****

Hip Button (formerly the Hip-Drive Button)

This Button is the primary area from which one horse drives another horse forward (fig. 3.26). However, it has several other uses and meanings, so going forward I will simply be calling it the *Hip Button*. A lead horse may use this Button to make movement happen. In hierarchy debates, you may see teeth marks around the top of the rump. This Button is actually a bit of a moving target because of this—any area on the top of the rump will do. However, I feel the highest point of the hip is the main focus.

3.26 One horse can steer another horse from the Hip Button. By changing the angle of approach, the lead horse can guide the other in front of him. This is an important function in being able to be the "rear guard."

3.27 The horse in the rear is using the Hip Button to tell the horse in front, "I have your back."

3.28 This mare was alone in the arena. She chose to communicate with me from the other side of the fence when she saw I understood how to do so. Within minutes she asked me, "Do you have my back?" Placing my hand on her hip is how I said, "Yes!"

When a horse is driving others forward in a healthy manner, he is also saying, "You go ahead, I'll bring up the rear and kick any predators that show up" (fig. 3.27). With this in mind, it is easy to see how the Hip Button is a huge asset to us in assuming a higher status in a horse's herd dynamics. A major shift in the relationship can happen *not* from driving a horse forward, per se, but from sending the "I've got your back" message (fig. 3.28).

SKILL-BUILDER

Giving the Message, "I've Got Your Back."

To tell your horse, "I've got your back," raise your Hold Hand (p. 51) to the height of the horse's hip in a relaxed manner and from a safe distance (even over a barrier will work). This implies that you are the "rear guard" and will remain alert and aware of any danger that may want to sneak up from behind. This is a high-ranking position in a herd, but it is also a dangerous, and therefore, serious one. I have witnessed this message turn a horse's world around. I have seen horses suddenly shudder, lowering their heads, release major tension, and in some cases, seek to "hide" behind their handlers.

In contrast, when you flash this message at a lead horse, I've seen them look at me with what can only pass as amusement. It is like he is saying, "Aren't you cute, little human? How nice to offer this...but...*ahem*...you are far too small to kick a lion." Still, even a leader likes a day off. Offering this message gives him the opportunity to let go of having to hold everything together. He may become deeply relaxed or let go of his usual stoicism and become playful.

When you feel comfortable and safe with a horse and have systematically gone through all the other Buttons, you may be able to rest your palm on the highest point of your horse's hip in a soothing manner. In fact, this can have a direct impact when riding, as well, because you can apply the same contact from the saddle.

My blind horse has always been a herd leader, and when she was losing her sight, she became difficult and even dangerous to be around. I began employing this direct contact onto her Hip Button whenever we were together. She would sigh with relief, lower her head, and generally become open to communication with me about working through this change in her world. She is now just as confident as she was before she went blind and remains incredibly brave about going out riding on trails despite her loss of vision. When I sense that she is worried, I can reach back to touch her Hip Button from her back, and she will relax and reset so we can go forward again.

SKILL-BUILDER

Using the Hip Button to Establish Hierarchy

When you have a pushy horse who seems to want to drive you from behind, try offering a Hold Hand (see p. 51) at the Hip Button, and then aim your pointer (Activating) finger at it, or even snap your fingers in the air near it to tell the horse's rump to *move*. You want to be the driver, not the driven. When you are the driver, you "own" the space behind the horse. "Drive forward: I've got your back," is the most important message we can foster with the Hip Button.

In my life training horses prior to Horse Speak, it seemed I was taught one baseline credo that I thought was written in stone: if a horse turns his hip to you, it is like giving a "horsey finger"—it is not only rude and disrespectful, but dangerous, and it must be punished right away.

It turns out that while yes, the hind end can send a maiming—even deadly—kick and should be treated with caution and awareness at all times, there is another very, very important aspect to some messages that originate there. I believe having "missed this memo" for decades has caused misunderstanding and even misery for both our species.

Yield-Over Button (also called the Stifle Button)

This Button is located in the fleshy area near the horse's stifle. Here several simple messages can be transferred, "Yield over, please. I am back here and need some room," "Please don't kick," "Let me pass," or "Let me be" (fig. 3.29). Activating this Button usually means the horse will step underneath himself with that same hind leg and make room, or he will lighten the weight on that leg, cocking

3.29 The Yield-Over Button is located near the stifle. Horses use it to ask another, "Hey, can you move your butt over?"

that hip to signal he is relaxed, not defensive. Often the other horse is nibbling bits of hay or grass; sometimes this message is used when a horse is just passing by. Other times a horse may be driving from behind and uses this Button to tell the horse ahead to move aside or not to kick (fig. 3.30). Occasionally, a horse bites at this Button to get the other horse's attention, but only a truly high-ranking horse would bite here because it is grounds for the offended horse to kick out.

For our purposes, the Yield-Over Button is often used in messages of driving the horse forward or yielding him over and away. We can also use it to

3.30 In a Low-Calorie Conversation, the Yield-Over Button also talks about having a "no-kick agreement." Here the chestnut has asked this of the black-and-white gelding, who has relaxed his leg in response.

SKILL-BUILDER

Building Rapport with the Yield-Over Button

If you cannot touch your horse's Yield-Over Button, it is a symptom of a deeper problem. You may want to use a light-weight stick, like a length of thin bamboo or a dressage whip (or a "Wand," as Linda Tellington-Jones calls it in her Tellington Method), to lightly stroke all the Buttons until you get to this one, then offer long, soothing down-strokes toward it. See if the distance the stick enables helps you gain access to it. In addition to lengthening your reaching, many horses are more open to being stroked with a stick than with your bare hand. I believe that our bare hands can bring too much intensity to touch for some horses at first. (For more information about using a stick in this fashion, I encourage you to refer to Linda's books, including *Training and Retraining Horses the Tellington Way*.)

You can usually activate this Button with eye contact or by pointing your finger at it while staring hard at it. You can of course aim a longe whip or swing a lead rope toward this Button if need be, but so often your simple body language is enough to ask the horse to step over.

Do not use your palm to ask the horse to move from this Button as this means, "Stay with me," or "Lean into me." I sometimes offer a Hold Hand at this Button to say, "Remain steady…no kick and no startle."

encourage a "gathering" of the hind leg for deeper, more active steps, such as those necessary for collection, or for lateral work. It has the ability to engage or disengage the power of the hind end.

There is a common training practice of yielding the hind end away, sometimes over and over again. Horses do not engage in this extreme action unless they are competing for positions in herd hierarchy and the battle is serious. Personally, I do not want to emulate battle positions with horses. There could be a one in 100 moments when this *is* the right message, but using it in the other 99 cases can cause a good deal of unnecessary conflict—sometimes even injury.

As with any other Button co-opted for human use, it is wise to learn how your horse really feels about the Yield-Over Button. Spend time getting to know him at this sensitive joint. Overuse injuries are common in the stifle area, so simply holding the Button, massaging it, or gently patting it can offer the horse relief and a new level of rapport with this important message center.

**** NEW BUTTON ****

Sit Button

This Button is located in the groove of the horse's hind leg (figs. 3.31 A & B). It is both an emotional and practical Button, similar to the Back-Up Button (p. 137), and in fact, in alignment with the action of the Back-Up Button, as well as the Bridge of the Nose

SKILL-BUILDER

Combining the Hip and Yield-Over Buttons

Logically, if you begin with your hand palm forward at the Hip Button in the air as a "broadcast" stating that you are the leader, you can then slide your hand down to the Yield-Over Button and Hold there with your palm on it for a moment to also indicate, "I might ask you to move your hind end." When your horse is comfortable with this in the air, then you may make full contact with your palm, sliding from the Buttons at the front of the horse to the Buttons of the hind end.

Fun fact: you can do this message (and many others) from a distance and when the horse is loose—no lead rope necessary. All it requires is patience and the willingness to observe the horse's responses. Sometimes the horse does not respond to your eyes or hands until you begin to move them away...so stay tuned in to his body language.

3.31 A & B The Sit Button is located at the back of the horse's stifle joint under the round part of the rump. It allows a horse to sit as he gets up and down from the ground (A). Horses use this Button to tell each other to "sit down and chill out." It can be used in fighting to cripple an opponent, but most of the time, this Button is used in play or as a soothing message of relaxation (B). When one horse wants another horse to rest, he may communicate with this Button, and we can, too.

(p. 122). If the horse backs up well, he also "sits down." The joints in the hind leg of the horse mirror the joints along the same plane in the front leg of the horse. They are all capable of folding, rearing, bucking, leaping, and jumping. They become stiff and inflexible when the horse feels stressed, and supple and strong in a horse who is in good athletic form.

Horses use this Button to mean, "Sit down; take a load off," such as when preparing to lie down. It is used as a correction when one horse bites another (offending) horse in this zone to say, "Sit down and cut it out!" Stallions nibble mares here as a request during mating: "Sit down and don't kick." A mare may bite her foal on this Button when he has become too playful. Fighting horses can bite here in an effort to injure the area and end the fight. Playful geldings will sometimes nibble at the Sit Button as part of a "Gotcha!" game, and when mares "duke it out" over hierarchy, they often kick at the Sit Button.

For our purposes, all advanced riders use this Button whether they know it or not: jumpers, reining horses, cutting horses, dressage horses, and even endurance horses (due to the steep terrain often traversed) all must "sit down" to collect. This Button

SKILL-BUILDER

How to Talk to the Sit Button

Although horses may place a well-timed nip to the Sit Button, I have found this is not what is needed from us. Instead, I have learned that *holding* the Sit Button and offering it soft, warm touch—often literally standing near the Button with a hand on it, no patting or motion at all—sends a ripple effect through the whole horse. No matter what the energy type or personality your horse has, this seems to be a universally welcome message.

When you can deliver such a calming message in the air as a "broadcast" or actually making contact, either with your hand or with a stick or whip, then if you do need to offer a "nip"—say on a particularly uppity youngster or an aggressive horse—you can tap the ground with a big X and look at the Button. This seems to send the same sort of message I have witnessed elder horses delivering, without a need for direct contact with the stick or a rope.

I prefer to have a "no strike" policy with horses, because I have learned that by doing so, they usually adopt a "no strike" policy with me as well. Given that I have worked with some extremely damaged and traumatized horses who were known for dangerous behavior, this choice is based on effectiveness, not "Pollyanna thinking." Certainly, there are rare instances where a physical reprimand is warranted, but with all I have learned, these are the rare exceptions, not the rule.

can mean "Power up" or "Power down." The Sit Button gathers power and coils it into the rest of the horse's body. Holding the Sit Button can help the horse's head and neck relax, too. Some people have reported their horses suddenly becoming very heavy in their hands when they hold them at this Button—almost as if they were literally going to sit on their owners' laps!

The two new Buttons I introduced—The Bridge of the Nose and the Sit Button—are actually "bookends" to the other 13 Buttons. Both these Buttons carry many meanings, can be very emotional for the horse, and are affected by each other. Interestingly, we often use these Buttons the most, without any awareness of the potential power of them. Pressure on the bridge of the nose goes all the way to the sit-down reflex. Sitting causes the bridge of the nose to want to tuck in toward the chest. (Picture a rearing horse, his hind end crouched in a "sit" and the bridge of the nose is tucked.) Because of this intrinsic connection, horses use these two Buttons for some of the most tender messages, and the most severe.

Talking to the Buttons

Spend time getting to know, enrich, touch, Hold, and Activate each Button. This can be a Low-Calorie, easy-to-understand, and quietly enriching time in your relationship with your horse. Get connected, build mutual respect, and offer gentle and quiet affection—that is the beginning of rapport. "Talking to the Buttons" is a great way to start the day, and once you know how, it normally only requires a few minutes.

To effectively interrupt an undesirable pattern of behavior (Red Zone) and actually begin laying down *new* patterns (Green Zone), going through the Buttons and combining Buttons in different ways is essential. In the case of a fear reaction in a horse, or even an aggressive one, for example, I will try to find the horse's "edge" by very gently going through all the Buttons. Inevitably, there will be a few that don't want any contact. In these cases, I will return to the ones that are okay, slowly making my way back to the ones that aren't in a predictable and careful way. Back and forth, over and over and over again, I repeat the touch of the Buttons. What I am *not* doing is some sort of behavioral conditioning to "teach the horse to accept the contact" or "react to the right cue." And I am *not* "desensitizing." What I *am* doing is "talking" to each Button with respect for the horse in front of me.

With this process, I ask the horse to allow me to *Linger Longer* (which is the term I use to mean "stay the course") as he learns to stretch his reaction memory to find the Yellow Light (see p. 20). If a horse shoots right to Red Light, then I pushed him off a cliff! I cannot help the horse renegotiate an old, embedded memory unless he can be met at the edge of that cliff with compassion and shown a way to develop. Only then, can we, together, as a team, move toward the Green Light. Talking to the Buttons can provide so much insight that if you learn nothing else from this book but just that, you will probably still take your horsemanship to the next level.

It is *very, very, very* important to have sessions (preferably three in a row—horses learn best when lessons are grouped in "threes") in which you do *not* ask for any movement at all, you just travel up and down the Buttons with your hand, Core Energy, X and O, and Hold position.

Set the horse up for success: Have a Safety Object in front of him to rub his nose on as needed. You can do it on cross-ties, but know that they limit the horse's ability to express himself, so pay close attention. You can also have this session in a stall with a horse you know and are comfortable with, or in a round pen or arena. Use a long lead rope to request the horse not leave the area completely, but allow a little wandering

SKILL-BUILDER

Finding the Button the Horse Wants to "Talk About"

- If the horses want to play, he will often engage the Play Button, then the Cheek, Mid-Neck, and even Shoulder Button (which can result in a squeal or strike), come back to a Greeting Check-In, and land on Play again (then fireworks happen).
- If he lands on the Jump-Up Button, then he wants to talk about intimacy and vulnerability.
- If he lands on the Shoulder Button, he wants to Buddy-Up and get comfortable.
- If he lands on the Girth Button, he may literally line up with you and ask to walk off together.

when it seems like the horse needs a pause or a break, or it appears the horse wants to point you at the Button he wants to "talk about." I advise having a session like this from the other side of a fence when talking with a horse who is very troubled.

Begin by Holding all the Buttons, offering your palm toward a Button in the air without touching at first. Touching the Buttons with your palm can reveal a lot, but it is more intimate and some horses are not ready for this at first. Once you have made contact all over the horse's body, you can then move on to a tap-like touch of each Button that says, "I want to talk to you *here*." (You can hold the Bridge of the Nose with one hand and reach back to touch as many Buttons as you can with the other hand, just pointing to the ones you may not be able to reach.) For example, you can ask the horse to be open to communication by tapping the Grooming Button three times, which says, "I want to have a deeper connection with you." You can also begin with Rocking the Baby on the Bridge of the Nose or the Friendly Button while offering contact on the Follow Me Button. This says, "I want to have a richer, more gentle connection with you."

Even if you think you know your horse, you will not know what he is "storing" in his Buttons until you take the time to be curious and interested in hearing about them from him. In body-centered therapies for humans (talk therapy combined with modalities such as massage, tai chi, qi gong, and yoga), we learn that emotional or psychological imprints can be stored in our bodies. These types of therapies work to encourage somatic release of memories and traumas. When I see a horse begin to process (see p. 113), it reminds me of what I have both experienced and witnessed during my own somatic release sessions. Realizing that the Buttons are centers of communication, and that horses indicate specific Buttons (by scratching one or displaying one to you) when they are communicating their thoughts or feelings led me to understand that they use the Buttons in a form of "Self-Talk." I have hundreds of anecdotal experiences, my own and those of others from all over the world, that support this.

Your goal is to open a door to discovery and offer consistent movement from front to back, then back to front, over the Buttons. You are showing your horse you know about the Buttons—you know where they are, you want to learn more about them, and your aim is to have more connection and Zero for both of you. Allow yourself to be open to "hearing" the horse as you offer connected contact. Keep your contact precise; do not linger too long and create stress. Be mindful and move methodically.

Combining the Buttons

Just as horses do with each other, you combine the Buttons whenever you move into more complete aspects of training or communication (figs. 3.32 A & B). Longeing is a pure example of this. You have a rope attached to the Bridge of the Nose and are asking the Cheek Button to "stay over there." Your Core Energy is directed at the Girth Button, while your following hand is aimed at the different Buttons of the hind end.

Riding, too, is a total combination of Buttons: reins talk to the head, neck, and front body; seat to the barrel; and legs to the hind end. And as you advance your abilities in the saddle, you can use the reins to talk to the hind end, your legs to talk to the front end, while your seat bridges both ends. (Eventually you can get fancy and talk to *all* the Buttons with just your seat, just your legs, or even just your mind...)

3.32 A & B Horses use the Cheek, Neck, Shoulder, and Back-Up Buttons, sometimes in combination, for relaxation, movement, and negotiating space (A). As an example of combinations we might use, Therapy Back-Up (see p. 255) can have different meanings when you add other Buttons, such as the Sit Button, to the Bridge of the Nose and Back-Up Buttons (B).

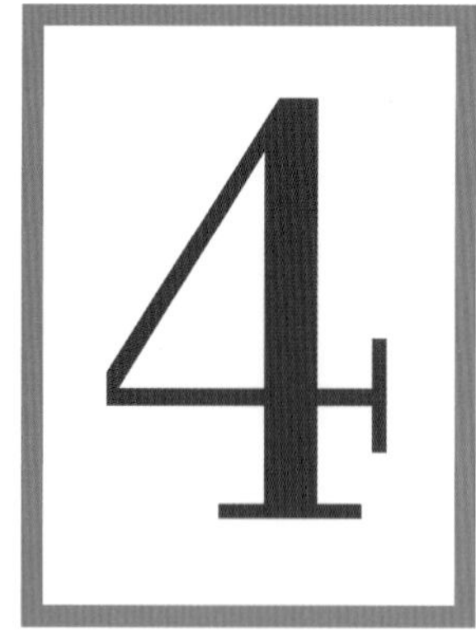

Understanding Herd Dynamics and Your Horse's Type

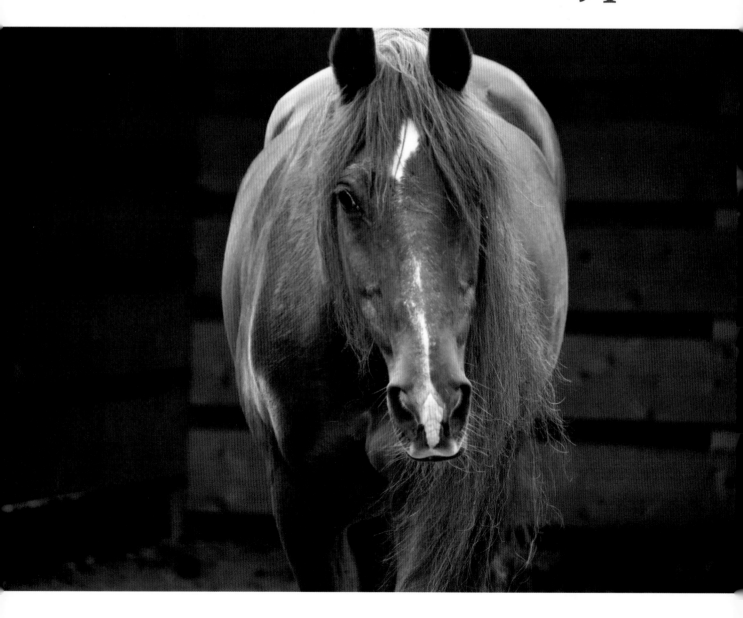

In this chapter, I take you inside the herd and how the members of a herd work together as a team. I identify *Energy Types, Roles in the Herd*, how to approach each Energy Type, how to assume the Role your horse wants you to hold in the herd, and herd management skills.

A Healthy Family System

I have sat and watched it take one horse twenty minutes to get the other horses in a field to all agree to go someplace different together. And in some cases, just when it seems like they all agree, one splits off and meanders in another direction—and the whole discussion starts over again. When horses have several hours to graze and be together, and there are no signs of danger, this lingering, "all-day" Conversation makes perfect sense.

One study of wild deer involved trying to determine how a large herd of deer agreed to move to one of the three water holes on a preserve. Cameras recorded the herd's movement and showed that a section of the herd would lift their heads and look toward one hole. Then a new section would raise their heads and look at another. When the largest section of deer looked toward a particular water hole, the whole herd moved off that way. The study suggested that this was a form of "voting." I have noticed horses using a similar communication method while at leisure. Lead horses may begin to aim for the water tank a good 30 minutes before actually getting the herd to agree to head there. It seems that during a large portion of the day, horses, like the deer, are voting.

4.1 Herd animals prefer to live in a state of Inner Zero. Both the horses and cattle in this photo are at Zero.

Of course, there can also be situations in which there is a fast scuffle and a quick argument. These instances may see the dust fly, but they also resolve quickly—everyone goes back to Zero as soon as possible in a healthy and balanced herd (fig. 4.1).

The baseline for how I view a herd is based on a "healthy family system." In the wild, groups of herd animals are typically made up of mothers, their children, and their children's children. Of course, this is different in a domestic horse-keeping situation, where your horse may be boarded and turned out alone, or you may have only two horses, or a horse and a single companion animal. The fact remains, however, that their quality of life as herd animals still reflects a family system.

My goal is to get away from the notion of an *alpha-dominant* projection on how horses band together. Horses want to get along with each other; it is in their very nature. Sure, sometimes they don't, but most horses *do* figure out how to live together, as well as how to live with us. They are born desiring to have a sense of belonging with a group.

Try to begin every day with this in mind, "My horse wants to be a part of my herd of two; it is up to me to figure out how to find the best way for us to fulfill this."

Three Energy Types

Every horse fills a Role on the Chessboard (see p. 89) and in the herd. Before we begin to describe these Roles, I want to identify the three Energy Types that linger beneath the surface of what we might label the horse's "personality"—*Stoic, Outgoing,* or *Hesitant.* I find that the Energy Types are a little easier to grapple with at first, and they can act as beacons to help you tune into the Role your horse plays—or would like to play. In addition, by understanding your horse's Energy Type and Role, you will be better positioned to use Horse Speak to communicate with him in specific ways that best suit with his unique personality.

SKILL-BUILDER

Energy Type Self-Assessment

While reading about horse Energy Types, think about yourself. What Energy Type are you? Have you attracted a horse who is like you, or one who is the opposite? Although you may be one Energy Type in one kind of setting, you may be a different Type in a different setting. Consider that the same is true for horses.

Think of the Energy Types as either *dominant* or a *trait*. A dominant Type is what the horse's baseline seems to be, while a trait is what emerges in a stressed setting. For instance, I have known tough Stoic guys to faint at the sight of blood. They act Hesitant around medical issues because the situation takes them out of their baseline (dominant) state and puts them into a state of energy they are uncomfortable with (trait).

My hope is that you are able to use the Energy Types as a barometer to gauge how your horse presents himself. Later, I will give you ideas on how you can be the best role model for your horse's particular Energy Type (see p. 182).

Stoic

Horses with a *Stoic* energy tend to put up and shut up. Stoic energy levels have a range from solid and trustworthy all the way across the spectrum to aloof and unreachable. They can sometimes be called "lazy," "oafish," "lackluster," or "boring." On the other hand, it can be said they are "aloof," "difficult to get to know," and "standoffish." When a Stoic horse gets mad, he means business—and he does not waste energy getting rid of whatever it is that is bothering him (dog, fence, another horse, person). However, normally, Stoic types keep to themselves, act as an anchor in the herd when moving is absolutely necessary, and "hold down the Chessboard."

Most good broodmares have some Stoic qualities; I believe they develop them from having and raising babies (fig. 4.2). I often find that Stoics are dependable, solid, and kid- or beginner-level friendly.

4.2 Mothers often develop a Stoic baseline Energy Type. The best mothers become quite unflappable. I have known mares who were not that nurturing toward their babies and remained really Hesitant (see p. 162). This is a "nature versus nurture" debate, but it does seem like the act of motherhood can bring the stoicism to the surface in certain mares.

How to Approach the Stoic Energy Type

Stoics need us to connect differently than the Outgoing and Hesitant types. They need us to show up and be their teammate. They want to know that *we* know what they are looking at on the Chessboard, how they are managing the other herd members, and how they are feeling. Stoics tend to have a feeling of confidence, and that's what they are looking for in us. Basically, a Stoic is saying to you, "I've got your back, do you have mine?"

This type likes to feel you will consider what they have to say, not just bowl them over with demands. When I have seen Stoics pushed into high-energy activities, they tend to stew internally until one day, they refuse... even going so far as to lie down and refuse to get up.

This type likes a clearly defined job. In the "old days," this horse would have been the best choice for the milkman: He would have pulled the morning milk cart to each and every house, stopping and waiting at each doorstep without ever needing to be told.

Outgoing

There are two main sorts of *Outgoing* horses: the super-friendly type and the frustrated type.

The *friendly type* is often "in your face," seeking attention, affection, and companionship with humans, but can be a bit of a "mosquito" to other horses, constantly buzzing everyone. This horse is desperate for Zero and usually does not know it. The *frustrated type* often has or had a friendly nature at one point, but felt betrayed, confused, or was bought and sold too often (changing hands/barns) and lost hope. This horse may act like a bully in a herd, and it may even seem like he prefers human company. Often, this horse is called "pushy" or "bipolar" by a confused owner because one minute the horse is super-cute and endearing, and the next he nips, flattens his ears, or becomes nervous or defensive.

People commonly mistake a pushy horse for the leader or "alpha" horse, but this is most often *not* the case. Pushy is just the way this horse *intrinsically deals with life*; it is not a representation of the horse's Role in the Herd. Frequently, being pushy also belies insecurity, and so these horses often need other horses with different personalities to help them find all three balances and Zero.

When a pushy horse has lost his Zero, he can be very defensive and will tend to "pop" others' bubbles. If he has been punished often or severely for this behavior, he may act out in inappropriate ways. This Outgoing type does not typically respond well to punishment, but rather gets worse—even dangerous. Most of the time, pushy, frustrated horses still have a glimmer of the friendliness in their Outgoing energy, and when I meet them, I try to help them rediscover this for themselves (fig. 4.3).

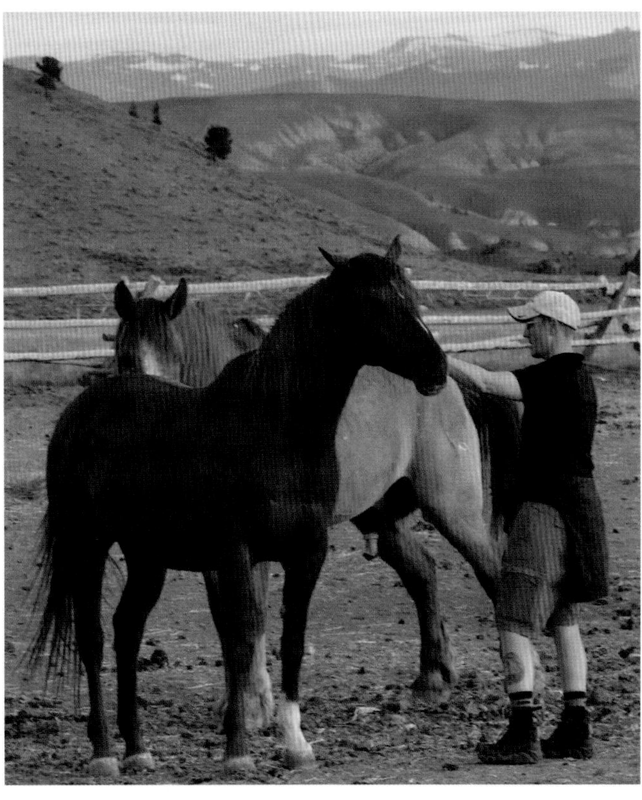

4.3 Outgoing horses, like the chestnut in the front here, have to be right there in the middle of everything and the center of attention!

How to Approach the Outgoing Energy Type

As we discussed, the Outgoing Energy Type (p. 160), whatever his Role in the Herd, ranges from showy to friendly to pushy. What he needs is extreme clarity. People who are wishy-washy in their body language or who don't have clear action plans make this sort of horse much more insecure. The Outgoing Energy Type needs black and white for clarity, but if he is harmed in any way, he takes it very personally. Think of a human toddler who needs to have clear boundaries because he is learning about limits. You have to set limits for the Outgoing horse, but you also have to offer a warm lap for him to "crawl up into" when he is tired and needs to be soothed. Luckily, pushy horses tend to evolve rather quickly once you have found that "sweet spot," which holds a clear line but offers plenty of enrichment and a dedication to Zero. In fact, I have met many pushy horses who were really difficult for the first few months we worked together but who ended up becoming attached to me—I dare say even loyal.

An Outgoing horse who is at Zero tends to become able to redirect his energy into being brave and forward. Because this type tends to react defensively sooner rather than later, they are often confused about the chaos they cause. Outgoing horses seem to feel as though *everyone else* is defensive and horrible, and they are simply trying to not be bothered.

When working with a confused Outgoing type, I usually need to start with the very basics: "This is what my X looks like, and this is what my O looks like. I will make a noticeably clear path to you. And here's lots of Aw-Shucks." I find that diffusing an aggressively pushy horse works best in this way. This is also where taking the time to start to offer a few Chessboard solutions, such as, "Here is a Safety Object," or "I will

Scan the Horizon for you," or "I will touch three objects on the Chessboard to show you things are okay here" can be invaluable.

Too often, Outgoing horses just *react* when they are confused. They are often the ones who act out with big displacement behaviors (p. 31) like rubbing their heads or necks on things, cribbing, pacing, and pawing. By taking the time to go over X, O, Core Energy, and even beginning to do some low-intensity Mirroring or Copycat (usually from the other side of a barrier like a fence or stall door so we can both keep our Zero), they often *begin* to mimic me, as though they want to make absolutely certain that we understand each other.

The Greeting Ritual (see p. 119) is very important for this type of horse, and they will be more likely to have a "Bubble-popping" issue when it comes to Greeting. Learning to respect the Bubble of Personal Space is the *hallmark* of this type. Unfortunately, when an Outgoing horse is friendly, it can be misunderstood, and early on in his training, this sort of horse is more likely to get reprimanded and mislabeled as overly dominant. In actuality, he is just needy.

Hesitant

Hesitant horses are the third most common Energy Types. They range from downright panicky to withdrawn and "faraway." Some of these horses are often also found at the bottom of the totem pole. They tend to want to be told what to do or be in the middle of a "horse sandwich." They don't want to make big decisions or choose where to go or have to defend themselves. These horses can also mask their Hesitant nature with an attitude that makes others think they "don't need much fuss." They usually aren't playful, nor do they look for a lot of stimulation, although they often respond quite well to positive reinforcement. They are happiest with someone to protect them in back and guide them in front—with some other pals on either side, as well. In other words, they like to be right in the middle of other horses' decisions and protections. In a herd of 20, you will find more of this type than any other. In nature, a herd doesn't need an army of leaders. It needs a group that is happy to follow along and doesn't argue all that much. Timidity ensures survival; when you are wary, you are less likely to wonder what that noise is behind that rock and go check it out.

Hesitant horses who are timid with people can sometimes become bullies, which seems counterintuitive. The reason is they carry so much internal stress from feeling unqualified to perform as brave, solitary, riding horses that they often suffer from anxiety. Displacement behavior (see p. 31), such as cribbing, weaving, or pacing is common.

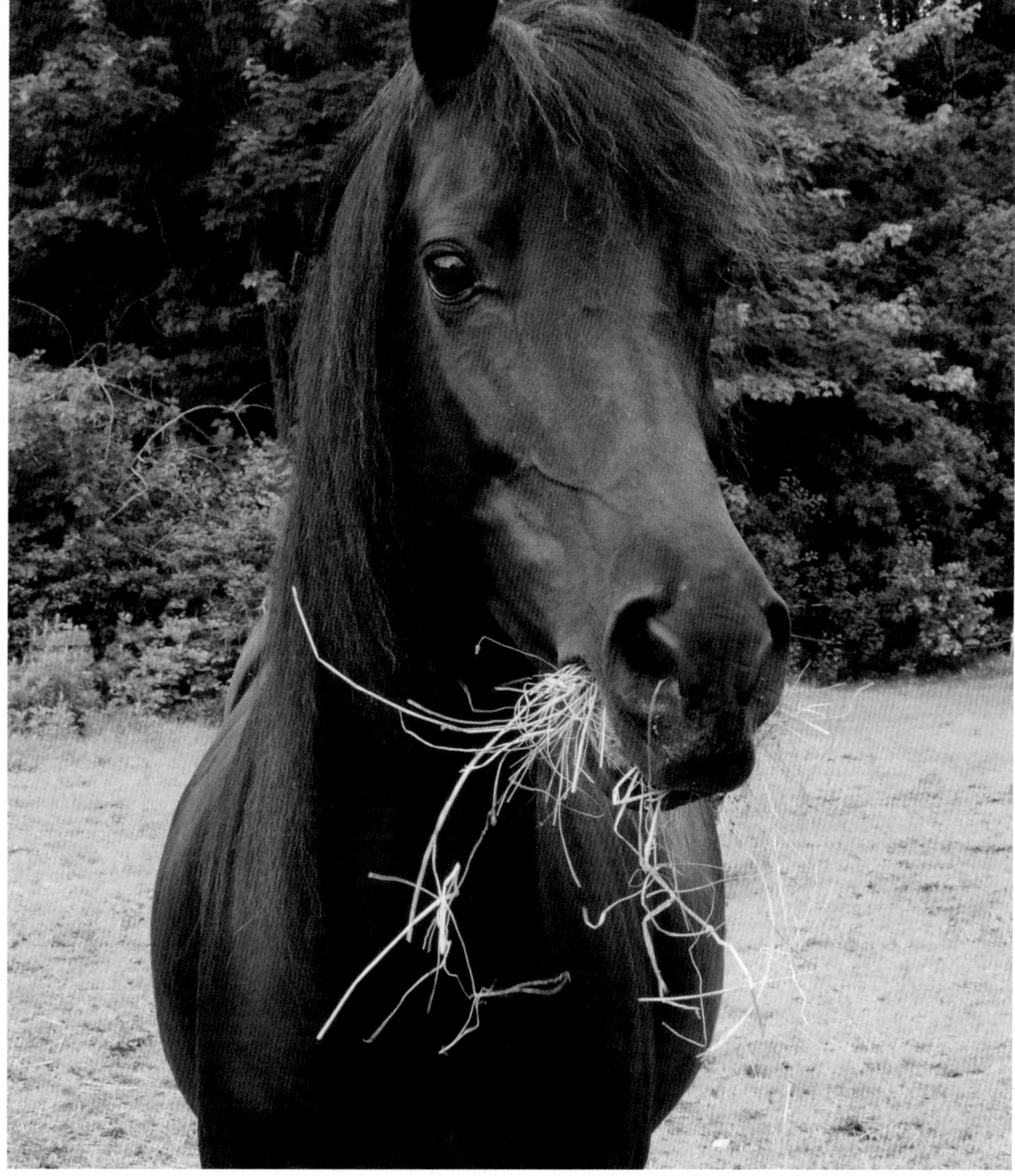

4.4 Hesitant horses may like people, they just need more time to warm up to them.

Hesitant horses can be overly concerned about the environment and like to have Safety Objects and find comfort in routine. They are sometimes barn- or buddy-bound, and typically like to have the people in their lives to fulfill their value for protection by being on the lookout for danger. I consider this Energy Type to be a bit moody, as Hesitant horses can seem sad and sweet and charming (fig. 4.4). Interestingly, horses with this energy type often have physical limitations that keep them more concerned and vigilant.

How to Approach the Hesitant Energy Type

To best work with a horse who is this type of energy, you need to grant a lot of messages requesting space. They often really like use of the Cheek Button (p. 124) and will even repeatedly offer that space to you as you approach them. Ironically, the more timid the horse is, the more he wants good definitions of space—being asked to take a step aside, for instance. However, due to his reclusive nature, the Hesitant horse is often highly sensitive, and if you ask for space with too much X, he will scurry away with no awareness of what he is doing, just pure reaction. You need a good deal of O with this sort.

The best way to connect with Hesitant horses, besides being very clear about "My Space, Your Space" (see p. 216), is to pay close attention to asking them to Copycat your steps on the ground, *one step at a time* (see p. 105). When you ride, you must make them focus on each of their steps, and they need a good deal of praise and Breath Messages. This type benefits when asked to focus on balance and organizing their movements carefully and predictably—not rushed. Too often, we see this energy in flashy show horses—their sharp, fast movements look attractive on the surface, but underneath, they are often suffering from anxiety and stress. You need to demonstrate very simple and direct X messages and be consistent in your intensity levels because of their tendency to scoot at the drop of a hat. (I sometimes say they are "allergic" to X"—see more about this on p. 47.) Get this kind of horse used to what your X looks like; how, why, and when you will use it; and the request you are making with it, ignoring the angsty reaction he often resorts to. Rushing or pushing this horse through activities will not result in anything beneficial over the long term. He may learn to tolerate an obstacle course, for example, but beneath the surface he will still not be Zero.

Roles in the Herd

Now that you have a sense of the three main Energy Types seen in horses, let's discuss the specific *Roles in the Herd* I have identified over my years of study. They are the:

- Mentor
- Teacher
- Sentry
- Protector
- Mapmaker
- Mother

- King/Queen
- Prince/Princess
- Joker
- Skeptic
- PBJ
- Peacemaker
- Pawn
- Mystic

These are the various Roles in the Herd that horses play, which impact their actions and movements on The Chessboard. Most horses fill a few Roles, which I believe is a result of Mother Nature making sure that a herd can balance itself out and stay safe. Most of us understand that a wild herd has leaders, but there has been a lot of misleading information and ideas related to what this looks like when it plays out in a domestic herd—which can be a bunch of horses, just a few, or even just a human and a horse.

You will find that most of the Roles in the Herd that I am about to discuss are responsible for varying degrees of protection, nurturing, and teaching. A few of the Roles are quite simple and these make up a good percentage of the "inside" of the herd (those who want no part of making major decisions, providing protection, or taking responsibility). This makes sense; you don't need that many cooks in the kitchen.

The list of Roles I've named is not perfect (I am always learning something new), but you can use it to help you aim in the direction of understanding your horse better, from a more rounded perspective. Similar to what I described for the Energy Types, horses have a dominant Role they like to play and a few other "traits" that surface as needed—for example, if a Mentor (see p. 166) finds himself in a group with other Mentors, he may shift and fill a different Role (fig. 4.5). However, the main traits will still cluster around a certain personality and Energy Type. A confident, stoic Mentor will not become a scared, insecure Pawn (see p. 178) and vice versa. *But* a horse who starts out insecure can still learn to have courage, and in doing so, other traits will emerge as the horse blossoms into his potential. This can happen when you understand his Role and Energy Type and how to nurture that evolution.

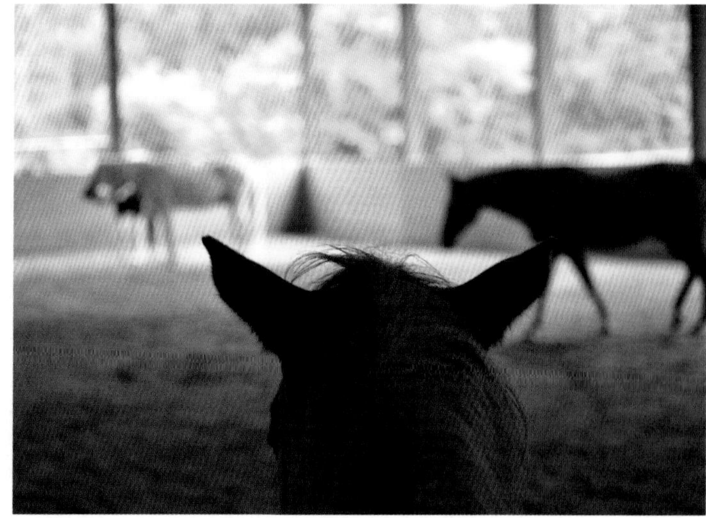

4.5 The view of the Mentor. The Mentor horse is worth his weight in gold. He may not be flashy, but he will always watch out for the good of everyone involved.

The most important thing is to remember that on a certain level it does not matter what Role your horse fills—*all horses want to find a deeper, better Zero while with human beings*. They can often find Zero by themselves out in a field, but the moment we show up, Zero melts like snow in the hot sun of our needs and wants. The deeper the Zero on the inside while with us (part of our "herd"), the better the behavior on the outside, and the easier it is to understand them and be understood by them. *This is the point of the whole thing.*

The Role in the Herd your horse fills gives you an idea of how you can communicate with him and perhaps helps you find out how to fill a Role that he needs from a companion. The goal here is not to lock your horse in a particular category; it's to arm you with information that helps you become the best member of your horse's herd with his needs in mind.

Before I go further, there is one label I would like to clarify because I referenced it in my first book: *bullies*. A bully is most often a horse who is acting out and displacing stress. A horse who is a bully is not a leader. He may drive all the others away from resources or demand no one bothers him, but these are not the actions of a leader. Leaders are inclusive. A leader may enact some rituals related to hierarchy or remind others that they need to move out of the way, but you will also see the leader eating and napping happily together with other horses. Bullies seem to never settle.

More often than not, in domestic horses, a bully is either undersocialized or in pain—or both. Stress is the driving force of the bully's behavior. Therefore, I do not consider this an authentic Role in the Herd, but rather an unfortunate stress-related "happening."

The Mentor

This is the horse we want to emulate the most in our Conversations with horses. This Role is compassionate, intelligent, and looks out for the welfare of others. Often the *Mentor* is an "all-around horse" with strong qualities of teaching, leading, and nurturing, and can take up the lead or follow behind as needed. This horse frequently has a Stoic energy; often he is solid, stocky in body; and sometimes he appears stubborn, lackluster, or "sticky" to get moving forward (figs. 4.6 A & B). The Mentor often holds a key position on the Chessboard, and when he moves, everyone else has to move, as well.

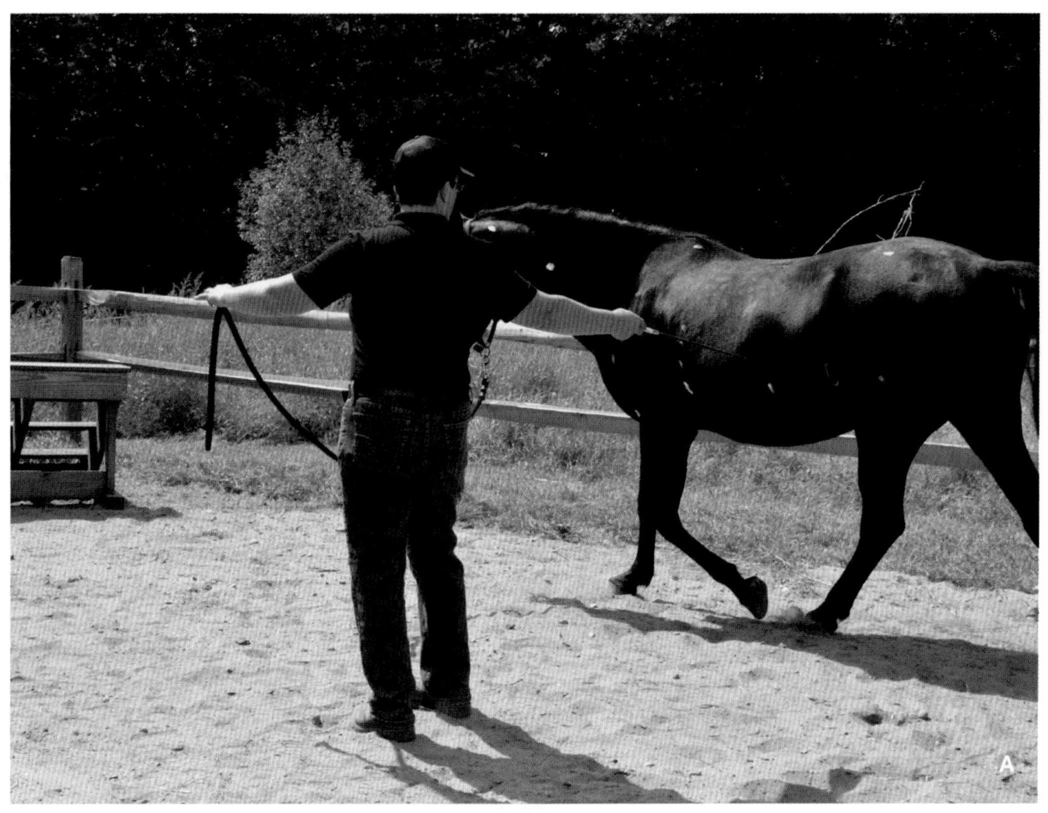

4.6 A & B Mentors are often Stoic (see p. 159). They may not want to move too quickly, and this is a choice out of wisdom, not stubborn resistance (A). I like to figure out who the Mentor is and Buddy-Up with him by aiming my shoulder to his shoulder (B). The Mentor helps me communicate with the rest of the herd.

4.7 A & B The gray horse is the Teacher and the black horse is a Joker (p. 175). Teachers will often play with a horse that they are trying to coach, but you can see the gray horse is using a Low-O posture to request the energy stays low (A). Teachers often have an "intelligent" expression (B). They can be stubborn if they feel that a lesson is not going well and can be demanding of their handlers and riders.

The Teacher

Teachers are often sticklers for the "rules" and enforce things more strongly than Mentors do. Teachers may have a playful side and are more ready to go forward than Mentors, showing they can either have an Outgoing or Stoic Energy Type (figs. 4.7 A & B). The horse who fills this Role is usually very trustworthy with young or new students but can be very demanding with older or more experienced ones. This horse has a tendency to "correct" other horses and humans alike with a quick nip, which isn't intended to hurt anyone but lets everyone know what is acceptable or not. Often, mares are Teachers, and they can double as Mapmakers (see p. 171) or Mentors as needed. Teachers are not always the best providers of protection—when they get worried, they would rather get to safety and then assess what just happened. I have noticed that, for some reason, Teachers often have one or two things they just cannot stand.

The Sentry

The *Sentry* has an Outgoing or Stoic Energy Type. In a herd, he may also double as a "scout" and move on ahead to check things out, coming back to the group to let it know what to expect (figs. 4.8 A & B). Usually, the Sentry is the one to take a serious

4.8 A & B The Sentry is the lookout (A). A good Sentry does not "sound the alarm" unless needed. We can be a horse's Sentry when he becomes concerned (B). I stroke the dun's Follow Me Button to suggest he follow my lead. He is a Mustang and I want to make sure that he trusts me.

look at possible danger, and if the Sentry says run, the whole herd gets going. This horse is often very brave. Interestingly, he may not be the highest in the pecking order and often doesn't seem to care. Even if he gets picked on, he is still the one to call the shots when it comes to potential threats. Often you will see this Role paired with one of the other strong leadership Roles we have already discussed. Usually not flashy or the most athletic, the Sentry can be great to ride but tends to worry about leaving his friends behind (what will happen to them without their Sentry around?) and is often a good group school horse or dude horse. If the Sentry feels his rider is hesitant, he may be reluctant to go forward and will try to spend time reassuring the rider that the environment is safe. Pushing a Sentry can cause him to become spooky if he doesn't feel like he has appropriate time to look things over. Just to be clear, the Sentry is not a horse who "cries wolf" and acts startled for no reason. He does not constantly look for boogeymen in a timid, excessive manner. On the contrary, a true Sentry often lifts his head "half-mast" and gazes off to the distance, but not in any alarming way. A horse who *needs* a Sentry will look to the distance with a chronic sense of alarm. The Sentry is the last to run and is the best at sorting out if there is cause to run or not.

4.9 A & B The Protector will often take up the rear guard (A). He may send others forward, but it is with a promise to "kick the coyotes." While they often have some nurturing qualities, they can also be demanding (B).

The Protector

The *Protector* is a horse who likes to drive others ahead but also will rest his chin on others' rumps in an action that is about fostering trust and showing the herd that he "has their backs" and will protect them from behind (figs. 4.9 A & B). (The Protector should *not* be confused with a bully—see p. 166. As I've mentioned, bullying behavior is typically a result of a horse with anxiety or poor socialization.) The Protector often walks the perimeter of the living area, checking for danger, as well as standing still in the Hold position, assuming watchfulness (see p. 113 for more about the Hold position). Often, a Mentor has Protector qualities. There can be a few Protectors in a large enough herd, but in a small group, members need to sort out who is driving. Sometimes two Protectors argue about who is in the stronger role and do not get along. Often you will see weaker personalities (the Pawn or Joker, for example) Buddy-Up and pair bond with the Protector. This kind of horse needs to be needed. With people, Protectors can be very safe and careful, but they sometimes refuse to do things they do not feel are good ideas. They usually have an Outgoing energy.

4.10 A & B The Mapmaker is the horse who is unafraid to leave others and go explore (A). He may not be the biggest or strongest, but he has a great ability to know where he is at all times. He seems to have a faraway look and loves going on adventures (B).

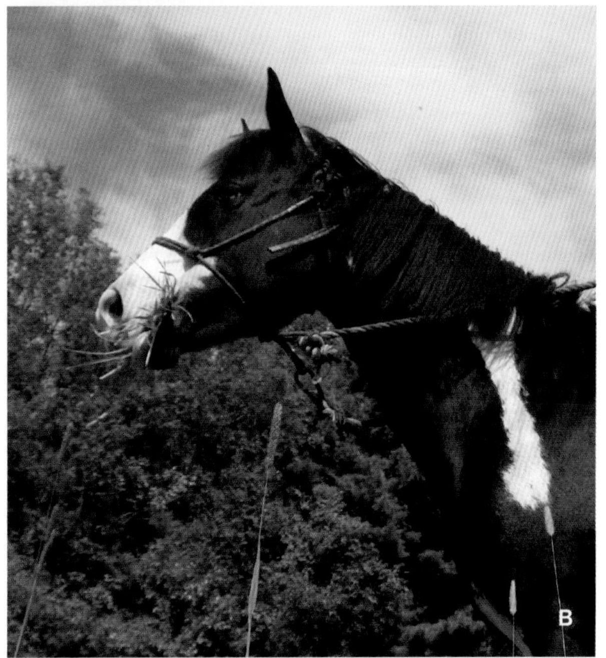

The Mapmaker

This role is in reference to the internal GPS that all horses have. The *Mapmaker* has the best one. These horses tend to be unruffled and move along at a quiet pace (figs. 4.10 A & B). They seem to keep track of time and get upset when dinner is late or the hour-long riding lesson should be over. The Mapmaker is fine if let loose on the property—he won't run around in excitement but will remain calm and sensible. This horse is great at herding cows and endurance riding but is typically not pleased with going around a riding ring. He loves to solve puzzles, complete obstacle courses, and perform tricks. The Mapmaker is either a Stoic or Outgoing Energy Type and is usually fine leaving others behind on a trail ride. This horse can often live alone. When coupled with the Joker Role (see p. 175), you have a real escape artist. This combo is most likely to climb into a child's wading pool for fun… or maybe just walk right into your house! They can have a low tolerance on the ground for petty things. I knew one Mapmaker who was sometimes aggressive on the ground, and we had to have strict boundaries in many scenarios, but she was a superb trail horse.

4.11 A & B The brown horse is a gelding with tendencies to be the caretaker, and therefore, the Mother (A). Mothers are also often displaying traits of Mentor, Teacher, Sentry, and Protector (B). A good Mother is an all-arounder.

The Mother

Real *Mother* type horses love babies—they are sweet with children, puppies, kittens, and miniature horses. They are very nurturing and forgiving and make great broodmares. This sort of horse can be protective and seem like a bully to other adult horses, but this is motivated by a big Bubble of Personal Space (think of it being big enough to encompass a foal). These horses are great for summer camp kids and therapy work, as they are usually willing to pack little kids around. I knew a Mother who was a Percheron and watched her win a gymkhana class with her tiny eight-year-old rider. The girl's legs were so wide on the back of this horse it would have been an effort to fall off, and that mare had a visible "grin" on the entire time. This horse was a great single driving horse and just a love to work with, but she was firm with all the other horses in her herd. Mares who are Mothers tend to have a strong cycle and can be a bit moody. Depending on her number of "off days" every month, she may need hormone support. A gelding who is this type will show strong qualities of a nurturer. This sort of gelding is great with colts.

Frequently a real Mother is a full-service horse: Teacher, Protector, Mentor, Sentry, and Mapmaker. The Mother may be more demanding of adult humans and have strong expectations (figs. 4.11 A & B). I have known people who say they feel "judged" by this kind of horse. Certain kinds of Mothers have an Outgoing energy.

4.12 A & B The Queen is a formidable lead mare (A). She knows her own worth and often gives people the sense that we must be deemed worthy. The King is usually very attractive (B). Like the Queen, he knows how special he is and will work very hard for the right rider.

The King/Queen

Horses do not have monarchies, so I admit it is a bit of a projection to say there are horses who are best described as "noble," "charming," or "gallant." I like to think they have the essence of the energy of a *King* or *Queen*—an air of glamour and the seeming ability to electrify the very air around themselves. Often stately and serious, this type also tends to show traits of the Protector, Mentor, or Mapmaker, with a real take-charge attitude but also patience (figs. 4.12 A & B). When this horse hits the show world, everyone pays attention. The King/Queen is often hard-working but can be

The Prince or Princess is usually a very attractive horse (A). Many people are drawn to them with high hopes of showmanship. However, they tend to have physical weakness or sensitivities and are not particularly good Mentor-type leaders in a herd (B).

demanding. This horse prefers one rider and enjoys the *best* riders (the King/Queen is not a child's horse). They are most often an Outgoing type.

The Prince/Princess

This type is not as regal as the King and Queen, but still possesses an air of the natural showoff. *Princes/Princesses* seem to know their value and enjoy being seen. They are natural show horses, but a bit more sensitive, even moody. Sometimes this type really hates ring work but will excel at a show by watching the competition. Princes/Princesses need to be admired, require companionship, and like to boss others around, but they are not particularly good Protectors, Teachers, or Mentors (figs. 4.13 A & B). They can, however, make good Sentries. These horses really only like one person to be their rider and are very selective. They love to do something every day but are more in it for the connection with their rider than because they enjoy the activity itself. They can be good trail horses and are often brave and free-spirited. This personality is most often an Outgoing energy type. I find they can be good horses for teenagers.

4.14 A & B The Joker often has a perky and interested expression (A). Whenever I see one, I can "hear" him thinking, "What can I get into?" or "Are we going to play?" This horse tends to act fearless and likes to play with objects (B). However, he may use "spookiness" as an excuse to run around (that is, as a way to entertain himself!).

The Joker

The *Joker* is a personality that many are drawn to but who can actually be a bit challenging. Jokers tend to be an Outgoing Energy Type: escape artists who get into trouble and are pushy, demanding, and needy... *but* are cute and tend to be very affectionate (figs. 4.14 A & B). The Joker sort of just tugs at your heart... right up until you try to train him. This horse doesn't see the point of training; once he has "the basics" down, he would just assume go out and do things together for the heck of it. This makes the Joker more of a candidate for endurance riding, trick training, team penning, or maybe just going swimming together (this personality tends to get right

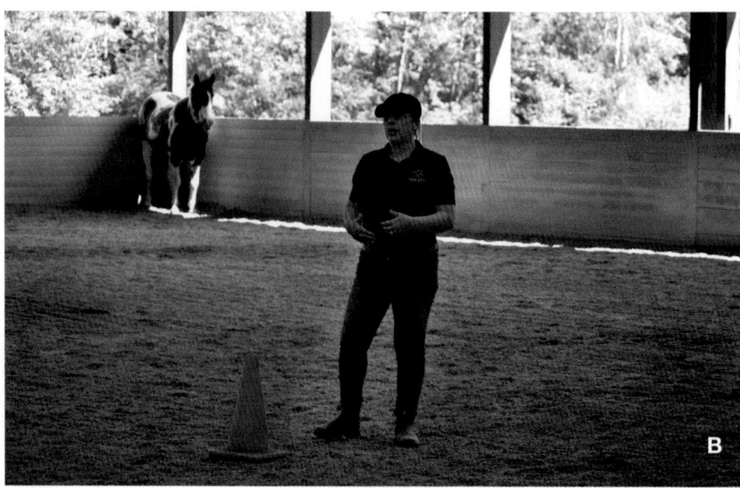

4.15 A & B The Skeptic is generally a "wary" horse (A). When I see a horse with an expression like this, I "hear" him saying, "Prove it to me." The Skeptic may have lost trust with people, so the more space you give him, the more comfortable he becomes (B).

into water). The Joker is often in your face, and he may think any limitations you apply are just another puzzle he should solve like a riddle. Although they are usually *overly* friendly, Jokers can degenerate into really aggressive horses if someone "gets after them." They can become fear-aggressive and inventive about making people go away.

Jokers often appear more athletic than they really are and have a tendency to be a bit weak in the back. This is a great candidate for a youth who has the time and energy to spend day and night with a horse—the joker will form a bond that can be extraordinary, as long as the ground rules get set up. As much as he will rebel against the idea of "My Space, Your Space" (see p. 216), he needs the boundary line drawn very clearly to gain real Zero and real courage, instead of relying on the false bravado he likely often exudes.

The Skeptic

This personality seems to be born with a sign that says, "Prove it." Skeptics can be timid and reclusive, or pushy, but their hallmark is an undertone of mistrust when it comes to people (figs. 4.15 A & B). They are most often Hesitant but occasionally Stoic. They need a lot of reassurance and can be very defensive. If you gain their trust, they will be very loyal. Skeptics do not make good school horses. They can be very clingy to other horses, yet on the other hand, they can act like bullies. When a trainer pushes this type, the horse either completely dissociates and shuts down, or becomes dangerous. The Skeptic is more prone to panic than anger or aggression, and there is often a sense of "sadness" about him. If the Skeptic has a chance to blossom, he can have qualities of the Mentor and can be surprisingly good in equine-facilitated psychotherapy with humans. Oddly enough, the more you give this horse space, the more comfortable with you he becomes. Skeptics hate feeling captured, so really respecting that Bubble of Personal Space makes them feel good.

The PBJ

The *PBJ* (Peanut Butter and Jelly) type is what I call the "middle of the sandwich" horse. This horse wants to be in the middle of the herd, and he can't handle stress, but he is often very affectionate and loves to follow directions. He wants to know the rules. The PBJ tends to pair-bond and is at his best with other horses around. It can be difficult for a PBJ to gain confidence on his own; he will require you to exhibit characteristics of the Sentry and to use Safety Objects. But he is simple, uncomplicated, and usually kind (figs. 4.16 A & B). I meet a lot of PBJ horses at summer camps or in equine therapy centers because they tend to be good with kids. It should be noted, however, that they often do not show any sign of a breakdown until it's too late—you really have to keep an eye on them. The PBJ tends to have a Hesitant Energy Type.

4.16 A & B The PBJ often gives the impression of wanting to hide (A). He prefers the company and guidance of other horses and can be very herd-bound. A PBJ who has been made to work beyond his physical or emotional capabilities may develop a poor disposition (B).

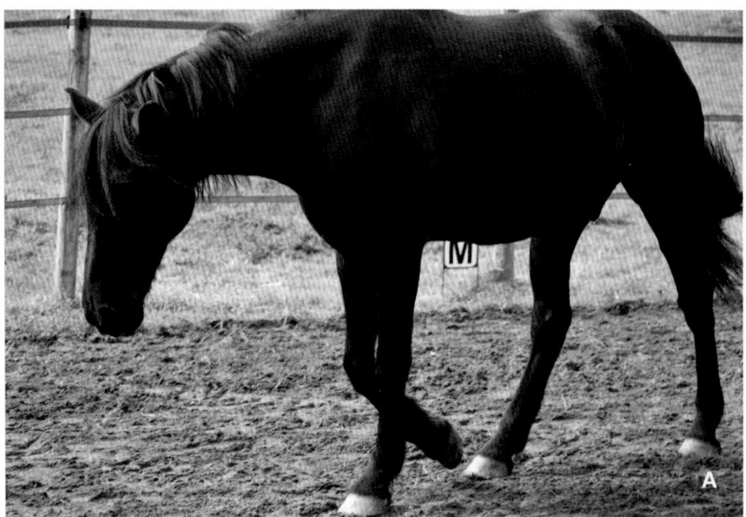

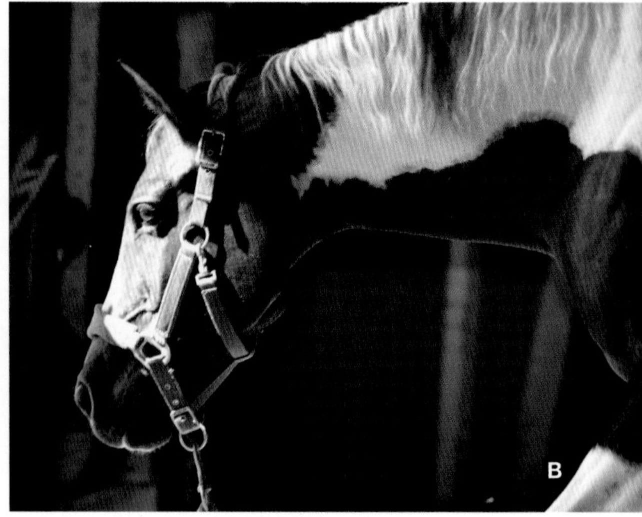

4.17 A & B The Peacemaker does not want to cause commotion. He may seem standoffish and Hesitant, but he does like other horses (A). Peacemakers can be soothing to be around, as they can feel like a "friend" and usually enjoy doing fun little activities with their handlers (B).

The Peacemaker

The *Peacemaker* is often standoffish with a Hesitant Energy Type; however, I have a Stoic Peacemaker in my herd. She swings from Hesitant about some new things to Outgoing about those she likes.

This horse personality tends to hang out on the edge of the group, sort of reclusive and doing his own thing (figs. 4.17 A & B). He is easygoing and usually gets along with all horses, no matter who he's turned out with. He doesn't want to cause a commotion. He can show some jealousy and loves attention.

Peacemakers can be hard to catch. They like to work a little, but not too much (they don't see the point of "raising dust"). They are not overly worried; however, if they develop a "phobia" it can be really challenging to get Peacemakers over it. When a trainer gets after them, they may shut down and stop moving, even to the point of laying down. When they say "NO" it's "NO." With the wrong trainer, this horse often becomes a kicker. Peacemakers can be hard to get into regular work—they prefer trail riding or hanging out, doing fun little things together, like trick training. This type of horse would like to just follow you around when loose and can feel like a "friend." Peacemakers tend to have teeth or hoof issues.

The Pawn

The *Pawn* is even more selfless than the PBJ and can come across as very primitive and simple. With a Hesitant Energy Type (although some can be Stoics) and preferring not to be the center of attention, this horse may not want your affection. The Pawn

4.18 A & B The Pawn is the "little guy," lowest in the herd hierarchy. Unlike a PBJ, he can be a loner. He is Hesitant, as you can see in the expression of the horse in photo A; however, if you get through to the Pawn, he can be quite lovely and good with children. The Pawn in photo B is the smaller horse on the left. He would be happy following his leader horse around all day.

is best as a buddy for the "primary" horse; he is frequently not a great riding horse as he has a hard time with learning even the basics (figs. 4.18 A & B). I have known so-called "alpha" horses who sort of "keep a Pawn around," almost like a mascot. The Pawn pair bonds with the horse seen as the leader and just follows him around all day. Pawns are good pack horses for this reason. Often, the Pawn responds well to young children or those with disabilities. These horses prefer uncomplicated and natural relationships. When they open up, they can be extremely sweet-natured and very tolerant.

The Mystic

This is a rare horse. *The Mystic* comes across like he is from some other place—a Pegasus or unicorn realm. This horse is sometimes awfully "hard to reach" in terms of connection and seems "faraway," but not in the way an abused or neglected horse would. The Mystic just has an airy quality that makes your heart skip a beat. If these horses are mistreated, they can lash out with rage or truly become completely unreachable. You *want* to win their affection, not just their tolerance, but this is really hard to gain access to. They can be difficult to train because they tend to have poor health the moment they get stressed. Sometimes this is the horse in the back of the stable who no one knows what to do with and requires a "special" person to bond

4.19 A & B The Mystic is a rare horse. Some of them give off the "air" of being hard to reach (A). But in these cases, consider the saying: "Still waters run deep." Most Mystics are easily insulted or injured by humans. They require a conscientious connection with a human (B). They are not always good riding horses—unless you truly expect nothing of them.

with—someone with no expectations. The Mystic tends to be extremely fast, and I have met a few who were off-track Thoroughbreds. These horses often give off an air of sadness but also can have fits of irritation and won't hold back when they do. I have met some Mystics who were gifted in equine-assisted psychotherapy work but couldn't be ridden. These horses need space, lots of space—*but* also require authentic connection, no BS. (As an interesting sidenote, I have met several mules and donkeys in the Mystic category.) Mystics can be any Energy Type, although I find the more difficult ones are Hesitant.

Don't Get Too Carried Away

I usually find it easier to interpret the horse's Energy Type than his Role in the Herd, because when a horse is in a withdrawn or agitated one (Red Zone), his "real self" may not be that apparent in the moment I meet him. Sometimes I am struck right away by features or movements that point in a clear direction in terms of the horse's Role, other times not.

I am a mother and a daughter. I am also a teacher and an artist. These are each different Roles, and they each put me into a different "frame." Similarly, horses can have traits from more than one Role in the Herd. Some horses seem to land right in the center of a Role and really exemplify that nature, and others seem "slippery" and hard to figure out. Have fun with determining your horse's type, and don't get too worried about being "right" or "wrong." Use these ideas as a fun place to start and see what you can come up with!

Other Type Considerations

Gender

Many people have asked me about the difference between mares, geldings, and stallions and how that affects communication.

What I can say is this: In general, mares seem to really value good, clear communication, and will often offer guidance, and even patiently take a Teacher role with human beings who are learning to use their bodies as a communication device. I have seen a mare look at someone in a clinic who just learned how to perform a formal Greeting with a quizzical and patient expression that implied she was thinking, "Yeeeeees.... Now, what comes next? Do you remember? Here's a hint—I will turn my head a little bit. There you go! Cheek comes next! Very good, Human!"

I often say that mares "own" the language. Geldings, on the other hand, I describe as "using" the language. Geldings seem to love it when people start to learn, just like mares, but they also tend to quickly arrive at a point with a person where they are hoping to communicate about their needs or concerns. Mares, on the other hand, seem to be happy just to finally be understood, and then count on you to not stop talking. They are like, "Okay, you know how to have a Conversation now, so no backing down."

Stallions seem to be somewhere between the two. They are really happy to finally be understood and listened to, but for some reason, I have met a vast number of stallions who seem to be really worried, or insecure. Geldings have a primary concern, like, "Where is the boogeyman?" Or, "Can you please use the toothy-brush, not the currycomb?" "Are you pleased with me?" Stallions, meanwhile, seem to be asking, "How close is too close?" "Do you want my 'big energy' all the time?" "When I bring my energy up, how do I know when to put it away again?" "By the way, can we snuggle?"

I find that stallions seem to be desperate for emotional connection. This can be from often being kept apart from other horses. A wild stallion has a whole band of mares to keep happy. I have met several people who have naturalized herds of horses where the breeding stallion lives out with the mares and foals. They all reported their stallions spend a good deal of energy soothing, connecting, nurturing, and teaching the young. In these situations, the owners also found that working with their stallions was very easy—he was almost eager to get away from the drama of his family life for a little while and let someone else call the shots! These stallions tend to be courteous and kind—real Mentors.

I have noticed that the most secure and grounded Mentors are often geldings. In these cases, it seems like the gelding retained some stallion-like qualities, but also lived in a big enough herd that they were able to develop their skills as a mature horse. Mares who are Mentors exist as well, but often they have more of the qualities of the Teacher or the Mother—sort of like "Super Momma." These mares usually have had a baby or two of their own, which served to help them gain wisdom and maturity.

I think the most important thing to think about with the gender of a horse and communication is to simply consider whether and how the horse has been allowed to mature into his or her role in the herd, and has the horse had a healthy family life with other horses?

How to Help a Horse "Mature" by Assuming Your Role in the Herd

One of the practices we use with horses is to force-wean them. This makes sense in terms of fitting into our needs for training and ownership: We need to switch a young horse's loyalty from attachment to "Mom" to attachment to a human being. However, there is a growing understanding that domestic horses are often not correctly developing emotionally. Many are psychologically stunted at about the age of two. It is common to meet a 20-year-old horse who still behaves like a young colt.

The way I think about it is that we have a whole world of domestic horses who have been put through a "foster care system." Far too many horses did not have a healthy, mature adult horse in their lives who could take the time to help them grow up. We now know that when elephants are orphaned and aren't taught by a mature older elephant, they can develop really destructive habits and do not learn how to properly behave as an elephant. I believe this is the same for horses in many ways.

My goal in outlining the Energy Types and Roles in the Herd is to not only offer a view of the "box of chocolates" that your horse could be, but to set you up to learn to assume the Mentor role in your relationship with your horse.

What Energy Type Are You?

Consider again the Energy Types I described for horses, beginning on p. 159. Under those parameters, what Energy Type do you think applies to you? You may want to ask your friends and family what they think your Energy Type is, as we are often not as aware of how we really come across to others.

In addition, look back at the Chessboard (p. 89) and the horses's values (p. 72), and start mapping out a version of how you move through your own world—what you value and how you problem-solve and what your comfort zones and areas of struggle are.

Next, look at the horse or horses you have in your life. Consider what Energy Type the horses you are attracted to have. How does that compare to the Energy Type you think you are? Is it "opposites attract" or are you "twinning"?

What Role in the Herd Are You?

Sometimes I think we are attracted to difficult horses who make us stretch ourselves into the zones and Roles where we are slightly uncomfortable. Other times, I find that people already have a skillset they didn't know about—perhaps they work in a profession that makes them accomplished in managing things—and so a Role comes easily once it is identified as key to your relationship with your horse. The trick when it comes to determining your Role in the Herd and how it can be used to connect with your horse and *his* Role in the Herd is to reach deep into the skills you may have earned in another area of your life and begin to apply them in your interactions with your horse.

Here's the bottom line: Horses do not have the brain structure to *strategize*. They are great problem-solvers (think opening a door), but their brains use emotionally embedded memories to help them problem-solve what is right in front of them *now*, not think about what happens next. How many horses figure out how to get outside the gate by learning how to open the lock, only to get on the other side and not know what to do? (Mapmakers seem to be the only ones who are better able to formulate some sort of "plan" when they get there.)

Our brains thrive on strategy. Predator-types need strategy to *outwit* prey, whereas the hunted rely on *outmaneuvering* the hunters. This is a basic difference when forming your herd of two: strategy versus direct problem-solving. (I am not a neuroscientist so I acknowledge this is overly simplified. I am using descriptions and terms that I believe are comfortable and make sense.)

How to Become a Leading Role for Your Horse

I already mentioned that using your Hold Hand puts you into the model of a "gate-keeper" or "guardian." Let's expand on that for a moment.

A Sentry, Protector, or Mentor is a role of higher rank in the horse's herd, but with an inclusive nature. Did you have a mom or dad or older sibling or coach who was always there for you? Is there a favorite superhero or figurehead that you admire or look up to?

Think about a crossing guard or traffic cop—this is like the Sentry.

Think about how gentle and compassionate Superman or Wonder Woman was—how they wanted to take care of everyone around them and never tried to show off. That is a Protector.

Think about Mr. Miyagi, the fictional karate master in the film *The Karate Kid.* He was an excellent Mentor.

Think about the character of John Keating played by actor Robin Williams in *Dead Poet Society,* inspiring his students, who called him "Captain." That is a Teacher.

Try to become the John Keating, or the Mr. Miyagi, or Superman or Wonder Woman in all your Horse Speak actions, and you will probably be in the right *mindset* and therefore, the right Role in the Herd.

Finding Your Way to the Role of "Mentor"

Emotionally stunted horses who have lacked having adult horses to provide guidance have not been allowed the learning curve needed in herd animals that is provided by older, wiser herd members. Without it, horses are at a loss as to how to develop self-regulation on their own. Equine herds have long relied upon the older, mature horses with a scope of experiences to be role models and teach the younger ones how to grow into mature responses. Most domestic horses, force-weaned, literally have not learned some basic lessons in behavior, and some of those lessons the equine brain cannot produce on its own. Horses can feel defensive and act neurotic as a result.

When you can use even a little bit of Horse Speak, however, you open the door to becoming the strategic Mentor of a horse who may literally be lost inside his own little world, not knowing how to "grow up."

Every single element I suggest in this book is, in fact, distilled from having studied how Mentor types—in horse rescues, in particular—can help troubled horses find Zero, begin to self-regulate, and grow out of their triggers. When I emulated the Mentor behaviors that I observed, I had breakthroughs with the horses I was working with. This was a driving force behind my passion for meticulously detailing, listing, and decoding the layers and layers that we now call Horse Speak. I really, really wanted

SKILL-BUILDER

What Is a Horse Looking for in a Human Mentor?

- We are Zero to the best of our abilities under all circumstances.
- We are aware of our footfalls. We walk with balance and precision. It's essential not to be "wiggly" in our movements.
- We are aware of our hands and arms: They move with purpose and give the direction of what our intention is in each moment.
- We are aware of our X and O postures and the intensity levels we hold apply in all activities.
- We listen to the horse's concerns because we understand their world view, Energy Type, and Role in the Herd.
- We take care of the Chessboard by Scanning the Horizon; walking around the edge of the arena, checking for bees, bears, and boogeymen; and creating a Safety Object or location in the area you are working in.
- We understand the Four Gs (p. 208) and apply them during every interaction. We pay particular attention to practicing a good Gone to give the horse time to process.
- Overall, we take responsibility for ourselves and have the best in mind for our horse at all times.

to help horses. But then, I really, really wanted to teach people how they can help horses, too.

At first, I wondered if an emotionally "stunted" horse was able to change. Luckily, I had incredible success helping a number of horses grow up. Knowing the Buttons (p. 117) and the Four Gs (p. 208) has meant that I can offer sequences of communications in the right order, starting with the Greeting Button, and moving all the way down the horse's body, talking to each Button, and seeing what each Button has to say. Having this Conversation with the horse's whole body (ideally, on both sides), not only tells us what is going on with the horse, it tells the horse *we know how to ask him* what is going on with him. The system of patterns of communication we can use with the Buttons is a breakdown of an otherwise totally organic process, but by making it into bite-sized chunks means we can learn it. This is what begins to set us up for the Mentor Role: Knowing the "order of operations" and being able to communicate that is part of what Mentors offer other horses. When we know this, too, we become trustworthy and important in the eyes of our horses.

Using Horse Speak, your big, strategic brain can come up with many solutions to help a horse have a new experience in the here and now, then help him process that experience and weigh it against those of the past in order to come to new conclusions about what he feels. This works not only well, but incredibly fast. Some things still take time because there are many little nuances of memory to process; a horse may need to repeatedly ask a similar question for a few weeks as every stored memory rises to the surface. However, the result is often that the new information is absorbed because it is rooted in the horse's own system of communication. You are "paddling with the current," so to speak.

The platform of a healthy baseline, including the ability to self-regulate, must be established if the horse is going to succeed in not only memorizing training cues, but performing with pride and emotional presence.

The importance of being the Mentor for your horse is why I developed so many tips and tricks for initiating contact with a horse from the opposite side of a barrier (see p. 43). When you have a good introduction with the aid of a barrier, you can get further, faster, because you won't lose your Zero, and then you will be modeling Mentorship.

One professional Mustang rehabilitator who has spent a year learning Horse Speak says, "I can now approach horses from outside their pens and work through initial sessions in half the time and with double the effectiveness. By the time I get inside

MYTH-BUSTER

Does Dominating Behavior Work?

Most horse training over the years has relied upon domination tactics. Even those who are committed to compassionate education of horses sometimes resort to domination tactics when things don't go well. The reason for this belief is simple: Dominating a horse often "works." To this I may say, "Of course it 'worked.' If someone dominated you for long enough, you would probably eventually give in just to make it stop."

Horses have a unique hierarchy structure that supports lead horses driving lower-energy-type ones around, so when we model this behavior, there is a certain part of the horse's brain that just gives in to instinct. However, lead horses drive others with the added agenda of, "I am driving you *because I will also protect you*. I need you to listen so if a tiger shows up, I don't have to argue with you in the middle of a crisis." And a return to Zero is always part of the picture.

What are some domination tactics? There are all sorts of methods, using flags, ropes, whips, and special halters. When a horse is really out of control and has dangerous habits, occasionally this can serve to renegotiate the relationship. However, very few people are actually skilled enough to do these kinds of activities with Zero inside. It is far too easy to slip into predator mode and not even realize it, or to feel threatened by an angry, charging horse, and so act like a threat right back at him. You also cannot "quit" in the middle of this renegotiation, and you must remain Zero *the whole time* or it can backfire. The truth is, most people are not going to be able to pull off a lesson in "domination," and I don't like the impression it leaves on certain people who have a predator brain that likes "big action." Horse Speak is more about "small action," and when using it to talk to your horse, you gain the ability to make better decisions in the moment for two reasons: First, with more awareness of the small communications the horse is giving, it's less likely the horse will build up to an explosive point. Second, if the horse does act out, you are armed with a quiver of many Conversations—pathways to understanding how your unique horse needs to be spoken to—in order to come to the best results.

Dominance tactics are typically used to force, bully, or coerce horses into the desired behavior the trainer is looking for. Horse Speak opens a door for the horse to seek to please us of his own accord.

Domination is often thought to go hand in hand with obedience, but it does not. For many horses, domination in training tactics can represent a high-intensity dispute over hierarchy. Remember, when horses live in a healthy group, they seek to return to Zero as soon as possible, and the Conversation goes two ways...both horses involved are saying something. But when a person uses dominance it is usually a one-way street: The horse has to figure out how to surrender to the position the trainer wants him in, and he also has to know to move away quickly (like he would if he was about to get bitten) if the trainer wants him to.

Bottom line: Horses in nature can have serious disputes over who is "in charge," but this is not a good model for horse-human interactions in the long run. What is normally reserved for high-intensity situations in the wild has been mistranslated into a training model dependent on running a horse around and "taking his breath away." Total surrender, like this requires, is traumatic for many horses. Yes, there are a few personality types who can move past it, and even seem okay with it, but so many more horses dive deep into themselves and retreat to a faraway place as a coping mechanism. This is not dead broke; it is dead broken.

the pens, the horses are eager to try and have lowered their defensiveness. This has allowed me to do my job with almost no struggle at all. In fact, even getting a halter on for the first time has been a completely new experience."

Herd Management

Some of us have multiple horses at home, and some of us only have one. Many people board their horses and may have to navigate the dynamics of other horses in an ever-changing environment. Some herds are not healthy for different reasons, and barn managers are often shuffling horses around, trying to make sure everyone is a good fit with their turnout buddies.

Herd management is probably a whole book by itself. If you have two or more horses who coexist, it is likely their Roles in the Herd create friction or unrest on occasion. Such behaviors can indicate underlying issues—for example, play-fighting can be an outlet for anxiety or displacement; bullying is often an outlet for social anxiety or undiscovered pain. Because of this, Horse Speak and assuming the role of the Mentor can be helpful in assisting a horse to find a "more comfortable place" in the herd, with you acting as the overseer. Believe it or not, when you are very simple and clear, you can have a positive effect on reminding everyone in the herd that you want them to go to Zero and *not* to play or fight all day and create disruption (figs. 4.20 A & B). My teaching has taken me to many establishments all over the world, and overall, you can always tell when the people at one barn are stressed or while at another barn, they are relaxed, because it is reflected in the horses and their interactions with each other.

You may find that other roles besides the Mentor are missing in your horse's herd at home. You can offer communication related to the values you know your horse feels are important and aimed at his Energy Type. Then consider that a healthy herd needs a Mapmaker, some sort of Mentor or Sentry, and a Protector. When horses that live together cannot seem to settle down for some reason, try to determine the types you have in the group. For instance, when you have two Protectors in one group, they could be competitive. I had a client who had two PBJs together, and they spent all day trying to hide behind each other. She introduced a Mentor donkey to the small herd, and he settled the PBJs down. Sometimes, simply adjusting your thinking to see your horse's and his herd's antics from a different perspective may provide the "Aha!" moment you need to come up with solutions for herd harmony. Horses tend

4.20 A & B **Managing more than one horse at a time requires diligence and self-control. Here, I use double Hold Hand to give an air message about Bubble space, mutual respect, and my Role in this herd of three (A). I use the Hip Button on both horses to say, "I have your back," and to place myself higher in the hierarchy as the Protector horse who also has the right to drive the other two forward or away (B).**

to respond well when we try to understand them better, even when you are not certain about how to deliver all the messages.

Should Horses Be Separated?

Separating horses because one is a bully or a group is too playful or just does not seem to get along is not the worst thing, as long as the horses continue to have some kind of access to each other. Living separately from other horses is part of being a horse in the domestic world. Most have been isolated in one form or another all of their lives. If they have adapted to it and are used to it, then it is not *necessarily* always bad for them. Not all horse personalities get along without the necessary balancing agents of the other Roles to guide and help them. Figuring out what Role your horse plays, and then adding the Energy Type and gender tendency, can help you figure out how you can help him live more happily, whether within a herd or separately.

A Strategy for Herd Harmony: The Hay Game

Here is one exercise I use for working out a variety of issues with one horse or a few horses at the same time. This communication serves a few purposes: First, the Hay Game is what horses do with each other very time they are served hay together. The pecking order is re-established at every single meal. Second, sharing a meal is also intimate and enriching. Plus, being at the top of the pecking order with your horse around the hay is a great way to have a real reason to ask him to move over and also to invite him back. Note that I *strongly* recommend you stay on the opposite side of a barrier when first practicing this strategy, for safety's sake.

Horses use eating as a way to communicate, connect, and practice social order, all at the same time (figs. 4.21 A–C). Being involved during meals presents you with an opportunity to discuss mutual respect, hierarchy, and clarity of intention. In addition, it gives you something to "talk about"—so much of what we do with horses translates to, "Let's talk about what I want to do," and this is simply, "Let's talk about how respectfully connected we can be around dinner" (fig. 4.22).

The Hay Game is useful for working with one horse, or a group. Set up several piles of hay along the fence of a paddock or ring, turn your horse or horses out, and move them *quietly* from hay pile to hay pile in a slow, conscientious manner by focusing on their Buttons with your Activation Finger (see p. 53) or a stick or dressage whip. (Because most horses won't want you to send them away from their hay, some sort of extension for your finger can be helpful at first.)

How to Do the Hay Game

1. Approach your horse. You *must* be Zero, demonstrating deep breathing, a comfortable smile, and what I call a *"How interesting?" attitude.*

2. Engage Going Somewhere down the Buttons, starting with a breath Greeting and inviting the horse with a Knuckle Touch (see p. 119) if he feels like it. He may just open his nostrils to you, saying, "Yup, there you are." Your horse may lift his head to Greet your knuckles, but it's fine if he doesn't.

3. Aim your finger or stick at the Cheek Button to Activate it, and see if the horse moves it away.

4. If he yields the Cheek nicely, step back and breathe, pretending to eat hay, as well.

5. Activate the Mid-Neck Button next, and see what happens. You may want to leave your Activation pointer in the air for a count of 10 seconds. This gives your horse a chance to process the request before you raise the intensity.

6. Every time you get an answer of *any* sort—even a grumpy one—remove the

4.21 A–C Horses move each other off hay piles as they settle a herd's hierarchy. The black horse in this group uses Laser Beam Eyes to create space (A and see p. 54). My horse Rocky, the grullo, is the Mentor of this group. He joins and uses a Hold position to settle the Chessboard (B). The mares reposition themselves around him. The Mentor settles the disputes and creates a quiet eating environment. You can see Rocky's "loud" tail swish, telling his companions, "We are done with moving around" (C).

4.22 Creating space between two horses who are eating hay sends an important message when we are finding our place in the herd because the horses who are higher in hierarchy can move those who are lower around.

pressure. You do not want to trigger food aggression. Breathe deeply and relax. Let the horse eat. (This is the proper use of the Gone phase of the Four Gs—see p. 208).

7 Go down all the Buttons this way, restarting each time with a Breath Message that says, "I'm back. Hi there."

8 Now move your finger or stick in a faster motion, again starting with Cheek and going over each Button rapidly in the air from outside the horse's Bubble.

9 Repeat this until you can aim your finger or stick at a Button and the horse moves off to a new pile of hay.

10 Over a few sessions, reduce your request so that if the horse merely yields his head, it is good enough. There is no need to send him away every single time.

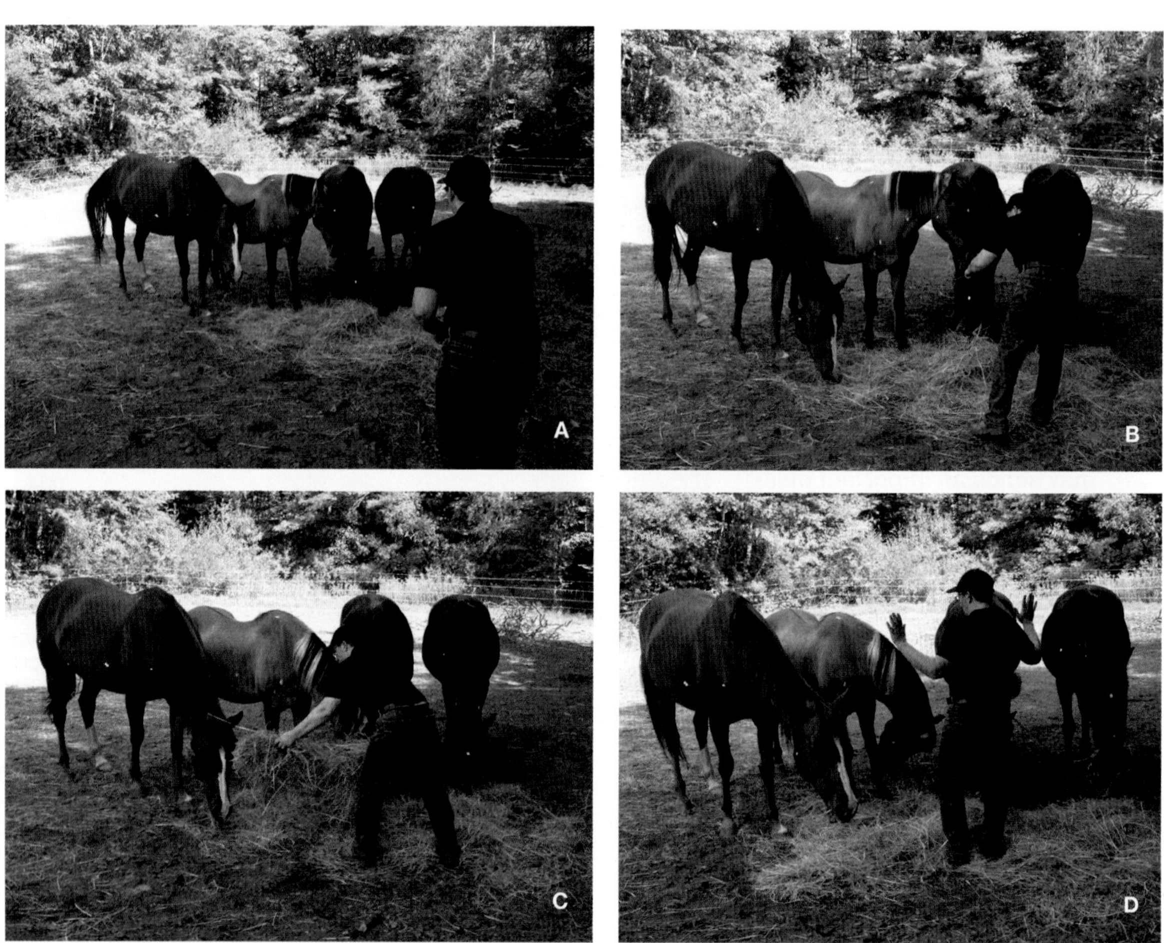

11 If you have several horses in the paddock, the end goal is to be able to do a quick Breath Message ("Hi"), then move your finger or stick in an arc from cheek to hip over the lead horse (because then the other members of the herd will see I mean them no harm), and have all the horses move off quietly to the next pile of hay. The lower-ranking horses will often follow the higher-ranking ones. They may scuffle with each other a bit during the move, which is why you stay on the opposite side of the fence, for now.

In the Hay Game, you aim to move a single horse or a whole group of horses, or to insert yourself in the group as they eat, with as little fuss as possible (figs. 4.23 A–G). It gives you a chance to learn which horse prefers to move off which Button, as well as more about the Activating the Buttons, in general. Practice being a benign leader; always allow rest and time to eat between movements. Keep the sessions

4.23 A–G I assume an O posture before the Hay Game to say, "Don't feel worried about my presence" (A). Because I am doing the Hay Game with a whole herd of horses, I will only use a very Low-Calorie Conversation. I Greet the Mentor to introduce my presence to the herd (B). Then I share out the hay to ensure the horses do not feel stressed by me (C). I offer X posture plus Hold Hand to say, "I am here, but you're okay" (D). (Rocky the Mentor is rubbing his nose, which means, "Is that all you want? Okay.") Combining Hold Hand with Activation tells the herd, "Get ready, here I come" (E), followed by, "Move aside, please. I am the leader around hay" (F). I then Blow Sentry in the middle of sharing resources (G). Now I am part of the herd, sharing hay and offering my role as a leader.

BUZZWORDS

"How Interesting"

The term "How Interesting" represents having a good mind set of openness, curiosity, and humor.

short. Do not become an annoyance to the horses—you are trying to use one of their own tactics to create a harmonious hierarchy in which everyone wins in the end. I prefer to end the game on a note of pure enrichment, offering hay by hand to the horses, and simply enjoying the sound of their chewing.

This exercise is excellent practice for becoming the Mentor. It provides a great way to enter into an important part of your horse's day and communicate about something of high value. As a rehabilitation technique, the Hay Game can work *wonders* on a horse with poor social skills.

The New Kid on the Block

Introducing a new horse into any herd is likely to produce a level or degree of fast-paced movement for a few days or weeks. Integrating into a new herd is a delicate thing, and although there will be plenty of Fire Drills, in which the Chessboard is maneuvered habitually and slowly, there will also be Sports Maneuvers, where movements are sudden and quick.

There are only a few *psychological* reasons why one horse chases another:

- There is a herd dispute, and one horse is driving another away from "his" herd, which models possessive stallion-type "ownership" or head matriarchal behavior.
- There is a hierarchy dispute, and two similar Roles in the Herd are figuring out who gets to play which role.
- One or all horses feel unprotected and do not know how to bond.
- One horse is stressed and has lost Zero and is displacing anxiety or stress through bullying others.
- A horse is in pain, and the others do not know how to help him, but empathy dictates they, too, feel stressed by the pain.
- Mating behaviors are being acted out—either wanted or unwanted attention.
- A horse does not have the right "smell." Some horses seem to love the smell of one buddy and not of others. And some horses just look and smell like "home," and others do not.

- There is a very troubled horse in the mix. An insecure horse can cause others undue stress, and they might not know how to handle it.

To help in this situation, use a strong double Hold Hand (both hands up—see p. 51), and walk with heavy, concentrating steps around the outside of the turnout area first. Then, if it's safe to do so, walk around the Bubbles of the horses in question, asking them to mirror your calm presence. (You can also separate the offending horses and give this message where they both can see you.) This says, "I am the Mentor. I want you all to settle down now, get grounded, and take a breath."

Always keep yourself safe. If horses are really acting up, aim your Activation Fingers at the Cheek Button on each horse, even at a distance or over the fence, and really *mean* it to say, "Hey, no monkey business while I am here."

Combining both of these messages while establishing Safety Objects to encourage the horses to settle can have surprising effects. You are saying, "I can see you guys don't know how to settle down. I am giving you a message to give each other space, a suggestion to keep things slow and relaxed, and a few Safety Objects to use to ground yourselves."

Working on Going Somewhere down the Buttons with one horse at a time (as you did with the Hay Game—see p. 189) while in view of the other horses tells the whole herd you are seeking to show them a better way and help them let go of any "stuck" feelings or energy in their bodies and minds. This gives the horses a new "map" of how to be and be together. It can be amazing.

5 Exploring the Circular Nature of Horse Conversations

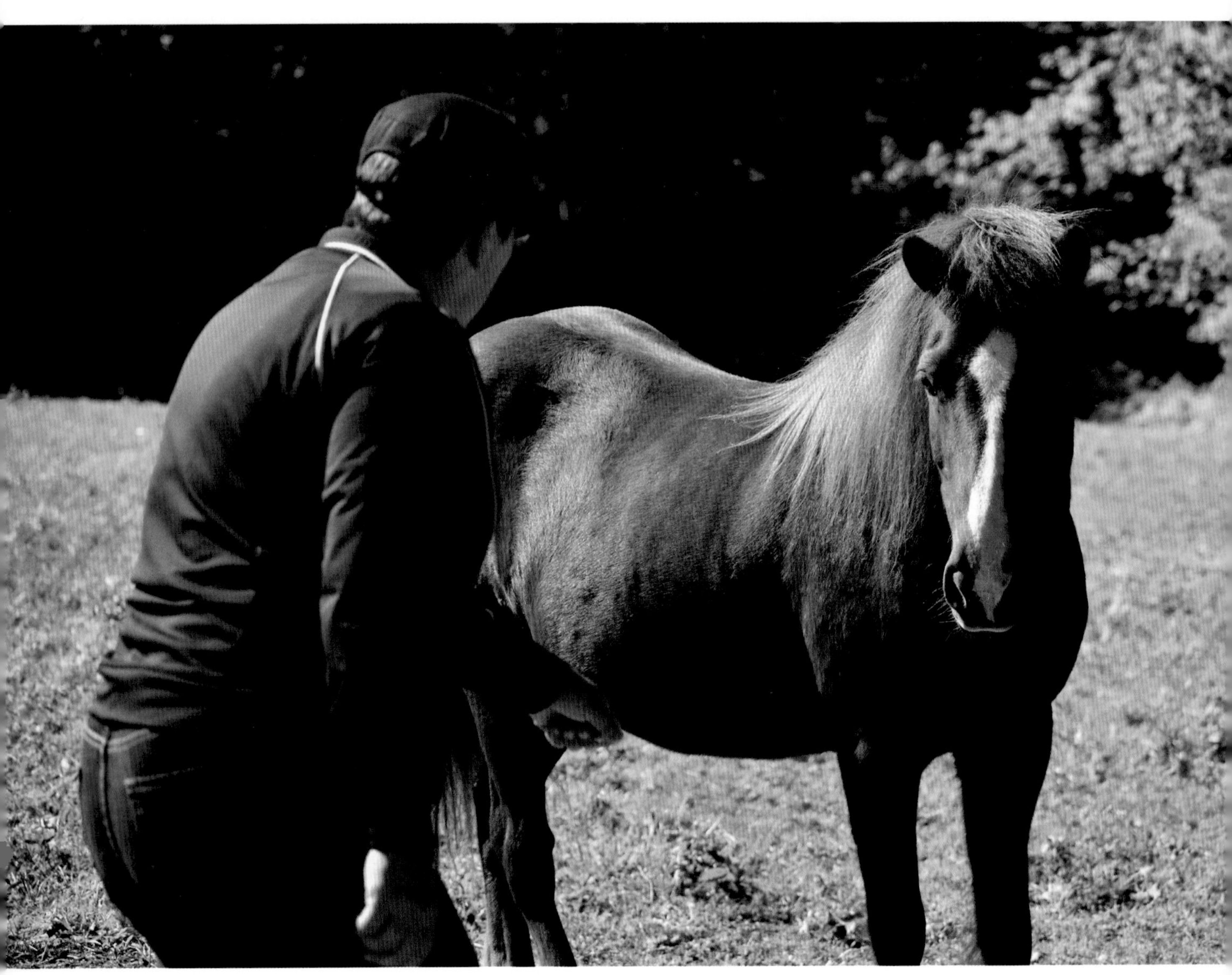

Earlier in this book, I identified the Four Gs—Greeting, Going Somewhere, Grooming, and Gone—as the circular "container" for how horses have Conversations with each other (we'll review the Four Gs and connect them to other Horse Speak skills later in this chapter—see p. 208). I have now created a second concept that my students have found useful when trying to remember what piece of a horse-human Conversation they are in and where they need to go.

IINN

IINN (Initiation, Introduction, Negotiation, Navigation) is an acronym referring to the four stages in the cycle of communication between horses, and between horses and humans. This cycle is so predictable that when we make it a habit to use the four stages in our work with horses, it can alleviate a tremendous amount of struggle, worry, and stress. The words I have chosen for this acronym are more relatable to humans, while the original Four Gs are conceived of from the horse's perspective.

BUZZWORDS

Approach and Retreat

This is how a horse or a person requests permission to enter another's Bubble of Personal Space. *Approach* is any sort of asking; *Retreat* is the reply from the asker once the horse has answered the Approach—it is the release of action, intensity, or asking.

Stage One: Initiation

The first step to having a Conversation is *Initiating* a connection with a horse, setting the stage (figs. 5.1 A–C). This can include Initiating a new encounter or a new level of training. It is whenever you Initiate an "idea of something" (like presenting a piece of tack for the horse to sniff), or an approach to the horse or paddock—you are working the Chessboard, creating a Safety Object, and suggesting a "safe space" where you are giving signals to the horse of being a Mentor, Protector, and all-around good herd leader. Think of actions like checking for bees and gopher holes (hidden threats) and "having the horse's

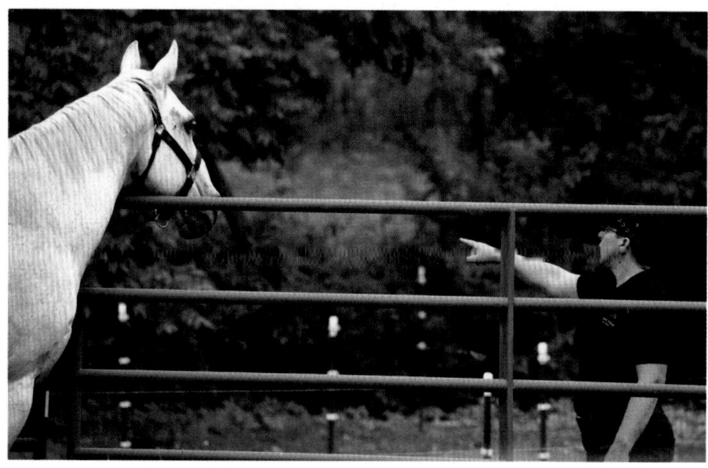

5.1 A The Initiation phase can take many forms. In photo A, the horse himself is a Sentry. I need to be convincing for him to let go and begin communicating with me. I need to become *his* Sentry.

5.1 B & C In B I use the outside of the pen to offer Initiation to the dun horse. I use the tools we've discussed to "make sure things are safe," proving my ability to be a leader. The horse then chooses to come to begin the Introduction (see below) himself. In C I use Hold Hand to the horse's Hip Button during Initiation. This horse needed to know I "had his back."

back." Initiation takes the old notion of *Approach and Retreat* to a whole new level (fig. 5.2).

What Generates Interest?
- Protection
- Resources
- Awareness of Space
- Breath Messages

5.2 The purpose of Initiation is to get the horse interested in communicating with you. Consider what he values and what you can offer him.

Stage Two: Introduction

Introducing yourself to a horse formally, or as a simple Check-In, is an echo of our own social dynamics (figs. 5.3 A & B). When we first meet someone, we Introduce ourselves in a complete and serious way (with horses, this would be the equivalent of the full Greeting Ritual I describe in *Horse Speak* and summarize on p. 119). Later, we reintroduce ourselves on a familiar and friendly level with those we like or know (with horses, our Knuckle Touch Greeting—see p. 59). Introduction can also mean Introducing a new item, like a piece of tack or the mounting block, or a new person. It can be Introducing a new arena or horse trailer. Introduction is different from desensitizing—in desensitizing, the horse is often made to stand still and learn tolerance. In an Introduction, we touch a targeted item, or the

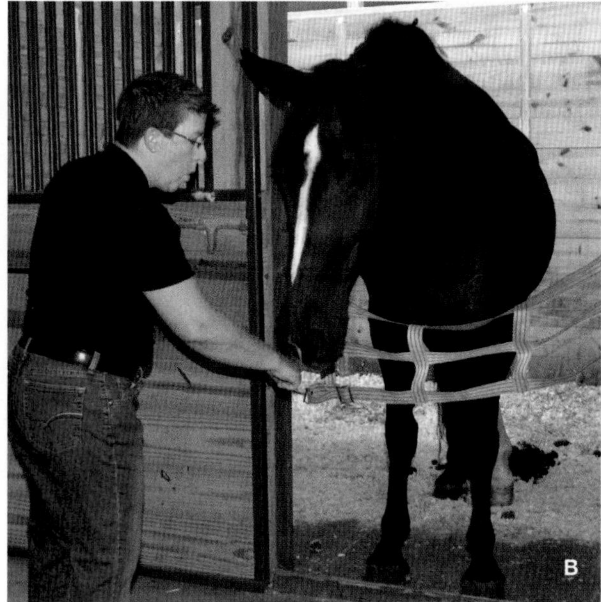

5.3 A & B **When Initiation is complete, most horses choose to come and offer a Greeting (A). This is the Introduction phase. A good Initiation usually sets up a calm Introduction (B).**

gate or the walls of the new arena, first. This is what lead horses do: They scope out the edges and *Thresholds* of the Chessboard and make sure it is safe for others.

Horses use their nose in the act of Introduction, not only with humans and other horses, but when they are learning about new objects and places, as well.

Remember that saying "Hello" to your horse when you see him is polite (fig. 5.4). Even co-workers who see each other every day have some form of a morning "Hello." Find a way to have a daily "Hello" Introduction with your horse that gives him a chance to say "Hello" to you, too.

5.4 **It is polite to say "Hello" to your horse when you first see him, but doing so over a barrier with respect for both your horse's Bubble and your own is important to the message.**

Stage Three: Negotiation

Like Introduction, *Negotiation* also echoes human social networking. Who is "one up" or "one down"? Who is the leader in an interaction or Conversation? Out of a group of five people in a think tank, each person probably has her own specialty—her own time to be "one up." This happens in equine groups, too.

BUZZWORDS

Threshold

This is the point or level at which something begins or changes. It can be physical or psychological. I discuss Thresholds in more detail beginning on p. 227.

With horses, the Negotiation cycle not only determines hierarchy, mutual respect, and Roles in the Herd, it also determines *each day* if the leaders are feeling well and up for the challenge of leading. Did the usual leader step in a gopher hole and so is not up to it today?

In the process of Negotiation, some horses need you to simply tilt your head to remind them, "Let's keep this mutually respectful, shall we?" Others need you to Activate the Buttons on their cheek, neck, and shoulder so they take a step back or over to yield space to you on purpose. Some horses are already yielding their head aside as you approach, eager to say, "Ahoy, Captain! Good to see you! I am ready to follow." (Note that if you turn your head aside a little when you see your horse do this, it is like a mutual "salute.")

Negotiation is directly linked to hierarchy, and the mechanism for determining hierarchy is directly linked to the movement of the head and neck—up and down, left and right (figs. 5.5 A & B). A high head is an X posture, so it is part of a display when there is a contest or invitation to play. A low head is used to stabilize another or a group, or to reduce intensity. A neutral head-and-neck position is often seen in horses in

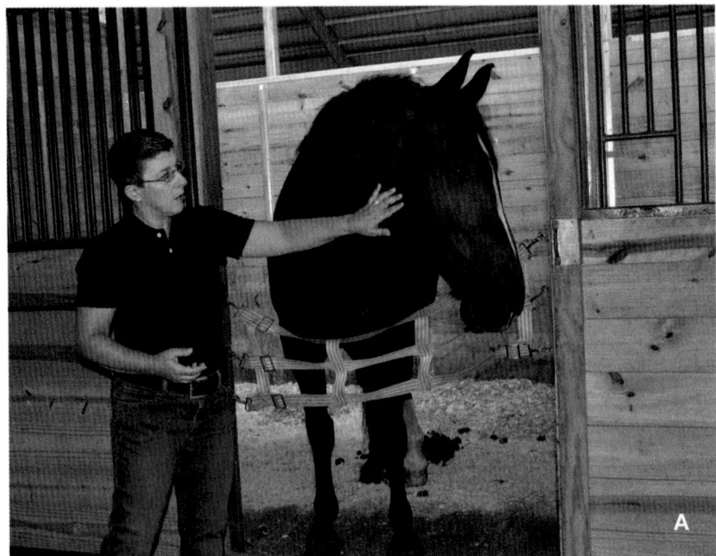

5.5 A & B Negotiation includes both asking the horse's head and neck to yield away and inviting it back to you. You are checking to see how easy or stiff the horse's movements are, and how well you both deal with each other's Bubbles. In photo A I check the Cheek Button: Is it soft and yielding, or stiff and unsure? In photo B my O posture invites the horse back for a Knuckle Touch.

Hold Position, such as when a leader offers calm and protection. Left and right are yields away, giving respectful space to another horse. In addition, they can be used as an inclusion gesture—what I often call *"Scooping"*—and this invites a horse to come closer or to begin to follow along in that direction.

Taken as a whole, the movement of the horse's head and neck is similar to our own gesturing with our hands and arms. Think of a waiter, inviting you, "Right this way," and the Scooping or sweeping use of his hand and arm. A grandmother, inviting her young grandchild onto her lap in a Low-O position with her arms open and wide—welcoming, soft, and safe. Friends asking you to follow them to come into their new home may sweep their hands and arms in a gesture, and duck their heads to the side as well, saying, "You gotta come see this!" A teacher, holding her palm toward her first-grade class as she gathers them together, using a "soft" version of the Hold Hand (see p. 51) to say, "Hold on there; let's get organized." She is the Mentor of the classroom.

Stage Four: Navigation

Navigation represents the phase of moving around the Chessboard of Life together (figs. 5.6 A & B). This includes problem-solving your relationship and relationships with others, strategies for the Chessboard, and consideration of Thresholds. This phase deals with locating resources, as well as dealing with potential threats and group cohesiveness.

5.6 A & B Navigation indicates all the other stages of IINN are working, and now you and the horse can move around the Chessboard together, as horse and handler are doing in a soft and fluid way in photo A. When Navigating, you still need to think about the Chessboard rules. For example, in photo B I have "claimed the fence," which puts me in the role of Mentor/Protector. I have also placed a Hold Hand on the horse's Girth Button to suggest we Buddy-Up and Go Somewhere together.

Horses are inclined to use problem-solving in this stage, so it is here we can find their Green Zone "Training Mind"—the best mindset for them to be in for *our purposes*.

In human social networking, Navigation is when we go somewhere together with people or groups we like and do activities we enjoy together—think of going to a museum and being ready to be open to learning from that environment while spending time with your friends. It is a sharing of space with those you feel comfortable with and doing things that are enriching to you.

In Horse Speak, Navigation includes being able to initiate Going Somewhere and Negotiate Thresholds, with the horse agreeing to pay attention to you and move along at the pace you recommend. He is introduced to Safety Objects and to other tools you may work with. Together you may need to deal with a Chessboard issue, such as a dog running by or a strong wind. During Navigation, you may need to have a good processing moment (see p. 113), offer the Hold Hand to the Buttons for reassurance, "blow away a boogeyman," or Check-In with the horse's muzzle to reconnect. This stage is the full summary of all the Horse Speak you have practiced—Navigation implies that you can, in fact, talk to your horse about anything and everything that comes up.

You can see Navigation requires all the facets of Horse Speak that we have already discussed to be understood, and for you to have at least cursory ability when it comes to the previous IINN stages.

MYTH-BUSTER

Is It Okay to Approach the Horse from His "Blind Spot"?

Traditionally, we are taught to not approach a horse head-on because there is a blind spot directly in front of him. However, when you watch two horses approach for a Greeting, this is how they do it: They walk straight toward each other, connecting center lines and the Greeting Button in between the nostrils. When horses lower their heads, the position changes the function of the eyes so they can better see what is in front of them. In addition, they can slightly adjust the position of the head to one side or the other in order to see you. This is why a Low-O posture is so important in Greeting.

IINN: Are you "IN?"

When you think in terms of the four stages of IINN, you can more easily locate the part of a Conversation you are *in* with a horse, or the part the horse is struggling most with. You can better deal with issues that arise like Thresholds (both psychological and physical) if you know how to best set up the Conversation. As mentioned already, a Threshold issue is usually dealt with in the Navigation phase, but if you had a poor Introduction, then how are you going to have a good Navigation? Maybe you had a poor Introduction because your Initiation wasn't up to par—you forgot to do it, or you didn't notice or ignored your horse's stare toward a far

SKILL-BUILDER

How to Approach Your Horse in His Stall

I think of a stall as the horse's bedroom. If the front of the stall is open so the horse can hang his head into the aisle, then he considers it to be his Bubble of Personal Space. If he can put his head into it, it is his.

The inside of a stall can either offer comfort and security, or a feeling of isolation and stress, depending on the horse and his associations with it. In nature, horses don't go into caves, so an enclosed box is not an intrinsic part of a horse's world view. That being said, some horses are happy in their stalls, and even prefer to be in one for a certain part of the day. Being stalled for most of a day is not good for their circulation or digestion, and without the needed mental simulation of being in the world, horses who spend too much time in stalls can become neurotic.

They are also social creatures by nature. As we've already discussed, when horses do not have proper socialization as they grow, they can miss out on how to become a healthy herd member. Horses must learn from older, wiser horses; or they can become mentally and emotionally stunted.

Using the stall as a micro-space to begin really good communication is powerfully effective in many cases. Although you may need time to practice learning and remembering the IINN ladder of success I have outlined in this chapter, once

(continued)

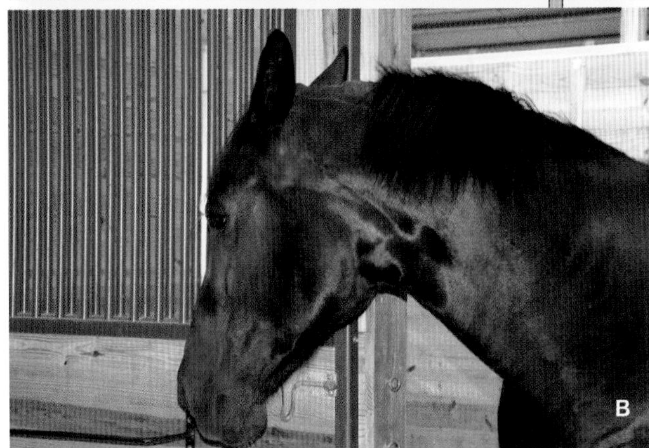

5.7 A & B Wherever the horse can put his head, he will consider part of his Bubble. This helps explain why some horses get so grumpy about other people or horses walking through and "popping" what they consider to be their personal space. Here you can see one person is standing directly in the front line of the mare's nose, and the mare appears to feel a bit claustrophobic about it. The person to the left is "entering" the horse's Bubble with her arm. There is another person sitting in a chair, also in her Bubble. Can you see how a horse may feel invaded (A)? As I begin the approach to gain this mare's interest, I can see she is skeptical and defensive in her expression and head and neck position (B).

SKILL-BUILDER

you have the "swing of it," you will be able to start your day with a horse in a much better state, having already worked out a whole cadre of protocols that set the horse up to be happy and invested in the activities you want to do. Not only that, but you can also arrive at this "happy place" in a matter of minutes.

What's not to love about this?

Every horse is different, and even if a horse does not like confinement and wants to get out of his stall in a hurry, or seems distracted or even grumpy, you still can arm yourself with a host of useful information that can help you alleviate some of his stall-related anxiety and frustration and get in line with you. You can now approach every single aspect of your time with a horse as an opportunity to communicate, forming boundaries, bonding, and problem-solving any little thing that may arise.

Approaching the horse in his stall requires all the information you've learned about finding Zero, getting into your observation mode, and using the IINN protocols of approaching, Greeting, and preparing to spend time together in a positive, "ready-to-go" state of mind. The way you approach the horse in his stall can mean the difference between starting the day distracted, defensive, or tuned out, or integrated with each other and emotionally ready to take on the tasks at hand. I go into more detail about Navigating the horse's stall in chapter 6 (p. 233).

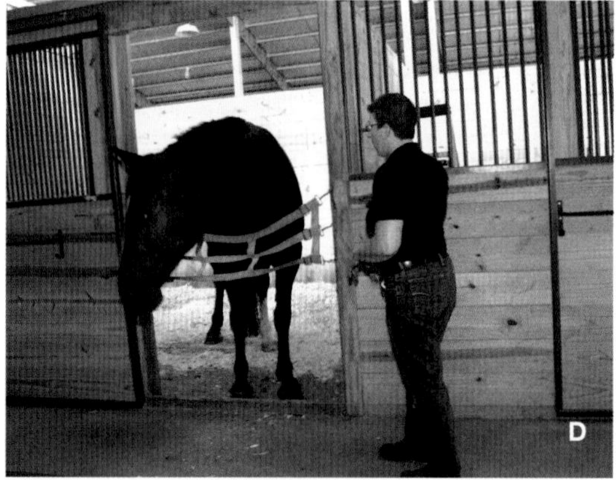

5.7 C–H I begin the Initiation stage by Securing the Environment: "Hmmm...how secure are these doors?" (C). After a few minutes of Initiation, the mare lowers her head and draws my attention to her concerns down the aisle (D), followed by a solid, Low-O Greeting (Introduction) in front of her Bubble (E). I Blow Sentry to say, "Hey, Boogeymen! Go away!" (F). We Share Space in O (F). Now that we have done Initiation and Introduction, it's time to Negotiate our leadership roles. I Go Somewhere down the Buttons, with attention to the Bridge of the Nose and Back-Up Buttons (H & I). I need to claim the space in front of her if we are to Navigate. I say, "Let's look for boogeymen together," taking a break from the Buttons to give a message of safety before we Navigate the Chessboard together (J).

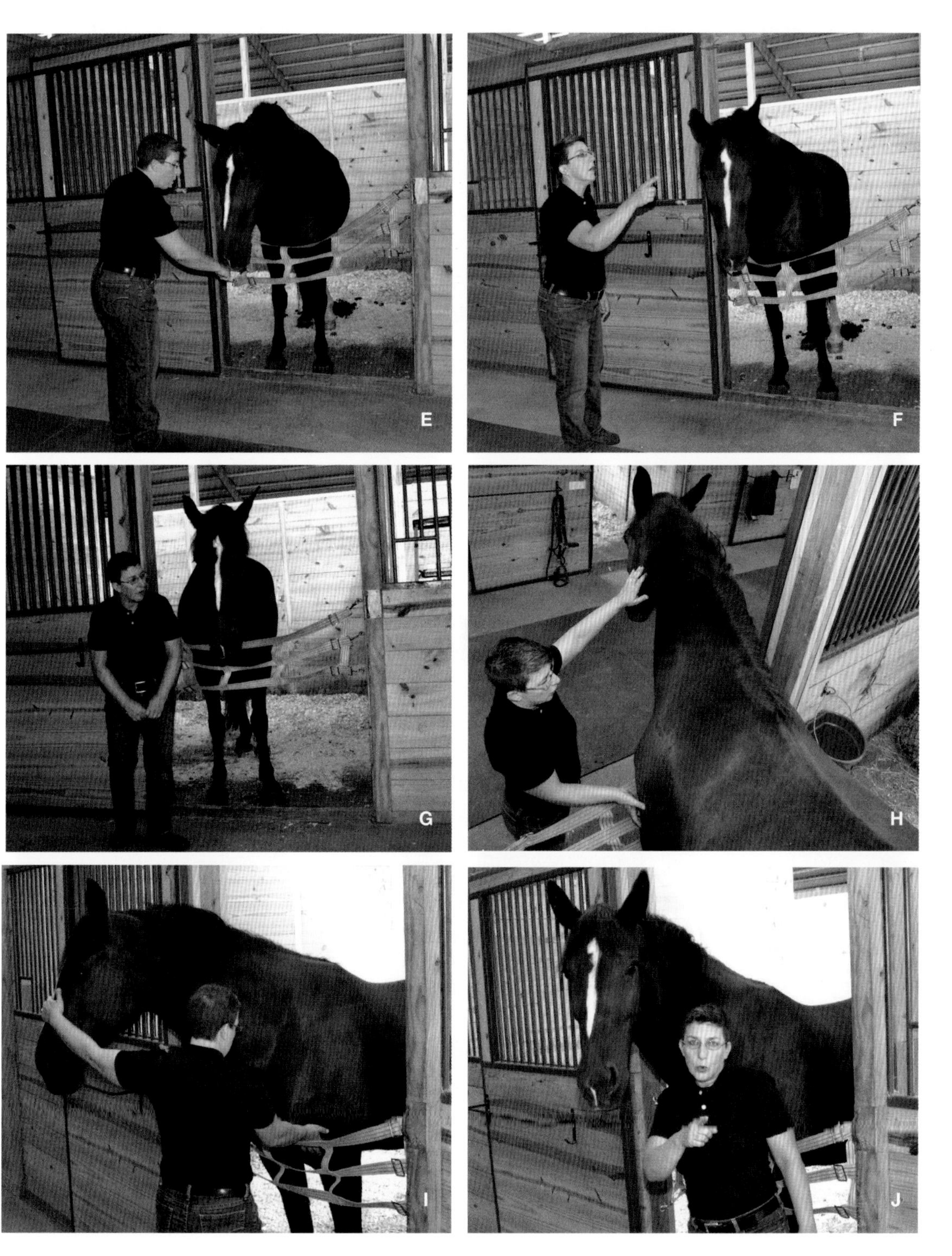
E
F
G
H
I
J

5.8 **Getting a Green Light for the Greeting Ritual (Introduction). Notice how I model the same energy and Bubble space as the horse.**

corner of the arena. Now the horse is worried you will not look out for him, and the psychological Thresholds are tougher to cross (I go into more detail about this in the next chapter—see p. 227).

I am aware that IINN could initially come across as mechanical and strange, but once you "get it," the cycle will suddenly snap into place. It really is a breakdown of what is normally subconscious or instinctive. The good news is, the subconscious will take over again, once you get the rhythm of it. The best thing about body language is it likes to flow out naturally (fig. 5.8).

Bubble Quadrants: Mechanics of Horse Speak

The Bubble of Personal Space, which I introduced in chapter 1 (p. 69), is broken into four main Quadrants: Picture an imaginary line running from the horse's nose to his tail and another perpendicular to the first, across the horse where the Girth Button is. When horses are moving around each other, they are aware of what Quadrant they are using, and why. We, however, are usually *not* aware of this, and our potential points of influence in those quadrants (fig. 5.9).

5.9 Every move we make in one of the four Quadrants says something to the horse about space, and the horse says something back.

Using the Quadrants

Because of the horse's awareness of the Quadrants, the Greeting Ritual (Introduction) is key to beginning a good rapport with a horse. Move straight down the center line at the horse's head for a formal, first-time Greeting, using a Low-O to ask for a low-intensity connection. After this, you move all the way to one side Quadrant or the other to Negotiate hierarchy, using the three Buttons of the Cheek, Mid-Neck, and Shoulder (see p. 140 and figs. 5.10 A–D). An informal or affectionate Greeting happens inside one of the front Quadrants. Your angles of approach when working with a horse carry significance, depending upon the Quadrant you are using or influencing—this is why you need to know what position or angle you are taking and why (figs. 5.11 A & B).

Much more about maneuvering within the Quadrants is revealed ahead as we'll spend more time practicing some of the skills I've already introduced: Observation, Mirroring, Copycat, and the "My Space, Your Space" Conversation (p. 216).

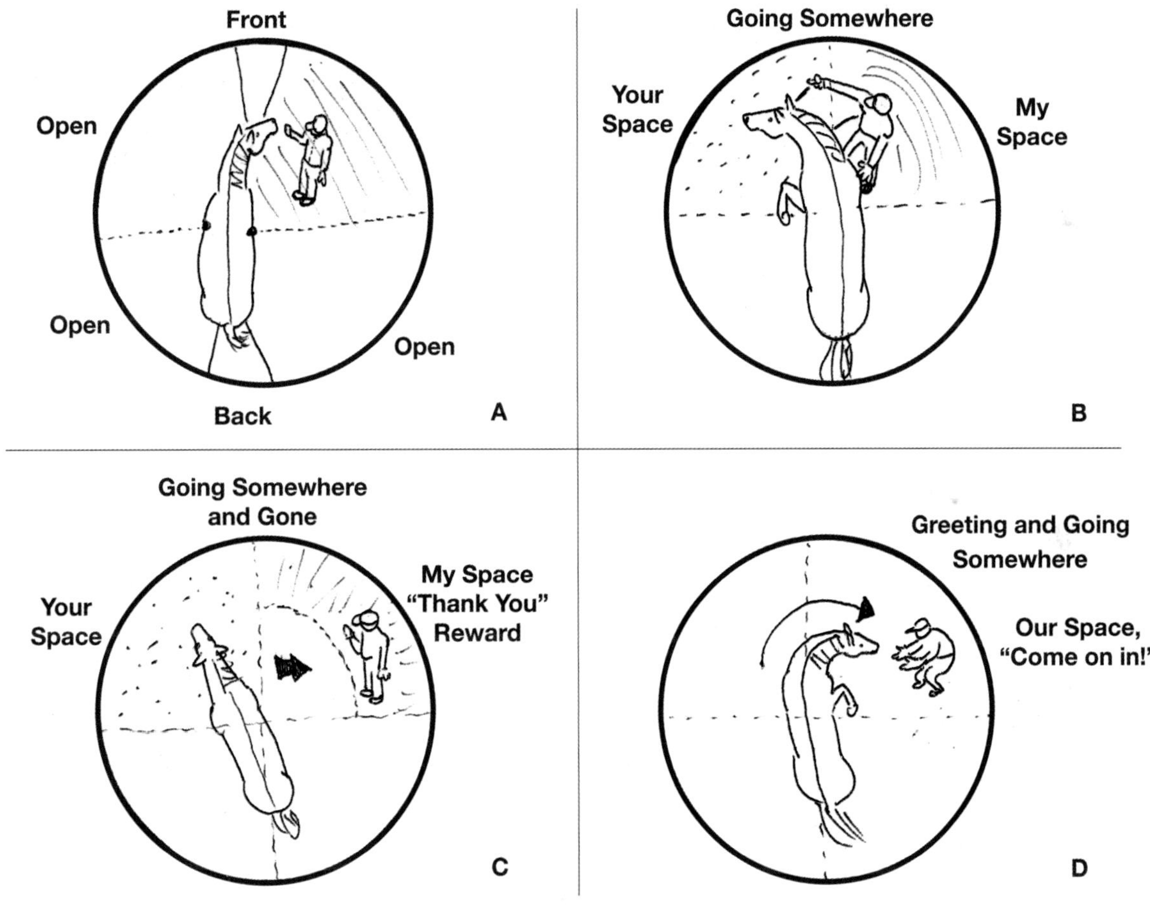

5.10 A–D Greeting a horse in the front and then moving to a side Quadrant sends a clear message, "I am occupying this Quadrant; you can have the other Quadrants" (A). Activating the Cheek, Neck, and Shoulder Buttons asks the horse to move into an open Quadrant (B). After you ask your horse to move to another Quadrant, taking a step backward sends the message, "Thank you," and is a reward (C). You can invite your horse back into your Quadrant by taking a step backward in O-posture (D).

5.11 These two horses Greet head-on with plenty of Bubble space.

Reviewing the Four Gs

We've already talked about the Four Gs as the circular form of horse communication. With the three main Energy Types and the Roles in the Herd in mind, every horse uses the Four Gs a little differently, but each of them still arrives at a deeper Zero, having gone through the cycle. You may ask, "Why or how exactly do the Four Gs help a horse feel more Zero?" The answer is simple: The Four Gs are a measurable and predictable interpretation of an otherwise strictly organic cycle, and the close of this cycle allows for a conclusion—a completion in a communication.

The primary gift of having learned the Four Gs and IINN is that, once you know them, you can help horses come to Zero, or a deeper Zero, when they need it. By providing this to your horse, he will see you as a benevolent leader and become emotionally and mentally "ready for the day" with you sooner and with more zest. In other words, your *presence* helps a horse focus and pay attention (finding that Green Zone of the Bell Curve—see p. 20), not your *techniques*.

Let's review the Four Gs very quickly:

- First, there is a *Greeting*, either formal or informal, as we've already discussed. It may be just be a Breath Message, or actually your knuckles touching the horse's muzzle (figs. 5.12 A & B).

- Next, you're *Going Somewhere*. Going Somewhere has three main actions:

  1 In many instances, the simple act of turning the head during a Quadrant discussion (see p. 207) is enough of a Going Somewhere communication (figs. 5.13 A & B). In these cases, it is more of an implied movement: "If we *were* to Go Somewhere, would you Mirror me? Would you follow me? Would you take direction? Or will you call the shots?"

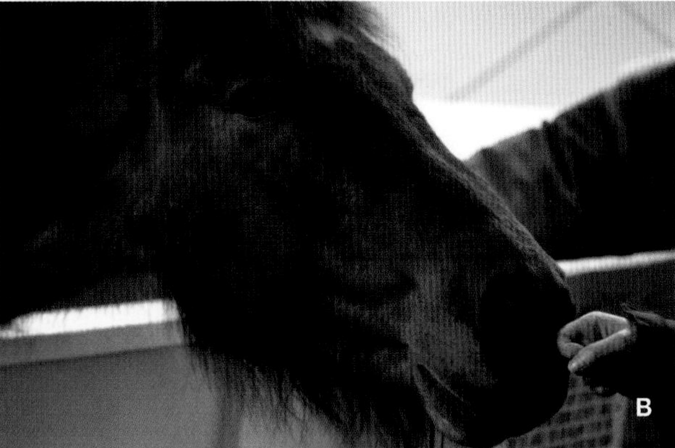

5.12 A & B The two horses in photo A demonstrate the Greeting Ritual in horses. They are nostril to nostril, breathing in each other's scent. When I Greet a horse, as I am in photo B, I aim for the Greeting Button first and foremost. Later, I may touch the horse's nostrils one at a time while breathing deeply.

5.13 A & B In photo A, the bay offers to lead by turning his head and gazing toward another area (the "idea" of Going Somewhere). The Cheek Button can be used to Activate away, or to draw and invite. When I first encounter the Cheek Button, I Activate the horse away, as I am in photo B. This is to set up the ground rules and boundaries before I welcome a horse into my personal space.

SKILL-BUILDER

Imagine the Four Gs in Human Terms

Let's consider the cycle of the Four Gs in human terms, to better illustrate:

You go to visit an old friend. When you arrive at her home, she opens the door and exclaims, "Hi! It's so nice to see you!" and you do as well, along with offering some sort of embrace. This is the *Greeting* Ritual. Your friend opens the door wide, beckoning you inside. You step into her house politely, without crowding her. This is the discussion of "My Space, Your Space"—you both agree to make space for each other and to respect that space (see more about this on p. 216).

Now, your friend escorts you to a chair and offers you a beverage. This is *Going Somewhere* to a Safety Object, as well as sharing resources. As you both settle in, she leans in and places her hand on your leg, saying in a hushed but excited voice, "Wait until you hear the latest gossip!" You are now Going Somewhere together in a deeper Conversation.

After you both explore your thoughts and opinions, a level of safety and trust arises. You suddenly feel compelled to open your arms and hug your friend, saying, "I just want you to know how much I love our get-togethers." This is a *Grooming Ritual*.

After sharing more smiles and affection, your friend offers another beverage and goes to the kitchen. You sit and look out the window, musing over your thoughts. This is a healthy *Gone*—a pause in the Conversation where you both can process. When she returns, you may say, "I have been thinking about what you said..." and this is a Check-In, which restarts the connection between you. Or you may say, "It's late. I really have to get going." This is the equivalent of a "tail swish," signaling your communication is complete.

Following this interaction, your friendship is renewed, comfortable, and enriched. You feel satisfied. You leave in a good mood and carry the feeling out into your day and the things you must do. This is finding *Inner Zero*.

The basis of the Four Gs is that there is a beginning, middle, and end to our Conversations with our horses. As I have said, it is a totally organic cycle—a natural process that I have simply broken into four parts so we can better understand and take advantage of it.

2 Going Somewhere can move down the Mid-Neck and Shoulder Buttons to include moving the horse's front feet forward, backward, left, or right. I may use this Conversation when preparing a horse to leave his stall, or if I am about to lead a horse and wish to check and make sure all our signals are working (figs. 5.14 A–C). This is more of a hierarchy discussion.

3 You may actually Go Somewhere together. When together in nature or during turnout, horses will take a walk, problem-solve the Chessboard, or begin to play during this phase of the cycle (figs. 5.15 A & B). When you can really Go Somewhere together, you are probably pretty comfortable with the horse and able to smoothly Greet him with either him yielding the Cheek Button or you asking ask for a *Horse Hug*. (During Greeting, the Cheek Button can either move away or toward you, depending on the needs of the relationship.) You can then begin Navigating the Chessboard—for example, walk to the cross-ties or move from paddock to stall.

MYTH-BUSTER

Should You Look into Your Horse's Eyes?

Horses use a lot of eye contact with each other because the eyes can convey silent messages, and prey animals use silent message as a survival tactic. However, we do not want to *stare* at our horses' eyes, because that can be intimidating. Instead, gaze softly with a fair amount of blinking. Horses appreciate the empathy that comes with pleasant eye contact.

- *Grooming* begins when Going Somewhere with the Buttons is complete. The horse has "talked about" whatever he needed to, and now it is time for a nap together, scratching the withers, or Rocking the Baby (see p. 137). This is where mutual shared connection can occur and a deeper Zero can be achieved (figs. 5.16 A & B). There can be contact or simply shared space. It is soft and warm and lovely. (Note that this is the best phase to begin bodywork.)

- The *Gone* phase has two main parts:

  1 This is the pause needed between messages to allow horses to "soak" on (process) what has been said, see what they think about it, and consider how they should respond (figs. 5.17 A & B). (We discussed this as part of the observation process, back on p. 113.) This pause should include you stepping out of the horse's Bubble of Personal Space for a moment to give him "breathing room." Nothing shuts Conversation down faster than crowding a horse.

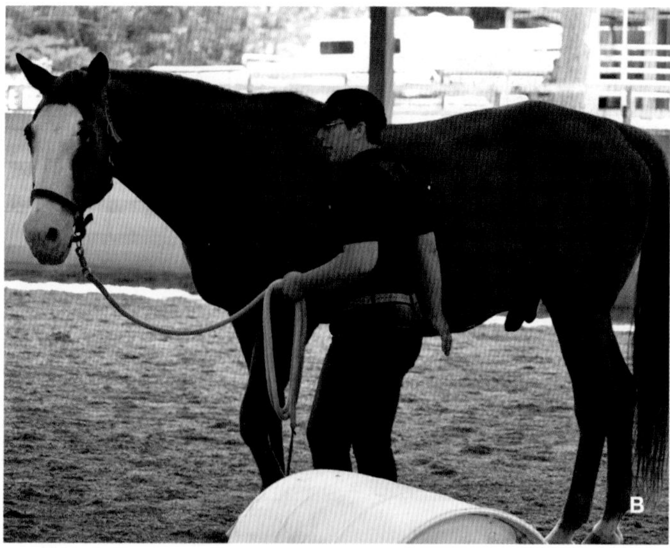

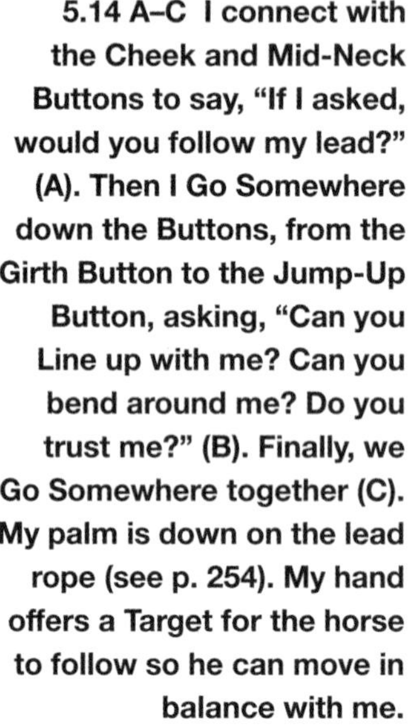

5.14 A–C I connect with the Cheek and Mid-Neck Buttons to say, "If I asked, would you follow my lead?" (A). Then I Go Somewhere down the Buttons, from the Girth Button to the Jump-Up Button, asking, "Can you Line up with me? Can you bend around me? Do you trust me?" (B). Finally, we Go Somewhere together (C). My palm is down on the lead rope (see p. 254). My hand offers a Target for the horse to follow so he can move in balance with me.

5.15 A & B Horses keep soft eye contact when they Go Somewhere together, as you can see in photo A. The pair's Greeting buttons are Targeting each other. Balance is essential in their movements for harmony to happen. Horses may decline to Go Somewhere together, which you can see in photo B. The black horse (a Joker) is asking, "Can we go over by that camera?" The white horse (a Teacher), looks at the black's Cheek Button to say, "You can go. I don't want to follow."

5.16 A & B The Grooming Ritual begins around the withers (A); however, it can include other Buttons. I Rock the Baby on Bridge of the Nose and Follow Me Buttons, for example (B).

5.17 A & B **When a horse begins to process, it can be a very meaningful part of the Gone phase (A). A horse in deep process goes inward to review his personal map of experiences (B).**

2. The second aspect of Gone is to actually be done with a Conversation. Often the horse signals this with one, sharp tail swish. You can offer the equivalent to the horse by moving your hand by your thigh in a quick flicking motion. Gone, either as a pause or statement that "I'm done for now," is *essential* in having a Conversation with a horse. Otherwise, it is a one-way monologue. After the Gone phase, there is a renewal demonstrated by a new Greeting (Check-In), and the cycle begins again.

The first time you formally review the Four Gs with a horse, it can take some time to go through it all, but after a while, you can complete the cycle in a few moments. Remember, the horse learned about the Four Gs with "Mom" in the first week of life. He knows this stuff—*it is you who is learning it*. You do not need to teach a horse this information unless for some reason you have a horse who is so immature and under-socialized that he has almost forgotten his own language. (I have seen this happen, and I can say they remember it with zest!)

Review the Skill-Builder on p. 210. The human friend in this exercise greets you with a big smile and a hug, but another friend may not be a hugger and could be quite shy. Still another may be to too high energy and you may find yourself trying to keep a piece of furniture between you in an attempt to not have your space invaded. Consider all these possibilities when you engage in a Conversation with your horse, and you will find a natural and comfortable way to settle into your daily Four Gs with him.

SKILL-BUILDER

How to Use the Horse Hug

It is not unusual to see one horse wrap his neck around another to express deep friendship. Not only is this a pleasant Conversation we can have with our horses, it can be helpful when preparing to Go Somewhere.

1 Begin the Horse Hug by standing with your back to the Shoulder Button on one side of the horse.

2 Reach one hand to the horse's cheek on the opposite side.

3 With your free hand, scratch under his jawbone, tickle his chin, or softly stroke under his throatlatch.

4 As you do this, encourage the horse to bring his head toward you and across your body with the hand that is on his cheek. Notice if he braces against your request. Don't put a lot of pressure on him but also don't quit easily.

5 Ask at least three times on each side. Don't be in a hurry. Just hang out with him, and when he does yield his face in your direction, even a little bit, release immediately and praise him.

6 When he wraps you in a full Horse Hug, reach up with your free hand and stroke his forehead at the Friendly Button at the base of the forelock. You are not training him to do a trick or forcing anything on him. You are just encouraging the horse to hear your request.

7 This can be an appropriate time to slide the halter or bridle on without stress.

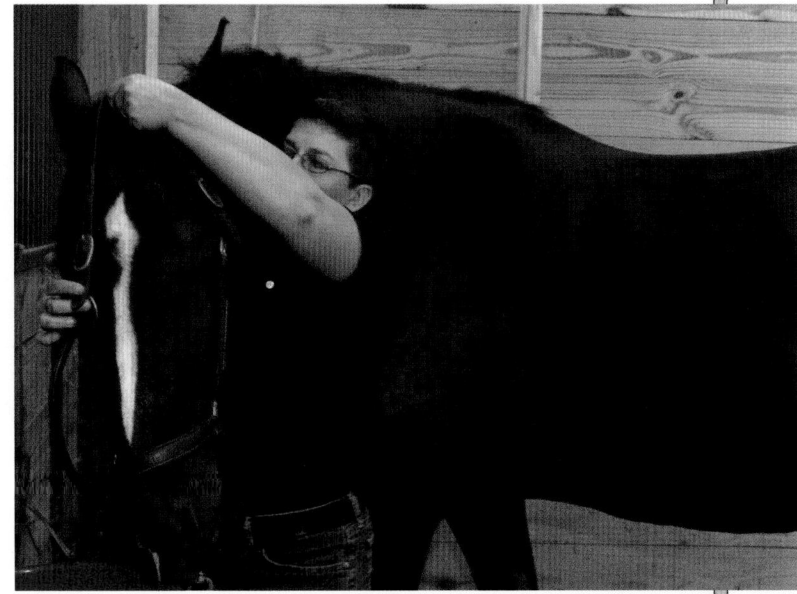

5.18 Using the Horse Hug can help us get tasks, such as haltering or bridling, done without stress. After inviting this horse's head and neck across my body with the Buttons, I slide the headstall on. Note both of our quiet, content expressions.

"My Space, Your Space": A Conversation About the Bubble

The Four Gs (and IINN) are important to negotiating the Quadrants and managing the Bubbles of Personal Space. To bring all the pieces we've learned in this chapter together, again consider the Greeting and asking to enter the horse's Bubble. What happens next is *"My Space, Your Space"*—one of the number-one rituals horses practice with each other (fig. 5.20). When we have this Conversation with our horses, it deals with the question of where the horse's head and neck should be, and where we should be in relation to his head and neck.

Here's how it works:

SKILL-BUILDER

Learning to See the Four Gs in Action

Confused about witnessing the Four Gs in horses? Don't be! They have quiet and prolonged Conversations over meals. When horses eat hay out of the same pile, many Conversations take place. So watching horses eat together is probably the easiest access you have to learning how to see this cycle for yourself.

Spend some time just watching two or more horses eat from one pile of hay. Watch their subtle movements and try to identify which phase of the Four Gs is in play. (I advise observing *after* the initial normal scuffle for best position is over as this is usually fast-paced and too difficult to follow, at first.)

5.19 Watching horses communicate while eating hay together is one of the best ways to learn the nuances of their language. Everything thing they do means something.

5.20 These two horses are having the "My Space, Your Space" Conversation about the front Quadrants of their Bubbles. How much space will each allow, and will each respect the other's space? We can see that the Haflinger is higher in the hierarchy because he is more balanced (standing squarely). The pony on the left is insecure (his legs are all askew).

- A Low-O Greeting is important to tell the horse, "I want to connect, but I want to keep it Zero." This is where a good Initiation phase (preparing to introduce yourself to the horse) will have hopefully created two things:

  1 You gave the horse a lot of signals that you want to make sure that there are no bees, bears, or boogeymen in the area so that it is *safe to get connected and say, "Hello."* This gains his interest.

  2 You and he have positioned yourselves to the front of his Bubble, on the center line of the two front Quadrants, where his Greeting Button is. He may even saunter over to Greet you.

- The very next thing in "My Space, Your Space" is a Going Somewhere Conversation to practice hierarchy. The Greeting Ritual lets the Bubbles "touch" (your knuckles touch the horse's muzzle). Now step to one side of the horse's head or the other to claim a Quadrant and begin the hierarchy discussion. Basically, it's a simple act saying, "I can have *this* Quadrant (my space) and you can yield your head into the *other* (your space)."
- You can do this in four ways with regard to the horse's Cheek Button:

  1 Tilt your own head away (what I call a "Mutual Salute").

  2 Aim your pointer finger at the Button (requesting distance respect).

  3 Physically touch the Button (asking for close-contact respect).

  4 Put your Hold Hand up in the air near the Cheek Button. This requires a little feel.

- Every horse is different and you may be an X person who has a big energy or an O person who tends to be very soft. Some horses are fine with us standing

SKILL-BUILDER

Learning to Pause

We talked about learning to recognize when a horse is "in process" back on p. 113. Allowing significant time for horses to pause and accepting when horses need to be "done" for a moment is vital to training. This alone can help alleviate a lot of the "acting out" we see in horses. A horse who feels overstimulated, rushed, emotionally congested, scared, frustrated, or confused is not going to feel better unless you give him a minute to take a breath.

Practice following this rule: Try something with your horse, walk away (or move to the end of the lead rope) after doing a tail swish (a flick of your hand by your thigh) to say, "Let's pause." This puts you outside the horse's Bubble (even if you are still connected by the lead rope). Another option is to take your horse to his favorite spot or Safety Object in the arena, then stand on the other side of it for a minute. In all three scenarios, you are creating a way for both of you to have a timeout. This is the best way to ensure a horse is able to stay in the Green Zone and learn the lessons you are trying to teach. It also helps keep you at your Zero because you have a chance to rest and reflect as well.

close, and some are not. Some people need to feel more space, and some do not. Both you and the horse need to sort this out. You need to experiment with the type of person you are and the type of horse you have. Energy Type plays a big role here: Some horses are so Hesitant that merely tilting your head induces them to turn their own heads away as they say, "Yup, I get it. You have my total respect. I won't pop your Bubble if you don't pop mine." Outgoing horses, on the other hand, often like connection and may not want you to send them away. When that's the case, inviting them into your space might be a more important message. Other Outgoing horses may need 200 touches on the Cheek Button because they are green or young or very confused or emotionally stunted. This type of Outgoing horse who is often invading your space—or the Stoic horse who tries to take over, or a Hesitant horse who panics and slams into you—needs you to move down the Buttons and include the Mid-Neck and Shoulder Buttons in the "My Space, Your Space" Conversation (one hand stays at the Cheek Button while the other aims the pointer finger at the Mid-Neck and then Shoulder). Remember, you are clarifying space in the Quadrant by asking, "Where should your head and neck be for comfort and mutual respect, and where should my body be for the same reason?"

- A really pushy or very confused horse needs to be told *to move his feet and yield the whole front Quadrant of the bubble either left or right*. When a horse is easily frustrated by the Conversation using the Cheek and Mid-Neck Buttons, move on and talk to the Shoulder Button and his front feet with the goal of setting boundaries but not adding stress. When "My Space, Your Space" includes the horse's feet, I like to call it "Stay in Your Lane," because I have encountered so many situations where either the horse or the handler is "wiggly" while walking. You not only want

SKILL-BUILDER

Having a Good Gone Phase

When you ask your horse for space and then remain in place and essentially crowd him, you are not setting a good example. On the other hand, a troubled horse may bounce back into your Bubble too soon or because he thinks your neutral posture is an O and you are calling him back. When this is the case, keep your Hold Hand in the air on the edge of the Bubble until the horse knows where the edge is, consistently, and knows how to maintain it with good manners. Do not assume your horse "knows what he should be doing" and then think, "He is just being a jerk." Help him know better *for real*, and he'll usually act better, too.

to keep the horse's head and neck in position, you want his feet to walk in a straight line as well. Leave your X posture active with your Hold Hand in the air to define that 6-Inch Rule I've talked about before, keeping the same amount of space between your bodies at all times (think of the double line on the road between lanes).

- Because you are claiming a Quadrant of the Bubble and asking the horse to "Stay in His Lane," it's important to be clear about also *inviting him into your space for connection and affection.* Be sure to also use O posture to beckon your horse to you when appropriate.

5.21 Good manners begin with us. When we can politely ask the horse for space, then he realizes he can politely ask for space when he needs it, too. This helps him to not feel that he has to drive us away when he becomes overwhelmed.

- When this has been completed, step outside the horse's Bubble and *give him his quadrant back*. This models good Bubble etiquette for the two front Quadrants where his head is. If the horse is intrigued and wants to follow you when you step outside his Bubble, then he may want to actually Go Somewhere with you. Take the hint and go for a walk around the Chessboard.

Don't be wishy-washy about "My Space, Your Space." Be clear when you ask your horse to "Stay in Your Lane," and be clear when you invite him to come closer or stay with you for Grooming. Affection and comfort are important values to both our species, but there needs to be healthy boundaries. Affection is only good if you can also say, "That's enough," when you are done with it, and it needs to be just as comfortable to stop as it would be to keep giving and receiving. *And the same is true for the horse*. When a horse can politely request space or comfort from you, then he does not need to impolitely drive you away or crowd you (fig. 5.21).

6 Starting the Conversation Outside the Box

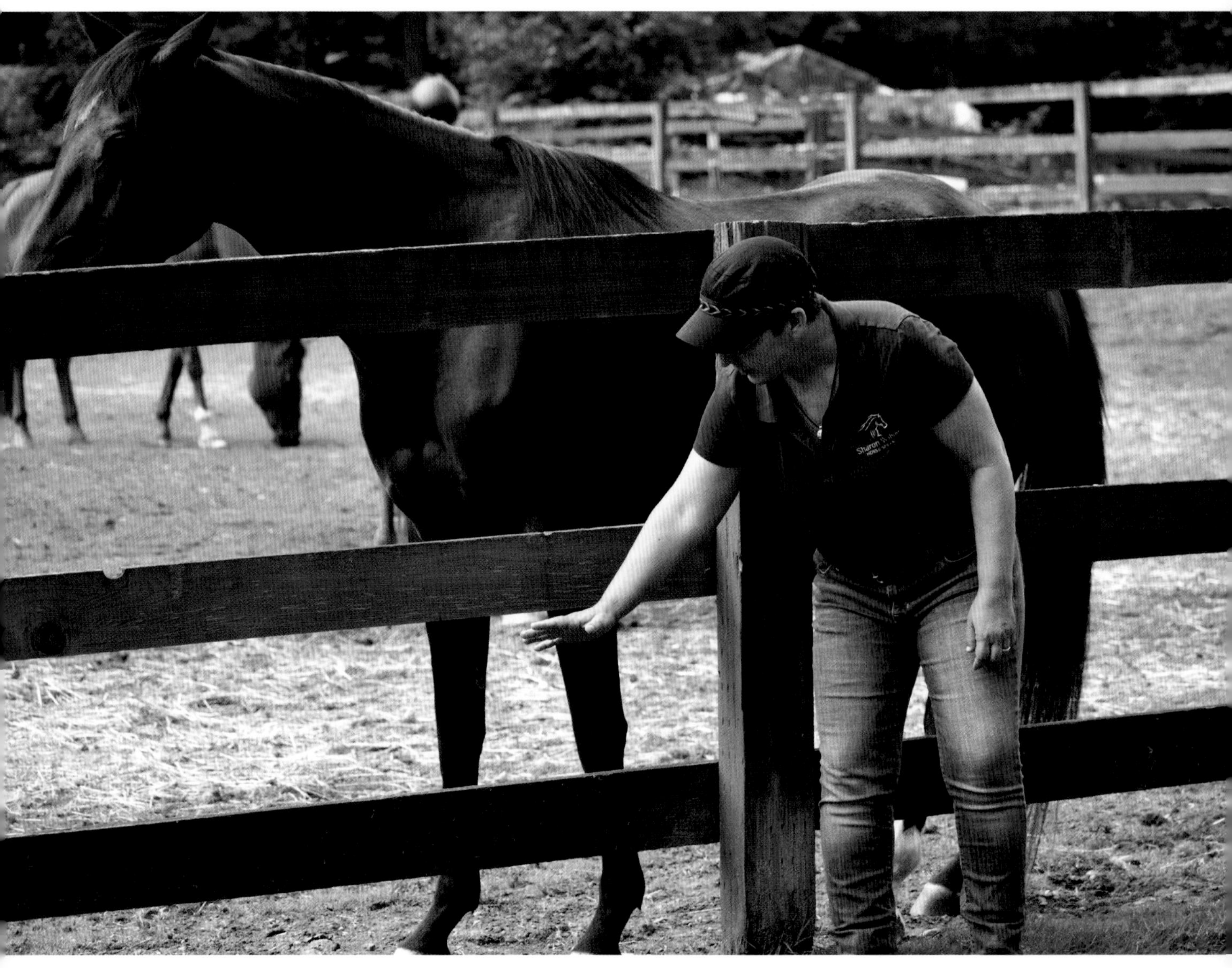

Horses are always watching. They are aware of the smallest details of their environment, and they are aware of what your body language is saying as you approach them. Every second you are near a horse is an opportunity for communicating. The fact is you have the potential to inspire your horse *to want to be with you*. You can achieve a *powerful end result*, within a reasonable amount of time, without raising any dust at all. Unless you're an "action junkie," why wouldn't you be interested in a fast-acting, high-potency, maximum impact with minimal effort strategy?

As we've explored in this book, Horse Speak offers us the possibility of beginning a Conversation from a place of introduction and then continuing with negotiations at a slow, steady pace that is mutually beneficial.

I was taught that you have to go get your horse, then get to the arena or round pen, and *then* the work begins. Now that I know Horse Speak, I can achieve amazing connection or work on resolving a horse's issues *without needing to touch him*. I know this may seem outlandish or overwhelming at first, but the power of being able to communicate from a distance means that horses begin talking to you the moment they see you—once they understand that you can, in fact, talk to them in their language. You do not need to do anything special to get and keep your horse's attention—you are interesting because you can talk!

I mentioned earlier in this book that talking over a barrier helps reduce risk and gives you an opportunity for better risk assessment. When we put a halter and lead rope on a horse, and *only then* begin to realize what the horse is feeling or thinking, we are stuck with dealing with whatever the situation might be in a way that might not be safe. Communicating first over a barrier—a fence line or stall door, for example—allows us time to find our Zero, and offer this to the horse as well (fig. 6.1).

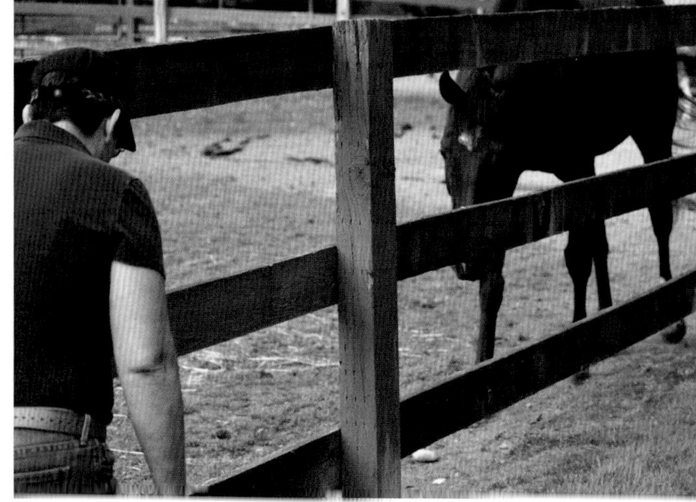

6.1 You can start your Conversation with a horse over a fence. One of the most fascinating things about Horse Speak is you do not have to touch a horse to talk with him.

When your horse lives in a large pasture and a smaller enclosure isn't available, the same effect can be accomplished by determining a set distance that is close enough for you to see each other, but not so close that your presence demands that the horse interact. Place a Safety Object in the field to use as a psychological barrier between you both. You can even lean on it to signal you want to have a calm safe place where you can begin a Conversation.

Introducing the Figure-Eight Hold Hand

There are a number of things we can do to prepare our horses to be with us. One is to offer enrichment, which I first touched upon in chapter 1 (p. 81). Luckily, there is a very simple but potentially powerful way to offer enrichment to your horse, and you can do it from over the fence or outside the stall. It is called the *Figure-Eight Hold Hand*. I stumbled upon this when observing elder Mentor horses who ambled around horse rescues, making stops by the paddocks that housed troubled horses. The Mentors would adopt certain "Hold" postures, and the horses on the other side of the fence would become calm.

How to Do the Figure-Eight Hold Hand

As you prepare to move around the world with your horse, offering Figure-Eight Hold Hand is one of the best ways to Check-In with the horse's entire body *first* (fig. 6.2). It is important to be aware of your Core Energy during this practice. You do not want to accidently drive your horse; you are offering a gentle gesture to say, "I see you; I see all of you."

6.2 Stand in one place on the other side of a barrier and imagine your palm can "see" every Button. Move your hand from one Button to the next, and then swoop back again, making a sort of figure-eight pattern. This is saying to the horse, "I see you."

1 Stand by the horse's shoulder and aim your palm at the Cheek Button.

2 In one fluid motion, move the palm to the horse's Mid-Neck Button, then the Shoulder Button, the Back-Up Button, the Girth Button, the Jump-Up Button, the Yield-Over Button, and finally, the Hip Button and Sit Button (figs. 6.3 A–D). You may want to linger at either the Hip or Sit Buttons, depending on which message your horse seems to prefer at that moment.

3 Swoop back toward the front again, passing over the Grooming Button at the withers, Follow Me, and Friendly. Just aim for the general area each Button is in, and linger a moment. If you notice that the horse turns to aim a certain Button to your hand, or he "twiggles" (twitch-wiggles) his skin when you breeze by a Button, he is drawing your attention to something specific.

4 When you complete the figure-eight pattern, sigh out loud and relax your hand. Notice how you feel. See what happens with your horse. Look for a subtle wiggle of flesh or a breath in or out. Look for tension or release. You may see many things, or nothing at all—but the horse *will* respond in some way. Allow him to have a moment to process (take that all-important step out of the front Quadrant of his Bubble that we discussed in chapter 5—p. 207), and then move to his other side and repeat the process. (In fact, many horses will yield their heads and necks away following Figure-Eight Hold Hand, which indicates they want you to switch sides.)

5 After doing both sides, the horse may go into a deep reverie, disappearing into his own world. This is particularly good. It means he feels "heard" and will now feel safe to release any "unfinished business." A horse who is processing like this is using the Gone phase to pause and recapitulate his experience. You will see him pass the information all the way through his body—each Button needs to "feel" the information. If he gets "stuck" in a Button, offer a breath or Hold Hand in that area, or stretch in some way, like nodding your head or touching your toes. Once the horse has passed the information all the way from his head to his hind end, he will experience some movement in the tail or pelvis, often followed by coming out of the reverie and wanting to move. Pay close attention to this processing. Note that at this moment a horse who has an undiscovered source of discomfort, such as ulcers, tooth pain, or hoof pain may try to display the hurting body part to you. I have found that once emotional release is provided by the Figure-Eight Hold Hand, many horses try to get help for their physical problems.

6.3 A–D **Figure-Eight Hold Hand, sweeping over the Buttons—very close to the horse, but not touching (A). This mare suggests that the Buddy-Up message at her Grooming Button is her "sweet spot" where her handler should linger (B), and notice the change in her eye as she processes (C). She seems to need her handler as her compassionate witness. Once she "shakes it off" after processing, the mare welcomes some soft touching at the Grooming Button (D).**

Horses don't want to hang on to old baggage. They want Zero. When you learn how to help them process, as well as add enrichment to their lives with Conversations like Figure-Eight Hold Hand, they begin to blossom into the best versions of themselves.

Enrichment on the Chessboard: Movement and Navigation

In chapter 2 I introduced the horse's surroundings as a Chessboard, with all his movements strategically related to the elements on the board with him at any one time (see p. 89). We learned to observe certain aspects of life on a Chessboard to help us better appreciate a horse's choices and behavior. Now, with the skills we've built between chapter 2 and now, let's consider how we can move and navigate with our horses in a way that is conscious of the rules of the game.

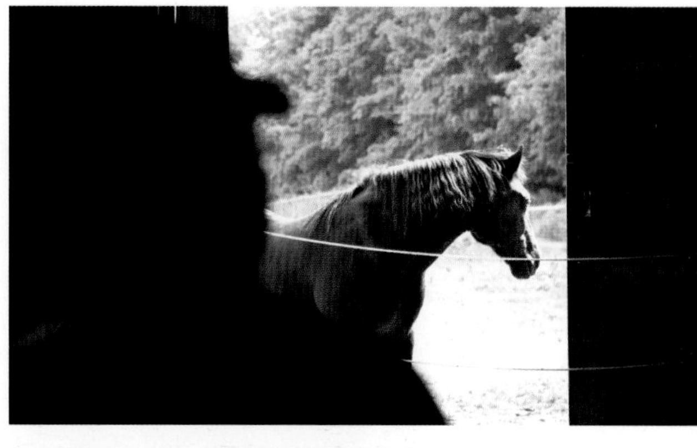

6.4 **For horses, the Threshold of the barn door is both physical and psychological. The light changes dramatically from outside to inside, and their eyes need several minutes to adjust. This can cause them to become very worried because if they cannot see that well, they are vulnerable to predators. Their instinct forbids them from ever letting go of the fact that they are prey animals.**

Thresholds: Physical and Psychological

For horses, a Threshold is the point or level at which something begins or changes (fig. 6.4). *Physical Thresholds*—tree lines, riverbeds, caves—pose potential danger simply because, in nature, this is where predators lurk.

Psychological Thresholds represent levels of requests you may ask of a horse—a mental Threshold is confronted whenever the horse feels he is reaching a deeper layer of having to trust in your judgement or overcome old conditioning that may have forced him

SKILL-BUILDER

Recognizing When Figure-Eight Hold Hand Goes Deep

When the Figure-Eight Hold Hand gives a horse the space to process, he may go into his own inner world. He may flutter his eyes, shiver, shake, tremble, and even occasionally lie down. For some horses, this message is very, very deep and important. I have witnessed a few dozen horses seem to go through what looked like a "trauma release" due to the level and severity of shaking they experienced. I have even seen horses appear to "pass out," and when they rose again to their feet, some needed to be escorted back to their stalls or paddocks to have a "timeout." However, within the same day, each and every horse who displayed this level of release appeared truly transformed afterward. Many had bright, happy expressions; some whinnied when we came back to check on them; some ran to their owners with pricked ears. These transformations were dramatic and each one was inspired from simply doing the Figure-Eight Hold Hand to say, "I see you."

It is important to understand that horses who slip into this kind of deep process are not necessarily dealing with some sort of trauma. I've seen plenty of plain old "lesson horses" slip into a deep process and come back a few minutes later, acting friendly and happy. Note: I do feel that when a horse experiences deep process it is wise to let him have the rest of the day off to completely unwind and reap the benefits of the release. You will find him refreshed and ready to engage tomorrow.

6.5 Laura pauses as she introduces the brush because it is a Psychological Threshold for this horse.

into things. For example, your horse may be okay walking and trotting under saddle, but cantering creates panic. When you ask your horse for something and he pauses and maybe looks like there is a boogeyman, he is saying there is a Psychological Threshold that makes him nervous.

In cases of trauma, horses may rapidly escalate to acting out when they hit a mental Threshold. Reading the signs of, "I need a minute," is essential in avoiding a meltdown. Pausing until the horse is ready is the safest and surest way to allow him to get ready to "jump into the pool." Think of how you may want to jump into a pool on a hot day, but you also know how the shock of cold water will feel, so you have to psyche yourself up a bit to do it. This is similar to a horse facing a Psychological Threshold related to something you are asking of him (fig. 6.5).

Practice Thresholds

By setting up controlled Thresholds, you can work with a particular horse's concerns, fears, or confusions. The Threshold represents a change of the Chessboard. By designing patterns and courses to work through with your horse, you can help allay his

SKILL-BUILDER

Thresholds and "Blowing Away the Boogeyman"

A horse will blow or snort forcefully at something in the environment that is of concern. As you learned in earlier chapters, you can calm him by Mirroring this short, forceful breath out with what I call Sentry Breath or "blowing away the boogeyman." When you answer a horse that is confronting a Physical or Psychological Threshold with a Sentry Breath, you are literally suggesting that your horse take a minute and get ready. You are saying, "I get it. I see your *internal boogeyman* right now. I also believe in you and think you will be safe doing what I ask." Use Sentry Breath consistently until it becomes a habit. Here's how:

1. Mirror the horse by holding your head up, looking in the direction he is.
2. Blow out audibly and forcefully, as if you are blowing out many birthday candles on a cake.
3. Give the "All's clear!" message by aiming your palm down (which says "Calm down") and breathing a soft sigh out. You can add other signals, like licking and chewing or blinking, or swish your "tail" (your hand by your thigh) to say, "We are all done with that boogeyman now."

Most horses are grateful when you blow Sentry Breath. They begin to trust you more and more, and will have fewer boogeymen. However, if you have a young green horse, a Joker, or an Outgoing Energy Type, you may find your horse trying to turn this into a game, like "The Boy Who Cried Wolf." If this happens, use your "tail swish" and then redirect the horse's focus onto something else. I also sometimes find that touching the Follow Me Button can help Hesitant horses trust you more when it seems that they are on constant alert, regardless of you being their Sentry. In this case, you may need to create more Safety Objects.

6.6 A & B Sometimes horses need you to protect their front *and* have their back. I put a Hold Hand toward what's behind this mare (A), then "blow away the boogeyman" with her (B). She needed both messages, at the back and the front, to really trust me.

6.7 A & B Thresholds are psychological and physical barriers between one Chessboard and another. Take time to make sure your horse is with you at every Threshold. Here, I look for the boogeyman down the aisle with him (A). My O posture, palm down on the lead rope, and the focus of my Core Energy help him Navigate the Threshold (B).

concerns about changing environments and prove to him that you will always watch for boogeymen at Thresholds (figs. 6.7 A & B).

Working with Physical Thresholds in this way can help a horse with his Psychological Thresholds, as well. On simple terms, this can mean that lingering at the "scary gate" while the horse is in hand, and going in and out of it several times in a row, can also help the horse under saddle, simply because you are instilling a good work ethic. The key is to construct a safe, controlled environment, talk to the horse's Buttons, and always have in mind the horse's values, Energy Type, and Role in the Herd. Manage your intensity levels wisely by demonstrating your X and O postures as needed, and use the Hold Hand to send soothing and supportive messagesfor example, Hold Hand to Hip Button ("I've got your back") or Hold Hand to Follow Me ("Relax and come forward").

Managing Your Core Energy and Thresholds

Pay close attention to your Core Energy when working with a horse's Thresholds. Even a Stoic horse is sensitive to your Core Energy. Sometimes when it seems like you're getting a strange response from a horse, the answer is simply that your Core Energy is angled slightly at him or too close to him. There are some horses who are so sensitive to this that they are very perceptive to you having "opened" or "shut the door," by accidently aiming your Core Energy into their path of movement. Imagine that there's a flashlight attached to your belly button—the path of imaginary light can help you understand what your horse is feeling. (I have known more than one person

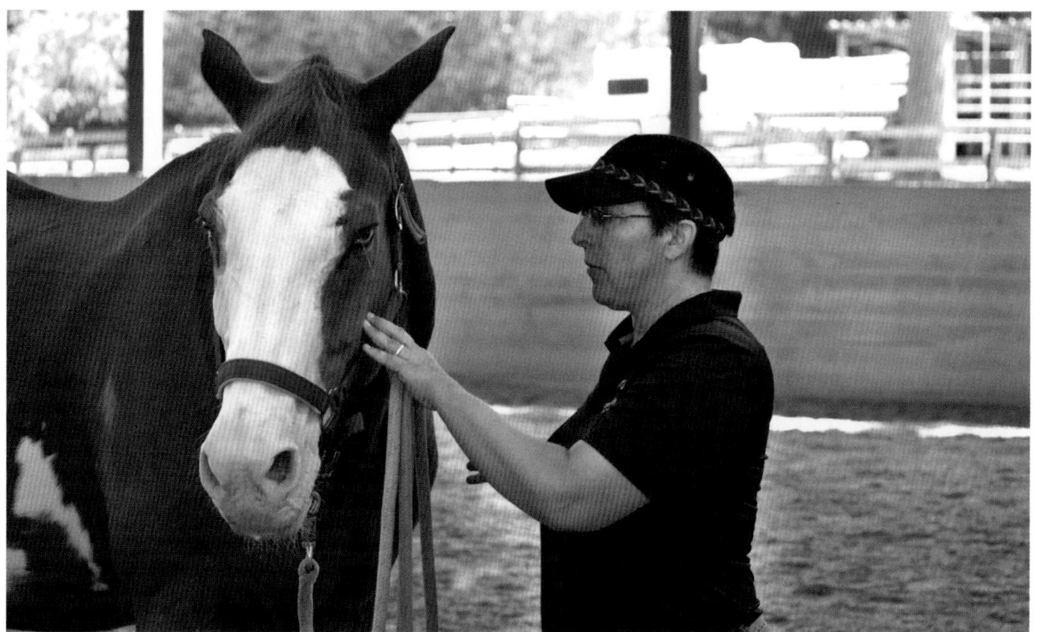

6.8 When talking to the Buttons, your Core Energy plays a role in the level of intensity or "believability" of your message. As I Activate the Cheek Button here, you can see how I have focused my Core Energy in the direction I wish the horse to yield his head.

who attached a small flashlight to their belt buckle... and found it quite illuminating!)

My goal with Horse Speak is to be able to move around the world with my horse paying attention to my subtle gestures, postures, and signals. There are moments, especially when working with Thresholds, when you may need to increase the intensity for a second and then go back to Zero. You can increase your X by adding your feet to it. A stomp, or a clear, solid step into the horse's Bubble "ups the ante." You can also add a strong out-breath, like martial artists use in their practice. All these messages together are "louder" than just making your hands or posture more dramatic. In some cases, adding a stick or even a stick with a bag on it, makes it easier for an O person to find her X, or for an Outgoing or Stoic horse to believe your X.

Practice moving around your horse while conscious of your Core Energy, its source, where it is aiming, and its intensity level (fig. 6.8).

Out the Stall Door and Through the Gate

The easiest way I have found to work out worries about Thresholds with a horse is to use the stall door as an impactful opportunity to practice moving across a Threshold *together.* I use X, O, Core Energy, Matching Steps, Fun with Feet, and clear gestures to contain the horse's forward and backward movement until he can come out of (or go back into) the stall with more Zero. When you do not have a stall, then a gate of any kind can serve the same function as a part of the Chessboard to be managed: Practice opening and closing the gate in hand, moving through it at Zero. So often I see people allowing horses to rush out of their stalls or through gates, just being mindless about it. I look at every door and gate and see *hundreds* of potential Conversations I can have with my horse, and useful skill-building opportunities for both of us.

In working the Chessboard in this way, there are a few general "rules" that horses use that will help you have a successful Conversation when using the stall or gate as a practice Threshold:

1. *Secure the Environment*: The leader sniffs the perimeter to test for safety or danger (remember you are looking for bees and gopher holes). The follower horses sniff second, if at all. This means you must touch the walls of the stall, the gate, and the fence line first.

2. *Scan the Horizon*: The leader will stand still, and stare off into the distance, demonstrating watchfulness.

3. *Sentry Breath*: If there is any lurking risk, blow one single, strong, outward breath. (This can vary from fairly quiet to very loud.)

4. *Create Safety Objects*: Make a Safety Object by relaxing at a specific item, such as a post, rock, tree, or even the mounting block will do. You are saying, "This is a nice place to rest, you are safe here."

5. *Problem-Solve the Chessboard*: Once all is established as secure, you can begin to work out the angles, corners, and any weird objects that are on the Chessboard. When you watch horses doing this, frequently they will spend time getting "stuck" in corners or knocking things over. This step determines how horses Navigate around not only the Chessboard, but each other. Thus, both Negotiation and Navigation are actively taking place (see p. 89).

As we already discussed, using the stall as a micro-space to begin really good communication is very effective (see p. 233). It can give you the ability to start your day with your horse in a much better state, having already worked through a whole cadre of protocols that set the horse up to be happy and invested in the activities you want to do with him. Not only that, but you can arrive at this "happy place" in a matter of minutes. Even if a horse does not like confinement and wants to get out of his stall in a hurry, or if he seems distracted or even grumpy, you still can arm yourself with a host of useful information that can help you alleviate some of his anxiety and frustration and get in line with you.

What you have learned in this book about finding Zero (p. 41), using your observation skills (p. 70), and using the IINN protocols to see what side of the stall the horse woke up on this morning (p. 197), prepares you to spend time together in a positive, "ready to go" state of mind. The key to remember is that the way you approach a horse in a stall can mean the difference between starting the day with the horse distracted, defensive, or tuned out, or with the two of you integrated with each other and emotionally ready to take on the tasks at hand. Review the Skill-Builder on p. 203, and then consider these tips for Navigating the Threshold of your horse's stall:

1 Begin with Initiation. Some horses can become stressed or pushy when you enter their stalls. When this is the case, check for "bees, bears, and boogeymen" outside the stall in the aisle first. Initiate entering the stall by opening and shutting the door three times before you step inside. (I find this little *Rule of Three* ritual can alleviate stress in the horse before you enter. It seems to give him a chance to prepare better.)

MYTH-BUSTER

Is Horse Play Just About Playing?

When horses begin problem-solving the Chessboard, Negotiation and Navigation can erupt into high-spirited play, with spinning, bucking, rolling, and running. Horses "playing" always symbolizes displays of protection, power, and prowess. The act of play for a prey animal includes the thought, "How do we get out of here?" as well as, "Where is the spookiest corner? And where is the safest one?"

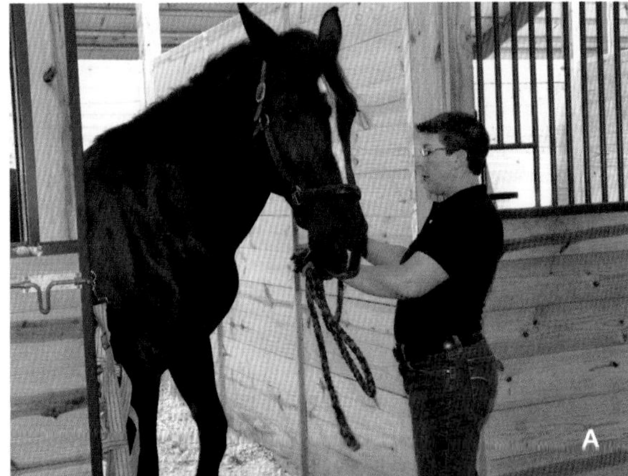

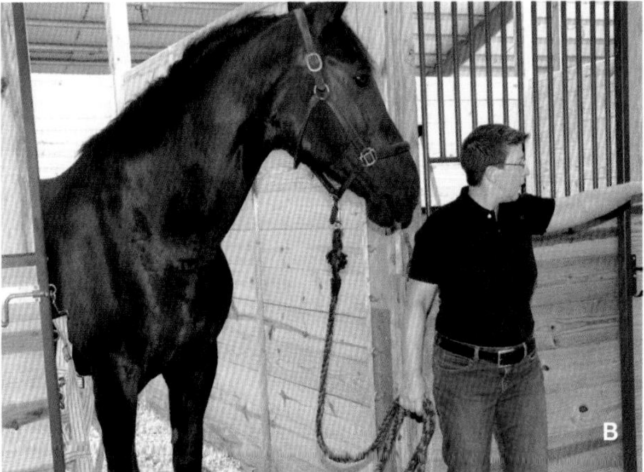

6.9 A & B Use your X and your Core Energy at the stall door to prevent rushing across the Threshold (A). When you are ready to go forward, take a big breath. You will notice a difference. Anytime your horse worries about the boogeyman at a Threshold, deal with it *before* trying to Go Somewhere (B). Look in that direction and blow a Sentry Breath.

2 When you are in your horse's stall, try to move around the edge of his Bubble without popping it, even though it's a very small space. This might mean that you simply touch the walls around the edge of the stall, or go in and touch the other objects in the stall and walk out again. This gives the horse a reassuring message by saying, "I want to move calmly around you before I touch you." (I again recommend that you repeat this three times in a row.)

3 Next begin the Introduction stage. Start with a Check-In over the stall door, if possible.

4 Perform a Greeting or Check-In inside the stall *before* moving to put the horse's halter on.

5 Negotiate how you would like to Go Somewhere by moving forward, backward, left, or right. This could be as simple as one step in each direction. Practice using all your body parts: feet, Core Energy, hands, breath, and eyes (softly blink at your horse's eyes saying, "Isn't this fun?").

6 Now Navigate the Threshold of the stall door. Open the door but don't go out yet. Do Fun with Feet (see p. 61) approaching the Threshold, stepping one foot over, then stepping it back, then left, and then right. Make it more about Fun with Feet at the Threshold than it is about getting out of the stall.

BUZZWORDS

Rule of Three

I find that horses learn about the world around them in processes of three or more. You have to do "three times three times three" in order for them to have a total understanding that a particular activity is the same no matter where you are or when you do it. Use the Rule of Three with all aspects of your education of the horse and for determining when to introduce the next level of lessons. For example, if you go to three new places and have three good experiences in each new place, you will round a corner in "generalizing" the horse's learning curve.

Horses learn in a "site specific" manner. They don't tend to "generalize" learning until the same information holds true in a variety of settings. This is why so many people say, "But…he is so good in the riding ring, why does he lose it on the trail?" and "She is so good on the trails back home, why is she losing it when I try to take her camping?" If you keep the Rule of Three in the back of your mind, it will help you ensure you have provided enough of these so your horse will be more well-rounded.

When I ran a therapeutic riding program, I had staff, students, and volunteers practice this stall Threshold routine in the first week of a new session. Not only did the horses calm down, but they also began to positively Greet anyone who came into the barn. By the end of week two, we no longer needed to go through the whole routine because a new level of awareness was instilled in human and horse alike. Everyone felt happier and more confident about getting horses out of their stalls, and all noticed that it set them up to have a much better day with the horses all around.

Common Movement Patterns of the Chessboard

One of the ways one horse moves around another horse's Bubble when Negotiating the Chessboard is what I call *Reverse Round Pen*. You will sometimes see a horse make a circle all the way around another horse (figs. 6.10 A & B). I have even watched a

6.10 A & B The lead horse (the chestnut Paint) walks all the way around the black-and-white herdmate to "gather and protect" him. I call this Reverse Round Pen.

6.11 After a Drive-By, the chestnut tells the entire herd to relax now. It's time to take a break.

horse do this while maintaining contact with the other horse's body the whole time.

There are a variety of different messages within this body language, but they all aim at a similar thing: It is a way for one horse to take the other horse into account, in his entirety. I have seen leaders do this to followers and followers do this to leaders and believe it is less a statement of hierarchy as it is a show of good faith from one horse to another. It is like saying, "I see all of you." The reasons leading up to this display vary widely, but usually the motivation is some sort of deeper connection or desire to really impress upon the horse, "I am really into you."

A related movement is what I call a *Drive-By* (fig. 6.11). This happens when one horse walks determinedly by another, then halts just outside that horse's Bubble, seemingly displaying all his Buttons. The horse who halts

SKILL-BUILDER

Standing Still

Simply staying still is a great way to encourage a horse to bring you one, or all, of his Buttons. I have witnessed a horse bring each and every Button to a quietly still person, starting with the Greeting Button and working the way down the body, even turning around and repeating the process on the other side. Practicing remaining still and waiting for a Button teaches you to trust that the horse is, in fact, talking to you, and makes you more aware of the process of equine communication and how you can begin to understand it.

is usually in a Hold position or in an Aw-Shucks with his nose down—Hold position is a signal for thinking things over or waiting patiently, and Aw-Shucks is a signal of reduced intensity that removes any pressure.

How We Can Use Reverse Round and Drive-By

Either a Drive-By or a Reverse Round Pen are useful for us to both regard and display. When a horse makes a full circle around you or walks determinedly by you and pauses outside your Bubble, in either case, it seems to represent the same sort of idea: "I want to talk to you, I am 'into' you, and here are all of my Buttons on display." If you remain still and have a palm up in Hold Hand position, the horse may then offer you one Button at a time to "talk to."

For our purposes, Reverse Round Pen is a great way to practice communication with your Horse (fig. 6.12). When you can put your Hold Hand in the air and walk all the way around a horse's Bubble without disturbing him, then you have "skated the edge of the horse's Bubble." This is terrific practice for developing trust and rapport, as well as learning which of your horse's Buttons are touchy and which are relaxed. If you can, try it while walking through a herd of horses in a pasture: Two Hold Hands up with the Reverse Round Pen or Drive-By means you are open and aware of everyone's Bubbles and Buttons, *but* you do not want contact, or to pop Bubbles, or to have any horse

6.12 I use Reverse Round Pen to say, "You stay there; I will Secure the Environment and walk all the way around you."

6.13 I walk around inside these horses' turnout with both Hold Hands out. This is a message of My Space, Your Space while I move through a Chessboard that the horse is familiar with, without popping anyone's Bubbles. This exercise is practice for the person, and an opportunity for the horse to watch.

pop your Bubble, either (fig. 6.13). It is like scooching down the row of seats in a movie theater, trying not to step on any toes and be as polite as possible in a small area.

I once used Reverse Round Pen to halter a mare who was terribly injured out in her field. She had been limping for two weeks and would not allow anyone near her. Her injuries were so bad, there was discussion of mercy-shooting her. I used Reverse Round Pen from 30 feet, then 20, then 10, then squatted down in a deep O posture. The mare dropped her nose to the ground, removing all intensity (Aw-Shucks), and at that moment I was able to move to her and slip her halter on. The process took me about 20 minutes. She made a full recovery.

Doing Reverse Round Pen in this case told the mare, "I can see you are injured. You stay on the inside of the circle, and I will walk the outside as your Protector."

SKILL-BUILDER

Cop Stop Hand

The Hold Hand up can be exaggerated when you are carrying food and become more of what I call *Cop Stop Hand*. This gesture is useful and helpful in many situations. Many people have learned to wave their hands around to keep horses outside their Bubble. This is ineffective. Waving your hands around makes you look weak. Imagine a policeman, flailing his hand wildly—it does not look impressive. The Cop Stop Hand is a solid, firm signal.

From the Outside, In

You can also use this Conversation with an *actual* round pen. In a way that is similar to first working with the horse from outside his stall before helping him Navigate the Threshold (see p. 233), I have also learned you can get more done when you begin by walking around the *outside* of the round pen, convincing the horse you are the Protector, before entering and continuing the Conversation inside. When you have gained sufficient connection from outside the enclosure, when you enter you are more likely to remain Zero with the horse. This, then, models the behavior you want the horse to copy.

Remember how we discussed Mirroring and Copycat earlier in this book (see p. 102)? These lessons were all about first learning to "get out of your own way," as well as fostering interest, trust, and loyalty in the horse. This is what we are doing with Reverse Round Pen.

Learning to move in rhythm, timing, and feel with a horse without any agenda (because you are literally not even near his Bubble) allows the human brain to go much further in memorizing the intentions of the horse's body language.

1 From outside the pen, Mirror the horse's gestures. Observe what happens. Mirroring is the best way to give the horse psychological space to be able to reveal to you who he really is, as well as what he may be feeling in that moment.

2 Next, play Copycat, simply reversing the Mirroring Conversation so that you are offering movement to the horse—again with no agenda—to see what body language the horse is interested in copying, if any. This is the best way to offer the body language of Horse Speak with fluidity and feel, and to gain insight and gather information that is beyond words.

3 Progress the Reverse Round Pen communication to include the whole IINN process, and go through all Four Gs from the outside the pen. I have known quite a number of horses who really benefited from having the opportunity to freely communicate with their handlers in this way. In most cases, the horses began following their people around, even though the fence was between them.

When you have done several Mirroring, Copycat, and IINN sessions, you should be able to step *inside* the enclosure with your horse and model the behavior you wish from him. Remember: all the aspects of the mechanics of the postures, signals, and gestures (the *science* of Horse Speak) come from hours and hours of Mirroring and Copycat sessions I've experienced in the years I have studied equine language. The final product (the *art* of Horse Speak) is achieved by integrating these essential lessons within the scope of agendas we really do have, such as catching our horses, haltering them, leading them, grooming them, and finally, riding them.

The Rules of Horse Chess

When first considering Negotiating and Navigating the Chessboard, it may seem overwhelming. I promise the idea will bring clarity and fun to your time with your horse, as well as making his behavior more regulated and maximizing your training time, whatever discipline you pursue or methodologies you favor.

The basic rules that follow lay the groundwork for your fluency in Horse Speak on the Chessboard (figs. 6.14 A–E). Use these on a regular basis, and your horse will look at you with newfound respect and trust.

How to Announce You Are Entering the Chessboard

- Change direction three times, according to the Rule of Three.
- Open and close the stall door or gate three times before entering (especially when entering an enclosure with loose horses that seem a little rowdy.
- Touch at least three things once you enter into the stall, paddock, or arena. This establishes a message of, "I'm here now; I'm taking charge of the Chessboard."
- Either blow a Sentry Breath or Scan the Horizon to demonstrate you are aware of the outer environment as well.
- Toss a rock *away* from the horse. If the horse spooks, then blow a Sentry Breath at the rock. (Watch a bold horse touch some new object, make it wiggle, and then spook at it while blowing out. He will usually do this three times before deciding the object is no problem.)

How to Approach a Loose Horse

- When possible, approach, use an O posture, and do a quick Check-In Greeting (see p. 119). Some horses want to Greet your knuckles three times—make it quick to say, "I'm busy. I have to check out this Chessboard " (figs. 6.15 A & B). The reason to be "busy" is because you don't necessarily want to enter into an entire Four Gs session with a loose horse. So, offering some sort of Check-In or quick Greeting should suffice. "Swish your tail" (wave your hand by your thigh) to say, "I am done." Horses tend to find you interesting when you are able to have short Conversations as well as extended ones.

6.14 A–E Horses see you right away when you enter the Chessboard, regardless of fences or distance (A). Therefore, the way you enter matters. I walk the edge of the fence to offer security to the herd (B). Since staying outside the fence is just as effective as going in, I touch the fence three times to Secure the Environment, and this action draws the horse near me (C). Messages of protection are pretty simple—imagine you're telling a child to wait before crossing the street with your Hold Hand and Core Energy (D). Blowing a Sentry Breath toward a source of concern is a stronger message of protection (E). Some horses need more of this than others. Always give the "All's clear!" when done by sighing out loud and looking down.

6.15 A & B After you have Secured the Environment, most horses are eager to offer a Greeting (A). When approaching a loose horse from inside an enclosure, make the Greeting a quick Check-In (B).

- If the horse is quiet and appears interested, then you can of course pursue a reasonable Conversation about whatever you feel like, if you wish.

Leaving One Chessboard for Another

- As you leave one part of the Chessboard (say, the paddock) and enter another (say, the barn aisle) with the horse in hand, use the same rules as when entering a new Chessboard. Touch three things in the space itself. Make a point of walking to the object or the wall, linger for about a minute, then walk on to the next thing. You are saying, "You can follow along while I make sure there are no bees, bears, or boogeymen" (fig. 6.16). Remember: You must touch the object *first* (p. 240). The mare touches the item before her colt does; using this tactic gives you the best results.
- After the three-touch check into the environment, pick a Safety Object and bring the horse there to rest. After resting, walk a small circle, and go back to the Safety Object at least three times (fig. 6.17).
- Remember to engage the Buttons. You never know which Button wants to say something or hear a message from you in new situations (fig. 6.18).

After a few weeks of providing this sort of consistency, most horses no longer require as much diligence. However, if one day there is something new, or it is windy, or some other distraction is happening, that time spent developing trust in your protection on every Chessboard scenario will pay off.

6.16 This mare Mirrors me as I tell her that she can follow along while I make sure all is safe.

6.17 I have entered the Chessboard, but the chestnut with the blaze doesn't know me. I use a Safety Object to help us connect.

6.18 Every new place we bring a horse is a new Chessboard. Every door or gate is a new Threshold. Remain aware as you Navigate these spaces, talk to the Buttons, and your horse will be able to maintain inner Zero. I use the Back-Up Button to balance this gelding as we Navigate the barn aisle.

6.19 A & B We use Turn the Key, Come to Me, to invite the horse to follow us from Safety Object to Safety Object. This makes the Chessboard more playful. The best part? No whips, no treats. You are enough.

How to Deepen Rapport Through Enrichment

- Spend quality time lingering nearby while your horse has some hay or grazes.
- Learn what your horse's favorite Safety Object is and invite him to hang out there with you (figs. 6.19 A & B).
- Determine what your horse's favorite thing to do is, and do it with him or just share space with him while he does it. For example, I knew one horse who loved to open gates. He and his handler would open them together whenever his handler wanted to just spend quality time with him.
- Learn how to do equine bodywork and offer some to your horse.
- Value spending time with your horse because you enjoy his company—and he enjoys yours (figs. 6.20 A & B).

6.20 A & B Enrichment means doing things both you and your horses enjoy—spending time together and maybe having Fun with Feet!

How to Engage with Desensitization as Needed

- Approach a "spooky" area or object, using some of the soothing Conversations we have described in the pages prior (fig. 6.21 and see pp. 153 and 229).
- When a horse is very worried about a particular thing, use the Three Times Rule along with a Safety Object as a resting point, or keep the Safety Object near as you approach the unfamiliar one. In extreme situations, plan on doing several sets of this approach, and then quit for a bit and come back after a break to try again (figs. 6.22 A & B).

6.21 Desensitizing is natural to horses. They build-up courage to check things out on their own. If we enter the Chessboard with this in mind, it can be so much easier when approaching "scary" objects, like this cone.

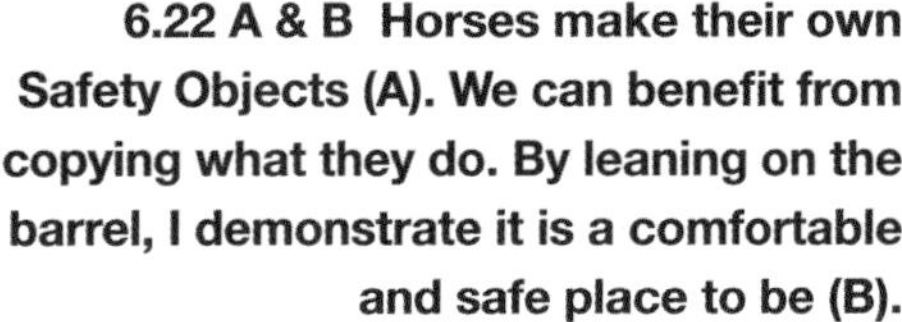

6.22 A & B Horses make their own Safety Objects (A). We can benefit from copying what they do. By leaning on the barrel, I demonstrate it is a comfortable and safe place to be (B).

- If possible, step on the scary object yourself, or otherwise touch it, without letting the horse touch it first. This suggests, "I am on it. Let me check this out while you stay back."
- Allow the horse to be loose with the object or in the location of the spooky area to see what he does with it after you have touched it or examined it.
- Clicker training can be a good tool to help a very Hesitant horse or a Stoic who has determined "No Way am I touching that thing." Some Stoics can become very hard to change, but food can help motivate them to at least try.

Remember, with desensitization, as well as other lessons, it is more effective to have several short 10-minute sessions rather than a single hour-long one.

SKILL-BUILDER

Desensitizing the Chessboard with a Ring of Cones

Outline a circle with a number of traffic cones. You can use as many cones as you like. Because every situation and horse are unique, use your best judgement, and try a variety of setups to see what works for you. I like to have about eight cones, six paces apart on a circle to begin. With a larger horse, I may have ten paces and a slightly larger circle, and with a shorter horse I may only have four paces and smaller circle. If you have a really Hesitant or panicky horse, you may need a smaller circle. An Outgoing or hot horse may need a bigger one. The best idea is to experiment with your particular horse to see what works best. While you can work with the horse both inside and outside the Ring of Cones, when the horse is on the inside track (between your body and the cones), he will often feel safer than if he is on the outside track (where your body is closer to the cones).

6.23 Create a circle of traffic cones and move from one to the next with your horse to practice Navigating the Chessboard together.

Walk with your horse from cone to cone, establishing each one as a Safety Object. Creating a Ring of Cones shrinks the Chessboard and provides a smaller focal point for you to use in Navigation practice.

Give the Horse a Place to Land

The most important part of working with a horse's Chessboard is to remember that he needs two essential things to be able to pay attention to you and remain relaxed enough to learn any lesson:

1 "A place to land," which means safety.

2 Time to process.

Many horses will bring their head toward you when they are seeking a Check-In, and if you do not offer them a place to land, such as your knuckles, they will choose a spot on your body or become nervous and start acting out (chewing on the rope or reins, or pawing). When they really emotionally need a place to land and you confuse this with space invasion, then their distress increases, and they act out more—maybe bumping you with their head or pulling away. Think of a toddler who needs to sit on Momma's lap because he is overstimulated or tired or nervous. If Mom shuns him, the likelihood of him falling apart on the carpet in a full tantrum increases. The tantrum is not because the child is bad, it is because he had a need that did not get met and his body and mind had to release the tension somehow. Note that this form of emotional-distress tantrum is very different from the sort in which a toddler demands his own way and uses a "fuss" to coerce Mom into giving in. Horses can do this, as well (especially those with a Joker personality).

When I give human examples like this, it is to provide what I hope is something more easily relatable. The fact is there are moments when a horse just wants his own way, and moments when he is truly struggling with something. The only way to know the difference is to learn to pay strict attention to his body language and facial expressions and try to get an impression from the horse without it being affected by too much personal bias.

By developing a pattern of helping a horse have a place to land, you both have a way to regroup and process. Having a moment to think can hopefully give you the space you need to determine what may truly be going on in your connection, communication, and Navigation so you can form a better action plan.

Merging Bubbles

When you are looking to work with a horse on any level on the Chessboard, you must understand that from the horse's perspective, what you are really asking is to *Merge Bubbles*. You are signaling your intention to take over as Mapmaker, Protector, Mentor, and Sentry. This is what the horse is looking for in sharing his space and decision-making with you.

The Horse Speak protocols I have offered, such as IINN (p. 197) and the Four Gs (p. 208), and Going Somewhere down the Buttons (p. 256), are all aimed at placing you in this trustworthy position, teaching you how to see and experience the Bubbles as real things, not imaginary ones. Merging Bubbles means the horse will choose the "follower" position in your herd of two because you are able to provide the psychological and physical tokens of trust and loyalty he needs. Horses want to follow; it's in their nature. They want to have quiet, Low-Calorie Conversations, and they want to live at Zero. They also want clear boundaries and good manners. They love to feel deeply bonded, and most of them want to come running to the gate when they see their favorite human show up.

7 Inviting the Horse to Come with You

How Leading Is Everything Else

There are a vast number of trainers who teach people how to lead horses better. Each of these trainers may have a different idea about what the best techniques are, but one thing they can all agree on is that leading is the foundation of everything else.

I agree that this statement is true. However, *if* the focus of leading is just to follow a set method, then the student may not inherently understand how the method relates to other aspects of horsemanship. Leading a horse well means he is giving you a Green Light to be his leader. When you understand what kind of leader he may be looking for (Does he need a Mapmaker? Is he looking for a Teacher? Does your youngster need a good Mentor?) you will be better able to fulfill more of your horse's values, which leads to him trusting in your leadership.

Beyond clarifying Roles in the Herd and indicating hierarchical patterns, walking with a horse on a rope has one primary focus as far as the *horse is concerned*: It is all about balance in connection.

Reconsidering Haltering and Leading the Horse

Before you can lead the horse, you have to get the halter on. It always amazes me when I get to work with a high-class horse who pins his ears or runs away from the halter. Sometimes this behavior is caused by mishandling; other times it is the horse's personality.

Haltering and leading a horse can be challenging for a variety of reasons, although if a horse was halter-trained well at a young age, there should be relatively few problems.

Help with Haltering

- I recommend laying a lead rope across the horse's neck if there is any chance he could get "wiggly" before you have finished putting on the halter and attaching the lead rope.
- When you have a very Hesitant horse, or one with a traumatic history, you may want to "Kill the Halter" (fig. 7.1). Lead horses in a herd will trample objects to ensure they won't cause the group harm. Step on the halter while the horse

watches. Encourage the horse to step on it as well. (In addition to helping the horse feel like you are a leader, this adds some humor to what can otherwise be a frustrating situation.)

- In extreme cases, leave a comfortable halter with a "break-away strap" on your horse all the time. In this way, the anxiety-producing issue is removed, and you can stay Zero while you use a *second* halter to practice putting one on and taking it off.

7.1 Lead horses (and curious ones) are inclined to step on, knock over, and move objects. On a practical level this determines if the object is safe. I discovered that for some horses, "killing" the object can really help them overcome skepticism about items they do not like.

Preparing to Lead

Now that you know how to use your X, O, and Core Energy, you may find that leading your horse is a bit easier! Every horse is unique, so a great place to begin your leading practice is by "asking good questions" about how to have leading become an enriching experience—one in which both you and the horse have a rapport and feel confident in one another (fig. 7.2). Consider these additional hints:

- The gestures to think about when leading are Hold, Activate, and Draw (see pp. 52, 53, and 57). For instance, you can Draw a horse to you while you are in O posture, and this encourages him to want to begin walking.
- Using Your X-posture, you can turn your Core Energy onto the horse's chest and ask him to halt with your Hold Hands (figs. 7.3 A & B).
- You can Activate the Buttons to ask the horse to come forward, especially those often used in combination, such as Cheek, Mid-Neck, and Shoulder. The Girth or Jump-Up Button work in some horses, and for others you can lightly tap the Hip Button.

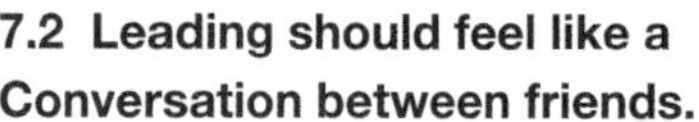

7.2 Leading should feel like a Conversation between friends.

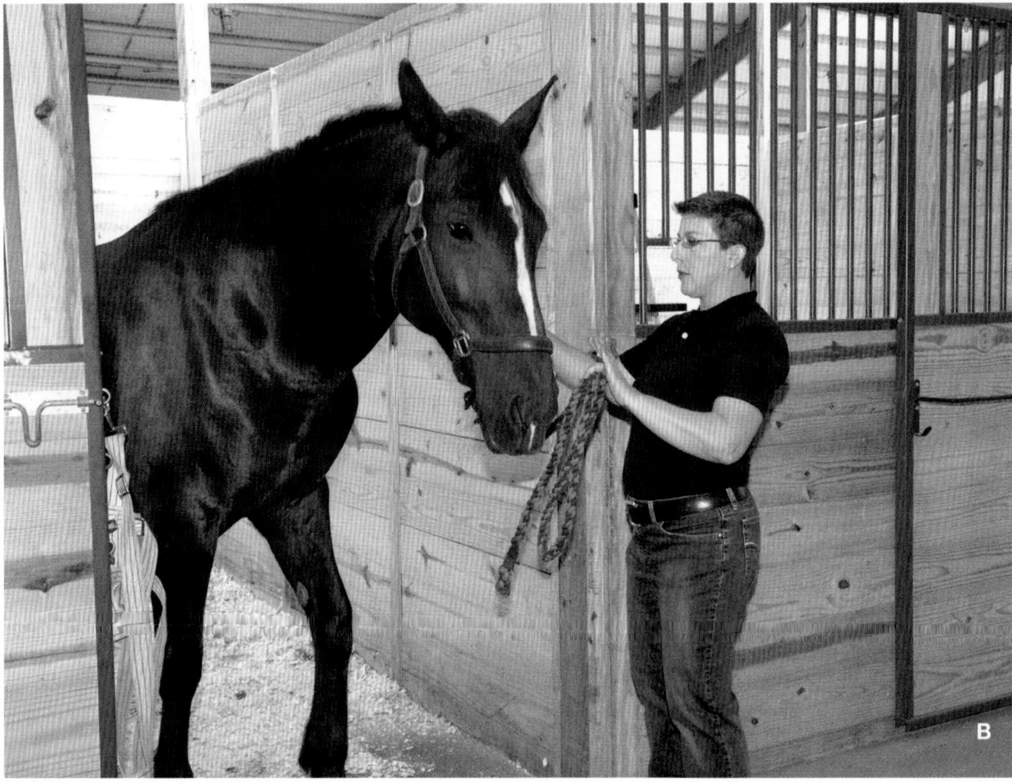

7.3 A & B I Draw the horse to me with my O posture. This encourages him to want to begin walking (A). I use my X posture, Core Energy, and Hold Hands to ask him to halt (B).

- Sometimes, a nice Therapy Back-Up (see p. 255) unlocks wariness and stiffness, and helps the horse come forward in balance.

Changing How You Hold the Lead Rope

You can hold the lead rope any way you want to, as long as it isn't wrapped around your wrist or neck. However, when you want to send a message of relaxation and trust to the horse's nervous system, then place your palm *downward* on the rope (fig. 7.4). With the palm down, there is an *intrinsic* calm that the horse feels; this is not something you need to train him, because your own nervous system has a positive reaction to this gesture. There are some things we do with our body language that are "hardwired," and this is one of them. When we are babies, we crawl before we can walk. Placing your palm in a downward position signals your brain to stabilize. I call this gesture *"Palm Down, Calm Down."*

From this position, you can offer a "scoop" upward on the lead to ask the horse to go or to halt. He will not be offended by this ask because it will not upset his balance. Sliding your hand along the lead is also a nice feeling and lets the horse know

7.4 Place your hand on the lead rope so your palm faces downward, what I call Palm Down, Calm Down. This signals both to you and the horse to stabilize.

a change is coming. This is another intrinsic gesture. A "scooping" motion causes circular rotations in your arm and shoulder joints. Circular rotations create a balancing effect. Think of walking on a balance beam and how your extended arms and hands automatically make little circling motions when you try to stay balanced. Doing this on purpose sends a balancing message to the horse (fig. 7.5). Therefore, adding scooping gestures to your leading practice not only encourages forward motion in the horse, but motion in balance. Scooping to a halt has a similar effect: halting in balance.

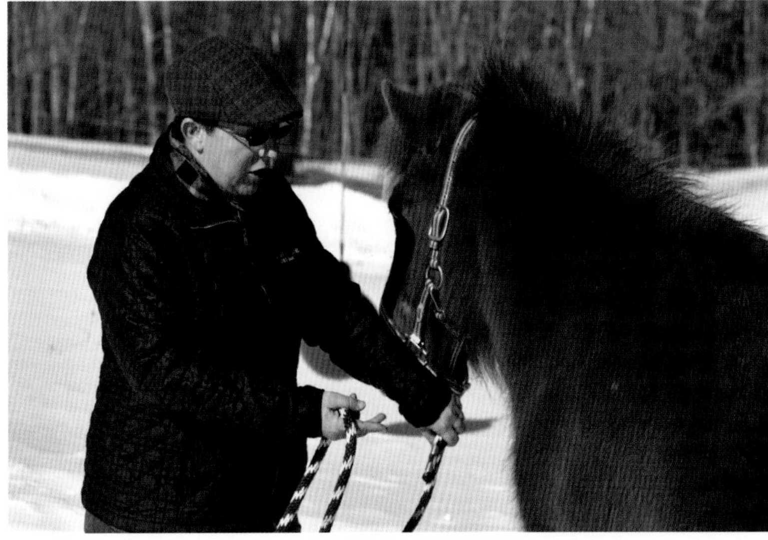

7.5 You can see in this picture both my hands are rotating. The one closest to the horse will "scoop" easily from this position. The other hand is scooping toward the Back-Up Button. I have found this motion removes resistance and stress.

Remember that if you are "herky-jerky" with the lead rope, you upset the horse's physical balance. And as we've discussed, poor physical balance makes poor emotional and mental balance.

Therapy Back-Up

The *Therapy Back-Up* releases physical tension in the horse, which in turn assists in releasing current or stored emotional tension. It can help a horse get "back in his body," and it is highly effective in getting the horse in harmony with you while you are together.

With every change of the Chessboard, there is an opportunity to offer a Therapy Back-Up. I have a saying: "Go backward if you want to go forward well." *But... please do not drill* or ask for more than a nice lean of the body or single step at first. If you do, you will invite resistance with something that should feel like smooth butter when done well.

How to Do the Therapy Back-Up

I teach the steps to this Conversation in my first book, where you can also find instructional photos, but let's review it here so we are ready to take it further in the pages ahead (fig. 7.7).

SKILL-BUILDER

Touching the Buttons Before You Go

Going Somewhere down the Buttons can mean the difference between a horse being ready to go with you on the lead, and one who does not feel connected enough to you. The following recommendations are especially important when working with a troubled, "sticky," or panicky horse. Horses who are more solid in their leading skills and usually follow along can benefit from this exercise, too, as it can help them overcome tense situations.

- Stand by the horse's shoulder and use Figure-Eight Hold Hand in the air along all the Buttons, on both sides is best (see p. 224). This just sends the message, "I want to connect with you. No pressure." Watch for wiggling Buttons and release of tension or increase of tension around certain Buttons. Talk to any Button that has issues with a longer linger of the Hold Hand over it.
- Touch the Buttons. Use your Hold Hand in contact, sliding it along the horse's body and linger a moment on each Button.
- Use your Activation Finger (very lightly), and tap each Button to make sure the horse is okay with being Activated at each one. Linger on a troubled one with a Hold Hand. Retreat to the last untroubled Button.
- After you form contact with the Buttons, stand still in Gone phase. Let out five sighs in a row. This tells the horse you are waiting for his answer.
- If a horse acts like he wants to move off carefully and slowly, he may want to show you a Button he needs to talk to you about. Allow a little room on the lead rope for the horse to move in this thoughtful, careful manner.
- As discussed on p. 245, it can be helpful to have a series of Safety Objects to walk to if the horse is really challenged. Too often we get going and just want to keep going, but horses want to pause every 10 steps or so to renegotiate the environment. If you take advantage of this fact and work a pause into your leading practice, they will tend to lean into their courage and remain Zero enough to try harder.

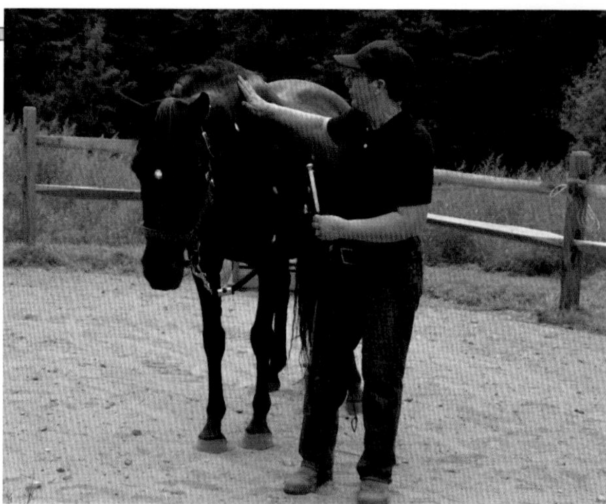

7.6 I use my Hold Hand to connect one Button to the next in a sweeping motion before leading. In this photo, I am sliding from Mid-Neck toward the Grooming Button, which this mare loves. As you get to know your horse's Buttons, you will learn what his favorites are, too.

1 Face toward your horse's chest on one side of his body (not directly in front of him).

2 Place your hand closest to the horse's face palm down on the lead rope, then slide your hand toward the clip at the end of the lead where it attaches to the halter ring under his chin.

3 Your other hand, which should be holding the bulk of the lead rope, now moves toward the point of the horse's shoulder, aiming at the Back-Up Button—aim your fingers up into the Button with a motion like you are scooping water up to it.

4 The hand holding the clip and ring of the halter now begins to rotate so that your thumb eventually faces upward with your elbow down. Engage this rotation all the way to your wing bone (scapula) and into your back. Scooping your hand on the lead rope like this puts a mild rotational sensation into the halter, inviting a kind of Rock the Baby (see p. 137) on the head of the horse.

5 Draw the lead rope toward the horse's chest so his head and poll are encouraged to drop and arch downward toward the chest. Again, use a scooping motion to make this feel "buttery" instead of pushy.

MYTH-BUSTER

Can Every Horse Do a Therapy Back-Up?

In almost every single case in which someone says to me, "My horse won't back up," the problem is 90 percent user error:

- The person is rigid, uses too much X, or is too demanding and trying to force it. We do not mean to be this way, but most of us have been conditioned to be "too X" with horses.
- The other side are those who are "too O"—they "feel bad" about asking the horse to back up.
- Then there are the cases when the horse completely replies with a lean or step back, but because it is so easy, the person doesn't think anything happened.
- At the most, I'd say 1 percent of cases are horses with such physical limitations that they cannot do this easily, *but* even they can find a lovely, buttery *lean backward* with the right touch.

7.7 **Your Therapy Back-Up should feel soft and easy, like smooth butter. Some horses have physical limitations that can affect their ability to back up, which is why I suggest only asking for one or two steps at a time.**

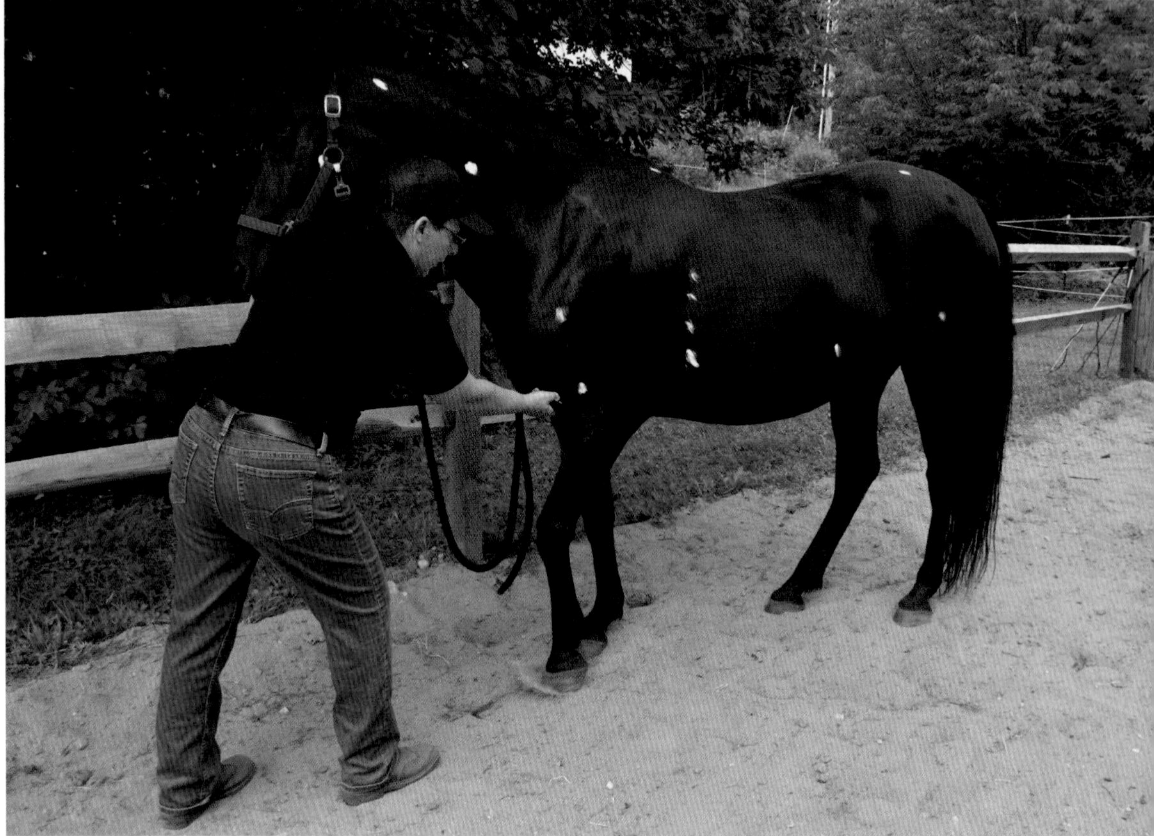

6 Take a firm, clear step toward the horse's front foot while using the appropriate amount of pressure on the lead for the horse you are working with. If the horse is "stuck," use your pointer finger to press into the Back-Up Button. Note: Do not push on the horse's chest as this will create resistance and will take away his sense of pride.

7 The moment the horse yields backward, even a little bit, return to Zero and praise him.

Advanced Therapy Back-Up

Advanced Therapy Back-Up engages both of the "new" Buttons I introduced in chapter 3 (p. 117), connecting the horse's skeleton from the Bridge of the Nose Button to the Sit Button. In essence, this Conversation engages all the joints of the horse in one action. When done well, with softness, and only one step at a time, most horses come to like it and even *ask* for it—it is *enrichment* rather than punishment. With some practice you will be able to ask for the movement with just the Bridge of the Nose instead of signals on the halter or lead. Then, you can do the Advanced Therapy Back-Up with your horse at liberty.

Advanced Therapy Back-Up:

- Releases mental, emotional, or physical tension in the horse, whether new or old.
- Claims the space in front of the horse in a benevolent way.
- Encourages the horse's chest and core muscles to lift up and engage.
- Helps refocus a distracted horse and keeps his attention on you.
- Increases rapport.
- Decreases stress and resistance.
- Enhances your awareness of micro-gestures.
- Improves the horse's ability to move in balance. (You're also improving your own balance.)

I have come to understand that this one activity has many layers of meaning and can be a door that opens the horse to better and better associations within himself, as well as in his connection to you. Think of this Conversation as carefully and compassionately witnessing your horse renegotiate old memories, feelings, or difficulties, as well as learning to feel more embodied.

Things to be aware of when using Advanced Therapy Back-Up:

- Watch for the slightest try.
- Look at your horse's facial expression for changes.
- Monitor your X and O posture.
- Be attentive to when a horse is ready to stop or is willing to continue.
- Encourage a Hesitant horse to Linger Longer, but do not use force. Watch to see if the horse offers the Bridge of the Nose Button toward you—this means he would like more.

BUZZWORDS

Hot Potato Release

This means release any hold or pressure with speed ("drop it like a hot potato").

- Watch to see if the horse moves his head one way or the other, which often signals he would like you to change sides. When changing sides, hold the horse steady (often horses are initially confused about this movement and think they should follow you).
- The lead rope "scoop" (see Step 5 on p. 257) accesses the Bridge of the Nose and is important for more advanced maneuvers that require trust.
- At any moment during this entire Conversation, step away and give the horse a chance to process. This is an opportunity for you to let go of the old belief that horses "resist for no reason" and that we must "make them do things."

When you are ready to try Advanced Therapy Back-Up:

1 Begin by Rocking the Baby on the Bridge of the Nose (figs. 7.8 A & B). You also can hold the noseband of the halter. This is done the same way you do it with the Grooming Button (see p. 136).

2 When it's difficult to touch the Bridge of the Nose Button, do several *Hot Potato Releases*, until the horse starts to relax.

3 When you are Rocking the Baby on the Bridge of the Nose you are affecting the whole skeleton. Wait for the horse to begin to enjoy this offer. The message you are sending is, "You can trust me; I am not going to hurt you."

4 Once you have achieved relaxation through the Bridge of the Nose Button, draw your attention to and look at the Mid-Neck Button while you continue to Rock the

7.8 A & B The Bridge of the Nose Button connects to the Sit Button through the horse's skeleton. Gently Rock the Baby here to Initiate a relaxed backward motion. *Do not push.*

7.9 Holding the Sit Button is another way to encourage the horse to back up—some will even back into your hand. Activating this Button promotes feel-good sensations between you and your horse. This horse, a Skeptic, is trying it out.

Baby. You are saying, "You are safe, you can let go with me." Horses often hold mental and emotional tension in their necks; watch for it to relax.

5 Next, continue Rocking the Baby while looking at the Mid-Neck Button and Activating the Back-Up Button as you step forward with your foot (figs. 7.4 A–C). Adding this helps achieve deeper levels of mental and emotional well-being for the horse. You are looking for a "buttery" lean back, and possibly a single step (at first).

6 As the horse leans back or takes a step back, you may look at or Activate any other Button on his body to continue to communicate a message of well-being, balance, and harmony (fig. 7.9). Take time to enjoy this interesting journey of Activating other Buttons as you do this exercise (fig. 7.10). You can engage a Button by touching it before the horse begins to back up or by looking at it when you ask the horse to begin. Any "sticky" Button is to be taken seriously, have patience, giving the horse plenty of processing time.

7 Do not do several steps backward or it starts to feel like punishment to the horse. Instead, use three or more sessions of Advanced Therapy Back-Up in which you get a single step or two each time.

7.10 Adding more to your Therapy Back-Up can keep it fun and interesting. Breathe out to make it smoother. Look at other Buttons to include them, and see what happens. Here I'm adding Fun with Feet!

8 When you are done, step aside with Palm Down, Calm Down on the lead rope.

9 If the horse seeks connection, offer your knuckles for a Check-In. If the horse acts a little "fresh" afterward, chewing on the rope, give him more room, moving one step away, and use Hold Hand over the Cheek or Mid-Neck Buttons.

I included so much about the Therapy Back-Up in this book because this Conversation has become one of those magic, overall "good things," like the old saying, "Shoulder-in fixes everything." Therapy Back-Up is physically, emotionally, and mentally healing. It assists horses in feeling calm and also strengthens their core. It promotes a sense of overall well-being and encourages them to stay attentive to us. It can take a little time to find the sweet spot where the actions begin to feel "buttery," but it is worth it.

Common Leading Misunderstandings

"The lead rope is what leads the horse."

This is probably where a lot of confusion begins. The lead rope *does not* lead the horse; it is meant to guide the motions of the horse and maintain a connection from his bubble to yours.

Your body language guides the horse. Horses follow footsteps; they also follow your Core Energy. This is why if you back away from a horse in an O posture, he is often tempted to follow you. The lead rope needs to feel like the *second level* of leading a horse, *not* the first.

"The horse should follow behind you."

Horses do not *necessarily* really prefer this. Occasionally, this is an acceptable position, and some horses do enjoy following a leader. However, when you are not aware and do not "feel" the horse back behind you, through the lead rope, but are instead just

SKILL-BUILDER

Therapy Back-Up Self-Assessment

Practice using your Core Energy and changing from facing front (as you are walking forward) to facing backward (to ask for Therapy Back-Up). Make a *Power Pivot*—a turn on your toes—to swing from walking forward to aiming your Core Energy at the Back-Up Button, asking the horse to perhaps suspend that forward step in the air and move it backward instead. In addition:

- Think of your Core Energy as if it is the flame on a gas stove, which gets adjusted for different levels of intensity. Pay attention to where your Core Energy is aiming and if the "flame" is "on" or "off" or in between. Don't blast your horse on "high heat."
- Breathe out when you ask the horse to back-up.
- When you step in with your foot to ask the horse to step back with his, notice whether one foot or the other has a different affect—does it close or open the door to the horse's Bubble?
- Practice Hot Potato Release when the horse makes the slightest move backward.

7.11 The horse following behind you on the lead rope is not the problem. Being inattentive to what the horse is thinking back there or how comfortably or uncomfortably they are moving *is*. For some horses, this makes them feel like they are "fish-tailing," and this upsets their balance.

sort of attached to the rope at one end with the horse attached on the other, then leading from the front is like a truck pulling a trailer with loose couplings. It is a "fish-tail" experience for horses, and some attempt to straighten out their leader by switching sides often. Others will try to "drive" the leader from this position, since it looks to them like their leader doesn't know what to do. And others just shuffle along, their equilibrium upset by the "dragging" effect. When leading from this position, you cannot see the horse, so cannot adjust if the horse becomes worried or is struggling. It can also put you in jeopardy, should the horse startle.

If you are leading two or three horses at a time, and one chooses to follow behind you, then herd formation has changed the dynamic. When it is just you and your horse, however, you need to be very "clued in" and aware, with "eyes in the back of your head." When a horse prefers to follow behind you on a loose lead rope, you must remain highly aware of what he is doing and if the position is making him feel disconnected from you or off balance (fig. 7.11).

"The horse should be led with your hand on the lead rope directly under his chin."

Horses definitely *do not* prefer this hand position. It can afford the leader a certain amount of control, limiting the horse's power to break away, because the lead rope is connected to the halter, which crosses the Bridge of the Nose Button, which is extremely sensitive.

Horses being led by the reins are often held like this—both reins are through the leader's fingers and the leader has more control of the horse through the bit. Usually, when a horse is led this way, his head and neck will be fully extended, and many will have a "lag" in their willingness to take first steps forward.

Often, this type of leading uses a chain, as well. (In more extreme cases, the chain goes through the mouth or over the gums of the horse, which is common with racehorses.) Horses have extremely sensitive and tiny little bones on the bridge of the nose (fig. 7.12). "Shanking"— especially with a chain—can cause damage, even to the point of fracture. Yes, it will often redirect a horse's energy if he is getting out of control or worried, but the change in behavior is due to pain. You have done nothing to improve rapport, trust, and willingness to follow.

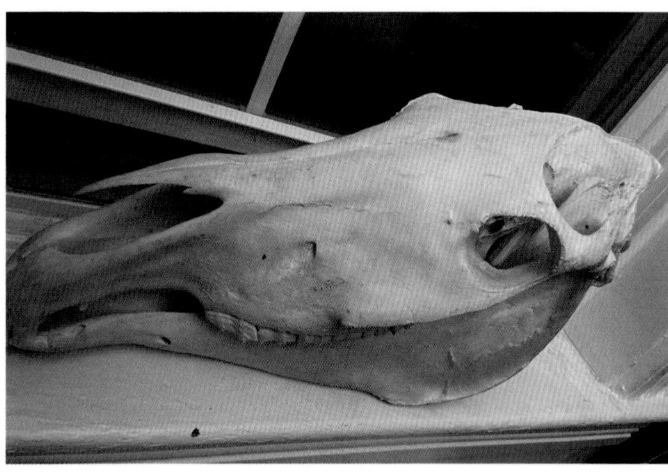

7.12 Look how delicate the bridge of the horse's nose is! Lead him and handle his head Buttons with this in mind.

The hand in a position right under the horse's chin activates the arm strength of the person, and when horses sense muscle strength, they find it offensive. They lead each other with agreements and signals, not by muscling each other around. Softness is valued in a herd to maintain Zero.

When you do need to lead a horse with a short lead rope or the reins, your hand must be very buoyant and light... like holding a beverage without a top while in a vehicle. You must be able to swiftly and softly adapt to the horse's balance needs and not hold on with a death grip.

"The horse should walk with his head at your shoulder or with his head low."

Again, this is often a standard set with the intention of controlling the horse's head. Most horses do not like having their head in a fixed position because it limits how they

SKILL-BUILDER

Lead and Feel

You can experience being led with a partner and a lead rope. One of you should adopt the leading position, holding the rope close to the clip, while the other holds the clip itself. The leader should step forward. It only takes a moment for the follower to feel out of balance or even defensive. Switch roles, and when the leader, practice having a light, buoyant hand.

Remember, if you have to pull a horse to start and pull a horse to stop, you are hijacking the horse's ability to balance and rebalance. Try this with your partner, and you will feel what I am talking about.

MYTH-BUSTER

Does Traditional Tack and Equipment Hurt the Horse?

I have come to understand that for some horses, a longeing cavesson is more subtle and provides better communication with the Bridge of the Nose Button than other forms of halters. However, too much weight or pressure on this Button can be quite uncomfortable for the horse.

Rope halters have become a common sight in the horsemanship world, and many horses seem to be comfortable enough in them. They can certainly be helpful for those horses who have a "strong head and neck" and seek to pull the rope away from people or become pushy during leading. They work because the rope of the halter is small enough in diameter to put more precise pressure on sensitive areas of the head. However, shaking the rope violently can severely disrupt the horse's sense of balance as well as cause nerve pain.

A chain that as affixed correctly over the Bridge of the Nose Button can act as a similar deterrent to a strong horse's urge to pull away or push through the person trying to lead him, but its best use is in only lightly jiggling the chain as a "reminder." Shanking, pulling, or jerking the chain can cause quite a lot of pain. I have seen horses who appear to have permanent tissue damage due to poor halter work.

Dropped nosebands, which are commonly used to "stabilize the bit" on an English bridle, can add severe pressure to the nose of the horse, as well as limit the nostrils' ability to breathe clearly. These nosebands need to be adjusted correctly and used only if absolutely necessary. This is not a necessary piece of tack except in specific cases.

Martingales and tie-downs can exude sharp, sudden pressure on the Bridge of the Nose Button. These are again pieces of tack that should only be used for specific applications in the horse's education. Most horses should not require one when ridden.

Of course, there are also the extreme cases of abusive tack that I've seen, such as nails in a noseband of a jumping horse, or wire in the noseband of a tie-down on a barrel racing horse. Some "bitless" mechanical hackamores put such extreme pressure on the nose that I have seen bleeding wounds.

Aside from the common sense that tells us that such pressure over the nose of a horse is harsh at least and cruel at worst, this Button has a subtle, emotionally sensitive, and tender message for us to communicate with, if we let the horse do so.

It breaks my heart to see these things.

7.13 If a horse chooses to walk with a low head because he is at Zero, it is soft and lovely. Training a horse to keep his head low can be a bandaid that doesn't truly address an issue of insecurity.

can rebalance themselves. Fixed positions like this are always for our benefit, not for the horse's sense of well-being.

If you choose to teach a horse to keep his head in a certain position while leading, it should not disturb his sense of balance or make him feel "shut down."

"You need a stick, whip, or flag when leading a horse to help motivate movement, correct any bad habits, or keep the horse in place."

Sometimes such a tool is useful with an uppity youngster or in a remedial case in which a horse has become a danger to himself and others; however, leading with a stick, whip, or flag as an everyday occurrence is *not needed*.

A stick of some sort can be helpful as an extension of your arm for offering support or soothing a stressed horse while maintaining distance. Sticks can certainly also help define personal space, create motivation, and block forward movement. But if you feel you *must* carry a stick to get a horse from A to B, then it would be wise to look at the sense of balance your horse has when with you.

You can use a stick, whip, or flag if you need to, but learning Horse Speak should also provide answers as to what your horse is really struggling with, eventually making one unnecessary. The fact is, I am not flat out against using a stick, but isn't it nice to be able to use your body language for most of what you do with your horse? When I teach classes or clinics, and I give everyone a stick of some sort but no direction, it normally only takes seconds for everyone to start fiddling with their sticks. More playful people taunt each other or even "sword fight." *We can't help ourselves!* When there is a long pokey thing in our hands, we tend to want to use it! This is my primary reason for suggesting people do not use sticks, whips, or flags with horses as a regular thing. When you are walking with a stick in your hand, your horse knows it. If you wiggle the stick unconsciously or rely on it too much, it can cause distraction or even problems. I challenge you to see how much you can do *without* needing to carry or use a stick. That way, you can keep your mind at Zero.

"Shaking a lead rope to make a horse back up is a reasonable gesture." Shaking a lead rope may indeed make a horse back up... but try it with a human partner like you did in the exercise on page 265. You will discover that not only does it knock you off balance, but it is surprising, threatening, and the first response from the person being asked to back up is to not know what to do and freeze.

From what I can find, it seems one of the origins of this technique was wranglers who may have been leading or ponying several horses at a time. "Putting life" into

SKILL-BUILDER

Rock the Baby with Halter

Many horses want something I introduced in *Horse Speak* called *Rock the Baby with Halter*. The horse wants to feel you balance his head either from the side of the halter or while standing directly in front of him. I find young or green horses, especially, like this when standing at the mounting block where they may be insecure about what to do with their heads when being mounted. Try it:

1 Stand in front of your horse, facing him. Alternatively, you can stand on one side of his head, facing forward, or in the Horse Hug position (figs. 7.14 A & B).

2 With one hand on the lead rope, place the other palm down on the halter noseband.

3 Shift your weight back and forth, breathing in as you rock in one direction and breath out when you rock in the other.

When the horse relaxes, even a little bit, let go and step away to let him process. This is the next level up from asking the Cheek Button to yield away. Instead, you are saying, "Come Here Face"—you are inviting a nicer Conversation with the horse about where to place his head and helping him find the best-balanced position for you both.

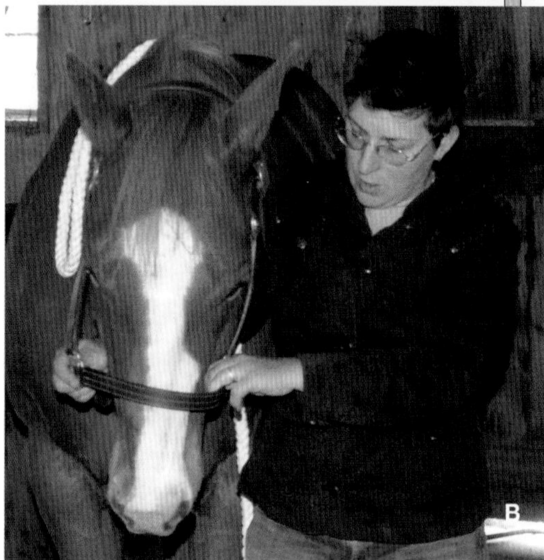

7.14 A & B Rock the Baby with Halter from the side (A) and in the Horse Hug position (B).

one lead rope allowed the person to communicate with a specific horse out of several in hand. However, once this strategy was adapted for the general horse public to use, it lost some of its original practicality. When you watch an experienced wrangler use a tiny bit of rope shake to "wake a horse up" or get his attention, you will see the *smallest action possible* and the fastest Hot Potato Release. It is just a *part* of that expert's body language; it is not a replacement for body language or an exaggerated version of body language.

Shocking or surprising a horse by shaking the lead rope, does usually (eventually) make a horse back up; however, you create an inversion in his spine as he hollows his back and lifts his chin to try to get away from the rope and escape the pain the shaking halter causes across the Bridge of the Nose. Inversion is bad for the horse's balance and well-being. It puts the horse into too much X, which can translate to tension and anxiety.

If you have learned to use a rope shake to ask your horse to back up, you have not ruined the relationship, but press pause on this gesture and replace it with the Therapy Back-Up (see p. 255). I have seen many people successfully replace one with the other and even link the two together. Therapy Back-Up makes a horse feel congruent, inwardly safe, and relaxed. It is good for his posture and emotions and serves as a great way to Activate his core to improve his ability to collect and balance. Linking a slight shake of the lead with Therapy Back-Up may take some finesse, but then the movement of the rope is the signal it was meant to be just a little "life" in the rope, with the horse engaging in a better use of his body.

"Horses should always be led on a loose lead rope."

There are times to lead a horse on a loose lead rope, so he doesn't feel too restricted or claustrophobic. When the rope is *too* loose, however, it may not be capable of sending useful messages to the horse. It's best to have a relaxed lead and knowing how to balance between close contact and loose contact.

Often horses who are used to being led on loose lead ropes have been motivated to keep up or stay within the leader's Bubble with the use of a stick or by twirling the loose end of the lead rope. A certain amount of striking the horse may have happened to reprimand him if he did not keep up and keep the loop in the lead. When this occurs, again the emphasis is on surprise and reprimand. These kinds of methods often fall under the title "pressure and release" or "make the wrong thing hard and the right thing easy." If someone slaps you every time you are in a position she does not like, then probably you will try to keep up, and if she is nice to you when you are in the position she likes, then probably you will learn to stay there. Of course, these techniques have some efficacy because horses are born followers. But when you use these techniques with your horse, while he may have learned to be in a specific position, he may in fact be worried whenever you change what you do with the lead rope, for fear he will be slapped for "getting it wrong." Luckily, horses are forgiving.

Change the idea of keeping the horse on a loose lead to: "release, release, release—pressure—release." You will be acting more like a horse and less like a predator. And adding Horse Speak to your usual signals when leading will add much value to your time on the ground together.

"Horses should be led on a tight lead rope."

While leading a horse, there are times to navigate with him in a close proximity, but the horse should still feel that he has freedom to move his head. Some people are afraid to ease up on the lead rope because they feel like their horses will break away from them, but walking them *exclusively* on a tight lead severely limits their balance.

How Horses Prefer to Be Led

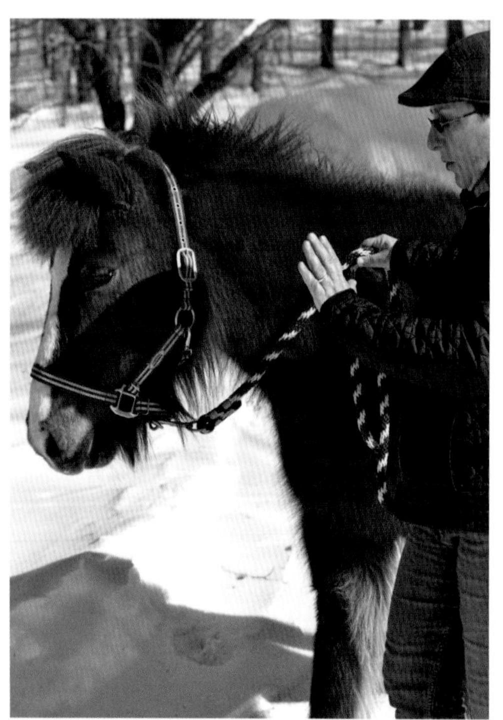

Given that there are a number of personalities as well as Energy Types (see chapter 4—p. 158), not all horses want and need the same things. A timid Pawn will want more closeness and security when being led, and so this kind of horse often needs to learn how to maintain distance from his leader. A Stoic Mentor may lead *you*, regardless of the position you put him in, because he just wants to take care of you. A pushy Joker may need a lot more discussions related to hierarchy, such as being led with one hand near his cheek (Cheek Button) at all times for a few days to remind him to stay in his own Bubble (fig. 7.15).

7.15 Here I offer Hold Hand to the Cheek Button as we make a change of direction on the lead. This simulates two horses with their cheeks near each other, so it helps your horse figure out how to keep his space clear when turning. You can use Hold Hand with either hand, so try this in both directions.

The Magic of Three

As I have mentioned numerous times throughout this book, in general, horses use a cycle of three to complete a thought, and this can be applied to everything you would like to do with them (see The Rule of Three on p. 234). One activity I find horses consistently like when being led is to stop and *linger* while you touch:

- Three things in the barn aisle.
- Three things on the pathway.
- Three things inside the riding arena.
- The mounting block three times and walk away before coming back to mount.

After you have lingered at an object, allow the horse to touch it. Remember: Do not let your horse touch items *first* because this puts *him* into the role of Protector instead of you.

Inviting Your Horse to Come with You

Even more important than using the Rule of Three is *inviting* the horse to be led. There are a few ways to do this.

O Posture

You can make an O posture and invite the horse to sniff your knuckles (Greeting or Check-In) or come toward you as you walk backward a few steps (fig. 7.16).

7.16 Using your Low-O posture, you begin your connection with your horse with a beckoning message (O posture, Knuckle Touch, backward steps). You have invited the horse to find his Zero with you; the O posture represents good leadership.

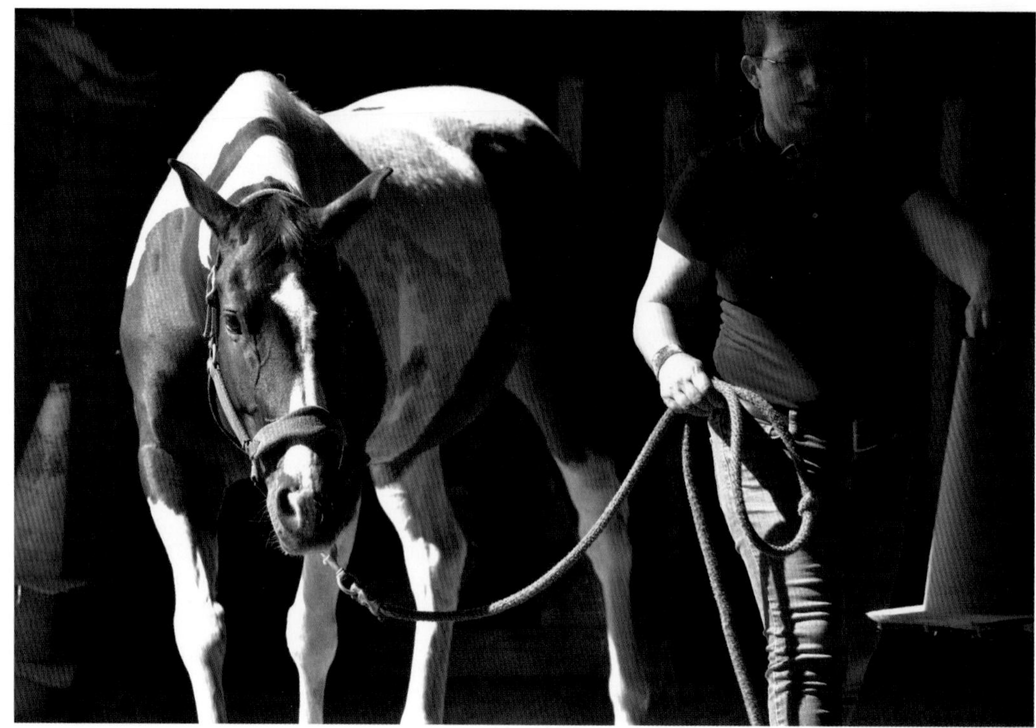

7.17 As you move toward leading your horse, your Palm Down, Calm Down gesture is a nice O message for him to continue following.

Palm Down, Calm Down

This is the gesture of soothing or grounding energy that I first described on p. 254. When you face your palm down toward the ground it tells the brain to stabilize (fig. 7.17). You will be difficult to "knock over" from a simple push to the sternum when your palms face down. However, if you lock your hands into fists, it is quite easy to push you over. At clinics, I have people experiment with this position of the hands, and they are surprised and delighted to realize how grounded they become. Try it yourself with a friend!

"Scoop" the Lead Rope

Creating a circular motion in the bones of your arm translates to the rope, and to the skull of the horse. The rotational sensation releases stress and encourages a desire to move. Even when a horse "sits back" against your arm motion, you can use a certain amount of strong contact with the scoop because this can "answer a question" for certain horses. The question is, "If I pull back, do you 'get after me,' or do you stay the course?" When I am answering this question for the horse, I Linger Longer, even if I have to stand "in the scoop" with a horse for a full minute. Every single time, the horse is satisfied when my reply is, "It won't get worse, I won't strike you. When you're ready, just come along." I have worked with a high number of rehab horses who were convinced I was going to get after them, and the only way to change their minds, and their behavior, was to *not* get after them.

If I give and take on the rope too quickly, it can cause a jarring or startling motion. Or if I feel outwitted and give on the rope too soon, the horse will just ask the question again. It is important to do this with one steady energy and stick to it until you see the horse indicate with his facial expression that he "gets it." Three of these scoops is usually all it takes for the horse to realize no one is going to hurt him, no one is angry, and he is not in trouble. Invariably, this specific gesture does wonders for the horse's confidence and helps him release really intense baggage related to leading.

Matching Steps

Horses follow the sound of each other's feet. I first learned this when working with a blind horse, but then realized all horses benefited from being able to hear my feet. You do not have to make loud stomping noises when moving with a horse, but it is best to march along at a good pace so that your footsteps are rhythmical and predictable.

Not all people and horses have a walk that complements the other. For best practices when working around horses, it is better to adopt a slower, more methodical stride in general. Mentors move in a slow methodical way, so if you practice moving like them, you are more likely to keep the horse's confidence in you. When you walk quickly, you are inadvertently sending a message to the horse: The only reason horses begin to walk quickly on their own is because there is tension or something intense happening.

Stomp to a Stop

Stomping your feet when you stop allows the horse to clearly hear that your feet have lined up. I have found that horses seem to prefer to line up their front feet with your feet when they hear your feet come to a stop. Breathe out as you stop; that way you have both breath and feet working together (fig. 7.18). In addition to this, make sure that you stop when you stop! *Many people are guilty of shuffling when they stop.* If the horse takes an extra step because he is uncertain about you stopping, and then you take an extra step because you are uncertain about him stopping, it can be very confusing for both of you. It is better to stop your feet and allow the horse to make the mistake of taking an extra step at first. Once he realizes he made a mistake and did not line up his feet with yours, most horses will do better next time.

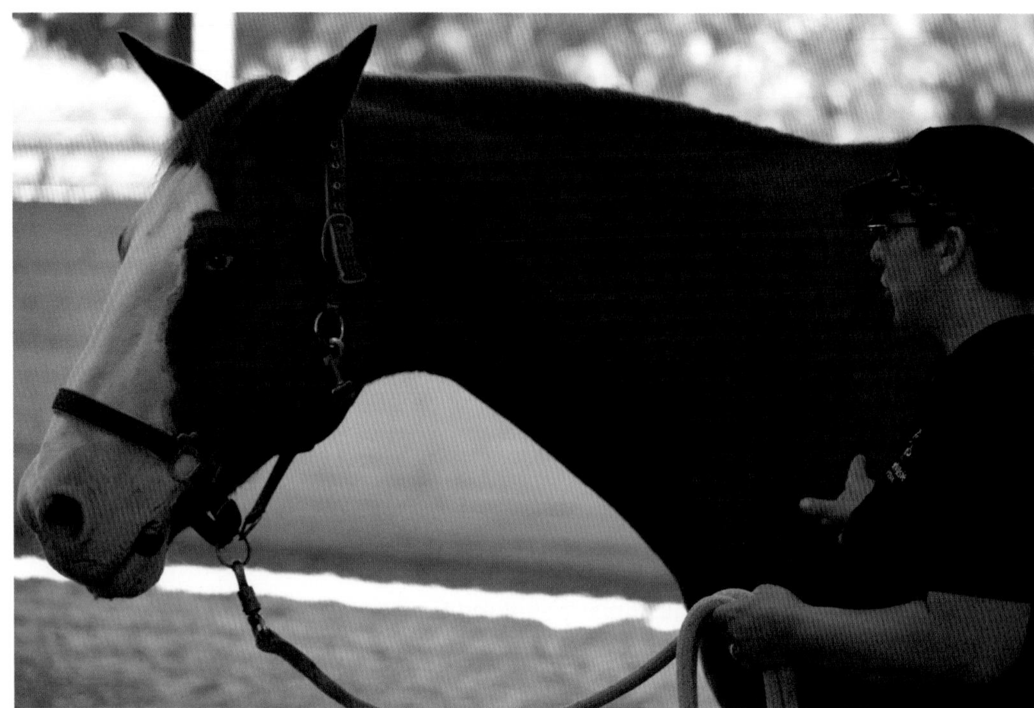

7.18 **Horses often like to halt with you in a Buddy-Up position after Stomping to a Stop. When you clearly stop your feet (breathing out audibly helps), you will notice the horses likes to stop with his front feet lined up with yours and his shoulder right next to yours. We just don't have the long head and neck like they do!**

In most cases when the horse continues to move past your Stomp to a Stop signal you can include your Core Energy, aiming it toward the horse's chest and even possibly stepping into a Therapy Back-Up. (As I said earlier, you have to be fast on your toes, pivoting quickly from walking forward to facing the horse, aiming your Core Energy at the horse's chest as you step into his space and ask for Therapy Back-Up.) For some horses who are confused or not paying attention or worried, you may have to step in and redirect them in this way. This answers their question about whether you are claiming the space in front of their Bubble. For Therapy Back-Up to be most effective, do not drive the horse backward several steps, merely ask for a single step backward. In most cases horses begin to not only halt but also gather themselves in collection as they stop. You shouldn't need to include Therapy Back-Up more than a few times for the horse to understand this message.

Turn the Key, Come to Me

This Conversation, which I describe on page 57, is very inviting—to the whole horse or to a specific Button. When inviting the whole horse, stand in front of the horse's Bubble in an O posture and "Turn the Key" from the horse's eyes to your belly button. When inviting a specific Button, then do the same gesture, but directed at the Button, then take three steps back (at least), and wait. Make sure you are aware of the angle of any turns so that you don't accidently ask the horse to do something that might be hard for him.

7.19 **Turn the Key, Come to Me can be added to any exercise when working with your horse. Most horses find this gesture irresistible. Here I aim it at the Mid-Neck Button to invite a turn.**

Ready, Set, Go

Activate the Cheek, Mid-Neck, and Shoulder Buttons in succession with a single tapping touch—not stabbing or jarring, just a little touch to each one as you say, "Ready, set, go!" Speaking the words out loud makes you congruent (your insides match your outsides—see p. 28). Horses draw their noses across these Buttons or look at each of these Buttons when they want another horse to follow. They may also lower and lift their heads, which is another way to say, "I am ready to go."

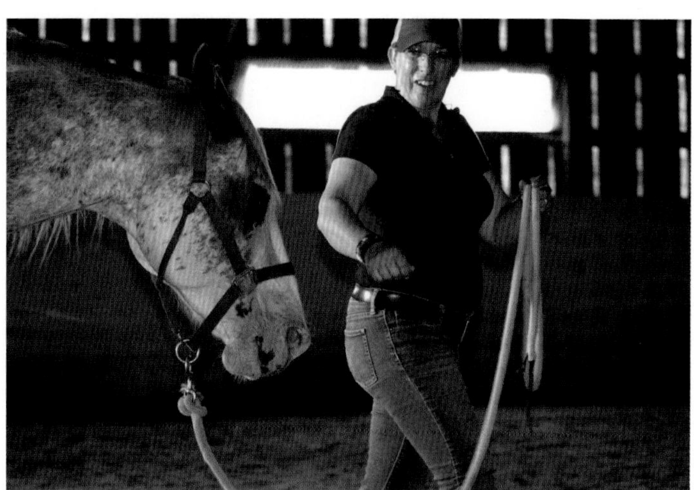

7.20 **Target hand in action! The Greeting knuckles can be something to follow.**

Targeting

We talked about using the Greeting knuckle (Knuckle Touch) as a target for the horse to follow on page 119 (fig. 7.20). More timid horses really like this, and some Mentors also really enjoy the pleasant contact. An outgoing Joker may like the contact but also want to play, so be mindful not to let that happen. You can also turn Targeting into Invitation Hand (p. 61) or point your finger at what you want to move toward. Try all three!

Follow Me

You can ask the Follow Me Button to come with you by touching the Button three times or Rocking the Baby there. Turn the Key, Come to Me will also work on this Button (see p. 128). After you invite the horse forward, take three steps back and wait.

Line Up

You invite your horse to come with you when you touch the Girth Button three times—again, not stabbing or striking, just three little taps. This is the Button that means, "Line up with me; we need to stick together." You can also use the Girth Button when you are moving the horse around your body into a different position—for instance, at the mounting block. It is good to be able to signal the Girth Button while walking with your horse as it reminds him that he needs to stay lined up with you as you move together without barging through your space.

"Don't worry, you can go forward with me."

When you tap or aim your energy toward the Jump-Up Button, you share this message with the horse. Due to its location on the horse's body, you may need to gently use the end of the lead rope or a stick to reach it. You can only talk to this Button on the lead rope when the horse is comfortable with you using Hold Hand with him there. A really sensitive or defensive horse may suck back and feel picked on, so know the temperament of your horse, and monitor your intensity levels. I have used this Button with horses I did not know and who were about to really panic, in combination with a quick Sentry Breath and a single eye blink or head turn on my part. In these cases, I said, "I mean you no harm. I am a Sentry; you can come along with me."

Tap the Hip Button

First offer Hold Hand to the hip, then tap the Button three times with your Activation Finger or a stick that can reach, or even the end of the lead rope. You are not slapping the horse, just Activating the Button. This is the "drive forward" Button, and you are saying, "I am the driver, and I want you to trust and follow me."

Use the Yield-Over Button

This may seem counterintuitive, but for a really "sticky" horse, asking him to yield over *first* before moving forward unlocks his mind and feelings. The horse's feelings are expressed in the pelvis once they have passed all the way through the Buttons (see p. 148). You may see the horse lower his head or lick and chew after you Activate this Button. Once he seems unlocked, begin to go forward.

Use Safety Objects

Set up several Safety Objects along the path you need to take, or come to agreements

7.21 Using Low-O posture to ask a horse to inspect an object placed between you is a part of checking out the Chessboard. I Draw the horse directly toward my belly button with the Greeting Ritual pattern.

with your horse about which items along the path are safe to stop at and touch or linger over (fig. 7.21). Invite the horse to explore the Chessboard with you instead of just trying to get from A to B.

High Hand, Low Hand

When your Target Hand is higher in the air, you change the way the horse balances through his Buttons. When your hand is lower in the air, you are also changing the way the horse balances. Try a little of each to see how your horse responds to your hand being higher or lower—especially when you change direction (fig. 7.22).

7.22 When the horse is following behind you, it is important to check in with him to see what he is thinking. Extending your arm away from your body—higher or lower or in the middle—helps him move in better balance because the line of the lead rope is clear and focused.

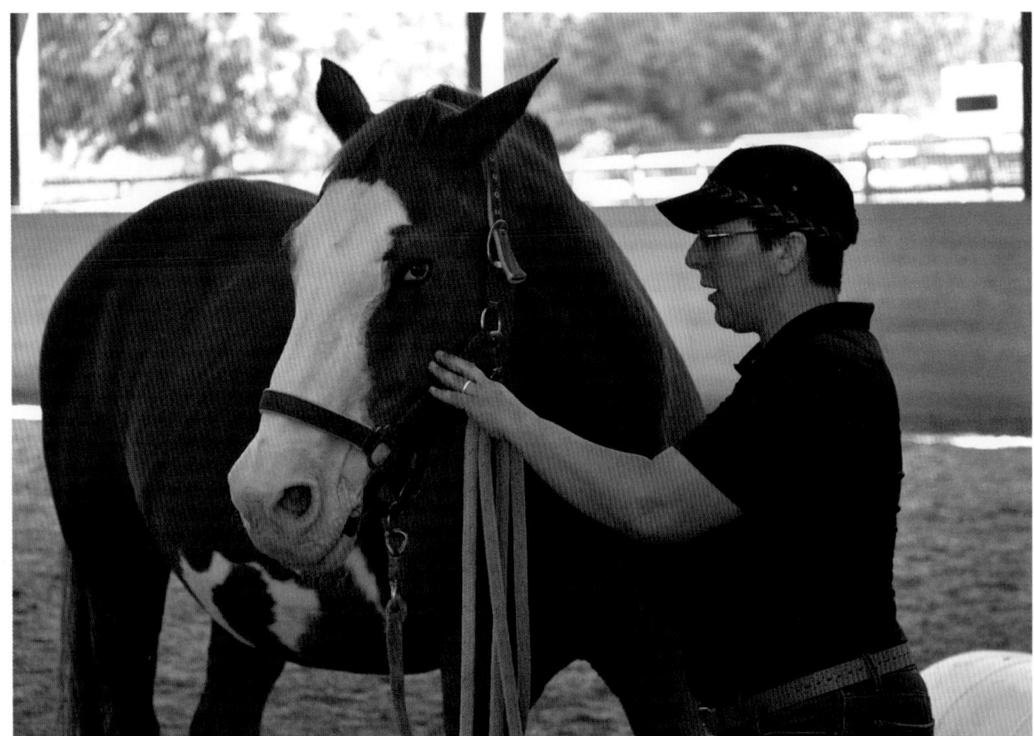

7.23 Activating the Cheek and Shoulder Buttons as a combination helps us both make a balanced turn away from my space. Because the horse's body is so much larger than mine, if he is on the inside of the turn, I need to be very mindful of how to help him create the necessary bend.

Change Direction with the Three Buttons of Respect

When you are moving the horse *away* from you to change direction, bring one hand out in front as your Target hand, and Activate the Cheek, Mid-Neck, and Shoulder Buttons to ask the horse to move over with your other hand (fig. 7.23). This helps to keep the balance in the horse's body better as you change direction *away from you.* If you are moving the horse *around your body* (toward you rather than away from you), keep your fingertips toward the Girth Button to encourage the horse to move circularly around you. In a sharp change of direction in a tight area, look over your shoulder at the horse's Hip Button, or step away from the horse as though in a "micro-longe" position, and ask the Yield-Over Button to step away while requesting the horse's head come in to you. In either case, the horse should swing his hip away from your gaze. Many people are delighted and amazed by this!

Other Messages

Secure the environment on the Chessboard in all the ways you know how: Scan the Horizon, blow a Sentry Breath, offer a good Aw-Shucks to lower intensity. Use Matching Steps to rate speed, and develop good rhythm, timing, and feel for

7.24 Keeping the 6-Inch Rule between your body and the horse's body also helps him move around you in better balance. All I need to do for both balance and space is keep my hand close to the Cheek Button and a little away from my body. Can you see the horse orienting his head to keep his cheek near my hand as well?

moving together. Try Fun with Feet while walking somewhere—pretend to walk over ice or lift your knees really high. Keep soft peripheral eye contact with your horse while walking. Horses do this! They use a good deal of soft eye contact to stay informed about moods,
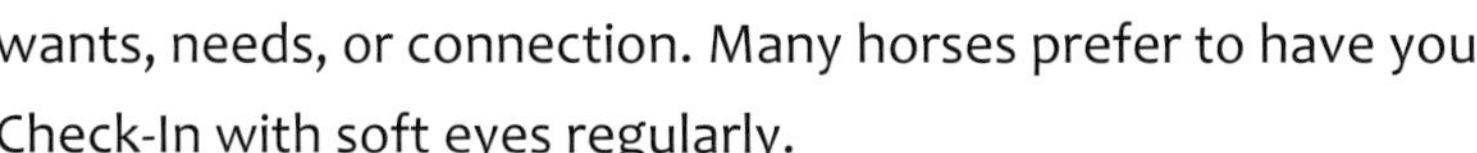
wants, needs, or connection. Many horses prefer to have you Check-In with soft eyes regularly.

6-Inch Rule

For safety purposes, the best position when leading a horse is with the 6-Inch Rule (see p. 128) between yourself and the horse, and with your shoulder between the Cheek and Mid-Neck Buttons (fig. 7.24). This allows your peripheral vision to see the horse's facial expressions. If you can drive a car, you can use your peripheral vision to see the horse's face as you walk forward, because this is the same skill.

Positioning yourself near the Cheek and Mid-Neck Buttons allows you to keep your Hold Hand up near the Cheek Button in the case of a pushy, nippy, young, green, or panicky horse. In any of these cases, the Hold Hand tells the horse's face to maintain its space at all times and refrain from tossing. This one message can really help horses stay in their own space and walk in their own lane. Most horses become very quiet when they receive this Hold Hand message.

MYTH-BUSTER

Is the Horse's Position Important?

Ultimately it is not about having the horse be in the "right place." It's not where the horse is, but what *you are talking about* as you lead him. If you have good rapport with a horse, you may be able to lead him from behind (like in long-lining, but with one lead rope) or it may be fine for him to follow along behind you. You could have an extra-long lead rope, or no lead rope at all. It isn't about position, it's about the Conversation.

Things Horses Tell You When Being Led

Bulging a Shoulder Toward You

When horses want to claim space in a Conversation about hierarchy with each other, they begin with the Greeting Button (even just a sniff), then move to the Cheek and Mid-Neck Buttons, and finally, they use a driving message aimed at the Shoulder Button. They can do this one Button at a time or in a fluid "cheek-neck-shoulder" motion. If you notice a horse reaching into your space, offer your knuckles as a Check-In to catch "leaky" energy before the horse engages his other Buttons.

Here are some other common messages from the shoulder:

- The shoulder is also used in Buddy-Up (see p. 118), when two horses walk or stand shoulder to shoulder in a relaxed manner, or even stand shoulder to hip in a mutual protective and restful manner (fig. 7.25).
- One horse can also use a "scooping" motion of his cheek and neck to indicate he wants to be included in another's Bubble. When the scoop includes the Shoulder Button, it is inviting the other to "come along."
- Walking past another horse, pausing at the horse's shoulder, then resuming motion is a quieter version of "scooping up your pal" to go somewhere together.
- A worried horse may touch you with his shoulder as he tries to Buddy-Up with you, asking you to protect him. Or he may be trying to scoop you up and get you to go with him to safety.
- In times of danger, a horse may push his shoulder into the shoulder of another horse to signal, "Come on! We gotta get out of here!" It is Buddy-Up in a rush.
- When a panicky horse wants to move past another higher-ranking one, he may use this same shoulder gesture like, "Sorry... I gotta get through here!" Of course, when this happens with a person, it can knock the person down.

7.25 When horses Buddy-Up, they Match Steps, and we can, too.

- If the horse feels like you are not a good leader, he may use the shoulder or his front foot to take space in the front Quadrant of the Bubble from you. Basically, in this situation he is putting his foot down and saying, "One of us has to lead, and I don't think it's you."

You must consider all these possibilities when determining why your horse is bulging a shoulder into you. This is why I emphasize the first part of Initiation,

SKILL-BUILDER

Be the Sandwich

In many cases there are two main signals that really help Hesitant or insecure horses feel you are offering them a chance to be in the middle of the sandwich—even though there is only one of you.

1. First, before walking, have a good Check-In. Make it as soft and kind as possible.
2. Then aim your Hold Hand toward the horse's hip in the air before walking.
3. Do a Therapy Back-Up, but only ask the horse to take one single step back. You are claiming the space in front, but improving the horse's balance and telling his hips to release tension. Remember, horses get emotional and express it through their pelvis and tail (see p. 225). The Therapy Back-Up encourages the pelvis to sit-down, which tells the horse to relax.
4. Move into *Dancer's Arms* for a few steps.
5. Walk in Dancer's Arms to a series of Safety Objects.
6. Repeat until the horse feels quieter, then try walking normally.

All these messages tell the horse, "I've got your front, I've got your back, and I will walk with you in the middle."

7.26 You can "be the sandwich," for your horse with Dancer's Arms that say, "I've got your front, I'm Matching Steps with your front feet, and I've got your back."

BUZZWORDS

Dancer's Arms

This is my solution to making our bodies more horizontal, like a horse's. Both arms are extended at shoulder height. One of your hands leads as the Target; the other sends the horse forward from the Girth Button (see p. 141 for more on this Conversation).

Introduction, and Negotiation is dedicated to resolving or developing better boundaries so that by the time you are in Navigation and *actually leading the horse somewhere*, these conditions are already more or less set to a better standard (see p. 197 for more about IINN).

Pushing Ahead

The term "alpha" has been used for a long time to denote a high position in a hierarchy. We often associate this word with a sense of power, dominance, and machismo. Although it is true that horses can display such impulses, especially in fighting stallions or high-ranking mares, in my opinion, it is important that we do not personally assign the value of "alpha male" or "alpha female" as we think of it in human terms. As we learned in chapter 4 (p. 156), horses who are the best leaders also behave like Protectors and Mentors; therefore, the best leaders tend to be quiet, self-assured, and predictable, and overall offer a sense of security to their followers.

Because of this, when a horse is pushing ahead while you are trying to lead him it is more often a sign of insecurity than anything else. Many horses prefer to be what I call "sandwiched": There is a horse in front of them who is leading the way and a horse behind them who is bringing up the rear and offering protection. Most horses want to be in the middle of a "sandwich." They don't want to make the big decisions about where to go, nor do they want the risk of being the Protector.

Make strong use of the Cheek, Mid-Neck, and Shoulder Buttons with a stronger 6-Inch Rule, keeping your hand in a light X position, out and toward the horse's body. Normally you only need to do this for a few days to a few weeks and the horse starts to understand, "Okay, you mean *always* stay out of your space and let you go forward first."

Hanging Back

Horses hang back for a simple reason—usually because they just don't want to go where you want to go. What you do about it depends on *why* the horse doesn't want to go where you are taking him. I usually treat this as a Threshold problem (see p. 227), in which case I'm inclined to use all the Chessboard concepts, as well as consider what Energy Type and Role in the Herd I am dealing with. A Stoic Mentor who hangs back may think my ideas about where to go are not good. A Stoic Skeptic could be waiting to see if I hold true to my word and do not fall apart and "get after him" when he balks. A Hesitant PBJ may not want to leave the protection of other horses.

With this information, I will go through the list of likely values each holds and the messages I might use to improve our connection:

- I could help the Stoic Mentor feel there are good resources where I want to go.
- I could try to go up in my intensity levels with the Stoic Skeptic, very, very precisely so he can see what my X looks like as I "add volume." This type of horse often wants to see "how bad it gets," only because many of them have had it bad. Once this sort sees that my Level Four intensity is just another volume and not full of anger or aggression, they tend to lick and chew and come along nicely.
- With the Hesitant PBJ, I could use the Follow Me and Sit Buttons, along with Safety Objects and Sentry Breath, while leading in Dancer's Arms until he believes in me.

SKILL-BUILDER

Turning up the Volume

You can add intensity to a "sticky" horse with fingertip pressure on the Button you wish to move. I use a three-times tapping motion: Your straightened fingertips go, "Tap, tap, tap!" This tends to work well on the Girth Button for forward or sideways motion.

You can also use a three-time tapping touch with the end of a stick on the Hip Button, Yield-Over Button, and in some cases, the Jump-Up Button. The tapping should not be punitive in feel. Instead, it should emulate the way you might tap a person on the shoulder to say, "Excuse me, I need to move past you."

The goal of thinking about the levels of intensity here is that you are increasing the volume of your requests by degrees. Reading your horse's body language and facial expressions should tune you in to see if a horse is resisting from fear, confusion, or pain or memory of pain. In my experience, most horses want to get along with you, so rather than thinking, "How hard do I need to be to *make* my horse do the thing?" you should be thinking, "Is there something I don't know about limiting my horse's abilities here?"

Remember: *The better your directions, the fewer your corrections.*

Crowding

Generally, horses crowd out of anxiety. Horses who are crowding tend to be anxious about where they're going or what they are leaving behind. Most often I will begin work with the Bubble of Personal Space keeping the 6-Inch Rule between us. For this to work I need to stay active at the three Buttons of respect: Cheek, Mid-Neck, and maybe even Shoulder Button. If a horse is crowding because he is resistant, then often he is also trying to pull away at the same time. With this situation I will not only use the Buttons of respect, but also a Therapy Back-Up, aiming my Core Energy at the horse's chest at least three times in a row. Because the Therapy Back-Up helps the horse feel calm and secure in his body, as well as yield the front of the Bubble to you, and because this method does not create more stress or tension for the horse but actually relieves it, it can work in many situations where a horse is being physically demanding.

The keynote with crowding is, when it is caused by anxiety, offer many calming messages. I like to stop more frequently while leading this horse to do a Check-In with him, which can mean offering my knuckles for him to sniff, stroking his neck, and looking at his eyes while blinking softly to encourage him to stop staring and being

SKILL-BUILDER

Working with Personalities

When a horse doesn't want to go forward because he is a Peacemaker and it is part of his personality to hold back, then I will go all the way down his Buttons until I find the Button that he responds best to. For example, often Peacemakers will respond well from the Jump-Up or Yield-Over Button. If the horse is a Mentor, sometimes he has a hard time leaving a buddy behind. In this case, I may personally take some time with the buddy horse being left behind, and when I am leaving with the Mentor, I may do a Hold Hand toward his Girth Button, and then toward his Hip Button for a moment to tell him, "You are with me now; everything is fine." I will take a big breath and let out an audible sigh or even a shuddering breath. I may include an Aw-Shucks to lower the intensity and flip my hand as a "tail swish" to say we are done for now. This allows for a nice Gone phase, which I find can help Mentors who worry about their buddies and experience separation anxiety.

When the horse is a Skeptic, PBJ, or Pawn, then I may offer "sandwiching" messages to him. I tell him that I know that he wants to stay between a horse who is leading and a horse who would be driving, and I will do my best to provide that.

stressed. I will also offer Sentry Breath, *Nurturing Breath*, and even stroke my hands down his front legs to draw the energy down and out and help get him grounded again. In this case, walking with a stick may help you keep your Zero. Use the stick to aim at Buttons and stroke the horse's legs and body. Licking and chewing as though you are chewing on a peanut butter sandwich is also helpful with anxious horses because other horses will not make chewing noises and sounds until the stress is gone and it's time to eat again. If you know your horse finds something specific to be relaxing or enriching, use it when you pause in your motion on the lead. This way you not only correct pushy or crowding energy, but also invite the horse to feel safe, protected, and comfortable.

BUZZWORDS

Nurturing Breath

This is the inward sniff or snort that sounds like what mares use with newborns to urge them to stand and nurse. You can mimic this breath by clearing your throat with an inhale—it can resemble the soft snort a pig might make.

Circling

There are some horses who seem to have so much going on inside of them that they have a hard time stopping when you do and want to circle you instead. Sometimes a horse really wants to get back to where he wants to be or to a friend—when you have a horse like this who is prancing about and is difficult to settle, allowing him to circle once or twice around you can be helpful *if* you have a focal point for him to pay attention to once the activity has stopped. In this situation, you need to be the calm center of the hurricane. When a horse circles you too many times, it may have the opposite effect from calming him down and may actually amp him up more.

When a horse is circling and getting worse, I Activate the Girth and Yield-Over Button. When the Yield-Over Button is Activated, the horse is tempted to cross his

SKILL-BUILDER

Dealing with "Leaking"

When a horse is what I call "leaking" into forward motion or away from you, it is a sign of stress. Provide calming messages by helping him stand in a balanced position and blocking the "leaky" motion. If the horse takes a step when you didn't ask him to, he is asking to take over the Conversation, and you need to be quick enough to catch that "leak" with your X posture and Core Energy, stopping the forward movement. This is not punishment; it is an important message. It's X *for* the horse, not against him.

hind legs and shift his pelvis away from you to allow him to look at you more directly. This can help him stop. I have had the best success with horses who circle by setting up an arena with many objects to step over, around, through, and under. Make sure to pause often as you add enrichment.

If a horse tends to circle you once he gets past a Threshold, then circling is the symptom, but the Threshold is the problem. In any case, a horse who has "big energy" like this needs to have everything laid out clearly *before* you get to the problem zone. This is why the Initiation, Introduction, and Negotiation aspects of beginning your day with a horse are so important. When you can prepare the horse mentally and emotionally before you ever put a halter on, you are more likely to keep him calm and also teach him how to keep himself calm.

I love the look of self-satisfaction on a horse's face when he begins to challenge himself and deal with situations that once were hard for him. We don't have to constantly manage the horse because he is unable to manage himself—remember, horses want to be at Zero, therefore, when you show them the way to modulate their own intensity levels, they tend to begin to learn how to do this for themselves.

SKILL-BUILDER

What's He Sniffing?

When the horse wants to put his nose on you and sniff your body at certain moments when you are leading him, most often he wants to have a Check-In with you. If he sniffs your arm or your belly or your shoulder or your leg, and you are comfortable with a Knuckle Touch, then offer your Greeting. If the horse sniffs your knuckles and then goes back to sniff the body part on you again, consider the following questions:

- Is the horse indicating a particular Button on your body? For instance, is he sniffing your shoulder or is he sniffing your tummy?
- Is the horse sniffing down your leg or onto your boot? Often this is either a request to start moving off, or a comment that you are standing too close or accidentally aiming your Core Energy at him or across the front of his Bubble.
- Is the horse intent on sniffing your belly button area? Is he also rubbing his forehead on you? Often these two things go together when the horse is seeking emotional connection of some kind.
- Is the horse trying to draw your attention to something? Is that something simply that he wants to have a nice moment with you?

Sniffing the Ground

Some horses seem to want to sniff the ground frequently when being led. In these cases, I like to first have their eyes checked. If all is well, it seems that some horses really want to smell the area they are in and get a lot of information in this way. There are actually horses in the herd who are taught to track. Horses have an amazing sense of smell, and if you find your horse wants to sniff the trail often and his eyesight is found to be normal, then it's really no big deal. Come up with an agreement with the horse about how often he can sniff, where he can sniff, or how much time you want him to linger there. It is fine to have agreements with horses about what you are or are not comfortable with. Having a worried or knee jerk reaction to a horse's curiosity or his need to "see what is going on" is not beneficial.

Leading Practice with Safety Objects

I like to use all the leading strategies we've discussed in this chapter in an arena for the sake of improving communication between myself and all the horse's Buttons. Many of the confusing moments between us and horses can be cleared up with consistent practice leading a horse and communicating with a specific Button.

I like to have several objects set up in an arena to work with and problem-solve as reasons to use the different Buttons for different things. When you see horses turned loose together in a pasture or arena with a few items in with them, you will see them explore and not only move their own bodies but also move as a group or pair in relation to the objects.

There is one thing to keep in mind when you are using obstacles: You want any potential obstacle in the arena to be a Safety Object. For this to work you must touch the objects before the horse does. There are a lot of desensitization programs out there that teach people to drive or send the horse to an object to sniff it. It is not that this is wrong or bad, but it does send a confusing message to the horse. Lead horses are the ones to sniff objects first. Protector horses are the ones to explore the Chessboard first. If you want to come across as your horse's leader and Protector, and you are telling him that all the objects in the arena are safe and offer potential places of rest, then you must touch the objects *before* he does. You will see surprising results from this simple adjustment.

8 Advancing Your Body Language at Liberty and on the Longe Line

The Magic of One Rider, One Horse

My goal is this: if we want to educate a horse to perform at a high level—be it in liberty performance, as a working cow horse, in the art of dressage, or in one of the many other forms of working with and riding horses—then the horse needs to be understood. The relationship between horse and human needs to be carefully cultivated *first*, not second. Then both the horse and the person are invested in each other and in the work they are doing together, and both take pride in the outcome.

Many famous riders and trainers got to where they are from an epic performance given on one or two favorite horses. Those riders and trainers may go on to work with many more horses and advise hundreds of other people, but their popularity and success came from the performance that *one horse in particular* gave them. Even those with long careers and a number of well-known horses still only name one or two as having been the "ultimate partner."

Like in any relationship, beyond any method applied or any gold belt buckle or blue ribbon, there is a baseline "chemistry" between horse and that rider that actually makes the difference.

Nurturing that chemistry is part of what Horse Speak promises to do, and I find that working with the horse on the ground—"at liberty" and on the longe line—is one of the keys to this. Time spent understanding the horse, and his balances and imbalances, on the ground translates to more success in the saddle.

Liberty Work

People have commented that in my first book, *Horse Speak,* I am often working with horses who are "free," at liberty, in the photographs. The reason for this is that I feel it demonstrates the *essence* of communication without the need for artificial forms of control. However, I also recommend in that book, and in this one, to make the best use of a barrier when first building rapport, if one is available (see p. 43). Instead of creating a smaller space to directly influence the horse from *within* (you inside the round pen with the horse, for example), I discovered that you could get more done to build trust and rapport if you use the smaller space to begin communicating from the *outside* (the horse inside, you outside). I can say that approaching a horse from outside while he is at liberty not only encourages him to communicate, but it also keeps both of you at a

8.1 Because Horse Speak is a language, you can talk to a horse from anywhere. This means you can create safety, harmony, and connection with a horse from the other side of a barrier. This allows the horse to *truly choose to be with you*.... There is such authentic connection when a horse, like this one who could move anywhere in this large arena, chooses to stick with you for the simple reason that *he wants to.*

better Zero, because the barrier does not allow the horse to become overly fixated or defensive (fig. 8.1).

I used to be a clinic-goer, and I noticed that often as a clinician approached a round pen, she tended to linger on the outside, talking to the audience, even if that round pen was on the inside of a bigger space with bleachers around for a large audience. This matched up with what I had been seeing with Mentor horses at rescue facilities approaching others in the herd from the outside their pens. Lo and behold, many clinicians got a lot of initial communicating with the horse accomplished as they talked to the audience and prepared to enter the ring. In some cases, the horses were already

8.2 A & B Liberty means freedom. When horses engage with us at liberty, it is important that they feel free (A). Good balance is achievable when the horse is relaxed. I had never worked with these horses before. Note how they are Matching Steps in harmony with each other and with me (B). There is rapport between us, and they are choosing to be near me within this large arena.

starting to Copycat them, before the clinicians ever went inside. And often, the clinicians had a better connection from *outside* the fence than they did once they got inside.

Liberty work doesn't have to be up close or flashy to be worthwhile (figs. 8.2 A & B). You and your horse can gain an understanding of each other and begin to have a feel for one another without contact, without much movement, and even with a barrier between you. Horse Speak acknowledges the finer points of communication and tries to make the most of them.

Conversations About Balance and Energy

When working with the horse at liberty, I like to use a structured environment, like a round pen or a Ring of Cones (see p. 247) in a larger arena or pasture to provide a reasonable space in which to manage "picking the energy up" and "putting it away." When longeing or riding, far too many of us were taught to just pick up a trot or canter and go. This only works on the horse's obedience to a cue; horses do not inherently know how to balance themselves on a small circle or balance the weight of a rider. When you are thinking about raising the intensity (asking for movement, for example), the most important thing is that your horse stays in balance—mentally, emotionally, and physically.

Using high-intensity activity can have a place in the horse's overall education; however, using it as a starting point or as a mainstay can create severe limitations and unwanted byproducts. The faster the horse moves, the harder it is to read the Conversation. I suggest practicing raising the intensity during a time when you both are at Zero, so you have a place to come back to. Moving the Conversation up a notch to a higher Intensity because it seems like the horse needs to sort something out is a decision to arrive at, having already gone through many layers of Low-Calorie communications.

> **MYTH-BUSTER**
>
> **Does the Horse's Form Matter at Liberty?**
>
> A good coach or trainer can see where an athlete (human or horse) is not using good form and is able to guide the athlete to use the body to its fullest. Good form enhances athletic ability, minimizes stress to the joints, and reduces the risk of injury. However, in the equestrian world, far too often there are misunderstandings and shortcuts when it comes to putting a horse into good form.

Dancer's Arms

I introduced Dancer's Arms in my first book *Horse Speak*. It is a way to open the door to a more authentic form of movement *with* a horse rather than making movement happen *to* a horse.

SKILL-BUILDER

Claiming "My Territory"

When you have an Outgoing or "hot" horse who seems to "need to move around," try the following at liberty:

1 Claim one spot on the Chessboard for yourself and let the horse run around the rest of the space. (This is what I call "My Territory.")

2 Stay close to a wall or fence so the horse can't get behind you. It is best to have a few objects on the Chessboard that the horse can "have" for himself. You may even place a little hay out as a place to settle.

3 Shoo the horse away from you using an *upward* motion on a whip, rope, or plastic bag. (Downward motions indicate reprimand.) Maintain your X to appropriate degrees as long as the horse is moving, but do not "throw gasoline on his fire."

4 Decide where the edge of your Bubble is. Do not be wishy-washy. Line the edge of your Bubble with Safety Objects if you can.

5 Shoo the horse away from your Bubble if he tries to come too close with a high head.

6 Watch for any signs he wants to renegotiate—for example, lowering the head, O posture, deeper breathing, blinking, rolling. When this happens, lower the intensity of your X posture, and turn your shoulder toward the horse.

7 If the horse begins to ask to connect with you, I find it is often better to walk toward him, and invite him to come halfway, rather than allowing him to come all the way to you. If he comes to you, sometimes it can be confusing as to whether or not he is now claiming the space, or you still are.

The goal with the hot horse at liberty is this: He can run around as long as he does not intrude into your territory. Once he shows signs of calming down, take control by saying, "Okay, now let's meet halfway." I find it is usually best to then halter the horse and either work in hand with a lead rope for a bit, or even put the horse away for the day. Do not try to get liberty work or concentrated work done when the horse just "blew off steam" because he will need at least 20 minutes to release all that adrenaline.

This process can be restorative and constructive when done correctly. Do not turn it into a game of chase. If you feel that you cannot keep your Zero for this activity, then I recommend you stay outside the arena or pasture and claim a section of the fence line as "My Territory." Sometimes, being outside the barrier is actually better for you both, because the horse can be witnessed without you ever losing your Zero.

In the past, I studied dance, and one of the forms was called "contact improvisation"—the exploration of one's body in relationship to others through the sharing of weight, touch, and movement awareness. I discovered that using some of these elements in conjunction with the horse invited the horse to have a Conversation about balance with me. I had also received training in classical in-hand work and combining those traditions with the insights of authentic movement through dance opened a door to the language of motion that horses speak.

The concept of Dancer's Arms is expanding your awareness of lateral motion not only in the horse's body but yours as well. It is intended to provide a *shared experience*. Most of the time when we think of having the horse do lateral work on the ground, we put his body into the position that we want him to take. We may not be aware that he is mimicking our body language more often than not—when our body language is not clear about lateral movement in our own spine and our own sense of balance, then we could be sending mixed messages without knowing it. When you see very skilled people who know how to create nice lateral movement on the ground in their horses, there are micro-gestures they are making to explain things to the horse that *they themselves* may not be conscious of.

The whole purpose of Dancer's Arms is to prepare you for advanced balancing maneuvers while on the ground. Your lead hand can be connected to the Buttons of the horse's head and neck, and the driving hand can be connected to the Buttons of the body and the hind end. Your Core Energy can act like a magnet and either attract the horse to you or move him farther away. Your feet can move with either the front or back feet of the horse or simply take up the general rhythm, pace, and timing of the horse's movement. Altogether, your body begins to move like a dancer. For the horse, this experience is about inviting him to move in a balanced way in straight lines, circles, and arcs with you. Rather than prescribing precise movements, this allows you and your horse to explore a beautiful experience.

Is This Like Traditional In-Hand Work?

There's nothing wrong with traditional lateral movements that are taught on the ground and in the saddle in many disciplines. It was when I worked with rescue horses and found they frequently needed balancing techniques to return to a state of well-being, but due to various limitations, could not participate in a classical conditioning program, that I invented Dancer's Arms. It provided a modality of physical therapy while also instilling pride and well-being. In addition, I discovered that Dancer's Arms

8.3 Dancer's Arms at liberty. Horses find this position to be a positive experience. We become "longer" and more horizontal, like them, and our hands and body are all talking to different Buttons at the same time—like they do with each other.

helped to prepare both humans and horses for better overall awareness and balance, which all contribute to better liberty, longeing, and ridden work (fig. 8.3).

The art of creating lateral movement in a horse is well-documented and understood, but the emphasis is always on teaching a horse how to move into a position that we have predetermined is the "right position." The limitation of this creates a vacuum in which you may not fully know or understand how your horse feels organically about his body and where it is in space. I have seen some horses performing technically good lateral movement according to principle; however, I can see that the sternum is locked, or the Sit Button is not engaged, or they are unable to fully mobilize their hyoid apparatus (the attachment of the tongue and pharynx).

Because I worked with so many horses who had severe balance problems from illness or injury or overwork in bad posture, I developed a desire to be present and open with every horse with the intention to help him rediscover his own body and tap into his innate sense of balance.

I did not want to "put" a horse into a frame or form and assume that this was good balance or good posture *for him*. By going slowly and working with the individual horse, lateral work turned into more of a physical therapy activity in which the horse had agency of self-discovery.

If you already have a system of lateral work that you and your horse know and enjoy, I suggest simply adding Dancer's Arms to your repertoire. Many people who have worked with me and this Conversation have been excited to discover new levels of openness, understanding, and willingness in their horses.

Getting in Position

When first practicing Dancer's Arms with your horse, you can use a halter and lead rope or longe line, and it is best to have several cones set up to walk toward so that you maintain a straight line as you learn to ask for movement. You can carry a stick or dressage whip to use as an extension of your arm if you wish.

1 Begin with your feet facing the horse with both arms outstretched, one hand extended toward the Bridge of the Nose and the other hand reaching toward the Girth Button (fig. 8.4). Your skin and body need to touch the horse's body for your nervous system and his to become entrained. Your Core Energy should be directed under the horse's neck.

2 When you are ready to move, turn your feet and your core completely forward—what I call "opening the door" (fig. 8.5).

8.4 Begin Dancer's Arms with your leading hand on the noseband of the halter near the Bridge of the Nose Button. Gently hold the halter with your lead hand; you don't want to "clasp" and get your fingers stuck.

8.5 Your legs will Match Steps with the horse's front legs and your other hand will touch the Girth Button to ask for movement. Expect this to feel awkward at first; your horse may stand there and look at you, saying, "What do you mean?" Just smile and breathe.

8.6 Ask the horse to bring his nose a little toward your belly button. This should be a gentle ask, nothing forced.

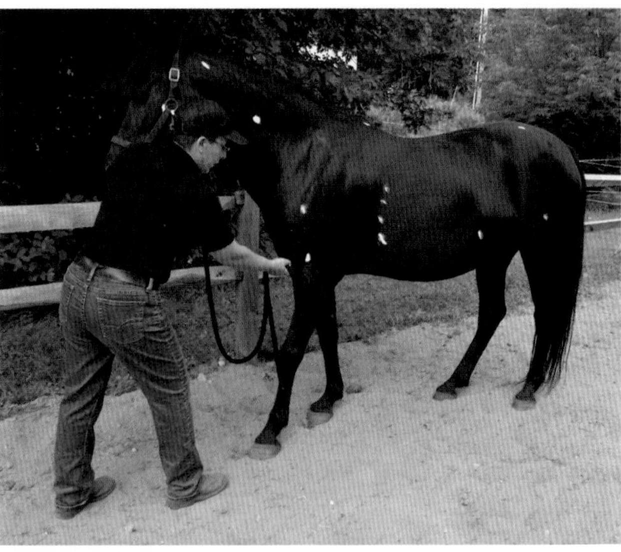

8.7 From Dancer's Arms, you can Power Pivot to go directly into Therapy Back-Up. You can use this to ask the horse to halt squarely or as a half-halt.

8.8 Here you can see the C-curve we hope to achieve from the horse's nose through his spine to the tail. This the horse is balanced through his whole body.

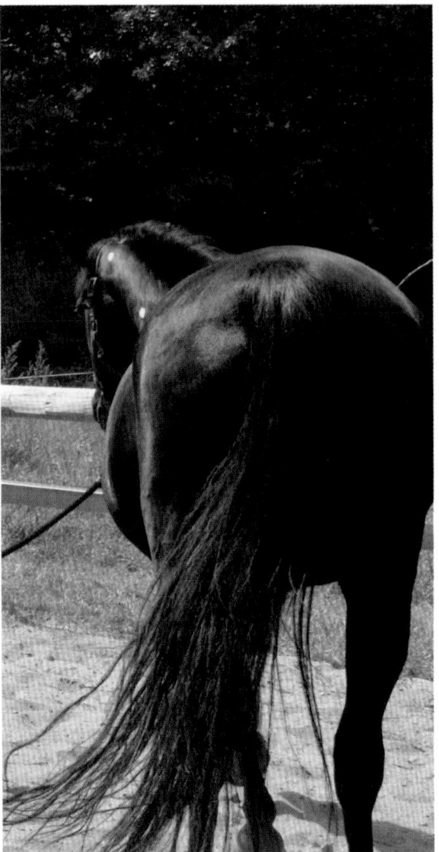

8.9 When you and your horse are comfortable, ask for the same movement, but stay farther back from the horse's body. Here I point the end of the stick at the Jump-Up Button to add a little "sparkle" to the forward motion.

3 Take a few steps toward a cone, then halt. Do not be too picky with the horse. When you begin this Conversation, it is more important for you to get your own body position correct. A horse who is trying to learn this may wiggle or circle or not fully understand what you want at first; do not complain about it. All you want to do is pick up the energy, move it along, and then stop the energy. Note that if your horse really has a hard time walking with you in a straight line, try along the wall or fence line of an arena first. You are not trying to create anything specific like shoulder-in or haunches-in. Rather, you are learning to put yourself and your horse into a posture of balance and explore that balance together. Just as with the tango or the waltz, you must only do a few steps at a time when you are both first learning.

4 When you both get good at moving from cone to cone, then you can go to the next step: Asking for the Bridge of the Nose to relax in the palm of your hand and aiming the horse's nose a little bit toward your belly button (fig. 8.6). Do this at least three times in a row, but do not overbend the horse's neck. You do not want him "rubber-necking." You are simply asking for a little flexion through the top of the poll. This should feel relaxing to the horse, not like you are being overbearing or pushy.

5 Now, use your fingertip pressure at the girth to invite the rib cage to move a little bit away from you as you move. When you halt, engage a Therapy Back-Up (p. 255) to help the horse balance into himself (fig. 8.7). You are balancing forward and backward; this is how it starts to feel like dancing!

6 The goal eventually is for the horse to create a lovely arc from his nose through his head and neck through the spine so that he forms a letter C from nose to tail (fig. 8.8). You may not be able to see it happening, but you will feel it! When the horse begins to find his lateral balance, often there is a lovely "floating" sensation in his body. The change is from encouraging somewhat awkward mechanical steps to becoming dance-like steps.

7 When you are comfortable creating the C curve, move away from the horse's body, but ask for the same steps without touching him (fig. 8.9). Having engaged a better sense of balance in your own body because of the spread of your arms and the flexibility of your core as you walk forward, you will be much more aware of the feeling between your body and the horse's body when you are both in balance—and when you are not. Dancer's Arms will help you notice little nuances in your horse's sense of balance that are otherwise difficult to observe or train your eye to see.

8.10 As you use the Advanced Therapy Back-Up, you can look at other Buttons, or even point to them. Doing this adds more rapport.

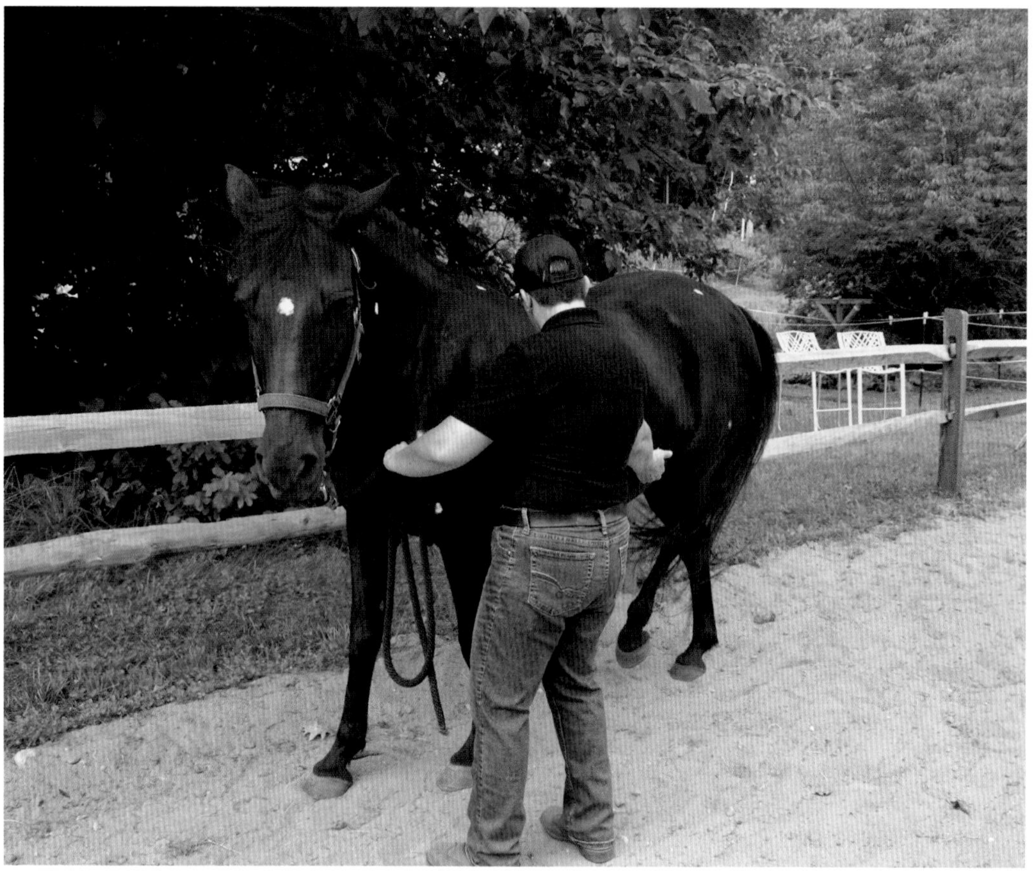

Dancer's Arms to Therapy Back-Up

Therapy Back-Up and Dancer's Arms really fit well together. When you offer an Advanced Therapy Back-Up, you can move from touching the Back-Up Button at the armpit groove and indicating every other Button besides that one: for example, with one hand either on the Bridge of the Nose or "scooping" the lead rope, the fingers of your other hand can Activate the Girth or the Jump-Up Button, or your eyes can look at the Mid-Neck, Shoulder, Hip, or Yield-Over Buttons. You will notice that the horse lifts his tummy and tucks his pelvis and yields his face and softens in general.

After an Advanced Therapy Back-Up using many of the Buttons as ways to balance and reorganize your horse's body, you will find it much easier to go forward in Dancer's Arms and also connect to other Buttons (fig. 8.10). Remember that each Button has its own meaning; when you go up and down the Buttons to go backward and forward again, it is having an effect on the horse's sense of communication, connection, and understanding. Try to not to think of it as a purely mechanical activity that just moves the horse this way and that.

Dancer's Arms to Longeing

You can extend Dancer's Arms naturally into longeing, on a line or free. In addition, by adopting variations of this position as your horse moves around you, you can address stiffness, tension, or other issues you notice in your horse with your own posture.

8.11 It is easy to segue Dancer's Arms into longeing. You can use Matching Steps and Fun with Feet to change rhythm and tempo in your horse's footwork.

SKILL-BUILDER

Feet Don't Fail Me

Now that you are able to pay closer attention to your horse's balance and connection through authentic movement, bring your attention to his feet. Use Matching Steps (p. 49) and Fun with Feet (p. 61) to begin to incorporate precise timing in his footwork.

I teach Fun with Feet in *Horse Speak*, so rather than give a list of instructions to follow here, I encourage you to experiment, and see what it takes to engage one of your horse's feet at a time and what it takes to engage that precise foot in either forward or backward steps.

Horses use single footsteps to communicate intention and meaning, so when you do this, you may begin to sense the horse is saying something. For instance, you may begin to not only notice when one foot is ahead of another one, but also interpret if that foot intends to go somewhere, is claiming space, indicates a concern, or is offering to connect.

Longeing How-To

If you work the Chessboard, including IINN to secure the environment for the horse (as needed) and prepare him for work, you will have negated many of the common issues horses have related to longeing. Consider the Four Gs as you establish the longe circle (figs. 8.12 A & B).

1. Greet the horse in the working space.
2. Go Somewhere by cuing the Cheek, Mid-Neck, and Shoulder Buttons to *begin* movement. Use your Dancer's Arms posture with your leading hand as the Invitation Hand to ask the horse to move forward.
3. Aim your belly button (and stick, if you use one) at the Girth Button to ask for more distance.
4. When you are ready to increase the intensity and ask for speed, cue the Jump-Up button or Hip Button.

MYTH-BUSTER

Can Horses Tell Us What Exercises They Need?

I believe they can. At one of my clinics, a horse who was exhibiting a certain amount of emotional imbalance was encouraged with Dancer's Arms and Advanced Therapy Back-Up at liberty. I held the Bridge of the Nose via the halter as an assist the first couple of times. Every time I released him to "soak" on the experience, he brought himself back to me and put himself back in position to do it again!

I used all the Buttons in his Therapy Back-Up to help him feel his body from different points of balance, and I then walked him forward in Dancer's Arms, including not only the Girth but also the Jump-Up Button.

The horse had previously tried to step over some ground poles and had been dragging his feet and tripping. After we completed five or six versions of Dancer's Arms to Advanced Therapy Back-Up, he walked over to his owner and invited her to walk over the poles with him again. This time he was able to lift his feet well and high! When he was done, he let out a huge sigh, blew out his nose loudly, shook like a dog shaking off water, from head to toe, and yawned deeply. There were about 40 people in this clinic, and everyone was smiling ear to ear sharing in his self-pride! In my work with Horse Speak, I have seen many examples of horses telling us what they need, once they discover we can understand them.

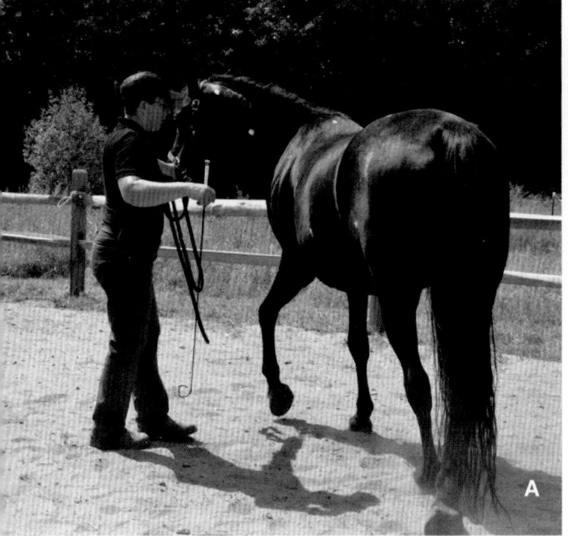

8.12 A & B Once you can move in Dancer's Arms, it is a logical next step as you increase the space between you and your horse to practice micro-longeing in half-circles (A). You can gradually expand the distance between you and your horse by asking for more Bubble space from the Girth Button. I am putting it all together with Dancer's Arms, Target Hand, and Matching Steps. My front hand and arm talks to the Buttons of the front end, my body is positioned in the middle of the horse near both the Girth and Jump-Up Buttons, and I am using my stick to ask the Sit Button to reach more deeply under the horse (B).

5 After a successful Going Somewhere, halt with O posture, look at the Yield-Over or Sit- Down Button, and offer Grooming.

6 Step away for a moment and pause with a big sigh—the Gone phase—before starting up again.

7 Most horses want to have a Check-In with a renewed Greeting of some kind before Going Somewhere in "Round Two." If your horse tries to come in on the circle too soon, aim your hand or stick back up at the Buttons of the Cheek, Mid-Neck, and Shoulder to ask for a few more steps around.

8 Note that when a horse asks to come back to you, at first, always allow it; he is checking in and making sure longeing is just an enrichment activity and you are not trying to drive him away from your herd of two.

MYTH-BUSTER

Is the Horse Being Respectful by Stopping Outside Your Bubble?

In Horse Speak, it is *polite* to stop outside the lead horse's Bubble of Personal Space, not on the edge of it where the lead horse could feel encroached upon. If you ask for halt and your horse moves farther away and *then* halts, this is why. To request a sharper halt that is more *with you*, focus on Matching Steps and use a Safety Object to stop at.

8.12 C **Modulating the X and O posture along with the Gestures and Matching Step messages can help create a relaxing "lift" into the trot. Here I am in more of an O posture to keep the pace steady.**

8.12 D **I am using Drop It to Stop It and beckoning with O posture to invite the horse back to me. My step backward helps the mare move into a good position directly in front of me.**

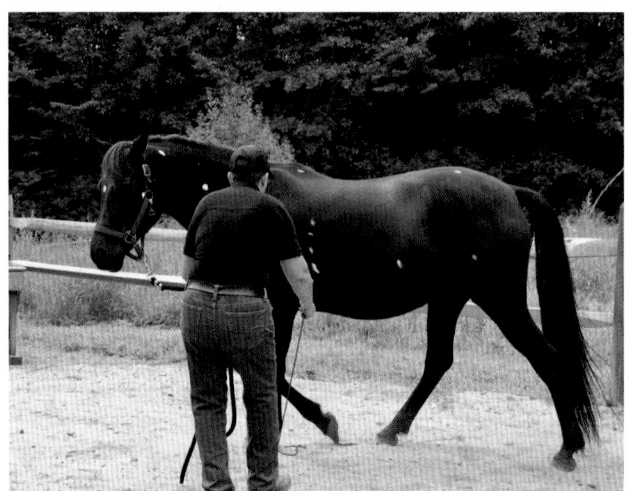

8.12 E **Your O posture combined with a "sit" motion asks the horse to slow down or halt (Drop It to Stop It). Here I asked the horse to slow down, which is why I am still facing her. You can try this message from different positions and aiming at different Buttons to see what your horse prefers.**

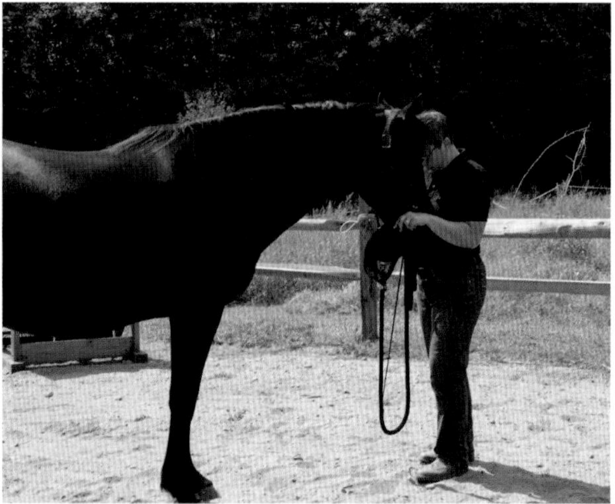

8.12 F **End with enrichment. I am always grateful to my horses. If I remember to treat everything as a gift from them, it helps me not slip into "task tunnel vision."**

9 Horses use half-circles to move away from and come back to each other. If your horse wants to come back to you after a half-circle on the longe, allow it a few times to reduce anxiety or concern.

10 Next link together two half-circles into one full circle, using Drop It to Stop It (see p. 61) or O posture to halt the horse. If you want the horse to halt on the outside of the circle, use your hand or stick to aim at the Mid-Neck or Girth Button.

11 If you want him to turn and face you, then step backward and invite him with Turn the Key, Come to Me or O posture. Give the horse a "place to land," using either the Greeting Knuckles or a Hold Hand.

By using all these signals, when you remove the longe line for free longeing or other liberty work, you will be able to use the Conversations and have the horse go, stop, and move around you with simple changes in your body language.

SKILL-BUILDER

Longeing the "Shut-Down" Horse

When a horse seems distant and "shut down" when you ask for longeing, he may be either imploding or getting ready to explode. He could be dealing with confusion, emotional distress, physical balance issues, or all three. As described previously, use IINN to prepare him for the activity. Use the Four Gs to him to move out on the longeing circle.

What will be different than your usual longeing session is your ready use of the Hot Potato Release and your praise for *anything*—even praise for *standing still* (as opposed to bolting or freaking out). The "secret sauce" for unlocking a frozen or shutdown horse is to *not* try to unlock him with big intensity, but try instead to enter into a communication of micromovements and very Low-Calorie Conversation with copious amounts of enrichment.

Slowly, you will see a frozen horse begin to trust and open up again. Sometimes you need to exaggerate your movements to demonstrate what you look like in X and O but without asking him to do anything about it. You can do this from a distance or up close, but have *no intensity* in your expression. You are sort of "talking someone off a ledge"; make no sudden movements.

I know what I am saying may go against the very grain of traditional methods, which push a horse to comply on the longe line or in the round pen. And there may come a time to "hold the horse's hand" and encourage him to try something, even if he doesn't think he wants to.

In my experience with rehabilitating horses, this process is a great way to instill different levels of balance and learn to rate speed with a sense of inner Zero for you and the horse. This activity can be a really useful part of the horse's overall education, so don't turn it into a doldrum or an argument. It is too hard to undo negative experiences, and fighting over longeing is something that can be avoided if you are reading the horse.

Balancing Intensity Levels and Activity

Do not try to get sustained trot or canter the first few times on the longe line. Just ask to "up" the intensity, and then drop right back down to "lower intensity." Lowering intensity on cue is *much more* important to the horse and to our safety than being able to get him going.

It is not hard to move a horse out—he will go forward and find a comfortable "play "or "work" engagement with you when he knows you can stop him also.

SKILL-BUILDER

Longeing with Cones Exercise

Set up a Ring of Cones (see p. 247) and walk around it with your horse. Then use Dancer's Arms around it, asking for Therapy Back-Up to center the horse at each cone. Reduce the cones to four in a big circle, and longe to each of the four cones, breaking the circle down into Quadrants. After a reasonable amount of time, take away two cones so there are two half circles, then take away one so only one remains, around which the horse makes a full circle and stops. Move the cone to the middle with you, and ask the horse to go two or three times around, then come to the cone.

PROBLEM-SOLVING WITH HORSE SPEAK: LONGEING

8.13 A This mare worked as a school horse. She was very trustworthy with kids, but she became rigid and frozen when asked to move out on the longe line. After IINN, I started offering enrichment.

8.13 B Her body became so tense the moment I asked for a few steps of micro-longe, I decided to stop and work on enrichment in the form of some light bodywork.

Mentors and Teachers and Sentries and Mothers are very good at *stopping* the energy.

This is one reason why I encourage all people to offer the horse as much Therapy Back-Up as they can, all the time, for any reason. The better your back-up, the better your halt. The more you back up in a calm, centered manner, the more the horse relaxes and follows your lead. You claim the space in front, and this allows the horse to *want* to follow because you do it in a way that makes them feel good.

Here are two horses I worked with using the skills we explored in this chapter. Both were shut down when we began talking, but in both cases, we could get to a nice place. I hope these demonstrate the potential that these small changes can have in how we interact with horses.

MYTH-BUSTER

Should You Longe to "Get the Bucks Out"?

Longeing was never intended to "get the bucks out" before riding. If you *practice* getting bucks out, you are *teaching* bucking. Look up "how to train a bucking horse" on the internet. Horses are trained to buck for rodeos using the same principles. Practicing Zero is what helps remove the anxiety or stress or overexcitement that leads to bucking.

If your horse prefers a little warm-up activity before carrying a rider, then longeing can be helpful, so you may want to keep it in your pre-ride work—perhaps just adjust your expectations.

8.13 C The "I have your back" message at the Hip Button was very important to this mare. After a few minutes, I turned that message into an Activation request to move forward. She swished her tail but decided it was safe enough to try.

8.13 D In Dancer's Arms, I asked for Activation of both Jump-Up ("you can be vulnerable with me") and Yield-Over Buttons. I was asking her to unwind some of the strong emotions she had about longeing.

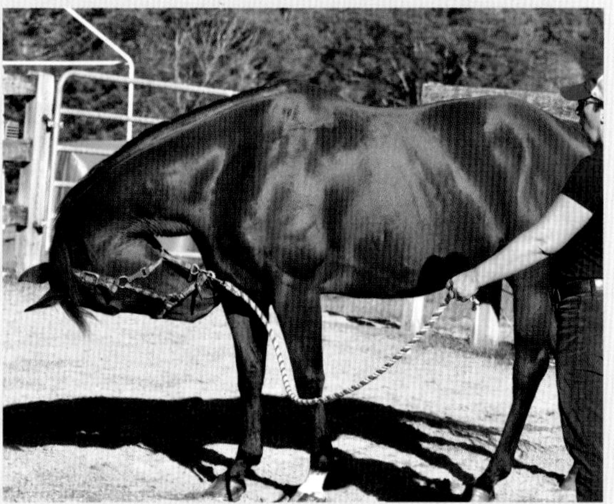

8.13 E Resting with a Hold Hand aimed to her Sit Button, she touched her own Back-Up Button. When this happens, I find it seems to say, "I am getting back in my body." Since she was frozen at first (see p. 65), this made sense.

8.13 F After I "held" her Hip Button for a full minute, the mare moved into a deep process.

8.13 G I turned the mare loose for a Gone phase and came back with a longer lead rope and a dressage whip. Normally these would both be triggers, but she was fine with them.

8.13 H I offered a "Yes" and "No" with my head, while sighing out loud and going to O posture. She offered to keep going all by herself, willing and engaged. The whole session was only about 30 minutes.

8.14 A This vaulting horse was well-trained to longe, but her owner was concerned that she wasn't "happy" in her job. She worked primarily with therapeutic riding students. The horse was totally obedient, but often looked stiff, no matter what she did.

8.14 B The owner had a lovely attitude and truly loved working with her horse. I could see that she had a bit of an X posture. After a reasonable warm-up, with the owner doing what she normally did, the horse did not get more relaxed.

8.14 C Just adding O posture to her handler allowed the mare to "hear" her owner say, "We are together." The transformation was amazing!

8.14 D All the owner had to do when the mare got stiff was remember to add some O posture—and the mare immediately mirrored her.

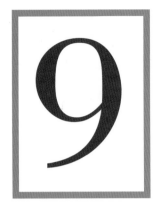

9 Riding with a New Perspective

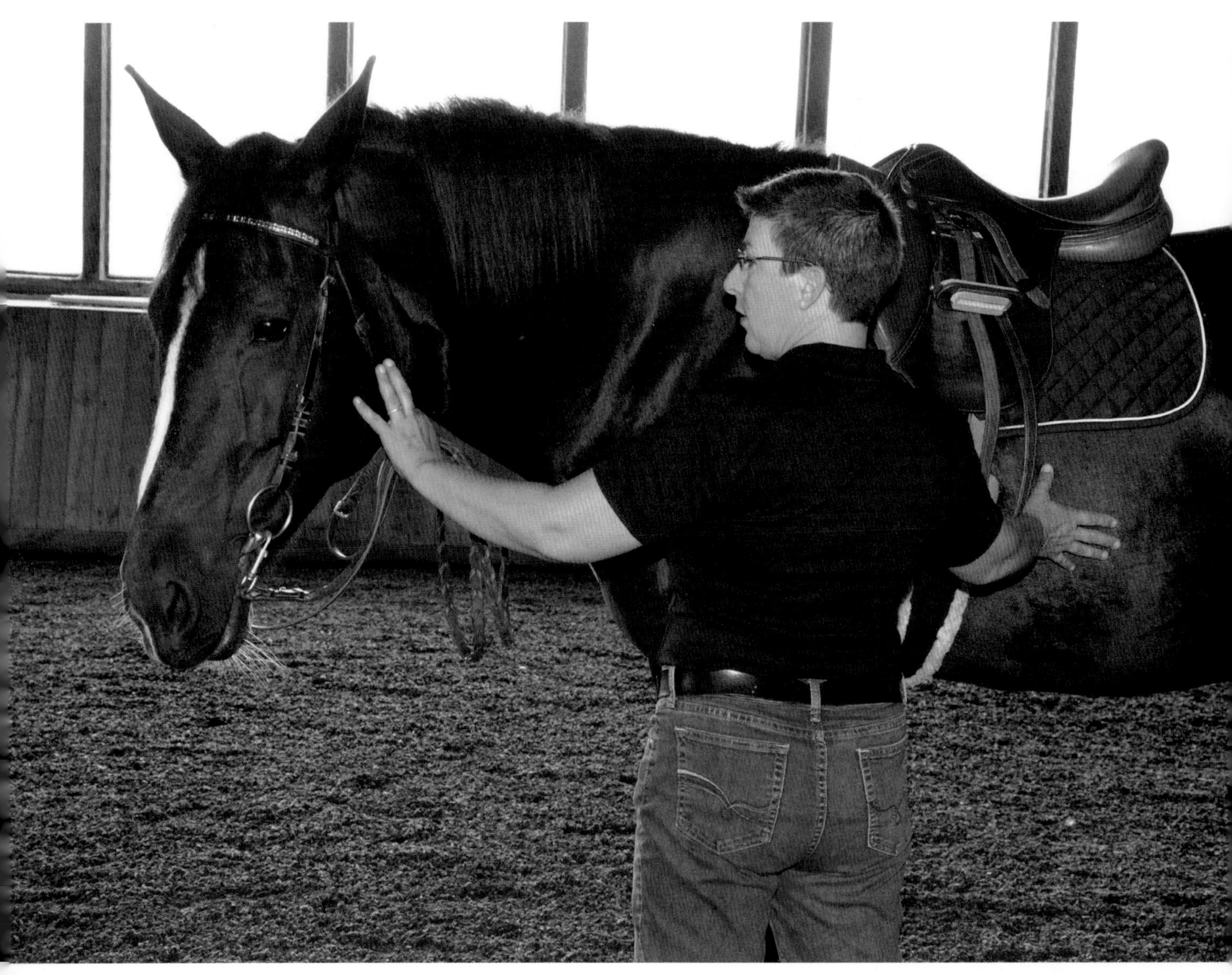

Horse Speak in the Saddle

9.1 Riding should be fun for you and your horse! Give your horse a chance to be involved in the process and tell you what he likes and doesn't like.

Riding is supposed to be fun; not only for us, but for the horse as well (fig. 9.1).

I have had a great deal of fun on the back of a horse. As I began to understand Horse Speak, the first question I had for horses was, "Do you like being ridden as much as I like riding?" As I talked about at the beginning of this book, the answer came after some time. It took effort for me to *not* ride for a while and remain dedicated to studying communication (I had a tendency to keep falling back into my "trainer brain").

But the days came when horses began to line up at mounting blocks and look at me with beckoning expressions. The answer was "Yes!" Horses *can* reach a place from which they also would like to have the experience of "going for a ride." Some seem to genuinely prefer it if we are on their backs. There have also been a number of horses who, when given the choice, said, "*No.*" My horse Zeke was one of them. However, after about six months of being allowed to tell humans for the first time in his life what *he* preferred, what he liked and disliked, he too made a bold decision to "go for a ride." There was no question at all about his decision: He marched over to a saddle I had placed on the riding ring rail (intended for a different horse) and lay down in front of it. Zeke was a horse of opinions, and that day, he wanted to put on that saddle and go for a ride—so we did.

What Horses Value in a Rider

Balance

As far as being ridden goes, the horse values his stability and balance above all things. An out-of-balance horse feels threatened. And I do not only mean good physical balance—I also mean emotional and mental balance. If you sit on a horse and your body is tense somewhere, this will change the horse's balance. And if you sit on a horse

9.2 Believe it or not, if you give horses options about their saddles, they will often sniff the one that they prefer. In this photo, we were having a "Pick-Your-Own-Tack Day."

and your *thoughts* are tense, this changes your micromovements, which changes the horse's balance. If you are *emotional*—maybe nervous and unaware that you are holding your breath or repressing some "black box" of stress—this changes your micromovements... and alters the horse's sense of balance.

Well-Fitted Gear

Horses need to be comfortable in their tack and gear (fig. 9.2). If they are in pain, it needs to be addressed for your riding experience to be optimal. Learning to read their signals with Horse Speak will help you interpret their comfort level and when there is an issue with their tack or equipment.

Knowledge of the Chessboard

Being able to use the Chessboard well is the next thing on the list of what horses care about. They feel differently about certain spaces and corners because of how they perceive things. For a long time, we have just pushed them through their spookiness, but how often does that really work? Some personalities can deal with this solution to fear or anxiety on the Chessboard, but others will literally shut down.

"Feel"

Gaining the skill of "feel" (see p. 35) means you can use your natural powers of perception to develop a repertoire inside your brain and nervous system for coding appropriate signals from the horse. Feel also enables you to understand and problem-solve from the horse's perspective. The cool thing about being a human being is that we can imagine. This is an unbelievable power. You can learn to think from the horse's perspective. He cannot think from your perspective; his brain does not have the apparatus to do so. However, horses are deeply feeling and empathic creatures; they feel us probably better than we feel ourselves. It's a great cooperative symbiotic connection, and this is the "one-ness" that people aspire to on horseback.

Empathy and Reason

If you saw a horse throw his head back when you first took riding lessons as an eight-year-old and heard your instructor say, "He is naughty!" as she smacked or punished the horse, then you learned, "This high head means 'bad horse,' and I should use force to correct it."

If the horse settled down and became "good" after harsh treatment, then the end seemed to justify the means. The term "bad" now applies to behaviors we do *not* like or want, and "good" to behaviors we *do* like or want. Force is applied to change from bad to good.

However, this is very black-and-white thinking such as we find in the developmental stage of a child between the ages of five and ten. Many people begin taking riding lessons around this age and absorb such beliefs from their instructors, who no doubt learned them from *their* own instructors and so on. Basically, I think that a good deal of the dominance-based horsemanship that is out there is largely a result of this generational attitude dogmatically being passed down

MYTH-BUSTER

Do Horses Act Out Just to Be "Bad" or "Naughty?"

When a horse acts out, it is always in response to three main causes: pain, confusion, or emotional distress. Horses do not have the same cognitive awareness of thoughts and ideas the way we do. They are "in the moment"—that is, if a horse *feels* bad, he may *behave* poorly. He does not have the type of brain that thinks, "AHA! I know just how I am going to get back at her! I will totally freak out at the show. That'll teach her..."

and enshrined. Kind horsemasters for thousands of years, ever since the days of Xenophon, have suggested that being harsh with horses has its toll—not only on them, but on us as well.

Understanding the Connection Between Movement, Thoughts, and Feelings

We have figured out that the horse needs to use his body in a particular manner in order to function at his best. Most good training is all about getting a horse into prime condition. However, we tend to look objectively at what the horse is doing—like "good forward movement" or "heavy on the forehand" or "uphill canter"—as a *physical response* to the function of riding a certain way.

The fact is, horses are not bodies devoid of thoughts or feelings; all three go together. If they learn to dissociate as a coping mechanism, it can be a dangerous situation. A horse who is dissociated or "slushy" (partly frozen and shut down) may mask it well and come across as a "good horse" or even a "dead-broke horse."

I *do* suggest that people find good riding instructors who can help them ride *physically* well; this is, in fact, an important part of the whole thing. But learning to witness the horse's sense of balance and movement as also a comment about what he is thinking and feeling is the next level. A good instructor will have some sense of this and will always consider the horse.

We are now in an era of choosing to ride horses because we want and seek a relationship or partnership with them. You cannot use standards of punishment in the development of real relationship.

MYTH-BUSTER

Are Horses Just a Collection of Behaviors?

We have long analyzed the horse's movements as though the horse is just a collection of behaviors and has no self-awareness of his own life experience. He does not possess the same brain we do and cannot do things like plan for next Tuesday, but he has more room in his brain for mapping territory and he has an amazing GPS. He has more room for scent—we now know he is on par with dogs in this department. Horses are also keenly aware of feeling connected to their family, their children, and the world they live in. They *feel*, and they are emotional creatures. Their senses are always "on," and they are in the "here and now" in a way most of us have forgotten how to be.

Preparing for a Ride

Tacking Up

Tack your horse up with awareness of your X, O, and Core Energy. Use IINN as you Initiate the idea of tack, then Introduce it enough times that the horse gives you a Green Light. Finally Negotiate putting the tack on: How much Core Energy can the horse handle? Does he react to your X and O? Can you get to a Green Light? Once the tack is on, Navigate the Chessboard on the ground for a few minutes before you mount.

Secure the Environment in the Arena

Use what you have learned to assess what your horse may value the most, how to help him be at his best, and what messages are his favorites. Each horse will need more or less of your messages of security. It may be a personal message to him, like Bridge of the Nose and Follow Me, plus Rock the Baby, to say, "You can use this arena as a special place to let go of fear and have fun." Or the horse may need direct messages about the arena itself (think blowing away the boogeyman, touching three things, creating Safety Objects, and so on).

Mounting with Confidence and Readiness

Initiate the idea of the mounting block, then Introduce it and make it a Safety Object. Make sure your horse knows the mounting block does not make you afraid. Believe it or not, many horses are leery of the mounting block because *we* get subconsciously hesitant there. Use a Protector horse's message of "killing the mounting block" if you have any discomfort getting up on one by stomping on it then letting out a big sigh, suggesting, "There, that's done." (This is similar to Killing the Halter—p.251.) Leader horses do this with objects left out in the paddock (like my horse Rocky did to my favorite lawn chair!). When you "kill" an object like the mounting block, you say, "This doesn't hurt us."

In addition, the following can help mounting go smoothly:

- The Horse Hug (see p. 215) is good to practice before mounting because it suggests two bodies getting connected. I have found that offering the Horse Hug before mounting can put many horses at ease.
- Use the Buttons and Therapy Back-Up to help the horse align better with the mounting block and be in balance before you get on. Follow up with Rock the Baby to further balance the horse in position.
- Mount three times in a row when you are building confidence or rapport, or as a form of enrichment from time to time. Mounting and dismounting is a worthy practice of balancing with your horse's body as you get on and off.

9.3 A & B Sniffing the horse's neck can be a good way to soothe both your nerves (A). It means, "You're my friend." Then use the Hold Hand on the horse's Hip and Grooming Buttons to say, "I have your back—this is supposed to be a comforting connection" (B).

Typically, mounting and dismounting upsets your horse's sense of balance to some degree, which is why practicing it over and over again tells your horse that you care about his sense of balance and want to make sure he is comfortable. Negotiate getting on and off until the process itself is a Green Light.

- Sniff the horse's neck as you mount. This is a message of friendship between horses (fig. 9.3 A).
- Touch the Buttons your horse might need for reassurance when you get on (9.3 B).

You will have an easier time mounting if you devote a few afternoons to getting a Green Light in all of these areas and making *that* the focus of your training session. Only then is a horse truly ready for Negotiating the Chessboard with you on his back.

Warming Up with Yoga Rein

The movements I call *Yoga Rein* can ease you and your horse into your under-saddle warm-up. This is a time to check for stiffness in both yourself and your horse. Consider it the warm-up before the warm-up. If your horse is open to it, I recommend actually doing a little yoga from the saddle, knowing that the horse may mirror you in some way. Instead of saying to him, "Stay still so I can move around," offer something like, "If I do *this* stretch, what sort of stretch do you want to do?"

The Yoga Rein exercises are designed to move through the Buttons, from Greeting Button to the Buttons of the hind end. They are intended to reveal many subjective experiences you or the horse may have had. In the following pages I explain ways to invite the Conversation into your warm-up or training session.

I have heard from both first-time horse owners learning to ride, and advanced horse trainers adept in the saddle that Yoga Rein helped them realize many little things that went a long way toward improving either themselves or their horses, or both. In my lesson and therapeutic riding programs, this was one of my secrets to maintaining my horses. I only had to ride them with Yoga Rein once a week, and it enabled them to deliver better balancing messages to the unbalanced riders coming to the program. In addition, the students who could learn even a little bit of Yoga Rein seemed to develop a better organic balance sooner and kept their sense of Zero while on the horse's back.

The key is, both horse and rider can benefit from this simple adaptation in numerous ways.

Gumby Pose

When you first get on your horse try to do some amount of *Gumby* (fig. 9.4). Gumby (which I explain in detail in *Horse Speak*) is the O posture of welcome, suggesting relaxation, and putting your "lizard brain" at ease about the fact that you are now on the back of a huge animal. This gives both you and the horse a moment to have a Check-

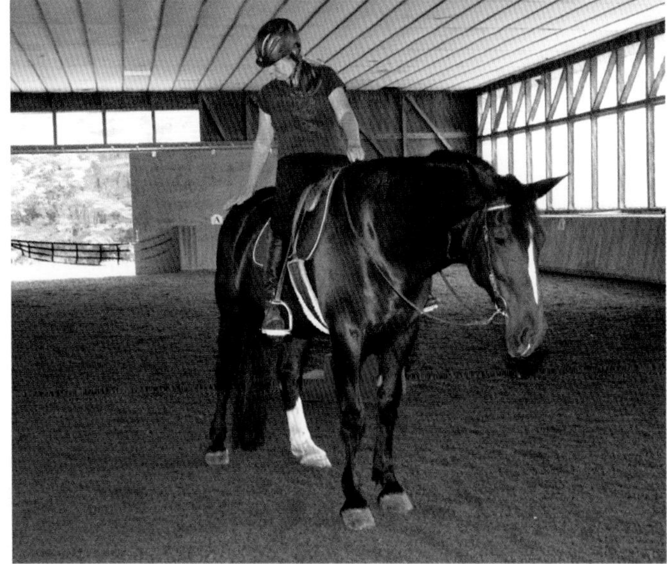

9.4 This mare had been bucking and bolting—and getting worse. She had all manner of bodywork done, as well as a thorough tack check, but she was still acting out. Her rider could never let the reins relax. Here the rider is saying, "You're okay. I have your back," with one hand on the Grooming Button and the other on the Hip Button while relaxing into her O posture in the saddle. This Gumby Pose encourages you to just let go and relax your frame so the horse can, too.

SKILL-BUILDER

Try to Be Gumby

1. Rest your hands, palm down, on either side of the horse's withers. Don't make contact with the horse's mouth.
2. Sit like a limp Gumby figure. Try and feel your horse's breath; see if you can sync your breath with his.
3. Walk forward in your slumped, relaxed position. Don't try to influence the horse, just follow his movements.

In with each other and make sure all is well. While in Gumby, you can offer to send messages of *calm*:

- Chew Gum (make a chewing motion and sound with your mouth, smacking your lips to mean, "All is clear").
- Nod your head "Yes" to ask the horse to mirror your message and release tension in his own neck.
- Rock the Baby from the saddle, shifting your weight gently side to side, or using your hands on the withers.

Palm-Down, Calm Down Yoga Rein

For the first section of Yoga Rein, it is important to use Palm Down, Calm Down, which we learned to apply on the lead rope in chapter 7 (p. 254). Those who are familiar with yoga will recognize a reference to Downward-Facing Dog Pose—I find that Palm Down, Calm Down effects a similar grounding energy in the rein.

Yoga Rein is primarily sending soothing and grounding messages, and inviting the horse to follow your directions forward, backward, left, and right, just as you have been doing on the ground. When you first practice this, please allow for big, broad gestures as both you and your horse explore opening joints, breathing, and contact. You may refine these gestures into an "invisible" message in short order, but at first you both need to feel the movement to understand it.

Yoga Rein in Practice

1. The Greeting Yoga Rein is a Check-In to say, "Hello, I have a rein" (fig. 9.5 A). Extend your Greeting Knuckles to the horse with one rein in your hand, palm down. Lean forward, extend your shoulder, soften your knuckles, relax your elbows, knees, and ankles. Invite the horse to either simply relax his jaw or actually turn and Greet you with his muzzle. With this "Hello Rein," you are practicing *conscious contact*—you are not trying to get the horse to do anything other than relax about the contact and perhaps say, "Hello," back to you.

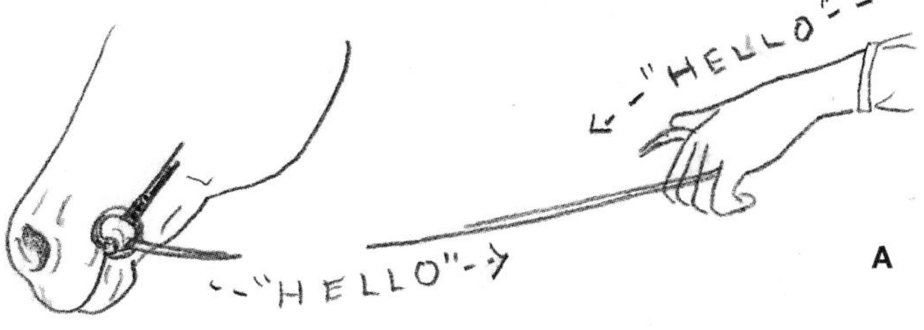

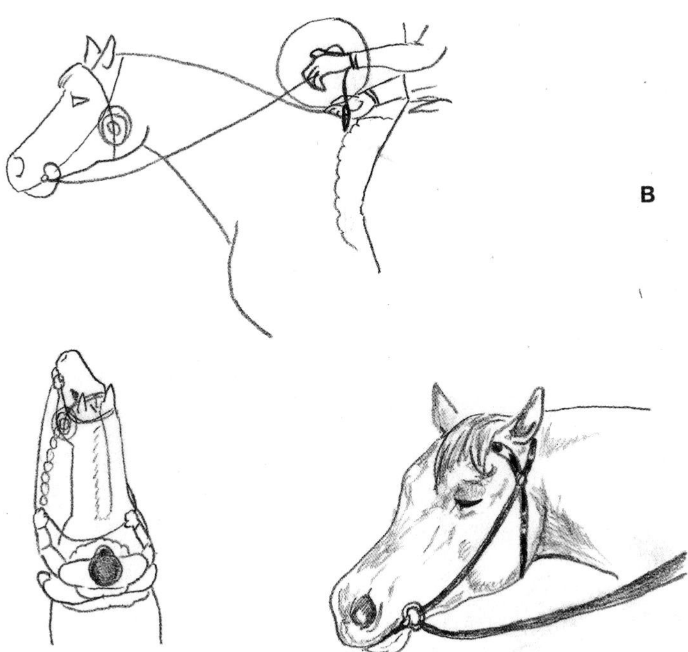

9.5 A & B Saying "Hello" with Yoga Rein is just lifting and sending the intention of welcoming, Greeting, and connection between your hands and the bit or noseband of a bitless (A). This is followed by "drawing a magic string" out of the Cheek Button (B).

---

2 In the next moment, extend your Hello Rein out away from your body to the side about 3 or 4 inches. Imagine you are connected to a "magic string" coming out of the horse's Cheek Button (fig. 9.5 B). Just like on the ground with Turn the Key, Come to Me, you are inviting the cheek into the Quadrant on the same side as the rein. This helps to release clamping down on the bit, locking the jaw, and tension in the horse's skull on any level. Relax your own jaw and neck to Mirror the activity. Keep your hand lifted for the correct leverage. *Don't* lower your hand to your thigh, which is a common mistake resulting in the horse losing balance.

3 Next connect Yoga Rein to the Mid-Neck Button (fig. 9.5 C). Stretch one arm forward, then draw it to the side, using your armpit to lift it and your shoulder to open it outward. Relax your neck and trapezius muscles. Allow your sides to lengthen. Feel your opposite-side seat and leg on the horse as a counterbalance (so if your right arm is engaged in Yoga Rein, your left seat and leg is the counterbalance). With the hand on the rein, draw an imaginary string out from the horse's

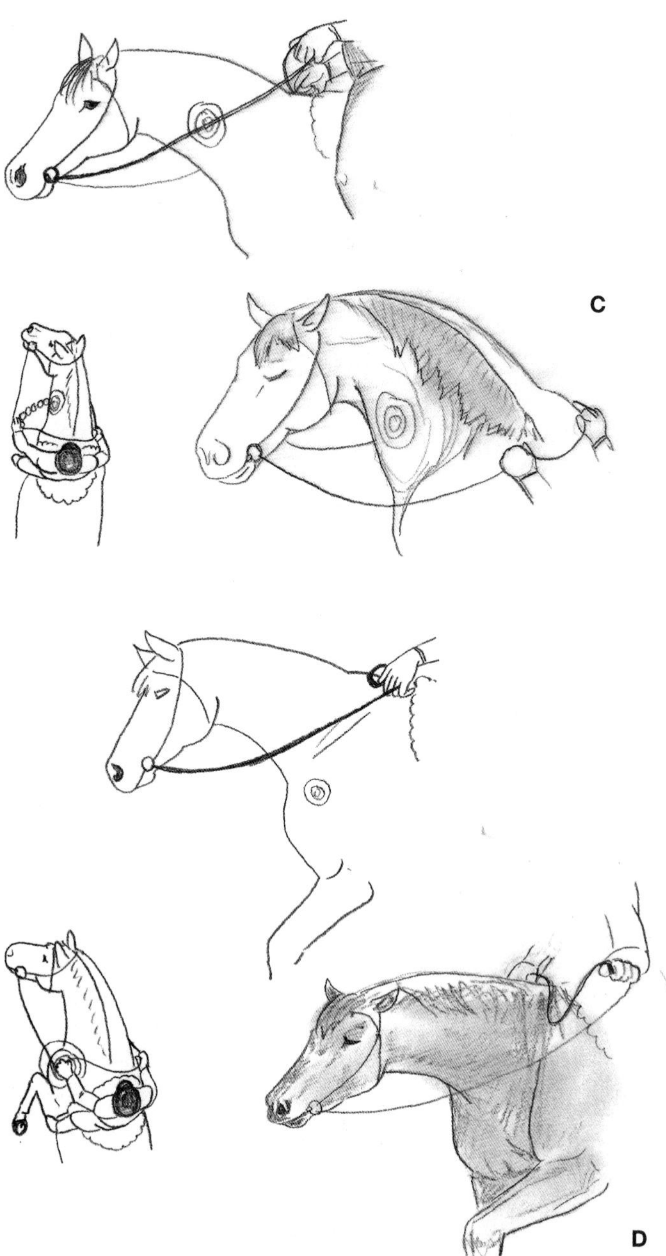

9.5 C & D Next invite the Mid-Neck Button to relax as the horse's head moves into the same Quadrant as the rein and the magic string comes out of the neck (C). Yoga Rein for the Shoulder Button invites the horse to take a single step into that Quadrant (D).

neck. Encourage the horse to connect his soft mouth, Cheek Button, and Mid-Neck Button in one fluid motion as he laterally flexes his neck. Do not demand anything of him; let him find it for himself.

4 Now use Yoga Rein with the Shoulder Button, pulling an imaginary string out of the horse's shoulder blade and to the side (fig. 9.5 D). Use the same arm motion as in Step 2, with the same opposite seat and leg awareness (don't hold tight with them—just feel they are there). The Shoulder Button is the next Button in the combination of Cheek, Mid-Neck, and Shoulder that you have learned to use in many scenarios. You are repeating the same Conversation you had on the ground about who follows who, and who gets to make the decisions. However, you want to also continue the Conversations you started on the ground about the horse feeling relaxed and happy. Use a little light encouragement to ask for a single step on the side of the shoulder your rein is connecting to (right rein, right shoulder). If the horse wants to start walking, that's okay, but if you can get a single step, it will have more meaning, because a single step is used by horses to determine hierarchy. Note that this is a good time to become aware of "leaky" energy from the horse. An out-of-balance horse may want to take more steps to rebalance, so it offers you a chance to make sure you

Cheek – Neck – Shoulder

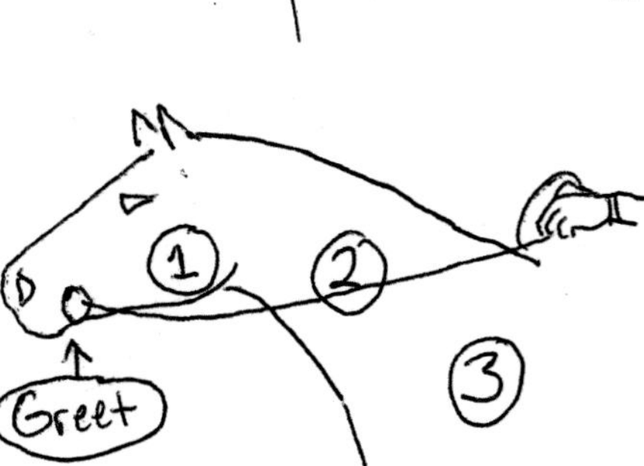

9.5 E–H Ask your horse to relax his Cheek, Neck, and Shoulder Buttons with Yoga Rein, envisioning that you are pulling a string from each of the Buttons as you release a sighing breath (E). Allow your horse time to process this "Hello Rein" (F). From the horse's perspective, the bit has little to do with these three Buttons (G). You need to scoop into your belly button—your own Core Energy needs to be in this Yoga Rein (H).

are offering balanced suggestions. Do not overbend the horse's neck. If your horse chooses to reach for a nice stretch, that is fine.

5 If you have been practicing Dancer's Arms, you should be relatively comfortable opening up your arms to the side. The idea is to have direct rein contact while imagining a magic string coming out from the Cheek, Mid-Neck, then the Shoulder Button (fig. 9.5 E). Don't make the mistake of drawing the rein down low across your thigh, below your belly button, which creates in imbalance. Lifting the rein at belly button height, or even higher, shifts the balance points through the horse's spine to the opposite hip and allows him to lift the shoulder of the same side of the rein that you are indicating (fig. 9.5 F). This is a sequence that connects to the natural flowing movement from the horse's head, through his neck, and then down and out one front foot. On the ground, a single foot can take space or give space, and is significant (see p. 61). You can signal the same degree of communication while you are on the horse's back. Isolating single foot movement is important to the horse for many reasons. Many misunderstandings common to riding a horse can be understood with new awareness from this one exercise alone (fig. 9.5 G).

6 Practice chunking down the Yoga Rein in this way until you and your horse have benefited from this simple but powerful set of front-end messages. Try to keep your horse's single footsteps pure. You don't want to let the horse just start walking off—*but* if your horse feels overwhelmed, don't drill this either. Do parts of it a little at a time. Focus on moving the front feet forward, backward, and side to side, while encouraging a Low-O swinging and relaxed head and neck in the horse. This is Fun with Feet on horseback (and can be returned to any time the horse becomes tense).

7 The last movement in Yoga Rein involves the rotation of your hand with your thumb outward, creating a "scooping" motion through your arm and all the way up to your scapula (fig. 9.5 H). This will look a little like you are "thumbing for a ride." If you have practiced scooping the lead rope to ask for forward movement

SKILL-BUILDER

The Art of the "Scoop"

The "scooping" motion through your arm that you have now used when leading on the ground and with Yoga Rein has many uses. For example:

- You can "scoop up" the horse's hind end while walking forward, or in an arc or on a circle.
- You can scoop while going down a steep hill to help the horse balance in the hind end and "sit down" or use a little bend to feel better about the hill.
- You can scoop one rein when taking a jump for more engagement from the hind end.
- You can scoop up the hind end for half-halt (one rein) or a full halt (both reins).
- You can scoop for deeper collection. (Don't be greedy; only ask for a few strides at a time at first.)
- You can scoop with one rein and "draw the magic string" with the other hand to create lovely "buttery" turns, bends, and lateral work.

on the lead rope (p. 254) and scooping as you do Therapy Back-Up (p. 255), then this gesture should be understood and easy for both you and your horse.

8 Bring this rein in toward your belly button. (Over time, you may find how little it takes—perhaps even just the thought of it—so your gestures become "invisible" and quiet.) This is a powerful Core Energy message, as well as a Conversation for the horse's hind end. When you scoop the rein on one side and draw the connection to your belly button, the organic signal goes to the horse's hip on the same side as the rein you are using. This is a matter of movement through your skeleton directly to the equine skeleton and is not something that needs to be trained. It is an intrinsic body language message that explains to both your body and the horse's body how

SKILL-BUILDER

Riding Mental Self-Assessment

While riding, ask yourself:

- How do the Buttons feel? Are there any that you know about from the ground that need more support? Which are the favorite Buttons for soothing, staying centered or Zero?
- Are you talking to the Buttons of the barrel? Does the Girth Button "hear" your seat and leg?
- The Girth Button says, "We are a team. Let's go!" Are you talking to the Jump-Up Button that says, "Stick with me—I'll help you feel good in this activity," or "Can you breathe deeply? Can you engage your tummy in more core strength?"
- Are you talking to the hind-end Buttons? The Hip Button for impulsion or protection? The Yield-Over Button for engaging the inside hind leg more fully? The Sit Button to ask the horse to sit more behind and come uphill in front?
- Are you engaging the Jump-Up Button on the outside of a turn with your lower leg when changing direction? (When turning left, use your right leg.) This seems to be much appreciated by horses, helping their balance and sending a security message during a maneuver that can be tricky for them.
- Does your horse need another message of support like Sentry Breath?
- Can you use Yoga Rein to place the horse's muzzle on a Safety Object?
- Can you use Safety Object messages to ask the horse to deal with something new on the Chessboard while you ride?

The art of connecting to the Buttons of the front end is what helps the most with calming messages and keeping the horse "with you" so he doesn't become distracted or spooky.

to create lateral feel, from the head of the horse all the way through to the hip on that same side. It asks him to engage or pick up that inside hind leg.

9 You can use this rein exercise to create the Therapy Back-Up from the horse's back. You can also use this rein when going forward to create lifting and collecting from the Sit Button forward. Many people find it helpful to sit more deeply or move into an O posture for best results. That way your body Mirrors the tummy-tuck and rounded back that you want the horse to discover in himself. The first attempts at this can be a little "sticky," so the more you sigh out loud, the better the message will be. Only ask for the littlest lean back at first—just like on the ground with Therapy Back-Up. (Note: Please be mindful to not overuse this Yoga Rein. Most people feel the inherent power and "smooth move" that this creates in their horses' bodies and love it. However, you are asking him to do a different movement than what he is used to, and he needs time to build up that endurance.)

Developing Yoga Rein Feel

Developing Yoga Rein is meant to be a *gross motor skill*. You are allowed to be clumsy at first as you sort it out (figs. 9.6 A–C). This is why doing so much Cheek, Mid-Neck, and Shoulder communication from the ground helps—your horse will probably know what you are aiming for and try to help you get there.

Enjoy "finding the flow" that starts between your body and your horse's body from Yoga Rein, and then pay more attention to the ways it adjusts your weight, your seat, your thighs, knees, calves, and feet. You should be able to discover that the rest of your body lines itself up in a good, logical arrangement.

The more you can tune into the smaller gestures, the more "invisible" your Yoga Rein can become. In fact, you can begin to switch to seat and leg messages along the Girth and Jump-Up Buttons, or use a touch of a dressage whip, with the rein only there as an assist. The nice thing is that Yoga Rein talks directly to the horse's body language, setting him up for a more "uphill" posture. Since horses would rather move in good balance, they often stick to what the Yoga Rein reveals to them.

9.6 A–C In this Hello Rein, the rider's wrist is too stiff and not in Palm Down, Calm Down. This is an X posture on the rein (A). Our wrists and hands need to be as "alive" and aware when we are riding as they have learned to become on the ground. Your posture needs to be a little more O to invite connection and offer welcoming messages to say, "Hey, it's just me up here" (B). The Yoga Rein is not about making the neck bend. It is an invitation to open up "stuck" places (C).

PROBLEM-SOLVING WITH HORSE SPEAK: YOGA REIN

9.7 A Despite the best efforts of his riders and trainers, this school horse was chronically out of balance, which made him "speedy" and hard to halt. His delightful personality made him a real asset to the riding school, so we hoped Yoga Rein would help him under saddle.

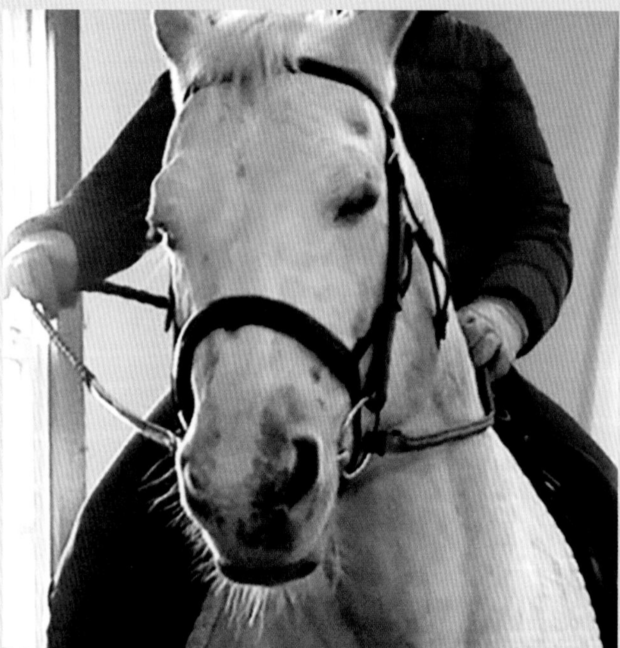

9.7 B After a few minutes of the gentle Yoga Rein, the horse began to really let go and relax into it. This helped him release tension in this jaw and neck. The rider reported feeling a deep calm from his back. Here you can see his ears are in deep concentration and his eyes have fluttered closed.

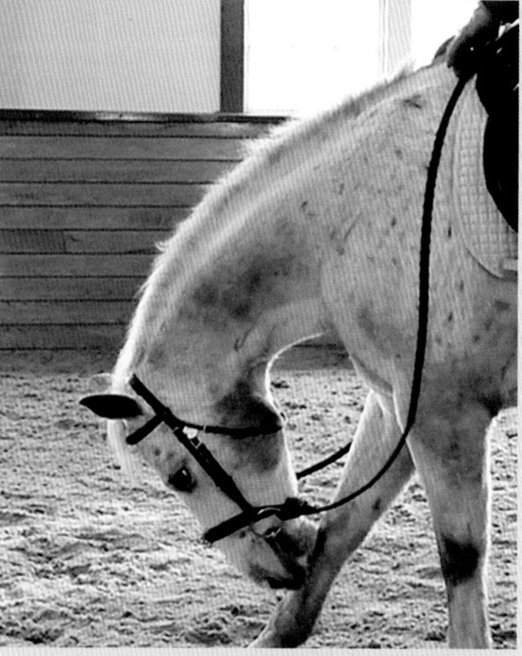

9.7 C After completing Yoga Rein on both sides, the horse was allowed a pause, in which he rubbed his front leg, sending the message he was "learning something." You could think of it as an "Aha!" moment.

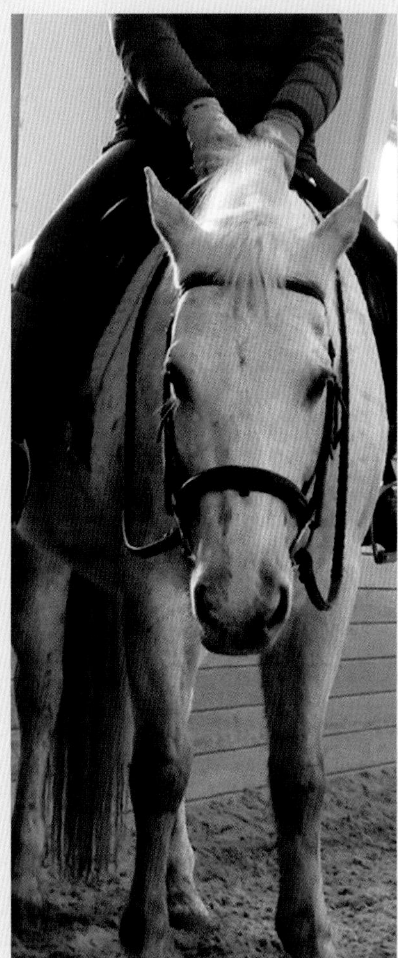

9.7 D He also began to rebalance his front end, lowering his head and licking and chewing.

9.7 E The rider only needed to bring the "scoop" Yoga Rein toward her belly button once, and the horse began reaching for the bit, and engaging his lower back and pelvis. Later in the session the rider used the scoop to half-halt while walking, achieving the same level of engagement.

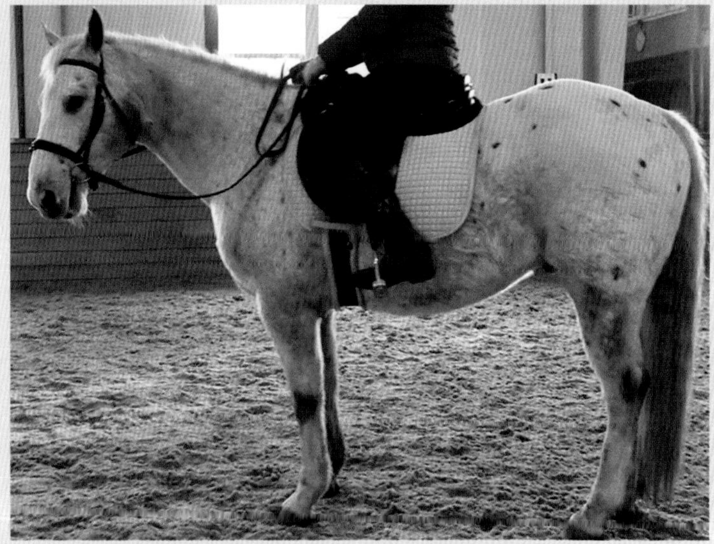

9.7 F After walking around for about 10 minutes and using some Yoga Rein to change direction and make a little serpentine pattern, the rider asked for halt using a scoop and immediately dropping her contact to Palm Down, Calm Down. The horse halted squarely. He had never felt so easy to halt.

PROBLEM-SOLVING WITH HORSE SPEAK:
YOGA REIN *(continued)*

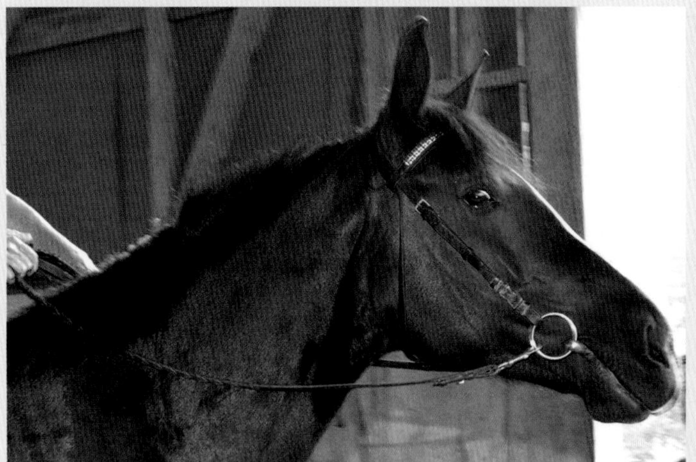

9.8 A When this mare was first introduced to the Palm Down, Calm Down Yoga Rein, she was both curious and skeptical about it, raising and lowering her head. She had become "uppity" and difficult to ride despite bodywork, tack adjustments, and alterations to her feed and nutrition.

9.8 B As the rider practiced the gentle Yoga Rein at the walk, the mare began to concentrate and search for the contact.

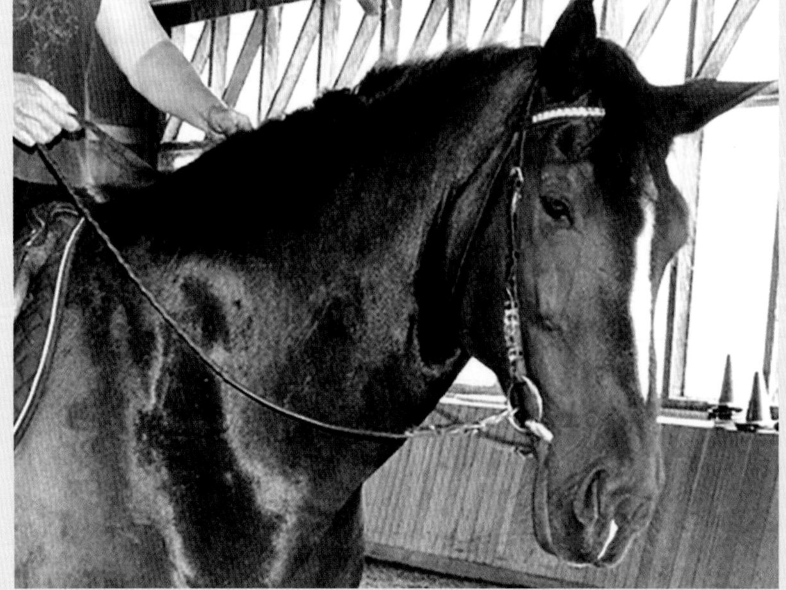

9.8 C After about 15 minutes, the mare was able to fully relax, taking deeper breaths, blinking, and licking and chewing. The pair were able to complete some nice walk-trot transitions with no resistance from the mare at all. The mare's rider reported a few weeks later that there had been a total turnaround in the horse's attitude—provided she got her morning yoga warm-up!

Ring of Cones Warm-Up

After Yoga Rein, you can continue your warm-up with a Ring of Cones to build confidence and rapport (see p. 247). Just like work on the ground with Dancer's Arms and longeing, the Ring of Cones offers a safer Chessboard to negotiate during a ridden session. Using the Ring of Cones at first allows you to master the art of picking up energy, moving it forward, and dropping it into a square and balanced halt on horseback. Using both Palm Down, Calm Down on the reins to get good, relaxed motion into the Buttons of the horse's front end, and then the scooping rein to connect to the Buttons of the hind end, you will create lovely, balanced movement through the horse's whole body. Using the cones gives the horse purpose—it is not just movement for no reason. It can also help the horse feel that the Chessboard is not too big or unmanageable.

SKILL-BUILDER

Ride the Chessboard with Awareness

Before trying to achieve our riding goals, try to make sure your use of the Chessboard is under control. It is very difficult for horses to focus on what we are asking if the boogeyman is threatening him at every turn.

You also cannot really master faster steps like trot and canter before you have mastered staying present for every walk step the horse takes, and knowing which foot is moving at what time and whether you need to "talk to that foot" through your rein, your seat, your leg, or even your breath. Horse hate it when our knees lock or our hands don't understand which foot they are supposed to talk to. They need us to breathe with them. They need us to unlock our jaws and nod our heads yes and no to remove tension there. We need to hold their Hip Button if they worry and blow away their boogeyman as needed. Ride the Chessboard with awareness; it's not just about what you are trying to *do on them* as a rider.

If you have good rapport with the Jump-Up Button on the ground, using either your leg or the touch of a dressage whip toward this Button will help your horse with balance. The message you are sending says, "You maybe a little vulnerable, but it's okay. You can stick with me." Unconscious spurring or smacking a horse on the Jump-Up Button has the opposite effect of making the horse feel *more* vulnerable.

From cone to cone, practice:

1. Picking up the energy and moving forward:
2. Dropping the energy and halting:
3. You can even ask for a Therapy Back-Up or a simple lean backward to gather the horse squarely.

A smaller Ring of Cones is easier to problem-solve and has fewer boogeymen. Pay attention to the angles the horse' body is in as he moves around the circle. Expand the Ring of Cones outward to the sides of the arena. Use particular spots on the wall or fence line to create Safety Objects. This helps keep the horse focused on *you*.

Regardless of the personality, Role in the Herd, or Energy Level of the horse, this activity has a million good uses. It shows your leadership is able to make the world a contained, manageable place, and that you want both of you to have a clear means of success. When your point-to-point movement is successful, you can try to increase speed or create lateral movement across the ring, or both.

Use the Ring of Cones in at least three different areas in your arena or on your property to "generalize" your horse's learning. Horses learn in "site-specific" map-making memories, so taking the same exercise to three areas on the Chessboard allows the brain to make an imprint of whatever you are doing and helps the horse understand "we can do this same thing no matter where we are in the world."

The Ring of Cones is good to try even with a seasoned horse because it affords you a great opportunity to communicate a host of possible "gray zones" where you or the horse had a misunderstanding that you may not even know about. Once you have completed this exercise, and you and your horse have a better rapport, you can move on; however, remember it can be an enrichment activity to use from time to time, like a "tune up."

Mirroring from the Saddle

Allow your body to move with the horse using Mirroring from the saddle. Try to let go and truly be a passenger. Ask a friend to lead you from the ground if necessary so you can truly relax and just feel the pleasant sensations of the horse's body moving beneath you.

While mirroring your horse's movements, follow his breathing patterns—as long as he is not breathing quickly in anxiety. In some cases, Mirroring may be just getting on, sitting still, breathing with the horse, and then getting off.

Copycat from the Saddle

Try aiming your eyes, belly button, and the toe of your boot on one side in the direction you wish to move. You can even point with your hand. This helps make sure your messages to the horse, outside and in, are congruent. See if his body Copycats you. Your outside leg can "hug" the Jump-Up Button; see how it affects the turn.

Once you feel you are communicating good basic messages with your horse without just "telling him what to do," minimize you motions down to the quietest gestures. Use the lowest intensity possible to see how simple and soft you can be and still be understood. Watch for the horse's neck getting stiff, rigid, or braced. Many horses compensate for a feeling of poor balance by bracing their neck. Keep the Mid-Neck Button relaxed using Yoga Rein if your horse becomes tense and move your own neck to help him copy and release.

The Question of Collection

Most of us know that horses need to carry a rider by learning to use their bodies in a more athletic manner. They need to become what we call "collected." To better balance us on their backs, we want them to focus on the middle of their bodies and lift us from the thoracic region, as well as "sit down" with their hips, resulting in an "uphill" use of the core. When this all comes together, the horse's pectoral muscles will become enlarged, and his poll will naturally engage. Gaining balance from the horse's inside (inside the bend) hind leg is important as the horse naturally uses the counterbalance of the head and neck like a ballast. The horse normally uses his inside shoulder to lean into a turn, and we want him to do the opposite in order to better use his body when under us. In the end, a more balanced, collected horse can carry a human being with less strain on his body.

Horses naturally know how to do this and will "collect" when out with other horses as part of their communication—not just a physical activity.

I've already told you about the old saying, "Relaxed and forward." This refers to one of the first things horses are supposed to learn how to do. If they are not forward enough, it is hard to get a good rhythm to work with, and that makes it hard to develop good cadence. Without good cadence, it is hard to cultivate specifics in the gait, like an extension or a slower rhythm, such as is found in a Western jog. The elevated and sultry gait of the piaffe cannot be reached under the weight of a rider until the horse has built up a certain amount of athletic power and coordination; however, horses can piaffe all by themselves if they want to show off to other horses.

So, forward is important, but as I mentioned earlier, the first word of the phrase is "relaxed." I have seen far too many well-intentioned riders and trainers who opt for forward only. Their feeling is often that in 20 minutes or so the horse relaxes, so if you trot around long enough, the horse will finally warm up enough to do real work.

Horses have told me that they really want to be relaxed *about* going forward. Many do indeed start to "get there" after a warm-up period; however, if they are carrying tension into their ride from the start, that tension is also emotional. Emotional tension does not get resolved by trotting forward. Through exercises it may be alleviated or energetically bypassed, but whatever was confusing, frustrating, or scary for the horse is still going to be there the next day.

Remember, the body position a horse is in reflects his thoughts and feelings and is a means of communication. Collection can be due to anxiety, frustration, fear, or aggression... or it can come from inner pride. The most beautiful energy to be a part of in a ride is when a horse is full of inner pride.

"Through" the Back

There are schools of training theory that say it is a good idea to have a horse move "through his back." This is sometimes achieved by inviting the horse to lower his head and make a healthy contact with the bit—the horse's biomechanics cause his back to lift as he lowers his head. Simply lowering the head does not guarantee that the horse has engaged his spine. But I believe, in fact, that lowering the head is a very good idea for other reasons than the over-the-back stretch.

Aw-Shucks (the horse putting his muzzle to the ground) can be offered when a horse is trotting or even cantering. Horses use this gesture to suggest lowering the intensity levels—either they want you to, or they are offering to. Sometimes they are saying, "Thanks for letting that go."

Training a horse to put his head down *exclusively* while you're riding can put him into a sort of zombie-like state. However, training a horse to pick his head up and round at the poll as a part of collection also has meaning. This says: "I am 'big stuff' and ready to go," or "We have to fight now....We are in danger now....We are defending ourselves now....We are super-tense." When a horse has to constantly keep his head up without being allowed to stretch down and lower the intensity, he can get overstressed and remain so.

Headset

A horse has a natural headset. Breeds have long been designed to have a higher or lower headset, depending on the work they are doing. It is best to really observe what your horse's natural headset is before you try to adopt a specific look for riding that you think is "correct." A horse who is feeling good will want to put his head where he feels most comfortable. If he is excited, it will become more X, and if he is lowering the intensity, it will go more O.

When a horse has his head held in too tight a collected frame, you can often see dimpling in the muscle and flesh behind the jaw, as well as bulging down the neck as poor muscle development had to compensate for lack of mobility.

MYTH-BUSTER

Does Floating My Horse's Teeth Fix His Headset?

It is very important to have a natural balance dentist, bodyworker, chiropractor, or osteopath look at your horse's jaw and hyoid apparatus. When teeth are even *slightly* off, a horse can develop a whole list of other imbalances through their body. When the teeth are off, the jaw will be off, and the set of the head on the first vertebra of the neck will be off. This will affect the entire spine. The hyoid apparatus—a collection of bones nestled under the mandible and in front of the cervical spine that provides attachment for several muscles, including the tongue—is like the gyroscope (a tool used to measure orientation) of the balancing act of the whole horse.

Relaxed Mid-Neck

If a horse cannot swing his neck from side to side while warming up, he cannot truly balance his body. When a training session is going to focus on collection, then the horse needs to be able to allow their head and neck to swing and sink into a deep, low stretch first. What you say by allowing it is, "I want you to feel naturally relaxed and balanced in your own way while I sit here," and, "Let go of any worries or tension. I am pleased with you." Tight knees (which I've already told you horses dislike) interfere with the ability to swing the neck, and not being able to fully swing the neck seems to inhibit the horse from being able to really lift his back.

Remember, the Mid-Neck Button deals with hierarchy and also friendship. Horses bite this Button when in a disagreement and sniff it as a sign of relationship. If we sniff the horse's neck, pat it in long strokes (do not slap it), Rock the Baby from the saddle, massage the withers, and use a deep O posture to reward him, we will encourage the horse to lower his neck and swing it side to side in rhythmic movement along with his stride. We are saying, "I am your friend. Thanks for letting me sit on you. Let me try to Mirror your movements and get in harmony with your body."

Warm Up the Way a Horse Would Appreciate

Horses like to warm up from front to back. First, they like to have us relax their heads, jaws, and necks. Then they like to find a nice, rhythmic, swinging walk, focusing on their front end. They want us to breathe deeply, sigh often, swing our body with theirs, and not "take over" the ride so fast. They like to move, stop, and move again, as we discussed in the Ring of Cones Conversation (p. 247). They like figure eights and ground poles and barrels to walk over and around. They like to wiggle their Greeting Buttons on the arena wall or on top of a barrel from time to time to "reset." They like to pause and process. They also enjoy it if we are pleased with the fact that they are letting us sit on them. In the beginning of a riding session, it is best when we are focused on the "relaxed" part of "Relaxed and forward." In fact, the more they can count on this being the case, the sooner they want to get to the forward part!

MYTH-BUSTER

Are Treats All Good or All Bad?

You can add enrichment to riding processes by learning what your horse loves—and that may include treats. The most important thing is to keep it Zero. Sometimes treats are the perfect enrichment, and sometimes they make a horse lose his Zero and move out of the Green Zone where learning and communication are most likely to happen.

Under-Saddle Training Can be Fun

Next, horses like the scooping rein we talked about at the beginning of the chapter (p. 320), and a little lateral movement. They seem to really enjoy leg-yielding and shoulder-in and haunches-in. They often like side-passing to a gate to open it. Remember, for horses, this kind of work is called "Fun with Feet." They *do not* like it if we are too fussy and picky and behave like their effort is not good enough.

Horses like to start with the front end, move to the hind end, and then bring that together into the middle. They like it when you learn to "hear" and "feel" every single one of their footfalls because *they* are so in tune with their footfalls and know they *mean something*. Horses listen to footsteps: It's one of their things. So often we are just sort of "going forward" on a horse, riding a wave of motion, but not really paying attention to the *meaning* of each footfall. The horse is walking on the Chessboard with you on him; the Chessboard is still real for him. It is not about the motion to them; it is about the motion in *combination* with whatever part of the Chessboard they are problem-solving. The collected trot may be easy and fun near the gate and may turn into scary collection at that spooky corner.

Don't Give the Wrong Message

When we ask a horse to be very forward and whip him or spur him into it, we are saying, "Hurry! Big emergency! Go, go, go!" But if we then just go around the Chessboard for an hour and never resolve (for them) what the big emergency was, they either assume riding is supposed to be a big emergency, or they shut down and dissociate.

See, horses prefer Low-Calorie communication for most of the day, so in domestic situations, if they are running, it is usually for "play." Part of play in a herd is engaging the herd's ability to create homeostasis—to get back to Zero. Dogs and cats "kill" a squeaky toy, feel satisfied, and lie down. Horses do not have this association. When there is no resolution to a game of power, they can become even more stressed due to the lack of Zero.

Common Questions About Horse Speak on Horseback

Should a horse have a long warm-up at the beginning of a ridden session?

The answer is yes and no. On one hand, we want any athlete to stretch and get warm, oxygenated blood to the muscles before playing sports. So, jumping fences without a proper warm-up is not a good idea. However, a warm-up can include more than simply getting on a horse and trotting for 20 minutes.

A Masterson Method® session on a horse can help him move out in nice balance from the start. A Tellington Method TTouch® session can get the same results right before a show. Put a horse on Sure Foot® Equine Balance Pads, and he will literally walk off them in good form and can perform a lovely, collected trot and canter in moments.

Horses helped me come up with Yoga Rein. Using these simple exercises and in only a few minutes, the horse is able to adjust himself and work with better body awareness, providing a starting place for deeper collection or lateral movement in moments. Riding is an athletic thing. This means it is ideal to get your horse to go forward with rhythm and free movement in his back and neck while using his core energy to lift you upward. You are either practicing good awareness and inviting strong athletic movement, which is good for the horse's body, or you are practicing poor awareness and repetitive motion muscle strain is a strong possibility for the horse. Warming up should be both relaxing and energizing—*that* is the bottom line.

Should I insist my horse go forward by any means necessary?

The horse is not a machine, and if you want to have a happy horse, then do not whip or spur him into movement. However, riding a horse that wants to stop every two minutes doesn't allow for good athletic practice and precludes both your ability to ride the motion and the horse's ability to learn to use his body well.

There are many ways to prepare a horse for the athletic activity of carrying a rider. A relaxing warm-up is one of them. However, insisting that a horse go forward immediately does not allow time to ensure he is mentally and emotionally relaxed. Remember: "Relaxed and forward." Notice how the word "relaxed" comes first. The more you do on the ground to have the horse's mind and heart engaged with you, the more likely it is that he can move off in good form under saddle, right from the start.

I have discovered that if you allow a "sauntering" forward motion at first, perhaps with "goals" of arriving at certain points and then halting and relaxing (see the Ring of Cones Conversation on p. 247), most horses get past the "Fire Drills" aspect of this stage of the Chessboard and are not only ready for "Sports Maneuvers" but start requesting them. I would rather have a horse ask me, "Hey, are we going to canter or what?" than to have to push him into canter after pushing him into trot.

Asking a horse to go forward includes helping him feel comfortable, safe, and interested in the Chessboard. Remember, where human beings can be riding a horse and focused on the movement, the horse is focused on the environment. Making the Chessboard smaller, as with Ring of Cones, can help the horse feel more confident in the movement you are asking of him. If you present a sense of direction to him, and a point of arrival, you can get the horse much more "on board" with the activity of being ridden. Eventually, this stage can even be bypassed, or reduced to the first few minutes.

Try not to just ride motion up there like it is all happening below you. Remember, the horse is expressing thoughts and feelings through his body language at the same time you are riding him. Learning to help horses carry themselves in different forms of balance *on the ground* first, before getting on, is usually interesting to them, and a good topic that they like talking about.

How do I make simple balance work interesting?

Actually, horses tend to become *very* interested and even ask for this sort of work. Therapy Back-Up and Dancer's Arms help inform deeper layers of balance while longeing (see p. 301), and as horses gain confidence through these groundwork skills, you will be better able to request similar responses under saddle.

I was taught to balance while riding with no reins and no stirrups on the longe line, on the flat and over jumps. Learning rider balance from an already well-balanced horse, like I did, is an important thing. Since most people do not get this chance these days, Horse Speak aims to educate your horse and you about good balance—and to influence it—through use of your X and from the ground *before* you get on. This will add so much value to your understanding and awareness once you start riding! Even interspersing a weekly riding routine with some days of just balance practice on the ground will add enrichment and value to training.

We have a responsibility to be centered and balanced as best as we can in the saddle, but the more we engage in Conversations about balance *with* our horses, rather than forcing an idea of balance onto them and doing things *to them*, the more interested our horses often become in practicing these things with us.

I have found over the years that these key elements of balance practice add up to a horse more likely to be in the Green Zone for learning and communicating, and who starts to ask, "Can we go faster?" The horse comes to a point where he feels satisfied with Fire Drills and *wants* to do some Sports Maneuvers.

What's the best way to raise the intensity level while riding?

What if your horse doesn't want to go forward, even with all this nice stuff we've been talking about? This is where you need to practice raising your intensity levels. If you have provided all opportunities for increased awareness and positive interactions, then upping the intensity can be part of the deal. Horses increase the intensity level with each other, so you can do it with your horse, too. In fact, some horses need to know you are their leader and may rise to the challenge, not because they are "punks" or stubborn; simply because nature wants horses to make sure that their leaders are fit to lead. The horse has to check sometimes to make sure you're not asleep at the wheel. It's nothing personal.

So, when it is time to raise the bar, go along the Buttons and raise the intensity until you find the sweet spot that the horse responds to the best. You can use your leg, or a touch from a dressage whip, or the swish of a quirt, or the tickle from the excess rein. It is not important to the horse what you use; it is important to him that you practice good intensity levels: think of turning the volume up one notch at a time, not cranking it to full blast, blowing your speakers, then trying to backtrack. To ensure that you are practicing good intensity levels, speak them out loud: "Going to Level One, Going to Level Two," and so on.

Remember; the more you can get from a lower level of intensity, the softer and more "invisible" all your cues will become. And while you can use more intensity, don't forget to then drop back to Zero and start over at Level One (see p. 41 for more about the levels of intensity).

How do I make sure my horse and I always get along?

Horses get grumpy with each other sometimes. If you get grumpy with your horse, apologize and do better next time. If your horse is grumpy with you, accept the same from him.

If you feel you need to make a point with a horse who is immature or just not being focused and is giving you a hard time for the sake of it (I can think of a few immature Jokers who really made me work), it is okay to make a point *one time*. If, however, you find you are getting drawn into more and more of a battle with a horse, then backtrack. Look at things from a fresh perspective and have an enrichment day instead.

Ultimately, we do sometimes need a horse to be compliant with our desire to go forward, maybe for longer than the horse wishes. This can be the case when we have athletic goals for the horse or if we really need to keep him in good shape.

My friend Heidi has a lovely Peacemaker horse who is happy strolling through the woods and not overly thrilled with the riding ring. She likes to keep him in good shape and competes in Western Dressage, so, she coined a phrase to use on the ringwork days: "Riley, it's time to go to the gym." She offers plenty of enrichment, and he gets to do his favorite rides in the woods, too.

Heidi started Riley off slowly and built his tolerance for ringwork over a few months. As he got stronger and more balanced, he began to enjoy this work, as well. Now, he is a very seasoned show horse who just loves spending time with his person, and the fact that he is in good physical shape means they can ride anywhere and do anything.

Following these ideas and blending them with your regular training schedule can have a significant effect on helping your horse be more invested in riding with you.

How Horse Speak Can Help You Ride Better

I suggest that riders take an inventory of their *own* athletic ability and consult with professional instructors if they feel truly limited in their strength or flexibility. But you now have options learned in these pages, and instead of getting on the horse and trying to improve his flexion and balance from his back, you have a lot of things you can create on the ground that work on these same balances.

In many cases, there can be a question of "the chicken and the egg," meaning, is the *horse* experiencing a limitation in *his* body that has caused the rider to become stiff? Or is the *rider* feeling a limitation in *her* body and that has caused the horse to become stiff?

If you are aware of a limitation in your riding, which could be affecting your horse, then when you get on the horse, be sure to do some warm-up for yourself. In this way you are suggesting to the horse that he relax about this "problem spot" in your body and not just Copycat it. I have mended bones from old breaks and riding limitations, like most people. But when I take the time to focus a bit on my stiff or weak places when I first get on my horses, I find they are much better at holding their own posture, rather than assuming any bad posture that could be coming from *my* issues.

9.9 Learning to use Yoga Rein and "opening gestures" from the saddle can unstick "stuck" and stiff places in the horse.

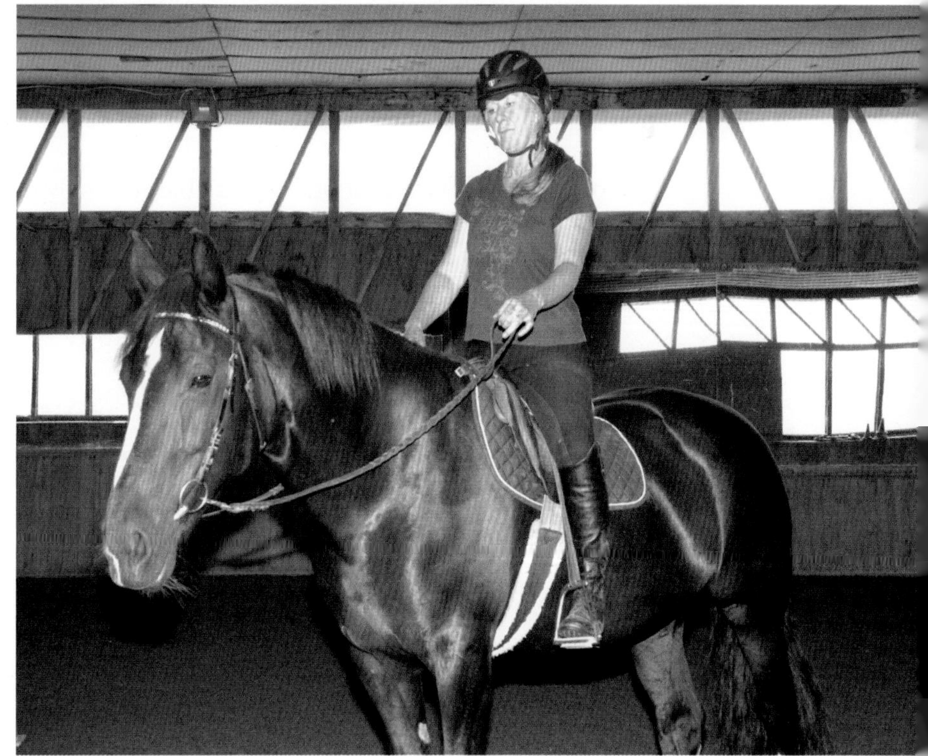

In the same light, I can relax a specific area on the horse's body by becoming aware of it as I ride and sending more breath or more "opening gestures" to that area (fig. 9.9). For instance, my horse Zeke had a very arthritic right hip. When we first started riding together, I would take the first five minutes and breathe deeply into my right hip *and* his right hip and allow both of those hips to relax with each

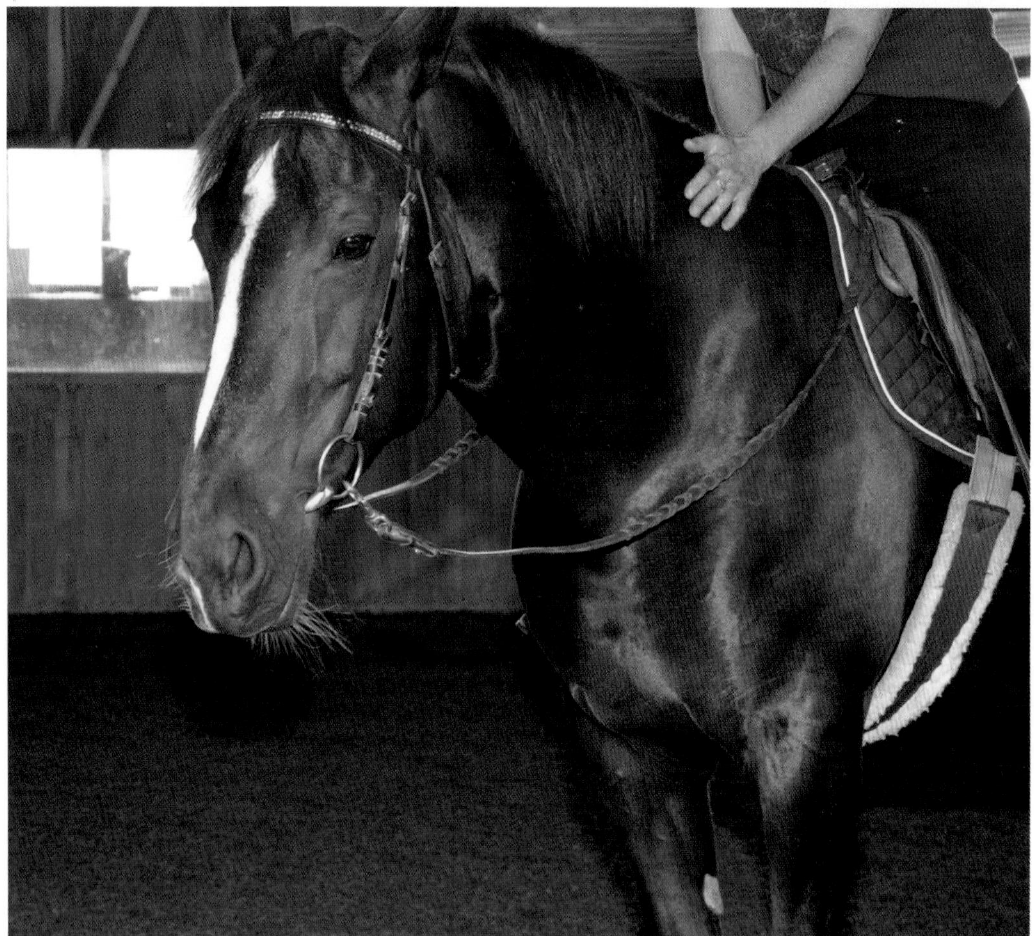

9.10 Remembering the horse is talking to you just as much when you are riding as he is when you are on the ground can transform the experience, for both of you.

other. In this way I found he was able to respond better to my riding, and as time went on, he actually gained more mobility in that hip.

The bottom line is that we both have bodies—we and our horses—and riding is body-to-body communication. Everything that you learn from the ground you can bring to the horse's back, and rather than have two worlds in your mind—one world of groundwork and the other of riding—consider it all one (fig. 9.10). When you're riding, your horse is still talking to you. Remember this, and *everything* will be better.

PART TWO

The Dictionary of Conversations

We all want to be able to hear what our horses are saying to us, and we want to be able to talk back. You now have the skills to create messages for your horse. In the pages ahead, find some of the many, many Conversations you can begin to have. As I have mentioned before, every horse and circumstance is individual, but these sample scenarios will give you some sense of how to begin communicating using the horse's language.

This Dictionary is broken into three sections: "How to Say…" (p. 340), "How to Fix…" (p. 348), and "Messages from the Horse" (p. 362). Note that you will find references throughout to the various terms and techniques I've explained in Part One. I encourage you to consult the index and then refer back for definitions, instructions, and deeper exploration.

How to Say...

HOW TO SAY, "I'M HERE AND I'M COMING TO SEE YOU."

When you arrive, try to find your Zero first. Ground your feet, check your Core Energy, and double check your inner feelings. It is better to talk out loud to your horse about your feelings than to keep them bottled up. Horses respond well to being congruent, and although they won't understand your spoken words, they will understand you are sharing feelings.

Next, pay attention to what your horse pays attention to. Mirroring in practice is this simple. Notice what they notice—because then you will probably notice when they see you. I cannot say how many times I am with a person or at a clinic and the horse is broadcasting "Hey there" from across the grass or over a pile of hay and the person has no idea.

The best way to announce your presence is to think about how you need to do your Initiation cycle: What does your horse value? Where is he in the Roles in the Herd? What sort of Energy Type is he? If I am meeting a politician or a teenager, I will have different approaches. This is the same for horses. Does your horse often worry? Well, show there is nothing to worry about rather than ignoring his concerns. Does your horse try to take over and lead you? Well, then, make sure you are offering the value of clarity; do not be wishy-washy in your approach.

Use this time wisely to gauge your horse's level of comfort, and learn to become the most interesting thing at the barn!

HOW TO SAY, "I WILL KEEP MY ZERO, NO MATTER WHAT YOU ARE DOING."

Why are you losing your Zero? Is it the horse? Is he a tough Energy Type for you? Are you an O person, and this is a young, fresh, Outgoing Joker who wants to chew on you the minute you get there? Or, are you an X person who has strong expectations, and you have a Peacemaker who would rather hang out with you and enjoy the sunset?

My partner Laura was a serious basketball player who won the state championships. Her Core Energy tends to be set to a high intensity. She frequently has to offer a Low-O by squatting until a new horse learns what her Zero looks like—what to pay attention to and what to ignore.

However, she can also be a pushover, so she finds she has to also give clear X messages and not allow any "leaky" energy, either from herself or from the horse. Leaky energy happens when you wiggle, shuffle, or make unclear "gray-area" movements. It can also come from the horse when he takes a step while on a lead rope that you didn't ask for, or he begins to pop your Bubble in ways that start "cute" but become bumping, pushing, or even nipping.

Zero starts to go away when there is a lack of clarity, so remaining clear is the best advice I can give for keeping your Zero. If you need to create a believable X, then try adding an aid like a crop or even just a rolled-up newspaper in your hand that helps you "believe in your X." Some horses need a good Level Four intensity to help them "know the limits," just like human toddlers do. Can you give this message and not get angry? If you need to create a believable O, you may need to squat all the way down like Laura, with your Core Energy completely off. I call this, "How Low Can Your O Go?"

HOW TO SAY, "HELLO," TO A HESITANT HORSE.

Hesitant horses are often harder to catch, more timid in general, and often more spooky than other Energy Types. However, they can also manifest a gentle, kind, and even affectionate nature. This is one of the types of horses that people frequently bring to my clinics.

The most important way to handle this Energy Type is to spiral into his Bubble with a lot of clarity about his need for safety and protection. Sometimes this horse does well with treat training because the food resource can help override the initial urge to panic. That said, I have also seen this type become over-excited by treats and cover up inner worries without actually resolving them, only to have the unsuspecting owner get run over or bucked off when the horse is spooked.

Dominance training makes this Energy Type freeze (see p. 65) and can make his anxiety worse.

When saying "Hello," keep your O posture in your shoulders, but do not "creep" around looking like a stalker. The horse needs to see your X to believe you can protect him. I have actually turned my back to the Shoulder Button to offer Buddy-Up with this type of horse. Breath messages, extended knuckles for an air Greeting, and lots of head nodding ("Yes" and "No") to ask him to relax his head and neck goes a long way. The Hesitant horse really needs your facial expressions to be soft: blink your eyes, make gum-chewing motions, look and point down to the ground and scuff your toe in the dirt for both Aw-Shucks and to tell the horse to look down and get grounded. Point to the ground where you intend to walk when you are ready to Go Somewhere, and then step into that spot. When horses graze, they indicate the next place they will put their nose and then step into that space. This Mirrors that pattern. You may also point to the horse's front foot, then point to the ground in front of your foot and sigh out loud. This says, "You can bring your foot (and your whole body) here."

HOW TO SAY, "I MEAN YOU NO HARM."

Be aware of your Core Energy and the Quadrants of the horse's Bubble; basically, turn your Core Energy away from the horse. Often, we approach with our toes angled toward the horse, which means our Core Energy is aiming at them. Certain horses find this very "loud" and react to it. Doing what I call "Core Off" can make all the difference with some sensitive horses.

The next thing to try is to step to the edge of the horse's Bubble, which means you need to be aware of where it is. Offer a Figure-Eight Hold Hand to his Buttons in the air. This says, "I see all of you, I just want to be here with you." I once did this to my horse Mommy when she was in the middle of receiving bodywork. She loves bodywork and her bodyworker, and she was standing still in the middle of the field with no restraint receiving her session, but she was not "letting go." The moment I thought to do the figure-eight pattern, she really released.

Simply standing with a Hold Hand to the Shoulder Button has been reported to be a potent help for horses getting their feet done. To be able to use the Hold Hand like this for moments when you need it, it is best to have practiced it beforehand.

For some horses, constant access to a Check-In is what helps them gain confidence. Pay attention to any time the horse brings his muzzle close, as this is a need to "hold your hand." (Think of a small child reaching for your hand whenever she is unsure.) You will need to touch the horse's Cheek Button and say, "Okay, now put your face back," to show you are in charge. He needs you to be in charge to know he can count on you.

HOW TO SAY, "I'M YOUR LEADER, PLEASE RESPECT MY SPACE."

Make sure you offer a satisfying Initiation and Introduction. When these steps get skipped, the horse can feel "jumped on." Use the Initiation and Introduction cycles to learn more about "what side of the barn your horse woke up on that day"—gathering information is crucial to good risk assessment and communication analysis.

Negotiate your hierarchy with your horse so that things are clear between you as needed. Depending on the horse's Role in the Herd and Energy Type, some horses need more Negotiation than others, and some horses need specific things addressed in their Negotiation that others may not need so much. At this stage, use the Three Buttons of Respect located at the cheek, the neck, and the shoulder, as well as the Back-Up Button. You may need to use them all together.

Remember to *step away* and give the horse space as a reward for giving you space (no matter how small, at first). It is not fair to claim space from a horse, asking him to yield away from you, while remaining too close to his Bubble.

The bottom line with gaining good spatial respect with horses is to stay clear, clean, and focused on the "rules." The 6-Inch Rule and "Stay in Your Lane," applies to both you and the horse. Horses have rules about "how close is too close." Watch a herd of horses and notice the constant affirmation of space between them. The rules set them free, so they feel comfortably connected at the edge of all the Bubbles at all times.

Move through all the Buttons, and make sure you can ask for movement and space Negotiation from each of them, but *please do not turn this into a drill*. You are "checking under the hood" not demanding obedience.

Jokers can have a really hard time respecting the Bubble, and it's nothing personal. It's just something you need to help them learn how to do. PBJs can act really "sticky" and want to "Velcro" themselves to you out of nervousness. Peacemakers can appear wonderfully comfortable with you scratching them and loving on them and may almost knock you over in an attempt to get more. Use Activation Fingers and hold on a Button for three seconds, either in the air or on the body, to say, "I want space, and I want quiet energy, too." Mentors or Sentries may seem very easy to get along with until they decide that they want their own way…and take you with them.

Using the Buttons of the front end for correction and redirection is the best way to practice reminding them that you have 51 percent of the vote in your relationship. For these leaders, the Therapy Back-Up is often key, although they can also seem to resist it, at first. Meet them in the middle, and start out only asking for a little lean backward. Too many people insist on several steps, and for a true leader-type horse, this can feel insulting or pushy.

If your horse has trouble with the Cheek Button being touched, then bring the "Stay in Your Lane" message to the feet. Draw a line in the sand and keep your feet on one side while keeping the horse's feet on the other. Keep a crop up between you as a physical representation of the line between your lane and his lane—just like there is a line in the middle of the road. More often than not, I find there is often human "user error" going on with this issue: We are unclear, "leaky," wiggly, or allow "cute" Bubble-popping.

Praise with deep, quiet messages, a low voice, and downhill stroking. Never use baby talk or high-energy scratching as they are overstimulating.

HOW TO SAY, "LET'S PUT ON THIS HALTER OR BRIDLE."

Use the Horse Hug position for haltering, bridling, and good old-fashioned hugging. Hugging a horse who resists it and seems tense will eventually help you "unblock" and relax his neck and shoulders. Think of the Horse Hug position as a sort of "trust fall" exercise for some horses. Ease into it with the knowledge that it can help solve many other issues.

Sniff the horse's neck to say, "I really like you" (horses do this to each other). Rock the Baby on the Bridge of the Nose or Follow Me Button. Offer a Hold Hand at the Shoulder Button to Buddy-Up. Also try offering Hold Hand to the Jump-up Button. This says, "I know you're vulnerable, but its okay."

Remember to give space back to the horse after he does something you requested that he maybe didn't really want to do right now—if you want a Yellow Light to turn Green, then acknowledge his "try."

HOW TO SAY, "I'M GOING TO BE CLEAR AND CONSISTENT WITH MY X AND O."

One of the big reasons you may need to do this is when working with a horse who has lived in isolation for a long time or who did not get to "be a horse" with other horses and so seems to have lost touch with his own language. I recommend staying on the other side of a barrier when first approaching this horse and making simple, slow changes in your body language. Start in O to begin on a welcoming note, move to a big X, and then go back to O. I often even speak out loud, saying "This is my X....and... this is my O." I find adding my voice helps send soothing feelings.

Do this several times, directing your Core Energy into new positions as you go. Supplement this with the Initiation you think this horse needs to let the horse know you are here to take charge, but you are working *for* him, not against him.

I have had this demonstration of X and O clarity literally work wonders with troubled stallions or horses who were weaned and trained way too early. In each case, when the X and O started to "get through," the horse began to Mirror me in delightful and humorous ways. It was a bit like "play therapy." Only after this could I really introduce myself properly and go through each stage of the Four Gs. I had to have a strong Gone cycle in between to let the horse soak up the lesson.

HOW TO SAY, "I REALLY NEED YOU TO STOP CROWDING OR TAKING OVER."

If you have to Negotiate space every single day with your horse, it indicates a few possible issues. One is that you are habitually too close (in his Bubble), and you are releasing your boundary message way too soon. Another possibility is that the horse is stunted in his development and has not learned good Bubble respect from other horses. Still one more possibility is that your Bubble definition is not consistent enough, and you have a Joker or leader-type horse who assumes control the moment you seem like you are not rising to the occasion. You do not need to become a strident or militant leader, but you do need to pay attention to wherever it is that is "leaking energy" and stop it.

Use Activation Fingers to ask for some space and hold your hand still for three seconds in the air after the horse complies. Slowly put your hand back down and take one defined step aside to reward the horse by giving some space back. See what happens. If he "leaks" right back to you, then you may have a confused horse who thinks your neutral position is actually an O, beckoning to him.

Remember, your X uses both your feet and your hands, so double-check what your feet are doing, what your Core Energy is doing, and whether you have "life" in your hands. Since single foot messages matter to horses, try adding a stomp to add energy to your X.

I often recommend people in this situation put one or both hands up in a Hold position for the duration of time spent working with such a horse for a few days, until both human and horse are more aware of the posture adjustment. Being diligent about the 6-Inch Rule and about your Hold Hand for a few days does wonders for crowding issues.

As a skill-builder, use a Safety Object between you as a visual aid if you can. Practice your space communications from over a fence to have a chance to see things from a new or fresh perspective. Leave your Hold Hand up the whole time you are with the horse, so you remain calm and consistent. Only lower your hand when the horse begins to self-regulate. Do not push the horse away, then quickly put your hand down fast—that is exactly how two horses initiate game play.

Do not *flail*, swishing your hands constantly, or shaking or flipping a rope, because this is on-again-off-again pressure with a too-quick release. *The horse cannot tell what you really mean.* If you feel you need a prop, then a stick with a plastic bag secured on one end, held by your side, and only used *sparingly* can be helpful. You may also use a horsemanship stick or wand to augment the message, "My Space, Your Space." I really love it when people feel empowered to give a message using just their body language, so remember, the stick is just supposed to be a long finger.

If you watch a Mentor horse deal with a silly youngster or immature herdmate, you will see that the Mentor remains in a strong Hold position the entire time, up to 10 minutes or more, until the troubled horse "gets it" and starts to relax. Only then does the Mentor ease up. Mentors, Teachers, and other leaders tend to be very patient with confused and immature horses. They Hold and Hold and Hold and Hold. Then, perhaps they make one, strong "statement" about putting their foot down by literally stomping, nipping, or squealing. This works for us, too. If you Hold and are clear about your boundary, allowing the horse to ask a ton of questions ("Is your boundary here? How about here? What about this spot? But what if I am cute? What if I look intimidating?") then, if you make one, strong Level Four intensity moment (I like to make noise on the ground or one huge swish with a bag on a stick so there is no doubt), you will have made a point. You must go back to Zero; leave the area to accomplish this if necessary. I like to do this type of thing from the *outside* of a round pen because the horse can scoot away, and I can go back to Zero, but the artificial barrier helps me never leave Zero in the first place.

HOW TO SAY, "I WOULD LIKE TO CONNECT WITH YOU."

Offer the Figure-Eight Hold Hand to Go Somewhere down all the Buttons. You can "scan" or engage each Button in a row from the cheek, down the neck, and move on in an even, calm pattern to cover all the Buttons. This says, "I see all of you." This can be accomplished by offering your palm in the air over each Button while your feet stay still, or by actually placing your palm on the horse's body where each Button is to the count of four seconds or four breaths before moving on the next Button, until you reach the Hip Button, which tells the horse, "I have your back," and the Sit Button, which says, "Relax, no need to worry about anything."

I know a therapeutic riding instructor who now moves down the aisle of the barn slowly each morning, lingering near each horse to offer a Figure-Eight Hold Hand. She reports that the horses often yawn, or even turn around to show her the Button they want to talk about. Every horse has his favorite Button message, and some horses have a real problem with one or two of their Buttons. Doing this activity gives you a chance to reassure them by using the Buttons that they like. Any buttons that are trouble indicates other things are going on—for example, pain or memory of pain, or confusion, or a traumatic past.

HOW TO SAY, "I'M GOING TO BE YOUR MAPMAKER."

Navigate the Chessboard of Life with your horse once you have completed the first initial aspects of creating good rapport between you. Remember to touch the objects of the horse's world *before* you let him touch them to remind him that *you* are the one in charge, and that you are also the Protector. Turning as many things as you can into Safety Objects is a great way to desensitize the horse to his environment. Thresholds are part of your Navigation process. Remember to use all of the calming messages: eye blinking, deep breathing, shuddering breath, and Aw-Shucks. Pause often to let him process.

The bottom line is make a plan, set up the right situation for your horse, and lead him through it.

HOW TO SAY, "I THINK YOU ARE A LITTLE HIGH STRUNG, AND I WOULD LIKE TO HELP YOU."

Figure out what messages your horse truly needs. Does he need messages about the Chessboard and the world around him or direct messages about how to self-regulate?

I often find that Rock the Baby on the Bridge of the Nose and Follow Me Buttons at the same time works wonders for a high-strung horse. The Hip and Sit Buttons are also great for whole-body soothing messages.

HOW TO SAY, "MAY I TOUCH YOU?"

Horses arrive at the Grooming Ritual when they have had a satisfying Greeting and Going Somewhere. This completion can be as simple as a breath of Greeting and Going Somewhere by asking the Cheek Button to yield or hold steady, followed by a sigh out loud and pausing for a moment, then reaching for the Grooming button to ask, "Can I touch you now?"

With my horse Rocky, he insists we touch the Greeting Button three times (although quickly), yield the head (Mutual Salute), pause for a breath (Gone) then he brings his jugular area to me to stroke. That is his favorite spot. It is funny that even though he wants the scratch, he prefers we go through the ritual first.

My horse Luna (an Outgoing Joker-Princess) ignores all protocols and runs me over to get a good scratch. She pushes other horses out of the way as well. I make her do the Greeting Ritual so she calms down and we can both enjoy Grooming.

In an insecure horse, or one who isn't always into being touched, I may tap the Grooming Button three times, then step away to wait for his answer. Most often, if the horse stands still, it is "Yes," while if he wiggles, flinches, or steps away it is "No."

HOW TO SAY, "I NEED MORE FROM YOU, BUT I WANT YOU TO STAY ZERO."

Initiate intensity levels on the other side of a fence or barrier to begin learning about this whenever you can. This allows the horse to express himself without risking that you will lose Zero. It also gives you a better vantage point to observe the messages he is sharing and take a break as needed.

Once you are inside an arena or pen, or have a horse on a lead rope, use objects to aim for and provide purpose. The Ring of Cones is perfect for Initiating higher intensity. All you both need to do is get from one cone to the next—pick the energy up, sustain it for a few steps, and put the energy away, staying Zero.

Most horses are more concerned about how you ask for halt than about how you ask to go forward. When the horse drops his nose to the dirt, this is a request to lower the intensity (Aw-Shucks). It means he is trying to self-regulate and is concerned about losing Zero.

The goal throughout is to practice higher intensity levels on the outside but keep your Zero and the horse's Zero on the inside. If you or your horse lose Zero, then go back to enrichment activities until you get it back again.

When your horse seems really sluggish and reluctant, he could be misinterpreting your request for intensity as somehow being "scolded" by you—a leader horse only sends a lesser horse away firmly when the horse is in trouble. Again, the Ring of Cones is great for dealing with this communication issue, because you can clearly define that you are saying, "You are not in trouble; we are practicing Sports Maneuvers."

Use the end of the lead rope or a stick to swish upward toward the Buttons. Starting with the Mid-Neck, move to the Shoulder, then Girth, then Jump-Up, then Hip. Each horse moves forward from each Button a little differently, so use this time to learn about how your horse feels about moving forward from all the Buttons, one at a time. When you do get good forward movement, aiming your intention toward the Sit or Jump-Up Button, combined with drawing the Greeting or Cheek Button toward you, will ask for different levels of collection and bend. The Yield-Over Button can create a nice stop if you look at it as you sit down in Drop It to Stop It, or even by pointing at it with Activation Fingers.

Ask for only a few steps of trot or canter at a time until you both can turn the volume up and down on the outside but stay Zero on the inside. Turn Fire Drills of slow predictable problem-solving into Sports Maneuvers a little at a time.

How to Fix...

**Issues listed in alphabetical order.*

DIFFICULT TO MOUNT

Use: What I call "kill the mounting block" works here. Nine times out of ten problems at the mounting block are related to internal nervousness that we bring to the mounting block, possibly on a total unconscious level. Our brain could be worried about slipping and falling, or the darn box could be unstable. Either way, stomp on it, and get up and down it several times like you are "King of the Hill," before working on how your horse stands next to it. Use the Therapy Back-Up to allow the horse to release any stored tension. You want to turn the mounting block into a Safety Object. I recommend getting on and off your horse three times in a row. In one case, I had a student get on and off over 20 times until both she and the horse felt they had "mastered" mounting.

DIFFICULTY CHANGING DIRECTION

Use: When on the ground, use the Cheek and Mid-Neck Buttons with one hand and aim your other hand out in front. The lead hand sends a directional message while the other gives a controlled yield message. You have two hands, so use them both when communicating with your horse. When changing direction toward you, use Turn the Key, Come to Me and back away in O posture, or just back away in O posture to beckon the horse to you. Lift your lead hand higher to encourage the horse to have a sharper swivel in his pivot; keep it low when you want him to do a low "come around" movement. Use your Core Energy to "open" and "close" the door of the horse's Core Energy (in his chest). Look over your outside shoulder while turning to ask the horse to "flip" his hip and give a sharp pivot. This also moves your Core Energy off the horse when done right.

Use the Horse Hug to ask the horse's head to come toward you, offer your other hand for him to sniff or even lick. Allow the horse to shift away if he gets worried but encourage him to Linger Longer.

DIFFICULTY WITH FLY SPRAY

Use: "Kill" the spray bottle to start. Get an old used one that is empty and have a nice afternoon stepping on it in front of your horse.

My friend did this with her donkey who had never been sprayed with fly repellent her whole life due to her panicky reactions. My friend left the spray bottle in the donkey's pen. When she came out later, the donkey went over to the bottle, pinned her ears, and squashed it with her hooves. Later my friend used a little treat training to help the donkey not slip into Red Zone so fast. She just exposed her to the bottle, gave her a treat, and then left. Next, she sprayed the Chessboard with the fly spray while the donkey followed on a lead rope. Then she sprayed only the donkey's front hooves. The following day, she sprayed the donkey's hooves, legs, and chest. By the end of the week, she could spray everything but the donkey's head.

DIFFICULTY SADDLING AND GIRTHING

Use: Incorporate the saddle in the Introduction stage. Greet the horse with the saddle and watch his expressions. Go away and come back with the saddle as many times as it takes for the horse to offer some sort of Green Light. Spend a whole afternoon getting Green Lights related to the pad, the saddle, and the girth. Keep your Core Energy off. If you get a Green Light, swing the saddle on and off the horse several times in a row before moving on to the girth.

Use the Negotiation stage with the girth. Lift the girth three times in a row with Hot Potato Releases. When you finally start to tighten it, breathe out as you do it up. We so often hold our breath around horses! Breathing out says, "Nothing wrong here." Do not expect a horse to ever really "like" girthing. Find a way to add enrichment to all tasks that are uncomfortable, like this one.

DIFFICULTY STANDING FOR FARRIER

Use: Enrichment! Add enrichment to the horse's daily routine by stroking his legs downward and slowly. Do not ask the horse to lift a leg until he is in an O posture. Then lift a leg and make little circles with it and put it down again. Repeat. Finally, pick out the hooves. Do this for a week before the farrier arrives. Consider allowing the horse to nibble hay while the farrier works, until you can wean him off the food reward. Any horse I have every rehabbed for this issue has responded well to this protocol.

DIFFICULTY STAYING FOCUSED

Use: Observation to ask, what does the horse truly need? What questions is he asking? If you are not sure, ask yourself, "If I *did* know, what would my best hunch be?"

Mirroring helps in this scenario: When you Mirror a horse, you let go of your agenda and help him realize you are seeking to be in harmony with him. This helps many Hesitant, nervous horses, as well as high-intensity horses, to start to key in to your body language. The secret is to offer him a slower, lower posture than the one he is in. For focus, you are aiming for Zero.

For the spooky horse: IINN, Four Gs to deepen trust and rapport, and then blow Sentry Breath. Secure the Environment; do X for the horse (yell at a tree, toss a stone); try

Hold Hand toward the Hip Button; be clear with X, O, and Core Energy. Use eye-blinking, head-nodding, lip-wiggling, and breathing out (all signals of letting go of stress, fear, and worries), while forging connection with you.

For the distracted horse: This horse needs very clear IINN with a good grasp of the Four Gs, and also usually needs *more time to process*. Offer to touch objects and create safe spaces and places. Ring of Cones makes a smaller Chessboard to manage. Aim an X message in the air near the horse's eyes, then a strong O message downward (bring your attention back to the ground). Aw-Shucks messages lower intensity. Lots of Therapy Back-Up and Dancer's Arms change the focus to suppling and helping the horse feel good in his body. A balanced body helps create a balanced mind/emotional state and better focus. Rock the Baby everywhere. Cupping or stroking the neck lowers stress or excitement levels and helps you aim for Zero. Occasionally, increase the intensity and create faster movement for a few minutes, then go back to Zero.

FEAR OF PHYSICAL THRESHOLDS

Use: Offer a good Initiation and Introduction cycle. Use the Four Gs a few times in a row to make sure you can Greet on some level, have a good Cheek Button Conversation, and can move down the Buttons of Respect (Cheek, Mid-Neck, Shoulder). Practice Therapy Back-Up, managing your Core Energy as well as being very clear with X and O. Use your Core Energy to "open" and "close" the door in front of the horse by swiveling toward him to ask for a sudden Therapy Back-Up every second or third step forward. Use Matching Steps to pace your feet and gain rhythmic movement together. Activate the Girth Button to "micro-longe" the horse around you, making sure he is yielding and bending through the Girth Button as he circles. Step up, halt, back up, halt, go around, halt, back up, halt, step up—repeat this series until you can manage the horse's steps when physically maneuvering over, around, and through Thresholds.

Audibly sigh and give the horse space as a reward. See if the horse likes long, downward stroking of the neck. Occasionally, horses with these issues like their eyelids stroked very lightly, creating a sensation like their mother's tail would have.

When leading: Try lifting your lead hand higher or moving it out farther away from your body, as you would when dancing with someone. Changing the angle or height of the lead hand sends a different balancing message to the horse. Some prefer it higher, lower, or farther away so they can shift their balance through a Threshold or in a sharp turn, like moving into a stall or through a paddock gate. Try arranging yourself to allow the horse to move through the Threshold while you stand still and send them through. You need to be able to tell the Buttons to move and also to ask the horse to turn back and face you once through the gate.

When riding: Make sure you have had success with the messages I just outlined on the ground. Use the same concepts when you are on the horse's back. Gain good control of a single step forward or backward from the saddle. This keeps the horse "talking" instead of "guessing." Use Safety Objects in a line to travel along or in a big circle to Navigate around. This makes the Chessboard smaller and less overwhelming, and it helps you be pinpoint the little things the horse has questions about. Learn to create predictable Safety Objects at Thresholds. Allow the horse to rest near the object or invite him to touch it with you. Once you have confirmed a Safety Object, the horse can touch it without you, because you have "given" it to him as a place to feel safe.

FEAR OF PSYCHOLOGICAL THRESHOLDS

Use: The physical maneuvering activities from Fear of Physical Thresholds (p. 227) help in this scenario, as well. Include psychological guides to Zero: Pay strict attention to rhythms of breathing and eye-blinking; release the horse's neck and poll by nodding your own head "Yes" and "No"; and offer lots of Aw-Shucks to lower the intensity. If the horse has too much X, adjust your expectations. Make sure your footstep messages are grounded and consistent! Use a Safety Object, blow away the boogeyman with Sentry Breath (followed by a strong "All's clear," pointing to the ground and breathing a soft sigh), and Secure the Environment by touching things as you move with the horse before he does. If you let your horse touch things first, he thinks he has to protect you and himself. You must convince him *you* are the Protector. Once you have established safe places to be and objects to touch, the horse may seek to be in those places and touch those objects on his own.

Psychological Thresholds need more time for processing. Do something three times and then put your horse away or turn him out to soak on the lesson.

As with everything, make sure your Initiation, Introduction, and Negotiation stages are decent. They set you up for next-level Navigation, which includes problem-solving the Chessboard with you. If the first three cycles are sloppy, then the horse is not really ready to problem-solve with you. (This applies to both on-the-ground and riding situations.)

When riding: Focus on the comfort of the horse's shoulders and his ability to lift his front feet one at a time. Make sure your knees follow the rhythm of the shoulders and are not clamping down. When in the saddle, your knees are almost directly in alignment with the horse's shoulder joints, and stiffness here is a common complaint horses have. Use a single step forward, halt, and step backward to get a better Conversation going rather than forcing them to take several steps or go forward blindly when a psychological Threshold seems to be an issue. Horses use *single* footsteps in both the Negotiation of trust, respect, and hierarchy, and Navigational problem-solving. Add as much enrichment to troubleshooting psychological Thresholds as you can.

FEAR OF THE VETERINARIAN

Use: The horse's Role in the Herd and Energy Type and determine his top value. Make sure he has his needs met before the vet arrives. If your vet is open to it, suggest she try a Greeting Ritual with your horse. Offer your horse his favorite Safety Object to put his nose on as well.

Hold Hand during procedures can be really helpful, and Hold Hand directly to the Sit or Hip Buttons.

Not all vets have great bedside manners, but we need to work with them, so talk to yours about what you are trying to do to help your horse.

Consider sedation when the fear is severe to help switch off the horse's Red Zone reaction. This means his memory of the situation will be colored by also being very relaxed.

FIGHTS

Use: In what is by far the most difficult situation, my best advice is to offer low, slow Mirroring and Copycat sessions from outside a barrier for a few days or even weeks. Make your X and O postures very clear, and keep your Core Energy on the horse when you demand space, even over the fence, but remove it like a Hot Potato for reward. Offer lots of Hold Hand to every single Button from a distance over and over again, until the horse starts to process. Slowly work up to creating movement from the other side of the fence, and then Drop It to Stop It or Stomp to a Stop with a sigh. Give lots of rewards like nodding, blinking, and turning your shoulder toward his shoulder for Buddy-Up.

Begin to give driving messages, but then make a Low O and welcome the horse back.

This is a good place to introduce the Hay Game along the fence line, or for you to play with My Territory along the fence line. You can evolve these messages into Matching Steps. As soon as the horse begins to walk, put Hold Hand in the air to Buddy-Up (at the Shoulder Button), and walk along with them over the fence.

You will need to show this horse Turn the Key, Come to Me and O posture beckoning to show him you *do* want him in your herd. You will need to invite him over, but his place to land should probably be an object at first. Point to where the horse can stop and stomp your feet.

HARD TO CATCH

Use: Initiation stage, spiraling in, Secure the Environment, breath and eye messages, Zero in action, and Sentry Breath. Toss a stone away, keep low O posture, change direction three times, find the edge of the horse's Bubble and back away, and try Reverse Round Pen. Determine if your horse is motivated by friendship, fear, or food, and if he is conditioned from past negative experiences.

If he is motivated by friendship, send messages to the Shoulder, Girth, and Jump-Up Buttons. Use Hold Hand at the Hip Button.

If he is motivated by fear, use the Hold Hand at the Hip Button for long periods, then let him process. "Chew gum" (smacking your lips means "all is clear"), sigh out loud, stay in a Low O posture with "Core Off" at all times.

If he is motivated by food, then plan to catch your horse timed around feeding to initiate a positive association with your presence. Or use specific food as a motivator three or four times, then wean off the food, and see if you can improve rapport with just your presence.

For past negative experiences, use everything I've mentioned, by degrees. Also, ironically, yielding the Cheek Button (very gently) can help you connect. The more you emphasize *respect for space,* the more a nervous horse relaxes because he doesn't feel so worried you're going to grab at him or "pop" his Bubble. Reverse Round Pen with Hold Hand is another way to talk to this horse and say, "My Bubble, your Bubble. Let's get comfortable with each other's Bubbles."

HARD TO HALT

Use: Matching Steps, Fun with Feet, and Stomp to a Stop. Make sure that your feet have *stopped.* The number one reason people have a hard time stopping a horse is they are trying to use the lead rope to stop them. When your feet can be heard stopping, the horse will pick up on it very quickly—usually only three or four tries. Breathe out and sigh when you stop. Once you both are tuned into stopping together, you should be able to sigh out and *quietly* stop your feet, and the horse will halt completely. Use the Ring of Cones to make a small practice area (and a smaller Chessboard). Walk around the cones, halting at each one. At first, do not "fuss with" the horse. Let him get it wrong. This teaches him to pay attention and learn how to self-adjust. If you fuss with him all the time, he will not learn to self-regulate. You are micromanaging the horse's steps with your own once you get in harmony, but this is different than fussing with them. Micro-gestures are the horse's way of having a Low-Calorie Conversation. Fussing with him in a quest for perfection will just frustrate you both.

When riding: Use a scooping rein to create a balanced halt within the horse's hind end. You can even use one scoop as a half-halt for collection, or to signal, "We are about to stop." This works best if you have first achieved a lovely, light, Therapy Back-Up from the ground. In fact, you can practice the scoop of a rein from the ground by standing at the horse's shoulder and using the reins as an "in-hand" skill-builder.

HARD TO SEPARATE FROM HERD

Use: A good Initiation stage is important. Open and close the gate three times for three days in a row before walking into the pasture. This tells *all the horses* to "cool their jets"—no rushing and no monkey business. Blow a Sentry Breath one time. This tells all the horses you are the guardian, and they must let you pass. Secure the Environment by touching three objects before engaging the horses (you can do this on the outside of the enclosure, first). Greet all the horses in some fashion, even if it is only a breath Greeting from a distance. Exchange Cheek Button messages with all of them, pointing in the air, even at a distance at their Cheek Buttons with your Activation Finger. Hot Potato Release when they make even a slight motion of respect away from you. Tilt your own head to say, "Good job," or "Thank you."

Expect to need to practice this formal "Greet the herd, walk onto the Chessboard" series of steps for a few days at least. Then, by the time you reach your horse, the whole herd should be in a calmer state, and ready to let you be the leader. If you need it or "just in case," carry a stick or a plastic shopping bag or even some bailing twine in your back pocket, which you can pull out and swish at a horse so you really mean it. Do not use it with your own horse, and make certain you are facing away from your horse and motioning toward a horse who needs to get out of your way. Remember, never flail around endlessly; this makes you look worried and weak.

You can also use Reverse Round Pen in this scenario: Use both hands in Hold position as you walk through the herd to say, "I am just walking by... I don't want anything from anyone." If you know the lead horse in the group turned out together, enlist his help: Put up your Hold Hand toward his Shoulder Button in Buddy-Up for a moment, sigh out loud, then move on toward your horse.

HARD TO TOUCH

Use: Figure-Eight Hold Hand outside the horse's Bubble aimed at all the Buttons. Use a stick or dressage whip to stroke downward along all the Buttons, then Hold Hand over each and every Button in a row. When you reach a "no-go" area, go back to the previous Button. Try Cupping (shaping your hand into a "cup" and rhythmically patting along the topline of the neck) or stroking down the neck or down the Friendly Button on the forehead and over the eyes. Use Reverse Round Pen. Also, ironically, Hold Hand at the Cheek Button can be key. The more you emphasize respect for space, the more a "touchy" horse feels safe with you and starts to let down his guard.

When this issue is related specifically to brushing or grooming, use IINN to begin a Conversation about brushes. Greet the horse with the different brushes and watch the horse's expressions. Try a brush out and observe the reaction. Some horses only like "toothy" brushes and some only like "soft" ones. We should not force a brush on them that they don't like. Keep your Core Energy off the horse as best you can because it can add pressure to the situation. Be open-minded about the horse's needs and add as much enrichment as you can. Watch for them to Green Light specific brushes or touches with soft expressions or Red Light them by leaning away or pinning the ears. Throughout, stand at the horse's side with a Hold Hand to send the message, "I want to connect with you."

HOT

Use: A bigger Bubble that includes My Territory, an object, or a spot on the Chessboard.

Be mindful of this exercise, because bully

horses will also use this tactic to claim the food or water access, and you do not want to look like a bully. Basically, you need to pick a spot that protects you—the edge of a wall, a fence line, a big tree, or several objects on the ground—that can be a natural barrier to inhibit the horse who might try to charge. This is easy to do on the outside of a round pen; place a barrel inside the pen for the horse to "have" but keep it near the fence. You will need a long whip, length of rope, or a stick and plastic bag for this exercise because with a truly hot horse things will get big fast.

You are not to hit the horse or throw the rope directly at him. You are going to claim a spot of territory that he wants for yourself.

Make a big X message while touching, keeping your back on, or claiming the fence, barrel, gate, water tub, or whatever. Walk slowly back and forth, but only a few feet left and right of the territory or object. Place your back to the object. When the horse moves off, turn your Core Energy down, relax, and sigh. If the horse charges and tries to take the spot back, go back to X. The moment the horse moves off, go O. Repeat until the horse lowers his head, circles away from you, or makes beckoning expressions.

Point to an area the horse may have for himself and dip your toe into the dirt. This says, "You can put your feet in that spot." When the horse settles a little, move quietly away from the spot you "owned" and move to the spot you said the horse could have. You are "switching sides," giving him access to the spot you had and taking the spot you said he could have.

After relaxing in the zone that was "his," swish your "tail" (wave your hand by your thigh), and exit. Wait a few minutes, then come back and get the horse and put him away for the day.

This Conversation has profound effects and should be used with as much compassion and Zero as possible. It is like the Hay Game, but on 12 cups of coffee. "My Territory" is an important message for uppity green horses, hot horses, or damaged, even traumatized ones, because you first claim the high-ranking spot (which may cause them to throw a fit) but then you give it to them when they self-soothe. You can take away, but you can also give. This is the prime leadership role.

Hot horses do sometimes need permission to run off steam, but My Territory gives purpose and focus to this need. Ultimately do not go out and use this Conversation as a weekly "fun way to get my horse some exercise." As an initial ice-breaker or as a way to redirect intense energy, it is superb. If you use it all the time, it will sour the horse.

Beginning with this message should set you up to be able to ask a hot or energetic horse to move thoughtfully through his paces with you on a longe line or at liberty to get the exercise he needs in a self-controlled manner, not in a "getting the bucks out" fireworks display.

KICKS

Use: Hold Hand in the air to the Hip Button and entire hind end, Reverse Round Pen, Mirroring, and Copycat. Get better with IINN and the Four Gs, especially the Greeting. Then, have him Greet a long stick (I like to use a piece of bamboo) and allow him to explore it. Starting with the Cheek Button and while standing near the Buddy-Up Shoulder Button, extend the stick to stroke all the way down the Buttons, one at a time, until you can get all the way down the legs. Secure the horse or have someone hold him, and walk all the way around him with the stick in the air and your other hand doing Hold Hand. Come back to the horse's muzzle and Greet again. Repeat until you can stroke the horse all the way around his body with the stick. Begin to get closer. The moment the horse gets tense (X posture), retreat with the stick to the last successful Button. Offer Hold Hand in the air to the Hip Button a lot. Allow the horse time to process.

Expect to spend a few days or weeks on this reconditioning. Watch for which Button is the most difficult one to touch; if it is the Jump-Up or Girth Button, your horse may have stomach problems or ulcers. If it is the Sit Button, he may have an injury or hormonal issues. Frequently, kickers need the Sit Button to be held with a soothing gesture that tells them, "Sit down with me; take a load off." I have known some horses who have this Conversation with a person and literally sit into her hand. In one case, I had a horse sit in the sand like a dog.

Use the Yield-Over Button on the stifle area to ask the horse to step aside one step. This request is also a "no kick agreement" between horses. However, if you whip the horse there or drive him there in a too-strong manner, it is like a dominant horse biting him. You may get the message across, but you have not built rapport. Only resort to Level Four intensity if you feel directly threatened, then go right back to Zero.

Use a length of soft rope to "embrace" one hind leg from a position standing near the shoulder area. Gently rub back and forth, up and down the whole leg. This often releases emotional tension and defensiveness. The hind end stores emotional messages and unfinished business that the horse was scared, offended, or confused by. You need to get that stored stuff out. Therapy Back-Up, all day long.

MOUTHY/NIPPY

Use: A decent Greeting of *some kind*. Most aggressive horses actually need their muzzles massaged to release positive hormones that reduce stress and help to "reset" their nervous systems. However, doing this on an aggressive horse is tricky. I like to offer the end of a crop or some other stubby stick for the horse to lip, mouth, and even chew on. Eventually, begin to "swipe" downward between the horse's nostrils in a Hot Potato Release. Swipe almost as fast as the stick touches the nostrils. Do not stab. Offer three swipes, and step away to let the horse process. Most horses will become very curious about this. While they need muzzle massage, they don't know what it is. As soon as they get a little feeling of it, most of them seem to suddenly realize this is what they want. *Do not* push the Play Button for any reason! This encourages biting and mouthiness.

Keep a Hold Hand up in the air near the Cheek Button for days or weeks until the horse has completely come to respect your Bubble. Only use the knuckles for contact—presenting the front of the palm to the horse's mouth is an invitation to lick or chew. Use lots and lots of Hot Potato contact. If you see the horse is going to nip in three seconds, then you stop at two seconds. Most of these horses are compensating for pain or emotional stress. Have the horse's teeth checked by a Natural Balance dentist.

NEEDS CONFIDENCE

Use: Ring of Cones. Walking on the outside and the inside of the Ring of Cones offer different messages: When the horse is on the inside, between you and cones, he is in the most protected place (between you and a Safety Object). When the horse is on the outside (you are between him and the cones), then he is in the least protected place. Also, every new cone is in a new placement on the Chessboard; some will be closer to the safe escape route and other will be closer to the boogeyman corner. Use the Ring of Cones both on the ground and when riding to work out any number of concerns, regain focus, increase the power of attention, resolve any issue with "go" or "whoa," and develop steady rhythm between elements. Stretch the cones out to get more steps between them, and eventually move them to the edges of the arena. Graduate to one cone in the middle of your work area to stop at if you or the horse needs to process or reboot. Place a cone as a Safety Object in the "spooky corner" to stop at as needed. Eventually, a cone can be an enriching addition to the day and a way to offer significant reward. Some horses outgrow it, and others love it. Most of them learn to self-regulate, and that means they learn to get themselves to Zero.

PUSHES OTHER HORSES AROUND

Use: The Initiation phase. You must act like a leader upon approach. Secure the Environment, blow Sentry Breath, change direction three times, open and close the gate three times, reverse round pen, or walk toward your horse with two Hold Hands up. Offer Hold Hand to the Hip Button of your horse to tell him you have his back; he does not have to push others (or at least you both can share the duties). Tell the other horses out loud, "*Don't look at my horse!*" Think that sounds crazy? Pair-bonded horses "claim" their friends and don't want other horse messing with them. Your horse will feel you have claimed the others in the herd; almost all horses really like this kind of demonstration. Model the behavior you want to see in your horse.

REFUSES TO GO FORWARD

Use: Your Initiation, Introduction, and Negotiation stages are key; make sure they are complete. Sometimes you can get more done to "fix" a situation by repeating the first three steps of IINN a few times—with breaks in between to allow any confusion, questions from the horse, or misunderstandings to surface—while the horse remains in a less tense, quiet environment like his own stall or paddock. By keeping the Conversation oriented where he has less stress, you can often have more success working out which stage of IINN is the most challenging for the horse, which G of the Four Gs the horse needs the most of, and which Buttons are "broken" or "shut off," and therefore are affecting his ability or desire to go forward. For instance, one horse may need dozens of Check-Ins because of underlying anxiety, but another horse needs dozens of Cheek Button messages.

Physically offer "Go forward" messages with Palm Down, Calm Down, then switch to a scoop on the lead rope forward. Also try a light tap on the Three Buttons of Respect (horses aim their eyes or muzzles in a fast motion across the cheek, neck, or shoulder of another horse when they tell him, "Ready, set, go" before moving off together). Tap the Girth or Jump-Up Button three times to say, "Keep up with me, I am the Mother or Mentor." Match Steps as you change direction three times and use Therapy Back-Up to "unlock" a stuck horse. Try offering Turn the Key, Come to Me or backing away in an O posture to invite the horse to follow you.

Increasing the intensity level is likely to come into play when asking for forward motion. Make sure you have good Level One, Two, and Three intensity awareness before using a Level Four. Aim to have all your messages working from Levels One and Two.

If you need a Level Four intensity, use the end of the lead rope or a dressage whip to swing upward toward the Girth Button. If more is needed, swing upward toward the Jump-Up Button. This says, "I know you're vulnerable. Stick with me; I've got you." A horse may drop his head after this message; however, if you do not have any connection established with the Jump-Up Button, this could send a horse into a defensive posture or action. Some horses respond well to a light tap, three times, on the top of the Hip Button. This says, "I'm the driver. Let's go."

Swinging upward toward these Buttons scoops the energy up from the horse's feet. I call it "sparking" the energy into motion. Don't swing downward to ask for forward, as this is like an attack from above. Try it on your own: Swing a rope overhand to slap the ground hard, and then swing a rope upward from the ground, as though trying to flick dirt from the end of the rope. Feel the difference in the inherent message. Downward feels punishing, and upward feels firm but inviting.

When riding: All the same messages and Buttons can be used in the same way as on the ground. First try unbracing the Cheek, Mid-Neck, and Shoulder Buttons, then the Girth Button, then the Jump-Up Button, then the Hip Button. When you know which Button works best for your horse, minimize the intensity. Only use Level Four intensity as a last resort. Making a point with Level Four intensity is fine to do as long as you do not lose your Zero. If you find you need a lot of Level Four, then back off and go through the IINN again. Look for the light to turn Green. If you're in the Yellow Zone, it could go to Red—and that is not good for anyone.

SPACE INVADER/PUSHY

Use: Practice a good Initiation/Introduction to look for any time the horse may naturally offer you a yield of the Cheek Button (any degree of looking away as you approach). Reward this *every single time,* and even offer one, as well, as a Mutual Salute (just a light tilt of your head will do). *You must step far outside this type of horse's Bubble to reward him for making any slight effort to learn about respecting your space.*

Horses consider respect for space *mutual,* so this Conversation is more about respectful connection than dominating their actions. When a horse still pushes you around, use the Cheek, Mid-Neck, and Shoulder Buttons all at the same time with two hands, and make him take a step away. Immediately step out of the horse's Bubble afterward. You cannot "win" this discussion. You are politely but firmly insisting on politeness in return from the horse.

I have yet to meet a horse who doesn't "get it" eventually. The only time people have a hard time with this is when they are either not using the side of the front Quadrant and are instead standing directly in front of the horse, or they forget to step back and give the horse space as a reward. Leaders reward followers by giving some space back to them after they have made their point.

For extra credit, use short, positive sessions of Therapy Back-Up to augment My Space, Your Space, sometimes even three or more times in a row. This works best when you only ask for a lean backward or a single step back each time. Do not push a pushy horse! Two negatives won't make a positive.

Understand that a horse who invades your space because he is *too friendly* is often allowed to get away with nosing your pockets and licking your hands, arms, or jacket. People tend to excuse this behavior because it is cute and a bit babyish. This is dangerous because it *is,* in fact, babyish behavior. Horses need to grow up and become mature to be their best selves and good partners to us. Do not punish the too-friendly horse, but use the tactics for the pushy horse with common sense. Do not hand-feed this type for the first two weeks of "renegotiating" rules of space. You may put a treat in a bucket at the end of the day, or offer a treat for a specific task, like bridling or putting on the girth, but consider the treat a reward for doing a good job with something, and don't use it as a bribe to get the horse to come close to you. Mother horses are walking treats, full of milk, and they manage to teach their foals to respect their personal space. You must behave the same or the possibility of a treat can actually create a lot of anxiety in the horse. Use the 6-Inch Rule and maintain My Space, Your Space between loving on them.

STIFF UNDER SADDLE

Use: Focus on the horse's inside (inside the bend) hind leg. Help that leg get strong and engaged with 20-meter circles. Think about that leg as you go forward, and adjust your body language to influence it. Do not "yield" the inside hind leg and force it to overwork, because this puts the horse into a "pretzel pose" and can make him feel out of balance and just stiffer. Use your outside (outside the bend) leg to "hold" the Jump-Up Button in a circle or change of direction, with your inside leg acting as a solid contact point for the horse to pivot around like you have done from the ground in many exercises. Aim your Core Energy into the arc. Use a measure of

O posture to relax the horse's body, and use Palm Down, Calm Down to release tension in the front end of the horse, as well. Nod your head "Yes" and "No" to release tension in the horse's head and neck. Breathe. Breathe again. Scoop up the inside hind leg with the rein to help both you and the horse dance through the movement better.

STRIKES

Use: Therapy Back-Up...but not as punishment. The Back-Up Button is full of nerves, and higher-ranking horses will use it to make a lower horse put a striking front foot down. Use the Bridge of the Nose in Advanced Therapy Back-Up. This Button is used by an elder with a lower stallion to say, "Ease up there; no monkey business." You must be gentle with this Button. Many horses resist being touched on the Bridge of the Nose at first, so use Hot Potato Release several times in a row until the horse allows you to place your palm across it. Tap the Mid-Neck Button three times in a row as a correction. Horses nip each other there as a warning or correction, and I have used this with good success.

TENDS TO PANIC

Use: The skills you've learned in this book in small degrees so you can accurately read the horse's messages and determine which of the Conversations are helpful. Keep the working area small and contained, and do not move around the Chessboard until you have mastered the area you are using. Make several Safety Objects and use them in new places as needed. Working the horse on the outside of you on the Ring of Cones may make things worse; keep the horse between your body and a Safety Object until you see him begin to develop a self-soothing ability. (Being on the outside of you is a vulnerable position; panicky horses want to be contained.) It can be helpful to have another horse in the arena when schooling, if you can. Work with a Mentor or Teacher or Sentry if you have one, leaving the panicky horse alone. Let him watch as you do all your work with the centered, level-headed herd members. Turn him loose with a Mentor or Teacher or Sentry and allow the lead horse to guide him, unless doing so could compromise one of them. Offer Therapy Back-Up every single time the horse loses Zero, as well as Rock the Baby on the Bridge of the Nose.

WON'T SLOW DOWN

Use: Your ability to slow down your own feet. Use three Therapy Back-Ups in a row. This says, "Hey there! Get back in your body. No reason to get worried or troubled." Lead with Hold Hand at the Cheek Button. You can actively hold the lead rope and lift your leading hand to be in alignment with the Cheek Button while opening your palm to it. Either touch it or keep the 6-Inch Rule. This works in most cases. It says, "I want your Bubble to respect my Bubble the whole time we are together." Offer Aw-Shucks when you stop to ask the horse to keep the intensity lower.

Open your outside hand as Hold Hand and aim it at the Buttons behind you, or over your shoulder to the Hip Button. Usually, you only have to do this a short while and the horse starts to believe you that you "have his back" while walking forward. Some horses crave being in the "middle" of the herd and feel exposed when at the back. If you offer a Hold Hand to the hind end you are telling him that even though you are up at his head, you still have his back.

In some cases, it may be okay to walk with a stick or dressage whip and touch it to the horse's chest when he tries to move ahead too much. I usually also offer to stroke down the horse's front legs when we stop to release the anxiety or tension.

When riding: The same is true under saddle. Practice from the ground so that you both are clear about the messages when you are on his back. Use your O posture to induce relaxation, and practice Drop It to Stop It in the saddle to get the same feeling you have practiced from the ground. Match Steps with the horse's shoulders through your knees, and slow your knees down. Use a scooping rein half-halt to rate speed as well.

WON'T SPEED UP

Use: Matching Steps first and foremost to both speed up and slow down. However, if you need help, use the end of the lead rope or a whip to tickle the Buttons from the Girth backward until you find the Button that the horse prefers. This puts you into more of a Dancer's Arms. You can move along that way or go back to forward-facing.

Try scooping upward on the lead rope. Even with a bit of pressure, the scoop doesn't knock a horse off balance, so it is not something they usually resist or become upset by. Scooping of a rein "gathers" the hip on that side and coils the energy there. Scooping a rein when asking for more speed can help the horse get the power back to the engine for a more collected *forward*. It will also create a body bend or lateral bend on the side you have scooped. Make sure the opposite rein is supportive or you will overbend the horse's neck, which interferes with uniformity through the spine and can overuse or severely limit the shoulder on that side, as well. The scooping motion also makes micro-adjustments to your own skeleton, which tends to make you balance better and therefore can make it easier for the horse to both balance and go forward. This little motion is very powerful, and like any new move, a little goes a long way. Think about it like trying a new pose in yoga or doing a new exercise routine—the first few times you do it may be very tiring, very quickly.

When riding: Think Matching Steps, just now on the horse's back. Make sure you can follow his footfalls as that is how you will adjust his speed. Use your Core Energy to Activate a higher intensity level—some describe the feeling like butterflies in your stomach before a roller coaster ride; some describe it like turning the flames up on the stove; some imagine there is a rolling ball inside them. If the horse still resists forward motion, use the Jump-Up or Hip Button.

Messages from the Horse

MESSAGE: HORSE SNIFFS YOUR LEG, AND MAYBE EVEN YOUR BOOT

This usually implies the desire to create movement. Either the horse wants you to move, or he is asking if he can.

- If you have been standing around with your horse and he does this, he is asking, "Can we leave now?" (A horse who wants to leave will often do an Aw-Shucks first. This is the signal to "lower intensity," and they are asking in a polite manner.
- He may be telling you that your feet or your Core Energy are too close; could you move over, or change your angle please?
- If he *nibbles* your boot, then he is insisting you move or is saying he wants to leave in a less polite manner. I will do a strong Hold or Activate to the Cheek, Mid-Neck, and Shoulder Buttons, then I will offer space or put him away. First, correct the bold energy; then, listen to the complaint.
- If the horse is young or a Joker and sniffs your leg with some *chewing or nibbling* involved, he is asking if you want to play. I send a horse away who asks this of me. You need to say, "No! I do not play horse games—those involve teeth, and I don't want any part of it." Instead, I may introduce a more appropriate game, like rolling a big ball or standing on a pedestal. Abide by the 6-Inch Rule all day with this one.

MESSAGE: HORSE TOUCHES YOUR SHOULDER

This message usually is requesting that you Buddy-Up.

- If the horse is bumping into your space with his shoulder and he is afraid, he is doing what's called "flocking," and trying to hide behind or with you. Establish the 6-Inch Rule here, and blow a Sentry Breath.
- If he is sniffing your shoulder, it is often an invitation for affection. We don't have withers, but this would be our equivalent.
- If he is bumping your shoulder with his head, he is feeling frustrated by something

and needs assistance. Bumping your Buddy-Up Button is like asking for help. Correct the bold energy, but listen to the problem.

MESSAGE: HORSE TURNS HIS HEAD

Head-turning is how the horse says, "I like you; you can have the front Quadrant of my Bubble," or, "I respect you. I will yield over for you." Or even, "Come on over!"

Negative head turning (turning away to decline interaction):

- A negative head-turn can be used if you are coming on too strong, and the horse feels insecure.

- If a horse turns his head away when you reach for him, and he has a sour face, he is making an effort to decline your request by removing himself from that Quadrant. The sour face is also telling you he doesn't want to do whatever it is.

- If a horse moves his head aside while you are approaching, and it looks like he intends to also move his whole body with it and leave, then pause, and back up three steps. Drop into a Low O posture. The horse is giving you space: He will respect your Bubble and leave the area, and technically, is still making an effort to tell you he knows you are above him in the pecking order. But for whatever reason he is feeling too sensitive, nervous, or confused.

- Head-turning in connection with the Greeting is usually in reaction to the Cheek Button. Just like in a formal handshake with a human being, you must step aside once the horse has given you the gesture of yielding the Cheek. Think about shaking someone's hand, and then they linger too close. This is precisely how the horse feels if he yields his head away, and you stand right inside his Quadrant.

- Keep in mind that even if a horse yields his head away from you in protest (doesn't want to put a halter or bridle on, doesn't want to come near, resists you coming toward him by turning away) he is *still* yielding the Quadrant to you. A horse who is lower in the pecking order will yield the space and leave when a higher-ranking horse moves in. It is still a respectful gesture, like he is saying, "I decline to engage in this activity... but I will not drive you away. I will leave instead."

Positive head turning:

- As you approach, you notice bright or soft eye contact, soft breathing, and a beckoning expression... and then the horse yields his head. This means, "Come on over! You're welcome into my space."

- After you groom one side of a horse, he turns his head away and leaves it there: "Can you please switch sides now?"

- After you Greet a horse, he turns his head to one side: "Now we show mutual Bubble respect."

- As you walk to your horse, he looks to one side: "I am ready for you, come over."

- A horse turns his head and steps toward you with one shoulder: "Come to my Shoulder Button and Buddy-Up."

MESSAGE: HORSE RUBS HIS FOREHEAD ON YOU

The forehead is the seat of the Friendly Button. Technically, it is a safe spot to rub for both people and horses, but only after the "How close is too close?" 6-Inch Rule is established.

- The Friendly Button is often *not* the horse's favorite spot to be rubbed when being worked. Work is one thing, and the Friendly Button is saved for the Grooming Ritual.

- Often, this is a sign of trying to relieve stress. Wearing a halter or bridle puts pressure on the cranial nerves of the face and tongue. Sometimes this feels harsh to horses.

- This message could be overfriendliness. A horse may feel very comfortable with you, and thus think it is okay to rub his head on you. I like the sense of friendliness, but I don't want to ignore it when he "pops" my Bubble. I first Hold him back at the Cheek Button; then I get into a better position to receive the head rub. This says, "Wait a minute. Don't just 'pop' my Bubble, but *yes* you can scratch." Only you can decide how much is too much and if you feel okay about this behavior or not.

MESSAGE: HORSE SNIFFS YOUR HAIR OR THE BACK OF YOUR NECK

Horses sniff each other's scents to bond. There are pheromones that get produced around the neck and ears. You can offer to sniff the horse's neck as a signal of deep affection and bonding, and to say, "We are friends."

- If a horse refuses a neck sniff from you, that is important information.

- You can allow a horse to sniff you if you feel safe, but always invoke the 6-Inch Rule, as well.
- This can be the precursor to a horse offering to groom you by nibbling on you, which is not what you want. Use common sense and decide how close is too close.

- Caution! Stallions who do this may be *flirting*... better to end it.

MESSAGE: AFTER A NICE GREETING, THE HORSE YIELDS HIS HEAD AND NECK FAR AWAY AND LEAVES IT THERE

- This may mean you are invited in closer.

- The horse could be asking you to change sides (it is helpful when changing sides to touch the Bridge of the Nose as you do to say you are switching).

- When the horse yields his head away and then takes a step, he is respectfully declining contact right now. Step to the other side or step away to see what he does next.

MESSAGE: HORSE SCRATCHES HIS OWN BACK-UP BUTTON

Horses often scratch a Button they want to draw your attention to, or that is "waking up" from the enriching Conversation they are having with you. Occasionally, when this happens, they literally mean they would like to back up.

- The Back-Up Button is also an acupuncture point related to immune system reboot. It releases relaxing sensations.
- A good Therapy Back-Up reduces physical, emotional, and mental stress; the horse may be requesting it.
- Between horses, scratching the Back-Up Button is a signal to "get back in yourself," after having, as we might say after a time of big stress, an "out-of-body experience." A fascinating function of our nervous system is to create a dissociation during a crisis. The same is true for horses. The Back Up Button helps them to "come back down."
- When a horse has been chronically dissociated, he may need frequent Back-Up Button stimulation.

MESSAGE: HORSE BUMPS YOUR BELLY WITH HIS NOSE OR HEAD

This is a strong message about your Core Energy. It can mean many things.

- Often used when a horse feels like your X is nonexistent. He is saying, "Where's my trusted leader?"
- It can also mean you are too X: "Please turn it down."
- Sometimes this is used to ask, "Are you feeling okay?"
- The horse may use this when you are unaware of your Core Energy and what it is doing. It may be blasting the horse.
- The horse senses you are sad, and this contact will be soft and gentle.
- You are not holding a 6-Inch Rule and the horse is frustrated by you being wishy-washy. (Horses prefer clear boundaries because they don't want to get in trouble; some Mentors will steadily put pressure on a person's Core Energy to get one of these messages across.)
- You keep treats in your pockets and the horse is "popping" the Bubble to get them. This is like a foal butting the udder of his mom to induce a letdown of milk. Like Mom, you need to have rules about food

on your body—she didn't let her baby nurse whenever he wanted. She had rules.

- The horse is immature.

MESSAGE: HORSE LOWERS THE HEAD IN AW-SHUCKS

Aw-Shucks got its name because I often witnessed it in moments of conflict resolution. It reflects the saying, "Aw-shucks, I didn't mean to cause a fuss."

- Any time a horse lowers his head to the ground and sniffs nothing in particular there, he is using this message.
- When the horse aims Aw-Shucks to you, it is a comment about reducing tension between you.
- When he aims it away from you, it is a comment about reducing tension and wanting to leave the situation.
- When he does it in response to you asking him to go forward (like in the beginning of a liberty or longeing session), he is requesting to keep the energy low, something is concerning him about getting too intense.
- If he tries to do it when you are riding, he is asking to lower the intensity.
- If he notices that you are tense or fearful and offers Aw-Shucks, he is trying to lower the intensity for your sake.
- If you got frustrated with your horse, or he got frustrated with you, and he offers it, he is desiring to let go of the tension.
- If you are round-penning a horse and he does Aw-Shucks, it is best to stop immediately because he is asking you to remove the intensity.
- Horses offer it to each other as sort of an apology if one is grumpy to another.

MESSAGE: HORSE RUBS HIS FRONT LEG WITH HIS MUZZLE OR FACE

This is the horse having an "Aha!" moment. When we are learning something or "getting it," we will often touch our faces around the mouth. This is a similar thing for horses.

- Horses will often pause to rub their front legs in response to a new lesson.
- This can also be in response to understanding something they were confused about.
- The message can be a response to *you* learning something.

MESSAGE: HORSE SCRATCHES A BUTTON WHILE YOU ARE WITH HIM

Yes, horses scratch at flies, but more often, this is a way for the horse to signal to you a Button he wants to talk about. As things get more comfortable, he may signal the Girth

Button. If he is feeling vulnerable, he may signal the Jump-Up Button, and so on.

- Sometimes a gesture is the horse talking to himself ("Darn flies! Grumble... grumble.") Sometimes he is sending you a direct message. Err on the side of caution and consider the possibility that if you are there, he may be talking to you.

- The horse may also be talking to other horses in the area. Pay attention to what the horse is focusing on.

Conclusion

Training horses has been around for thousands of years, but learning to communicate with them from the perspective of being interested in their species just for the love of it is something new.

A training practice will usually have much to offer about the horse's best use of his body. Many people know an awful lot about structure, anatomy, and the rider's responsibility for the horse's development. However, the mindset, and even the way people habitually talk about riding and training, tends to focus on the mechanics and *physical* nature of getting both horse and rider into some kind of frame.

The simple fact is that the horse is not just a body. He is not a blank slate upon which we can paint whatever picture of horsemanship we want. More than this—horses use their bodies to talk. If we put a horse into a frame, that frame means something to him. A collected horse can be in a state of alarm, a state of defensiveness, a state of fighting back, or a state of pride. We want him to be in the one that looks and feels the best. That's the one that also requires that we pay attention to the horse's feelings and read his facial expressions and overall body language.

Imagine having been forced to keep your mouth shut, and yet all the world around you was chattering away. I sometimes feel like this is a horse's experience. They know they can talk, and they know we have never listened before. Imagine how amazing it must feel to have one person come to you and say, in your language, "Let's talk about it!"

I like riding, and I enjoy training because I love teaching. However, I most of all enjoy *listening* to my horses. I believe in a horse wanting his Zero while in the presence of a human being. I have seen it over and over again, and I prepare work with a horse with this in mind. Looking at any vices or negative behaviors in this way helps me problem-solve what is really happening.

This is why I crammed so much information into this book. Somewhere in these pages you should be able to glean a nugget of useful knowledge that can help make the difference with your horse. The power of small things delivered in the right way at the right time blows my mind, over and over again.

May this work find those who truly want to go past the past. Now that I can talk to horses, all I ever want is to share this ability with as many people as I can, as fast as I can. There is this whole other world... and the veil is lifting. For generations, horses have transported us from A to B. Now, I believe they are trying to take us on the next level of our journey—a journey of realizing we have barely scratched the surface of what is possible with enough heart, compassion, and willingness to stretch ourselves.

As a small child, I remember seeing my first horse and feeling that the world had stopped. This animal completely captivated me, body and soul. This book is my devotional, and my legacy back to him. Thank you, thank you, thank you.

Most of all, this is my horse Rocky's idea. Had he not welcomed me into his world, I don't know that I ever would have seen it. Had he not challenged me to step up, I don't know that I ever would have taken the plunge.

Rocky, you are my friend, my Mentor and my companion. I hope your lessons have been represented here with due diligence, and may your astounding heart spread into every heart who reads these words...

X and O

Index

Page numbers in *italics* indicate illustrations.

C

I

N

O

P

Q

R

S

T

V

W

X

Y

Z